TREE OF LIFE, TREE OF KNOWLEDGE

TREE OF LIFE, TREE OF KNOWLEDGE

Conversations with the Torah

Michael Rosenak

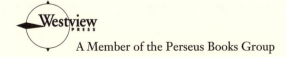

A Member of the Perseus Books Group

Copyright © 2001 by Westview Press, A Member of the Perseus Books Group

Westview Press books are available at special discounts for bulk purchases in the United States by corporations, institutions, and other organizations. For more information, please contact the Special Markets Department at The Perseus Books Group, 11 Cambridge Center, Cambridge MA 02142, or call (617) 252-5298.

Published in 2001 in the United States of America by Westview Press, 5500 Central Avenue, Boulder, Colorado 80301–2877, and in the United Kingdom by Westview Press, 12 Hid's Copse Road, Cumnor Hill, Oxford OX2 9JJ

Find us on the World Wide Web at www.westviewpress.com

The author and publisher would like to thank the Eisenbrauns of Winona Lake, IN, for permission to use text from *Tehillah La-Moshe* (ed. Mordecai Cogan, Barry L. Eichler, and Jeffery H. Tigay, 1997) on pp. 307–313; and Ben Gurion University of the Negev Press of Beersheva, Israel, for permission to use text from *Judaism and Education* (ed. Haim Marantz, 1998) on pp. 87–95.

Text design by Cynthia Young. Set in 11-point Janson by Perseus Publishing Services.

Library of Congress Cataloging-in-Publication Data

Rosenak, Michael
    Tree of life, tree of knowledge : conversations with the Torah/by Michael Rosenak.
        p.   cm.—(Radical Traditions ; 8)
    Includes bibliographical references and index.
    ISBN 0-8133-6561-9
        1. Jewish religious education—Philosophy.   2. Judaism—Study and teaching.   3. Bible. O.T. Pentateuch—Criticism, interpretation, etc.   I. Title.   II. Series.

BM103.R635   2001
296.6'8—dc21   2001023367

10   9   8   7   6   5   4   3   2   1

In loving memory of my dear parents,
Dr. Ignatz I. Rosenak and Minnie Rosenak
(née Neumann)

CONTENTS

PREFACE

THE IDEA OF THIS BOOK came to my mind many years ago, after several conversations with my friend and colleague in Jewish educational studies Joseph Lukinsky, professor at the Jewish Theological Seminary in New York. He had suggested that an educated Jew is, among other things, one who lives in some spiritual and cognitive proximity to the weekly Torah reading, the *parashat hashavua*, "portion of the week." He insisted that issues in the philosophy of education might be found in the liturgy's scriptural readings, that even the way the sages of tradition divided the Torah into "portions" reflected discrete modes of teaching Torah.

As this book developed, largely through my own study of texts and commentaries, I came to realize the enormous influence the revered Bible teacher of the generation now passed, Nehama Leibowitz, known widely simply as Nehama, had on my reading of Torah. Nehama's way of teaching was to line up commentaries and commentators on the Bible, ranging from midrashic teachers to contemporary scholars, to invite learners to discover "what is difficult in the text" for each of those exegetes, and then to thoughtfully choose and accept approaches that spoke to them. This methodology changed my view of what Bible study is. I came upon her superb teaching when first I studied in Jerusalem at the age of twenty-one; many years later, I was privileged to discuss with her the work of my (then) doctoral student, Marla Frankel, who explored Nehama's theory of instruction. At that time the grande dame of Torah teaching was at the edge of her ninetieth year and she was of two minds whether she wished to be portrayed as having anything as "highfalutin" as a theory of instruction.

Perhaps because of Nehama, who found her themes for study staring at her from within exegetical literature on the portion of the week and who thus required no overarching conceptions, I found myself wondering whether it was appropriate to do what I wished to do, namely, to tie Torah study to educational-philosophical questions. Wouldn't Nehama ask me pointedly, as was her wont, on what grounds I presumed to write my own "commentary"? Or whether I was not using the text of the Torah to talk about something else? It was only when she had expressed interest and even encouragement that I felt more comfortable with the project.

In this book, theoretical conceptions, garnered from many places, even if they do not precede reading of Torah, are certainly prisms through which I can read it. Throughout most of my educational career, I have been an academic teacher of teachers and have seen my task as helping educators clarify their thinking about what is worth transmitting to the young and about the paradoxes involved in instruction: between passing on the goods of our civilization with dedication while yet protecting the freedom and dignity of the learner; between supporting and nurturing the young and empowering them; between norms and spontaneity. Some of my teachers, either in person or through their writings, in particular, Rabbi Joseph D. Soloveitchik, who taught at Yeshiva University in New York, impressed upon me the idea that taking hold of only half of such paradoxes is not a 50 percent achievement of truth but a total falsehood, that having norms without dignity, just as having dignity without norms, is an evasion that portends not only the distortion of historic heritage but also the caricaturing of common sense. In discussing these and related issues with students at the Hebrew University in Jerusalem, I have attempted to show how these universal concerns arise within the Jewish religious and cultural tradition, how this tradition is a specific "language," articulating its own sense of "spirit" and suggesting its own avenues of search and anchoredness in the world. Often I found myself referring, as Joseph Lukinsky said one should, to the weekly "portion" of Torah reading to make a point. Frequently, I found that making a point in that way fructified discussion. When it did not, when my students, especially the secular ones, found my remarks sermonic, I learned something about distinguishing between legitimate "translations" of philosophy of education into Jewish idiom and illegitimate ones that pleaded more than they enlightened.

The philosophical-educational issue that navigates the stormy waters between order and freedom is one that has always agitated me. Is every enlargement of freedom necessarily a threat to order, or vice versa? Can we live without either order or freedom? When is the binding together of the two concepts simply special pleading for the forces of order, and when is it pointing to a road that leads to freedom? When is it merely a slogan, presaging thought control, on the one hand, or nihilism and anarchy, on the other? The questions associated with this issue, which are the backdrop of most discussions of moral education in general and "value" education in particular, first occurred to me long before I "did" philosophy of education, as an adolescent sitting at the Passover Seder, wondering why the celebration of freedom (from Egyptian bondage) should be called *Seder*, meaning "order." Later, I came upon the differentiation made by commentators, kabbalists, and even modern thinkers, such as Erich Fromm, between the Tree of Knowledge and the Tree of Life in the Garden of Eden as symbolic of order and restraint, and freedom and potentiality, respectively. That seemed a good way to light my way toward locating educational issues in the Jewish exegetical tradition of Bible study. I have found it fruitful and hope readers will as well.

ACKNOWLEDGMENTS

WITH REGARD TO A BOOK that took as long to write as this one, there are many people to thank: those who discussed the conception with me throughout the years I played with it, those who read chapters, and those who gently suggested that I rethink the entire project. Among the readers of preliminary chapters special thanks go to Arnold Eisen, professor at Stanford University, and to Lee Shulman, of the Carnegie Foundation and also professor at Stanford, who invited me to teach the basic ideas of what was to become this book to his doctoral seminar in Jewish Education. David Resnick of Bar-Ilan University in Ramat Gan, Israel, also made significant comments on many chapters, as did Jonathan Cohen of the Hebrew University and my son-in-law, Alik Isaacs, a doctoral student there. Our discussions sent me back to the manuscript on many occasions. I am also grateful to my son, Avinoam Rosenak, also of the Hebrew University, and Nessa Rappoport of the Mandel Center for Jewish Education in New York. Avinoam's keen sense of textual scholarship and his great sympathy for my project of "educational translation" made his reading both critical and reassuring. Nessa Rappoport kindly read the entire text and made copious notes and suggestions that were all worthy of incorporation and, in great measure, are reflected in the final version. For his reading and comments, I must also thank Barry Holtz, professor at the Jewish Theological Seminary of America, who has always been accessible to me when I wished to bend his ear about this and other enterprises. He read and commented on the outline of this book before a single chapter had been written, and I thank him for being available for me from that beginning and throughout. My special thanks go to Peter Ochs: Not only did he read the manuscript carefully and comment copiously and critically, but he did so in a manner that encouraged me to entertain the thought that he thought highly of my endeavor.

Not less than these readers, I wish to thank my colleagues at the Melton Center for Jewish Education of the Hebrew University. I have found working at this center to be a feast of comradeship, encouragement, and dialogue. My special thanks go to Seymour Fox, who was always engaged with my work, to the center's directors, Ze'ev Mankowitz and to Marc Hirshman, who constantly offered and gave encouragement and helped "schedule" me in a way that gave me room and time; to the administrative head of the center, Carmen Sharon, who always made me feel that any project of mine was a project of the center itself, and to Hinda Hoffman, dean of students, who thoughtfully and wisely read parts of the manuscript, and who also helped me find time without neglecting my students.

Two individuals who were indispensable in making the ideas in this book reasonably clear are Rachel Ebner and Vivienne Burstein. Ebner did a superb job of editing and Burstein, in preparing the book for submission, edited my writing and advised and helped me, with both professional competence and tact, to rethink not only words and sentences but also ideas. Without their work, the chapters of this book would have come across as (sometimes rambling) lectures. If they occasionally still do, the fault is mine. I am also deeply grateful to Sarah Warner, acquisitions editor, and Katharine Chandler, project editor, both at Westview Press, and Marian Safran, freelance copy editor, who also made my manuscript more lucid and turned it into an attractive book.

Very special thanks go to my friend Yitzhak Zohar. For many years we have been studying Midrash together, and the insights that I have gained from our conversation on Torah have enriched me immensely. I am grateful both for our friendship and for our learning.

Again, I thank my family. For this book, it is reasonable that I first mention my parents, Ignatz and Minnie Rosenak. They taught me the meaning of critical loyalty within the parameters of warm and demanding tradition. Each taught me a different aspect of Jewish belief and practice. For my father, Judaism educated to a kind of aristocracy: The good life was the normative and moral one, but the norms, for him, were overhung by high clouds of aesthetics. They did not conflict with enthusiasm for great poetry and music (mostly German) and a cultural reverence for tradition (English, American, but mostly Jewish). Mother, a reflective as well as a communal person, was a rationalist but unmistakably enthusiastic about what Jews were doing in pre-state Israel, despite the Holocaust. When we were children, Father would often read poetry to us at the Sabbath table: On Sabbath afternoons, Mother told us about the drainers of swamps in the malaria-infested valleys of Eretz Yisrael, the Land of Israel. To her, pioneers were bold spirits, something new and heroic in Jewish life, but she remained loyal, albeit with historical perspective, to tradition. With Father she shared a life of daring and danger in pre-Holocaust Germany; to his courage—as an attorney, in standing up to Nazi authorities on behalf of his often battered Jewish clients, usually securing for them visas to lands of refuge—Mother added the spice of social care and initiative. When Father insisted he needed to stay in his office in Bremen to save more Jews, Mother insisted that his and her family were also Jews who required saving. (They compromised and we escaped at the eleventh hour.) I am grateful for what both have given me, placing me in the shade of both the Tree of Knowledge and the Tree of Life even when the serpent ruled our native land. To their memory, I dedicate this book.

Finally, I am grateful to my children and my children-in-law who, with their children, have on many occasions heard me air the ideas that constitute this book. I am not sure that was what they most wanted to do on every such occasion, but for the times they listened, asked, and contributed to the discussion at our Sabbath table, I thank them. Above all, I thank my wife, Geulah, who made all this possible: our home, which reflects her inner understanding of what a Jewish home is like, where she and I, and our entire family, can conduct the ongoing, often surprising, wide-ranging, and ordered conversation that articulates our sense of where we are in the world and who we are to one another.

INTRODUCTION: THE GREAT CONVERSATION

About This Book

THROUGHOUT THE GENERATIONS of humankind, people have carried on a conversation about the possible meaning of life and the allegedly good or correct ways of conducting it. This conversation has apparently always been framed by tradition and habit, yet, at times, was refreshed by new reflection, itself generated by new—threatening or promising—experience. In our time and in our place, the vocabulary and agenda of the conversation are primarily, albeit now self-consciously, that of the powerful and secularized civilization that we call modernity.

In this book, as suggested by its title, I shall raise questions, suggest avenues of approach, and carry on the conversation about humans in their world through the prism of Jewish civilization, seeing this civilization always in interaction with its surroundings and yet stubbornly adhering to its own rhetoric in which it insistently says its own things. The reader and I shall enter what Robert M. Hutchins calls the Great Conversation by way of Judaism:[1] its texts and the voluminous interpretations through which all Jewish generations seek to make better sense of the texts. In doing this, we shall come upon some of its encounters with other cultures and faiths, as well as the determination of its scholars and saints to see the world whole. We shall see these sages finding everything of

1

value within Jewish teaching and yet recognizing truth wherever they find it, reshaping it if necessary to fit the contours of the civilization that they, and Jews in general, call Torah.

Our particular vantage point for engaging in this Great Conversation is that of education. *Tree of Life, Tree of Knowledge* is not only about understanding some texts within the religious tradition of Judaism but also about the specific conversations these texts have generated that reflect and illuminate fundamental philosophical questions arising in Jewish education and, to a large degree, in all education. As Hutchins notes, education is the effort of human society to keep the Great Conversation going by initiating the young into it and making them participants within it.

Questions in the philosophy of education are neither abstract nor pristinely metaphysical. They are inquiries into two focal issues that underlie all that parents, teachers, and other educators do when they transmit sensibilities, competencies, ideas, and valuable information to the young. The first issue revolves around the questions: What is worth knowing? Conversely, What is a waste of time, or corrosive of character, or simply useless? The second issue has to do with the following questions: *How do we know* which goods are worthwhile and which are trivial or harmful? *On what grounds do we distinguish* between the true and the insignificant or false? What gives us the right to make such decisions?[2]

My assumption is that the texts of the Jewish tradition are an important source for philosophical discussion of questions in Jewish education and beyond. In this introductory chapter, as throughout this book, I argue that the quandaries and debates, questions and puzzlings, in the ancient sources of Judaism may retain their vitality in educational conversation even now and that they may thus nourish educational thought that makes the young person a member of the community of culture.

A Dialogical Approach

All significant life, Martin Buber taught, is encounter.[3] If one agrees with the dialogical thrust behind this teaching, namely, that encounters develop into conversations, one may describe education as the reflective and responsible task of inviting young people to encounters: encouraging them to "show up" for them, helping out in the ensuing conversation, interpreting what happens there, and giving these conversations context and direction when necessary.

The right of parents and teachers to do all that is based on two interlocked assumptions. The first is that parents and teachers have had more experience with significant life than children and thus are likely to know something about how encounters are set up and to know which are most promising and worthy. The second is that they are members of communities that "speak" a language of significance and structure that has shaped and channeled their experience, which they, in turn, can transmit to the coming generation.

Parents and teachers, then, initiate children into conversation while teaching them a *language*.[4] Some of the most formative of these conversations are conducted in the immediate family environment. Others are initiated by the community and largely negotiated through its schools, informal educational frameworks, and religious institutions. There, encounters between the learner and an "outside" world are explored and sometimes, for good or bad reasons, held at a distance. These conversations introduce children into ways of thinking, feeling, and acting that together constitute a framework of order and, one hopes, for self-discovery. The *language* they are taught, therefore, provides young people with parameters for both restraint and achievement.

The young person, through the *language* she or he learns, is enabled to come to encounters. She or he gets to know the rules of each particular type of conversation and to understand what is being said, grows in the ability to participate in such conversations, to experience the fellowship and responsibility evoked by them, and, where appropriate, to have pleasure and joy through them. And perhaps most important, she or he learns that one never knows in advance exactly which conversation will take place when and where, that encounters are, despite rules and responsibilities, often surprising and challenging.

Language and Literature

When I refer to the *language* parents and teachers transmit, I have
in mind not merely one of the spoken tongues of humankind but
also a basic world picture and the distinct forms of rhetoric that
make communication about that world picture possible. In this
broad sense, *language* is a network of paradigms: of order, coherence, and a sense for the self-understood. Language underlies the
norms that nourish particular conceptions of heroism and nobility,
expressed and reflected in the narratives, memories, and hopes that
flow from it. It provides grounds for making matters plausible, yet
seems also to pose problems, in one sense long resolved, yet ever to
be addressed anew. For example, a particular language may be
based on the reality of an all-powerful and beneficent God who has
"come down" to meet humans. Yet those who "speak" the language
must deal with the unexplained evil in the world and the experience
of God's "absence."[5]

Each language offers its basic explanation of reality and gives
rise to prescriptions for living within it. Each points to an understanding of what it means to "meet" others and how, through
meeting, we may, or should, "see" ourselves as well as those others. By teaching a language, parents and teachers may well see
themselves bestowing life and truth on their charges, rescuing
them from disorder, confusion, and chaos. They are also trying to
make sure that they will have someone to talk to in the overlap of
generations, and that the beloved language, "the world," will go
on after them.

Yet, for what we teach and how we live, language is insufficient.
In itself, language is only a *way* of seeing and doing things; it is a
world of beliefs, dispositions, and a kind of grammatical code for
"correct" speaking. Language becomes a social and spiritual reality
only when *literature* is initially made in it, when it is first "spoken."
A language comes alive when what it means is interpreted, when its
ground principles, assumptions, and aspirations are negotiated in
the crucible of experience, when it "speaks to" the circumstances of
those who are addressed by it. Similarly, for a language to be

learned, there is a need to examine and then master its *literature*, to open the "texts" that have been written or otherwise articulated in this language. For *literature*, the most recent as well as the most primordial, tells us what can be said in the *language*, how it can be articulated, interpreted, and expanded.

The language's *foundational literature* enjoys special status, for it brings the language onto the stage of history and culture, making it more than an airy "way of thinking" or a blurry set of pointers. This paradigmatic *literature*,[6] or text, may be called classic, for it establishes the concrete existence and functioning of the language. If the language in question is religious, we may call this literature *holy*. Were there no "classic" or "holy" literature, the language would remain a shadowy realm of rules (without instances), procedures (without practice), poetic "imagination" without poetry, a vague recollection of revelation without religious life. Thus, foundational literatures, though, strictly speaking, texts within the language, are culturally and normatively indistinguishable from the language itself. In "holy" literature that is foundational for a religion of revelation, the writers are often said to understand so well what the divinely revealed language says and demands that the "text" is actually envisioned as spoken by God to the bearer of the foundational literature, the prophet.

But latter *literatures* are no less important than former ones, even if less entitled. For the making of literature is not simply a historical or prehistorical series of formative events or episodes. It is an ongoing and never-ending process that, although taking off from the paradigmatic, foundational, and "holy" literature, goes on to say its own things. Ongoing literature is the consequence of genuine life within the language, for the language must again and again be shown to be capable of addressing new problems, situations, and sensibilities. Paradoxically, the loyalty to the language of those who live within it is optimally expressed by their desire to show how its meanings may be expanded through interpretation. Their pride in the language that gives them their identity is expressed in the literature they make in it, and in their use of it in conducting their lives. This literature, they believe, shows the power of their language to provide a home in differing circumstances for those who cherish it and hold fast to their identity through it.

Were it not for the ever new literature of commentary, controversy, and invention that arises within a *language*, the language would readily become archaic. Without new literature, the original statements made in the foundational texts of the language, however venerable and majestic, would quickly become brittle, incomprehensible, and outlandish. Thus in every generation those who speak the language that gives them their identity are intent on protecting it and their identity (as speakers of the language) by saying new things in it. New *literature* brings the *language* up-to-date. It saves the language from sublime irrelevance, and it protects the public designated by it from either obstinate dogmatism or ultimate disloyalty.

The *language* of Jewish life, its *holy literature* that is considered indistinguishable from the language itself, and also the voluminous literature generated within it throughout millennia of encounter with new circumstances and with other languages and literatures is called Torah. More precisely, the foundational body of text that exposes the language to view may best be called *the* Torah. That, together with the subsequent literature that is generated in "protecting" the Torah and broadening its applicability and significance, is simply *Torah*. The later literature, throughout at least one thousand years of literature making, is called Oral Torah. There are significant differences of opinion as to where the Oral Torah ends and the commentary on it, a tertiary literature of "doing Torah," begins.

The distinction between the two is important, for Oral Torah, the corpus that paradigmatically shows how the language is both protected and expanded, is also, like the holy (foundational) literature, in a sense revealed. Just as the language could not be *known* without holy literature that "brings it down to earth," so could it not be *used* but for the literature that articulates and demonstrates its powers of application. Hence it too shares in the original revelation (of the language). It, too, is somehow "from Heaven."

The foundational literature is ascribed to prophets, especially to Moses, the father of prophets, who spoke to God "face to face."

The classic and holy literature of the Oral Torah, which models how the "language-holy literature" is protected and expanded, is ascribed to generations of scholars and teachers who lived in the millennium before and after the advent of the Christian era. These are known as *hakhamim*, "sages."[7] The tertiary literature, which carries the life of Torah through the generations, is the work of philosophers, mystics, exegetes, halakhic (legal) authorities, and, to a degree, of all Jews who "learn Torah" and live by it.

The language of Torah, I have suggested, is "philosophically" located at the very beginning of the historical memory and experience, inviting literature that will transform its ideas and ideals into norms and culture. But it is also, existentially, ever being fleshed out by literature that reflects language. Specifically, such an institution of Judaism as Jewish law, the halakhah, "translates" God's sovereignty over humanity and His covenant with Israel (language) into social reality. But even a contemporary analysis of the halakhah that makes sense of it as a religious phenomenon also teaches us about the world picture behind it and may illuminate the language itself. Thus the language reaches and instructs us, not only through the primordial revelation of language that holy literature always "recollects," but also through the prism of diverse, even tertiary, literatures.[8]

Teaching Through Torah

As said, this book is about Torah as a *language-literature* for education. It is an illustrative walk through some texts and through some problems together with those who are charged with arranging encounters and conversations between the young and their parents, between the individual and his or her community, between "our" world and "theirs," between the human being and the situations that confront him or her. The language of Torah, like other languages, constantly explores through its literature new ways of speaking about encounters and of arranging them, new ways, then, of understanding the act of teaching. This literature, one may expect, will be rich in educational prescriptions. Moreover, these prescriptions can expose aspects of Judaism's language and may give us glimpses of a Jewish philosophy of education.

Yet why embark on this exercise? Who needs it? And why trust the process of doing it? These questions arise because many persons in our civilization approach the language of Torah with suspicion, and even the majority of those who have recourse to it speak other *languages* with greater fluency and are more at home in other *literatures* that probably provide them with a greater sense of self-identification. This "foreign" fluency-cum-identification is helped along by the widespread cultural assumption that Torah is a *dead* language, meaning that it is no longer represented and vitalized by ongoing literature; that, therefore, it can no longer point to paths of genuine confrontation or encounter. Consequently, there is a wariness about "philosophy" in Torah. There is a suspicion that addressing it philosophically is mere apologetics, simple sermonics.

Yet the language-literature of Torah has functioned with singular power throughout its history. And I shall argue that the three historic features of Torah and its study can be imbued with comparable power in the present if we generate new literature that (1) recognizes the distinctive valuative status of individuals in modern culture; and (2) does not hide from the pervasive presence of diverse literatures and competing languages in the contemporary world and also does not shirk "encountering" them.

What are these historical features? The first is that Torah was the focus of a bold venture designed to make of the Jews, throughout their communities, what Alasdair MacIntyre has described as an "educated public,"[9] that is, a community of mostly ordinary people who shared texts (paradigmatic narratives, events, patterns of life) in familiarity, commitment, and reverence, with their scholars. The aim of this venture was that this "public" would understand enough of what these virtuosi were doing in literature making to be engaged associates, if not actual partners, in their conversation of learning, and to identify with what they did. Creating this educated public, although the records show that it was not an easy task,[10] was eventually achieved. It came into being largely through universal Torah study, through the legislation of liturgically ordered times and texts for reading it. The second feature coming out of the same literature orientation was the exegetical, midrashic, enterprise of the Talmudic sages of constantly engaging the holy literature and illuminating it by piling new literature on top of it.

The outcome of the liturgically ordered study and the midrashic exegesis of the rabbinic sages is the third feature: namely, that study of Torah brought to light what can be said in the language of Judaism about the central questions that preoccupy human beings in general, and Jews throughout their singular historical experience in particular. This bringing to light of what Judaism has "said," or can be shown to say, was the primary enterprise of philosophical, legal, mystical, pietistic, and sermonic teachers, who spelled out or otherwise articulated the issues, difficulties, and responses that together constitute the Jewish "worldview."[11] A brief look at each of these features of Jewish language and literature teaching may be helpful before I proceed.

"Three Days Without Water": Creating an Educated Public

The Talmudic rabbis made a cultural-educational decision of great consequence when they decided that a fixed regimen of public Torah reading would be a staple of Jewish life. For this decision, based on their understanding of the language itself, they sought authorization from the hoary past when Torah was all "language-holy literature," thus, clearly "from Heaven" and unmistakably binding. So, we find Rabbi Yehoshua declaring that public reading of the five Mosaic books, *the* Torah itself—although *re*legislated by Ezra, the restorer of Judaism in Babylonian times—actually originated in the immediate post-Exodus weeks. Rabbi Yehoshua thus paradoxically places this momentous decision before the actual revelation of the Torah at Mount Sinai, where Israel was given its (divinely ordained) language and "heard" the literature that brought it down to earth.

Here is the context as the rabbinic sage, in his midrashic "text," imagined it. The Israelites have miraculously passed through the Red Sea and need no longer fear their former oppressors, the Egyptians, for they lie dead at the sea. But the Israelites still find themselves, not in the well-watered fields of the Promised Land, but in the wilderness of Shur, a place midrashically pictured as hostile and even gruesome. The Israelites, although they are free, are now thirsty and becoming bitter. As the Torah depicts the situation: "And Moses led Israel onward from the Red Sea and they went out into the wilderness of Shur and they went three days in the wilderness and found no water" (Exod. 15:22).

After so many miracles, so much wilderness! With so much trustworthy and inspired leadership, so helpless! Only weeks away from encountering God and His Torah language of life, such disorder and foreboding of death! On this verse the Talmud taught:

> Those who understood hidden meanings [in Scripture] said, "Water" [really] means Torah. As it is written (Isa. 55:1), "Ho, everyone who is thirsty, come for water." Since [the Israelites] went for three days without Torah, they became fatigued. Hence the prophets among them ordained that they read the Torah on the Sabbath . . . [and] on Mondays . . . [and] on Thursdays so that they not go through [any series of] three days without Torah. (*Baba Kamma* 82a)[12]

It was not the desert with its fiery serpents and its parched ground that made them fatigued and thirsty. It was going three days without Torah! Understanding fatigue and thirst as spiritual deprivation, as a kind of "desert of language," and Torah as the well of refreshment and recuperation, is a remarkable tour de force, based, perhaps, on the insight of "the prophets among them" that there were wildernesses yet to come, that the desert of spiritual chaos, where there was no way of knowing "what can be said," constantly threatened to encroach on human civilization.

It was the decision to make the reading of the Torah a central feature of the liturgy that eventually created "an educated public," a community conversant with the language within which its scholars create literature. This momentous educational decision has come down to us by way of the Babylonian tradition, and its still current annual cycle of Torah reading. The Babylonian cycle divides the Torah, and the year, for both the scholar and the simple, into *parashot hashavua*, "portions of the week," study units equally present for all, designating universal "Jewish time" by what *parashah*, "portion," is read any given week.

Thus, for about two millennia, each member of the community has been enjoined to ponder the Creation and the Patriarchs each autumn (at least in the Northern Hemisphere, where all Jews once lived); to spend the early winter Sabbaths with Joseph and his brothers and the later ones with the Exodus and the construction of the Tabernacle. With spring comes the time, willy-nilly, to think about the sacrifices and the priestly laws. At the approach of summer, all are asked to endure together the forty years of wandering, the murmurings and insurrections. Then, in the heat of summer, all are to travel the last stretch of desert with their ancestors as they circled—and conquered—at the edge of the Land. Late summer is spent with the instructions and warnings of Moses' last days. Then, on the concluding day of the autumn festivals, there is Simhat Torah, the "rejoicing of the Torah." The liturgy of that day mandates the reading of Moses' final blessings and, minutes later, after the Torah has been rolled back to "the beginning," the creation of heaven and earth, where everything is declared good. Except, remarkably, for the human being. (Why not? It is clearly a problem. How may we understand it? What do the commentators say? Who agrees, or disagrees, and with whom? Why?) And so, a new year has begun.

Reading the Torah, until the recent past, accomplished universally what language-holy literature could do for a community whose leaders were educators and who uninhibitedly obliged cultural involvement. It supplied memories, anticipations, associations, order, and coherence. It created excitement and bodies of competence (like reading the Torah in public) and expertise (like navigating the "sea of the Talmud," replete with the commentaries of its early and late interpreters). And not least, it created problems and thus generated a demand for new *literature*. For although in every epoch some of the passages and portions of the week were experienced as exciting, alive, winning ready consent, others were mysterious and "difficult." What is more, over scores of generations, Jews, endowed with diverse discernments and thus alive to diverse "problems," proceeded to surround all of the text with commentaries. These commentaries elaborated, asked questions, posed difficulties, suggested solutions. In turn, this literature, this cumulative body of philosophical, legal, moralistic, literary, and theological exegesis, reflected and illuminated diverse paths of lifelong pilgrimage through the text. The abundance of exegesis permitted even learned and sophisticated and spiritually unquiet souls to choose from a rich store of meanings and thus to reaffirm the Torah constantly as the word of God, as the divinely given language of Judaism. Those less accomplished yet adequately schooled followed the holy text with the commentary of Rashi, the medieval savant who made the "literature" of Midrash accessible: asking questions, solving difficulties, telling stories, and making salient halakhic points where necessary.

The Bible of the Synagogue

Together, the scholars and more ordinary readers, inspired by midrashic masters of "literature," developed what Jakob Petuchowski once called the "Bible of the Synagogue," to be distinguished from the Bible of modern scholarship, studied at universities, and from the other traditional Bible, that of individual piety and edification.[13]

The Bible of the Synagogue has something in common with the Bible of individual piety insofar as the person seeking inner illumination may, by chance, be sitting in the synagogue or House of Study or "going over the weekly portion." But the Bible of the Synagogue is much more than a place of private inspiration. It is an ongoing festival of *literature*. It places before us an open and unending book of plain meanings (*pshat*), homiletics (*drash*), allegory (*remez*), and mysticism (*sod*). The Bible of the Synagogue is the totality of rabbinic text. It is the Bible (or rather, Torah) of Jewish instruction, of the well-versed Jew, and of Jewishly educated communities.

As the Bible of the Synagogue is a perennial conversation, it is subtly ahistorical, for everything within it jostles for a place beside the holy *literature* of the *language* and wishes to be recorded as part of what was actually "said at Mount Sinai." The inspired and the wise of different generations speak to one another within the Bible of the Synagogue as contemporaries, making even of Moses, whom the Torah knows as its prophet, Moshe Rabbenu, "Moses our (rabbi and) teacher." Having become what it is through layer upon layer of questioning, dispute, and inner development, the Bible of the Synagogue reaches us mysteriously endowed with an inner unity, as a network of solutions to all problems. Yet it is also and always like a puzzle, awaiting the learned and pious yet playful sage who will help us see the jagged pieces whole.

The Bible of the Synagogue seeks to make every text of the Torah comprehensible, for only thus can God's will and presence be experienced and only thus can Jews do what God demands of them. But it thrives on "difficulties." Thus it valiantly, but with zest, engages passages about lepers, Tabernacle furnishings, or sin offerings. It relates these sometimes opaque passages to cryptic verses in Job or Proverbs or Psalms, hearing, learning and teaching God's eternal Word through the prism of comparisons, (unlikely) connections, and controversies. The Bible of the Synagogue is with us wherever Jews learn Torah, wherever a halakhic problem arises, wherever a sermon at a synagogue service or a *d'var Torah* (literally, "a word of Torah") at the dinner table addresses a matter of perplexity in anticipation of instruction and enlightenment.

This "Bible," then, generates questions for modern as it did for ancient and medieval people. It invites them to encounter the language and its concerns through its literature's ways of thinking and talking about them—and through the literature acting upon them, even while encouraging them to articulate their own concerns.

One central issue within this Great Conversation of education and culture is undoubtedly in the relationship between "encounter" and "control." The questions that arise include: What is desirable knowledge or enlarging experience? Does all knowledge enhance life, or may some of it, at times, distort or stifle it? What is the relationship between wisdom and goodness? What is involved in genuine encounter? When does knowledge for use undermine wisdom?

Knowledge and Life

In the language called Torah, those are also crucial questions, often addressed in its holy literature: in law, in prophetic rebuke, in epic tales. The narrative at the beginning of Genesis sets the stage. Here is vintage Torah "language-holy text" standing open to the midrashic literature that will address its difficulties. Here is the Garden of Eden.

In the garden, we recall, there are lush and pleasant plants, rivers, and animals. There are two human beings, male and female. There is the serpent, who claims to know about God and therefore to have the key to knowledge, but being sly, he intentionally gets it wrong. And there are two signified trees: the Tree of the Knowledge of Good and Evil and the Tree of Life.

To begin with, these trees seem unconnected. It is only of the Tree of Knowledge that Adam and Eve are not to eat: "On the day you eat thereof you shall surely die," Adam was told. But the Tree of Life, despite its perhaps wondrous qualities and gifts, even eternal life, does not seem to have concerned God at first. Nor are we told that it tempted the humans. Apparently it seemed no different from any of the other trees of the garden from which the man and the woman were permitted to "freely eat."

Why did God prohibit eating of the Tree of Knowledge of Good and Evil? What was the knowledge that God wished to keep from the humans? And why did the Tree of Life become a problem for God after Adam and Eve ate from the Tree of Knowledge, so that God expelled them from the garden lest they become like God and "live forever"?

There are a number of possibilities. Perhaps the knowledge in question is about human obedience to God, so that it was not they, but He, who was for a time "ignorant." God did not yet know, as it were, whether humans would choose good (obedience) or evil (rebellion). Or, perhaps, God's commandment was intended to deny them the knowledge of evil, the potential for malice and misuse inherent in all knowledge. Note that once they know about evil, a knowledge that the serpent depicts as wisdom, they become ashamed, self-conscious, alienated from each other and from God, and even from the pastoral garden and the natural world it embodies so abundantly. Transgression, it is intimated, precludes encounter.

Yet God is not portrayed as wishing to deny knowledge as such to His human creatures. After all, the Tree of Life also represents knowledge. It is a knowledge of human potentialities for control, of the "magical" possibilities open to humanity. But by using knowledge that runs counter to the benign purposes of the Creator—evidenced by their eating of the Tree of Knowledge—Adam and Eve have given God, as it were, disturbing "knowledge" of their dubious intentions. Should they then be given access to this fount of wisdom? Being disobedient and lacking self-control, will they not use the life-giving properties of the Tree of Life for unbridled, evil purposes? Learning how life can be transformed through speech, won't they waste this precious knowledge to lie and quarrel? Perhaps natural resources they will know how to exploit will be wasted on weaponry? Perhaps they will discover such marvels of the created world as the atom and use it, whether viciously or haplessly, to destroy Creation? If so, humans must be kept away from the magic of the Tree of Life. If they live forever, what will contain the chaos and havoc they and their creativity will bring into the world?

Building a relationship between knowledge that is both valuable and useful and lives that are worthy, "well-lived," is the focal ideal of educational activity and the central concern of educational thought. What should one know? How best to use the magic of life? What to do about knowledge that is alienating, destructive of life? How much restraint is needed to envision significant achievement?

The Tree of Knowledge arranged avenues of encounter between people and God, between the man and the woman, and between people and their natural environment. Through God's command, the Tree of Knowledge set limits within the world. However, the Tree of Life pointed to the "magic" potential for knowledge that humans possess. In a seeming paradox, the Torah suggests that the blessing of such knowledge may freely be given to humans who accept the restraint of commandment but should be denied to disobedient ones. In the Bible at least, humans who eat of the Tree of Knowledge of Good and Evil are kept away from the Tree of Life.

"It Is a Tree of Life . . . "

In the Jewish literature of learning, the two trees seem to stand in the same place, their roots intertwined. Knowledge is transformed through the covenant of commandment and relationship. The Torah is to be found both in restraint and in discovery. Humans are to obey God, to curb their appetites through His commandments, and "to conquer the earth."

Over time a rich vein of midrashic literature, of Torah, sees the two trees becoming one. The Torah, most prominently but not exclusively in its negative commandments, is itself the "Tree of Knowledge" (Will you obey? Will you do what I command? Will you refrain from what I forbid?). But it is also, as Jews recite when concluding its reading in the synagogue, "a tree of life for all who hold fast to it." The serpent slyly promised Eve that human beings would live forever if they ate from the Tree of Life. In a stunning response to that, Jewish liturgy, in the blessing after reading from the Torah, declares that God has "planted eternal life in our midst"—not by magic, but by Torah. The serpent promised Eve that she and the man would be like God if they ate of the tree. But the Torah later teaches, "You shall be holy, for I [God] am holy" (Lev. 19:2). The way to be like God passes through the Tree of Knowledge of Good and Evil![14] Where there is knowledge of Torah, there is encounter with God, with life. Outside is the wilderness. The wondrous Tree of Life, when unrestrained by the restrictions the Tree of Knowledge places on humans, brings them death.

In our time, such conclusions readily become sermonic and simplistic. As noted, we live within other meaningful languages and literatures in addition (perhaps!) to the Jewish ones called Torah. Naturally, then, our questions, reflecting the concerns of all of us, are often formulated primarily in the language of the contemporary and mostly secular West. And so we ask, What does knowledge of

Torah include? (The assumption is that there is other knowledge, also accessible, also valuable.) And when we ask, How much control—and knowledge and experience—must be restrained or somehow locked away for the desired eternal life to come into view? We also ask, Where is such restraint to come from? Who legitimately imposes it? And where will it lead? Is the restraint that the Torah considers so basic to its language even remotely possible without the loss of the freedom and dignity that we (modern people) require and celebrate?

One central way the tradition of Torah approaches this problem is by pointing to the halakhah, the law, that is commanded, yet presented for choice. But is there as yet enough contemporary *literature* to flesh out as an option for a secularized world the halakhic principle that not everything possible is also permissible?

Conversely, how much else must we learn in humanities and sciences for discoveries to become fruits of the Tree of Life that yet stands together with the Tree of Knowledge, tempering the magic of discovery and achievement and thus giving them a human perspective? How much restraint for our medicine to become more compassionate, for our empathy to be less calculating, for our technology to learn ecologically oriented self-control? And how shall we learn it? How can the Torah instruct us in regaining ground for the benign, the life enhancing, in a world filled with knowledge that we cannot do without? For encounter and not only control?

These issues underlie educational conversation with Torah in our generation. *Tree of Life, Tree of Knowledge* is an attempt to participate in that conversation of learning. It is addressed to men and women who wish to arrange encounters for their children, their pupils, and themselves, encounters that "take off" from the language and literature that constitute Torah. These men and women admit that they cannot readily learn from Torah without bringing it into dialogue, sometimes even confrontation, with everything else in their spiritual and cultural worlds. Thus, the questions they may pose to the sources of Torah are suggested not only by classical "difficulties" in the text but also by the dilemmas and goods of modernity that urgently, and sometimes radically, suggest new ones.

At the same time, I envision these readers wishing, however self-consciously, to approach Torah with a rhetoric of trust, to relate to difficulties in the text as problems that invite literature rather than as patent absurdities, moral or theological, that disqualify the language. These readers, I allow myself to assume, want to see Torah as a locus of their identity and of their children's, as *language* to be protected and as *literatures* respectfully listened to and midrashically explored.

If this study helps to spark conversations among men and women and children of diverse "literary" inclinations, who yet share common foundations and draw upon a common language, I shall be profoundly grateful.

An Overview

Tree of Life, Tree of Knowledge is divided into an Introduction, followed by four parts, each dealing with a different avenue of educational initiation and encounter. In Part 1, my concern is with the parent-child relationship. I suggest that "the beginning" of that relationship, with its happy but also fearful anticipation, may well bring parents to inquire about beginnings: Where did "we" begin and who were our first parents? What were the hopes of these ancestors, and what did they anticipate for us? Perhaps more crucially, what did later generations, upon becoming parents themselves, think about their first parents?

This concern leads, in Chapter 1, to an exploration of quite diverse characteristics that midrashic and philosophical literature have "found" in Abraham and Sarah. I present diverse models for thinking about what we want our children to become.

In Chapter 2, I look at the kind of educational encounters the home can initiate by observing the "four children" the Passover service draws out of the Torah. Two of them, the "wise" and the "wicked," seem greatly concerned with what is going on at this festive family affair, whereas the other two, the "simple" and the "unquestioning," are mildly or not at all interested. The distinction between the first pair and the second suggests that the "wicked" child is a more promising type than the "simple" questioner. Here I also discuss how the education of the home is essentially different from that of the school.

The issue of trust in a mysterious, often confusing, and at times incomprehensibly cruel world, is the subject of Chapter 3. What is the sense of Abraham's "walking together" with Isaac to the binding and anticipated sacrifice of his son? What kind of a father is he? Who is the God he serves? Is there anything educational about all this? Psalm 73, attributed to Assaf, an educational personality of King David's time, sheds some light on the significance of "holding hands" in times of trouble.

Chapter 4 treats of what in Jewish tradition is the "evil inclination," which often seems to sabotage education and to undermine the "good inclination," which parents and teachers wish to foster. To illuminate the question of "nature versus nurture," I examine some midrashic attitudes towards Esau, the Bible's best-known "problem child." Was he born problematic, or was he miseducated? Must we view Isaac and Rebecca as unsuccessful in the education of their older son or as victims of his evil inclination?

Finally, if we think of parental education not only as getting children to do things right, but also as guiding them toward thinking and solving unanticipated problems, can the language and literature of Torah be helpful, or is it too narrowly normative to make room for novelty and innovation? In Chapter 5, I examine the question of how children can learn to make decisions against the backdrop of an impending disaster: of (Israel's) being caught between Egyptian chariots behind them and the menacing waters of the Red Sea in front, immediately after the Exodus. The desperate question, What shall we do now? is not what the Israelites anticipated when joyfully leaving Egypt. Our biblical text and the midrashic commentary on it help us to discuss some crucial questions. How can children be prepared for addressing deliberative issues intelligently within a normative tradition? How can they become responsible through the guidance of trustworthy mentors?

The issues discussed in Part 1 seem to belong primarily in the home. But even in the best of times—and for family life these are

not the best of times—the community too is entrusted with teach-
ing its *language* through the *literature* that sustains its collective life.
Examples of how the community teaches its *literature* is the focus of
Part 2.

As Part 1 opened with family "beginnings," so Part 2 begins with
the community's teaching, through Torah, about *the* beginning—of
the "world." For this *language-literature* of beginnings to make
sense to the young, it must be related to the manner in which children understand beginnings. This issue is explored in Chapter 6,
with an assist from the medieval commentator Rashi. He teaches us
to be concrete when initiating children into our world, even at the
expense of theological finesse.

Chapter 7, like the previous one, is centered on a single "portion
of the week," but one seemingly far less interesting or relevant. It is
the section of Leviticus that details the garments worn by the High
Priest. In the tradition of the Bible of the Synagogue, I connect
these splendid garments of Aaron, in contradistinction to the
undistinguished apparel of Moses, to the conception of "honor"
suggested by a team of sociologists, and juxtapose it to their conception of "dignity." What may we learn from these priestly
clothes, from Moses' "informal" dress, and from the ceremonies of
Yom Kippur, if we wish to help our children move toward dignified
autonomous lives that are yet endowed with socially significant
meanings and "honor"? Truly a midrashic enterprise.

Chapter 8 addresses the issue of Jewish law, the halakhah, a focus
of Jewish *literature*, and a window to its *language*. Following
midrashic sages, and with an assist from the contemporary moral
philosopher, John Kekes, I relate diverse legitimations of the halakhah to diverse understandings of human character. Here we
come upon the polemical question whether the "halakhically educated" child is a curious one or a conformist.

Chapter 9, which closes Part 2, is a midrashic and historical-soci-
ological journey through ways of understanding two verses in
Deuteronomy that state succinctly "what God asks of you." If at
first it seems quite simple to educate children to be "ideal persons,"
the task, once analyzed and explored, appears impossible. What do

commentators, ancient and modern, have to say about it? Is the community to educate each person to only one aspect of the educational ideal? And if that seems overly organic and hierarchical, what other options are there?

In Part 3, the problem, which arises within the home but is intractable without the community and its public presence, is how, in the face of other, sometimes "idolatrous" *languages* and sometimes pagan *literatures*, shall we defend ours? Can the integrity of Jewish identity be maintained without parochialism and closed mindedness? What is there in the *language* and *literature* of Judaism that mandates apartness and even seclusion? Conversely, which options and even demands for empathy, participation, and fellowship do we find there? What is really "inside" and what "outside" for the educated Jewish person?

Four chapters are devoted to this issue. In Chapter 10, we find ourselves in a seemingly simple world of "we" and "they," of Jacob and Esau. Jacob here is zealously concerned with self-defense, with keeping away from Esau, even when, and perhaps especially when, that stranger-brother seems "nice and cultured." The question arises, Is that paradigm of segregation and alienation still tenable in the open society of today? Or has it perhaps been horribly reconfirmed by the Holocaust?

Chapter 11 treats of the opposite phenomenon: Joseph's brothers, and even his father, have been invited to Egypt by Pharaoh who gave them "the land of Goshen" for their settlement, and they learn to feel very much at home there. Joseph and his sons develop a dual identity, an insider-outsider set of languages. Even portents of impending slavery do not suffice to get the family to return to Canaan, to really go home. Later, too, in the Greco-Roman world as well as in our own, we find Diaspora appearing as a normal component of Jewish life. Is it, then, hypocritical to teach love for the Land of Israel and prayers for a speedy return to it?

In speaking of "our" vis-à-vis "their" language, we tend to assume that "ours" is always particularistic, whereas the "general" culture is universalistic. But that assumption is based on the axiom that Jewish tradition is zealously solicitous about Jewish identity at the expense of universalism and in almost sneering disregard of it. In Chapter 12, I examine this view through the prism of the Noah story and take issue with it. I argue that the messianic aspect of Torah makes universalism an internal value. Jewish education, I submit, must teach covenantal commitment as a universal as well as a particular imperative.

Chapter 13 addresses an academic challenge to the conversation of Torah: The universal world of the university sponsors research into the holy literature of Judaism, the Torah, armed with a rhetoric of suspicion. Does that make the university "them," as in the Jacob-Esau model? Or is it possible to maintain the faith of Judaism without alienation from scientific inquiry? In educating young people to blanket denials of modern research into biblical texts, are we creating a false model of authenticity that, for the sake of wholeness, denies comprehensive intellectual and spiritual development? I suggest a tentative and personal approach for linking tradition to modern biblical scholarship.

Part 4 brings us to those later stages of life in which all education is, in fact, self-education. Neither the home nor the community can now tell us what to do or who we are, though we have been shaped, given a *language*, by both. Yet we must now understand that "putting it all together" is our responsibility, and that the ways we do so are our choices.

To begin this part, I return, in Chapter 14, to the family of Jacob, specifically, to the "spoiled brat" of the family, Joseph. How did this fascinating figure, many years after leaving his family, earn the title of "Joseph the righteous"? What happened? When did he achieve moral maturity? Is it possible for a person to change? In looking at these questions, I have recourse to the model of "four perfections" as the predominant thinker of the Jewish Middle Ages, Moses Maimonides, depicts them.

Then in Chapter 15, I return to Jacob himself. How did he learn, in his own old age, to make his peace with the memory of his father Isaac, who blatantly favored his brother, Esau, over him? How we cope with what we remember is a significant feature of who we are. It is, like the growth for which we are ourselves responsible, an aspect of *teshuvah*, "returning," "getting somewhere" in the search for ourselves.

The family, the community, and the school are involved in our infirmities and illnesses, but in a profound sense, we are left alone with them. The way that Midrash and biblical exegesis deal with the Torah's laws of leprosy and the leper is a blatant example of how sages and exegetes interpret the holy text to convey a message that is innovative yet within the rhetoric and the spirit of the *language*. The delicate balance between the community's tendency to stand in judgment over the ill and the understanding that it does not deserve to do so initiates the exercise in social relations and self-knowledge that is the subject of Chapter 16.

The subject of dying is one usually ignored by modern education and considered by contemporary adult society an unmentionable accident. The midrashic discussion of Moses' death at age one hundred and twenty, in conjunction with some halakhic literature, leads me to suggest what might be meant by being "one hundred and twenty years old." How do texts of Torah view death and how they relate it to life? The way the texts of Torah and Midrash consider this anthropological issue and some ramifications of it for education are the subject of Chapter 17.

Underlying the concept of self-education is the developing ability of individuals and communities to decide what and who they are. This ability involves philosophical acumen and practical competence to determine what is really worth knowing, not because it is useful in achieving other ends, but because this knowledge defines us and gives us a perspective for seeing things whole. Learning "for its own sake" begins in the home, continues in the humanistic segment of schooling, yet eventually becomes a personal quest. In the classic Jewish idiom the question is, What does *Torah lishmah*, "Torah for its own sake," mean? With an assist from a contemporary philosopher of education, M. A. B. Degenhardt, I examine in Chapter 18 how this concept can guide curriculum scholars and teachers and allow learners to discover, perhaps after the passage of many years and far from the educational limelight, what the intrinsic learning that they know as "Torah for its own sake" is.

My postscript brings us back explicitly to the mysterious trees that give this book its name. I note that each of the issues raised in this book has something to tell us about the questions: How does the Tree of Knowledge of Good and Evil stand together with the Tree of Life? Is restraint indeed linked at the roots with self-realization? How much obedience and how much autonomy characterize the well-educated person? In the spirit of the book, I conclude with questions like these.

PART 1

Parents and Children: Within the Family

The father is obligated to teach his child Torah. From whence do we know this? It is written (Deut. 11:19), "And you shall teach your children."

—Kiddushin 29b

ONE PASSOVER EVE, not long after our immigration to the United States from our native Germany, my father presented me with my first Haggadah, the narrative liturgy of the Seder service. Father was a somewhat formal and solemn person and his inscription on the first page of my new Haggadah was true to his character and manner, impressive but heavy fare for a child of eight. "No matter what happens in your life," he wrote, "always remember Judaism as you have seen it practiced in your parents' home." Later that evening, as I listened to the Haggadah reading on the Seder night, I picked up the rabbinic statement proclaimed in the Pesah service: "In every generation each person is obligated to see him or herself as having gone forth out of Egypt." The "always remember" of my father and the "always remember" of the Talmudic sages seemed to me to be more or less the same thing. In later years I realized, of course, that it was not exactly so. But even then, on those festive evenings when the specialness of the celebration and the lateness of the hour made things hazy, they still seemed to be coming from the same place and pointing in the same direction.

1

WHO ARE OUR
FIRST PARENTS?

WHAT SHOULD BE TAUGHT FIRST? That is a significant question in Jewish education. When the child is told
his or her first story about how it was and how it is and how it
should be, where should that story come from? In selecting "The
Beginning," where do we look?

Why not begin at "in the beginning," the first words about the
first things? For reasons that I shall discuss later on, it has not generally been done that way. Apparently, those beginnings, of heaven
and earth, say too much, or not enough, to children. Peculiarly, a
traditional approach was to begin with Leviticus and its sacrificial
order. The rational for this strange priority was that "just as sacrifices are pure, so are children. Therefore, let the pure learn about
the pure" (*Leviticus Rabbah* 7:3). But surely there is some real reason
hiding behind that. Could it be that the toddlers who studied Torah
in a distant past were the children of priestly families, who were
"socialized" into the guild as quickly as possible?

A survey of where adults today place the portals through which
children enter the world of Torah indicates that it all begins with
Abraham and Sarah going to the Promised Land. Everybody knows
about their hospitality, that Abraham's tent had four doors, one on
each side, so that he would not miss the appearance of any potential

guest. Less known is Sarah's tent, in which the light of industry never went out and delicacies were constantly being prepared for guests.

Every male child is first publicly mentioned in one breath with Abraham, for upon being welcomed in the synagogue before his circumcision, the child is blessed with the wish that he enter the covenant of our father, Abraham. Also, proselytes, those who have just been born into the community of Israel, take on the names of Abraham and Sarah as their own. And parents, looking at their first newborn child, who moves them up a generation and makes them responsible for a person of the "next" generation, may well ask: Who is this child in the chain of being, in the chain of our "language" and culture? How will we keep our children within the chain of our specific being, so that they not be the last ones, even amidst the loosening of all bonds? These questions suggest looking in the other direction: What is it that we wish to continue? Where did it all begin? Who were the first links in the chain and what made them forge this beginning? And they are likely to stop at Abraham and Sarah.

Where Is the Beginning?
The Wellspring of Tradition

Why begin with Abraham and Sarah? Why not, say, with Shem, Noah's son, father of all Semites? Or Terach, Abraham's father, admittedly an obstinate old idolater, but the first who started off on the road to settle in Canaan, the Land of Israel? The reason is suggested by the great German novelist of the twentieth century, Thomas Mann, in the Prelude to his monumental work, *Joseph and His Brothers*.[1] Mann ponders what he calls "the well of the past." It is deep, he reflects; it seems bottomless. "For the deeper we sound, the further down into the lower world of the past we probe and press, the more do we find that the earliest foundations of humanity, its history and culture, reveal themselves unfathomable." Yet we all, says Mann, "come to rest" on some point that forms "the beginnings of the particular tradition held by a given community, folk or communion of faith."

For those who read the Torah in search of both origins and destiny, the point on which we come to rest, where we find our first father and mother, is in the story of Abraham and Sarah. They are the beginning, for they are associated with the beginning of our historical community. Since they initiated our family and set an example of how the family is to live, they are family mentors and heroes.

At the same time, the ideals their children associate with them, through which they transmit conscious membership in the historical people, which is also a community of faith, are sifted in the remembering. Throughout the millennia, the children of Abraham and Sarah, having themselves become parents and grandparents, not only transmit but also "do literature" that expands on and sometimes reshapes what those primary parents represent. As a result of their own experience and reflection, they discuss who Abraham and Sarah must have been and even argue about what constitutes a good and loyal son or daughter of Sarah and Abraham. This argument intimates that the matter is not clear-cut but is itself a "well of the past," probed and pressed with the tools of diverse intellects and imaginings to nourish the present and to teach those who are our future, our children.

Who are the patriarch and the matriarch we wish them to have as first parents? What we choose as an answer to that question reflects, through the prism of an endless conversation of the generations, whom we wish them to become, how we wish to "raise" them.

Let us speak mainly at first of Father Abraham and then about Mother Sarah. What kind of father was he for us? What may his children learn from him? Looking at the newborn child, we ask: "What would we wish this child to think of when he thinks of Abraham? With what can we ourselves identify?"

Abraham, as the Jewish tradition sees him, was first and foremost a man of faith. In the language that the Hebrew text reflects, that means that he trusted God and God saw him as trustworthy. Hence, on the verse "And Abram took Sarai his wife and Lot his nephew and all the property they had acquired and the souls they

had made in Haran, and they went out to go to the land of Canaan"
(Gen. 12:5), Rashi, on the basis of a midrash, states: "'. . . the souls
they had made in Haran': those they had brought under the wings
of the *Shekhinah* [the divine Presence]. Abraham converted the men
and Sarah converted the women, and Scripture looks upon them as
having 'made' them."

What was the nature of this faith through which they "made
souls"? What was the difference that made them teach separately?
What are the waters that we are invited to drink from this deep
well?

The Faith of Abraham: Two Views

With regard to Abraham, two of the great thinkers of our Middle
Ages suggest very different portraits of the man. According to
Moses Maimonides, or Rambam, medieval Jewry's outstanding
philosopher, it was philosophical reflection that led Abraham to
recognize God: His faith was a philosophical one. Maimonides envisions the course of spiritual events as follows:

> While [Abraham was] still an infant, [his] mind began to reflect. By
> day and by night he was thinking and wondering, "How is it possible
> that this [celestial] sphere should be continually guiding the world
> and [yet] have no one to guide it and cause it to turn round; for it can-
> not be that it turns round of itself." He had no teacher, no one to in-
> struct him in anything. He was submerged in Ur Casdim, among silly
> idolaters. His father and mother and the entire population worshiped
> idols, and he worshiped with them. But his mind was busily working
> and reflecting until he had attained the way of truth, apprehended the
> correct line of thought, and knew that there was one God, that He
> guides the celestial spheres and created everything, and that . . . there
> is no god besides Him. . . . Abraham was forty years old when he rec-
> ognized his Creator. (*Mishneh Torah, Avodah Zarah* 1:2)

Having attained this knowledge, he began to refute the inhabi-
tants of Ur Casdim, arguing with them and saying to them, "The

course you are following is not the way of truth." He then proceeded to teach his sons. "Abraham implanted in their hearts this
great doctrine, composed books on it, and [especially] taught it to
Isaac, his son. . . . [Isaac] imparted the doctrine to Jacob and ordained him to teach it. He too, settled down, taught and morally
strengthened all who joined him."[2]

The Abraham that Maimonides portrays becomes capable of acting morally and faithfully by virtue of his knowledge, carefully garnered from childhood and fully appropriated in adulthood. He recognizes that knowing the truth implies pursuing a certain course of
life, but this understanding of "the right way" is primarily an intellectual achievement. This Abraham writes books and his son and
grandson are "ordained" to instruct others. He is the first philosopher who, through his speculations, learns "the way of God" and
teaches his children enlightened service, justice, and moral
strength. In fact, all who recognize God and act justly are his disciples and children.

Yehudah Halevi, a century before Maimonides, had presented a
different Abraham. This poet and thinker wrote a famous dialogue,
The Kuzari, fictionally conducted some four centuries earlier with a
Kuzar king who then converted to Judaism together with many of
his subjects. *The Kuzari* "records" the discussions between the king
and the *haver*, "rabbi-teacher," and the arguments that convinced
the pagan king to embrace Judaism.

In *The Kuzari* Yehudah Halevi draws a distinction between
knowledge of God *(Elohim)* and of the Lord (the Eternal, *HaShem*,
literally, "the Name"), presenting them as two different kinds of
understanding. The former knowledge, he explains, is the product
of applied intelligence and adequate training and confers competence and expertise: Such knowledge is the mark of the philosophically and scientifically sophisticated person. It is what we might call
a scientific mode of understanding. (Abraham, in Maimonides' de-
piction, indeed proceeds scientifically: He questions, probes, draws
conclusions, and states them systemically.) In contradiction to this,
the knowledge of the Eternal is "a matter of love, taste and conviction." Attachment to *Elohim*, declares Yehudah Halevi, is based on

speculation, but to *HaShem*, on passion, moral commitment, nearness, and caring. And Yehudah Halevi finds that these latter qualities characterized Abraham. Through the trials imposed upon him,
he became a paragon of righteousness. As Yehudah Halevi sums up
the soul of his passionate Abraham:

> Abraham bore his burden honestly, viz., the life in Ur Casdim, emi-
> gration, circumcision, the removal of Ishmael and the distress of the
> sacrifice of Isaac, because his share of the divine Influence had come
> to him through love, but not through speculation. He observed that
> not the smallest detail could escape God, that he was quickly re-
> warded for his piety and guided on the right path to such an extent
> that he did everything in the order dictated by God. How could he do
> otherwise than deprecate his former speculation?[3]

Yehudah Halevi, as though criticizing the future Maimonides, has
Abraham "repent" of his "former speculation." His Abraham is in-
stantly rewarded for his faithful deeds by the proximity of God,
whom he experiences as reciprocating his love. To summarize his
position, Yehudah Halevi has the king of the Kuzars muse on the
distinction between philosophy and innocent love:

> Now I understand the difference between *Elohim* and *HaShem*, and I
> see how far the God of Abraham is different from that of Aristotle.
> Man yearns for *HaShem* as a matter of love, taste [as an immediately
> experienced sense] and conviction, while attachment to *Elohim* is the
> result of speculation. A feeling of the former kind invites its adherents
> to give their lives for His sake and to prefer death to His absence.
> Speculation, however, makes veneration only a necessity as long as it
> entails no harm, but bears no pain for its sake.[4]

And the teacher-rabbi, seeing that his royal pupil is making good
progress, sums it all up: "He who follows the divine law follows the
representatives of this view. . . . The masses do not follow [the
philosophers] with their eloquence and fine teachings, . . . because
the human soul has a presentiment of the truth, as it is said, 'The
words of truth will be recognized.'"[5]

Abraham's Philosophical Musings

Which Abraham should be our model for living spiritual Jewish lives and educating our children? Is it to be the person who scorns the conventional truths and ways of foolish neighbors, who carefully and intelligently searches for the truth through reflection and reason and becomes a teacher of truth and moral justice? Or should our model be the loving and obedient Abraham, who "bears his burden honestly," who teaches through the example of his own, often painful, experience that all people find familiar and through the redeeming commandment they all need? Do we want our children, in the name of their Jewish commitments, to be rational and just, or do we hope that they will be loving, caring, and passionately identified? Or do the two viewpoints, seemingly contradictory, complement each other?

Let us begin to examine this problem by way of a midrash in *Genesis Rabbah* that, in typical "Bible of the Synagogue" fashion, draws on the imagery of Psalm 45, a wedding song of a Judaean king newly married to a foreign wife, a "daughter of Tyre":

And God said to Abram. "Go ye out of your land" (Gen. 12:1). R. Yitzhak began [by expounding the verse]: "Hearken, O daughter, and consider, and incline your ear; forget also your own people, and your father's house" (Ps. 45:11). This may be compared to one who was going on his way from one place to another and saw a castle in flames. He said, "Can one say that this castle has no master?" The master of the castle looked out on him and said to him: "I am the master of the castle." So too, Abraham our father said, "Is it possible that the world is without a guide?" [Whereupon] the Holy One looked out at him and said, "I am the guide of the world." "So shall the king desire your beauty" (Ps. 45:11), to make you beautiful in the world. "For He is your lord, and do homage to Him" (Ps. 45:12). Hence, "And the Lord said to Abram, go ye out of your land." (Gen. 12:1)

The request to the bride, that she see her Hebrew husband as lord, is transformed by the midrash into a command to Abraham

that he pay homage to *the Lord*. This demand arises in the context
of Abram's search for understanding. Wherever he goes in the
world Abram finds "the castle burning," and he comes to wonder,
as every young parent looking fondly, yet fearfully, at a newborn
child well might ask: "Is it possible that there is no ruler in the
world? What is this world into which we have brought this child?"

Abram, looking around him, sees only flames, havoc, and anarchy. God "looks out" and informs Abram that there is a ruler; God
is the master. Yet this intriguing information makes matters even
more problematic. If there is an owner, why is the castle burning?
All that God says is that He wishes Abram to render Him homage,
to be beautified, to "go to the land that I shall show you." There
Abram is to do it differently. God will not have to peek out of the
window of a burning castle; Abram will be beautiful by creating a
different world, a world that acknowledges the master, the king,
and pays Him homage.

On the one hand, the discovery of this "burden" is the result of
the very speculation ("Can it be . . . ?") that Yehudah Halevi de-
rides. On the other hand, the rabbinic allegory presents this psalm,
which urges a foreign bride to be loyal to her new husband-king, as
a call to Israel (Abraham) to forget his former people, to be obedient to the king who desires his "beauty," who desires the homage of
beautiful and faithful deeds. Abraham (Israel), like the bride of our
psalm, is being urged into a new personal relationship.[6]

Justice and Caring

In our midrash, then, we may find two aspects of covenantal relationship. God Himself needs, as it were, someone to "deal with the
fire," with the chaos in the world. He is asking Abram to establish a
society in which God's castle does not burn, where the destructive
fires have been put out. In Abram, the seeker after truth and justice,
He finds one who can shape the world according to His plan. The
covenant is with a pioneer of a wise and loyal humanity. No wonder, then, that God "reports" to Abraham before destroying the
wicked cities of the plain. In making a covenant of righteousness

with him, God has singled Abraham out so that he may instruct his children and posterity to keep the way of the Lord by doing what is just and right (Gen. 18:19). Abraham is to become a great nation so that "all the nations will be blessed through [him]" (12:3). This Abraham will defend pagans with the same cogency and urgency as those of his "household"; he will look for the righteous even among the wicked. He has no compunctions in warning God that He "dare not" destroy the righteous with the wicked. A man of justice, Abraham can demand that "the judge of the whole world deal justly" (18:25). Even for God, Abraham is a moral force to be reckoned with.

But our midrash intimates a second and contrary aspect of covenant that is seemingly more limited, but appears even more demanding. Its thrust: Forget the others. Love me! Be caring and I shall care for you. I shall call you by name and I shall be your God. You shall be mine and I will give you a land. Here it is not the whole world that concerns us, but a special inheritance; not abstract justice, or even universal malaise, but the particularity of genuine responsibility, caring, and attentiveness toward the other in the midst of the flames. The king wishes to beautify Israel (Abraham) but not through "humankind in general." God wants evidence that Abraham belongs to Him, just as the king in Psalm 45 wants the exclusive loyalty of his bride, of her *in particular.*

These two aspects of covenant represent the two sides of all human value and thus, two "pure" educational options. On the one hand, there is the ability to see matters in a universal and morally reciprocal fashion, and this requires dispassionate knowledge and reflection. On the other hand, there is identity, loyalty, and genuine empathy with the neighbor. And there is love, not as a generalized sentiment of good will, but as dedication, restraint, and sacrifice.

Is there a "natural" tendency for members of one gender to be more inclined to the first and for members of the other gender to be innately oriented to the second? Some modern scholars believe so. For example, Nel Noddings ascribes to women a "natural" inclination to caring, whereas men are associated with an inclination toward rules and abstract concepts of justice.[7] And some traditional texts and practices seem to support this ascription. In Jewish liturgy there is the prayer for a sick person, in which he or she is identified as the son or daughter of the mother, say, Yitzhak *ben* Sarah or Dinah *bat* Leah. Only the mother's name is mentioned, for the human being with a womb *(rehem)* is associated with the *rahamim* (compassion) that we seek from God for the sick person. But of course, every fine and educated human being, on the basis of her or his (perhaps!) gender-related inclination must strive for a personality that is both "systematically" moral and "subjectively" loving. Every noble human being recognizes the tensions between these two dispositions and attempts to negotiate judiciously and diversely between them. A moral and compassionate human being will attempt both to concretize and to personalize justice, even though it is in principle universal, and at the same time to stretch the frontiers of love, though it is always contextual and addressed to the one who is close and cared for.

Caring and the "Burden" of Circumcision

One of the trials visited upon Abraham, as Yehudah Halevi reminds us, is *brit milah* (circumcision). There can be little doubt that it was, as he says, a burden for the old man.

Let us recall the context of this "burden." God has decided to give new names to Abram and Sarai; their names will henceforth be Abraham and Sarah. Moreover, God calls this renaming "My covenant with you" (Gen. 17:7). It establishes a special relationship. It means that He will perpetually remain their God and give the land to their descendants. Yet, interestingly, it is only in the case of Abraham that the change of name is associated with circumcision; Sarah is given her new name without a bodily mark of covenant.[8]

A possible reason for this difference follows from the distinction we have just made between "justice" and "caring." Circumcision obviously has nothing to do with universal justice, with putting out the fires of violence and evil. It is a family matter, a token of identity and of relationship. Like the name given by parents to a newborn child, it is a mark of distinctiveness, of special attentiveness and love. It is about a fate of involvement, about togetherness and caring. Attentiveness, love, and caring is what we consider mothers, who have borne pain for their children, to have naturally.

With regard to *brit milah*, a mishnah teaches:

> R. Jose says: Great is circumcision which overrides even the rigorous [laws of the] Sabbath. R. Yehoshua ben Karha says: Great is circumcision, which even for the sake of Moses, the righteous one, was not suspended for as much as an hour. R. Nehemiah says: Great is circumcision which overrides the laws of leprosy-signs. Rabbi [Judah the prince] says: Great is circumcision, for despite all the religious duties Abraham our father fulfilled, he was not called perfect until he was circumcised, as it is written, "Walk before Me and be perfect" (Gen. 17:1). After another fashion it is said, Great is circumcision, since but for it the Holy One blessed be He would not have created His world, as it is written, "Thus says the Lord, but for My covenant day and night, I had not set forth the ordinances of heaven and earth" (Jer. 33:25). (*Nedarim* 3:11)

From this mishnah one may deduce that the covenant of circumcision is indeed about caring. It draws people together. Even the Sabbath, in its rigorous aspect of forbidden labor and stringent observance of its ordinances, may hold people apart, for each person may become ashamed of his or her laxity, or self-righteous about his or her punctiliousness in "doing what the rules demand." Hence, the duty of circumcision overrides the restrictive laws of the Sabbath, nullifying restrictions that may push people apart. And what better expresses the distancing between persons than leprosy, in which the afflicted are removed from "the camp" and live in isolation! The fact that the halakhah ordains the removal of even a leprous foreskin, though it prohibits the removal of any other diseased tissue, symbolizes the "overcoming" of the alienation associated with leprosy. And "heaven and earth," the spiritual and the concrete, must also be brought together. The world could not exist were there no covenant binding together the sublime and the everyday, body and soul, human frailty and absolute justice, the ideal and the real.

Note that our mishnah does not spare two of its heroes, Moses and Abraham. Moses delayed the circumcision of his son; he had been sent on a mission and occupied himself with "hotel arrangements" for returning to Egypt before performing the *brit milah* (Rashi on Exodus 4:24). Perhaps he saw himself as simply "too busy" acting on behalf of everybody to concern himself with one mere baby that "happened" to be his. As for Abraham, he was a man of many good deeds, but he was not "perfect" until he underwent circumcision and understood what it symbolized, namely, that next to moral intelligence and disinterested justice, there is involvement, the overcoming of alienation, the interpenetration of heaven and earth, living with the tension between knowledge and commitment.

The spiritual lives of Abraham and Sarah were more complicated than those of humanity's first parents, Adam and Eve. Those primordial ancients merely had to choose between good and evil; they lived in a world of "value" and "antivalue." What they confronted was either eating from the tree that had been forbidden to them or not eating from it. We do not find them having to decide between values: We do not hear of them deliberating about justice versus caring. They did not have to be "perfect," living a covenant between heaven and earth; they just had to be obedient. Abraham and Sarah, however, had to face dilemmas.

For Sarah, the covenant had to include the caring that extends beyond those obviously and concretely bound to her. Her new name, Sarah (replacing Sarai) indicated to the Talmudic rabbis that she was now to be the princess of all peoples and not only of her own (*Brakhot* 13a).

Sarah's covenantal trait of caring is never in doubt. Seeing her husband afraid, she agreed to lie for him, saying that she was his sister. Seeing his distress at her childlessness, she gave him her maidservant to bear him a son. The midrash finds that she was even solicitous of the pregnant Hagar until the latter defamed her (*Genesis Rabbah* 45:4). Then, like many caring people who discover their love unrequited, she took offense and it made her fierce. Her passionate love of Isaac and what she foresaw for him led her to demand the expulsion of Hagar and Ishmael. Isaac, after all, was hers.

The sages declare that Sarah's powers of broad understanding, albeit based on concrete situations of love and suffering, were also exceptional; they submit that she was a greater prophet(ess) than Abraham (Rashi on Gen. 21:12). On the verse "And God has made laughter for me; everyone who hears will laugh on my account" (21:6), Rashi explains: Everyone will rejoice with me. A midrash teaches that Sarah laughed with happiness at the birth of Isaac and she heard that people everywhere were "laughing" (i.e., happy) on this occasion because, at the birth of Isaac, they were cured of sterility too, as well as of blindness and disease (*Genesis Rabbah* 53:8). Her own private family joy radiated out to others, including, of course many whom she did not know. Her rejoicing caused others to rejoice.

This joy of others, we may imagine, caused her to rejoice for them. Caring that started at home was stretched to its limits, to take in the other, the stranger. Yet the sages of the midrash have drawn our attention to this quality of caring in Sarah before: Note that she, together with Abraham, "made souls," brought people "under the wings of the *Shekhinah*," the divine Presence, even while still in Haran (*Genesis Rabbah* 39:12)! Despite her modesty, staying "within the tent," even when angels came to visit, it seems likely that in "making souls," drawing people near, she led the way. Abraham, after all, knew that joining his household, like circumcision, was not a moral requirement of all humankind. Yehudah Halevi might say that the Abraham who was engaged in speculation and abstract reflections on justice had to learn about the burdens of caring—from circumcision.

A particularly bold midrash presents Abraham "deliberating" about this divine commandment, "thoughtfully" seeking the advice of his friends about it (*Genesis Rabbah* 42:8). He consulted, states the midrash, with three Canaanite friends, Aner, Eshkol, and Mamre, about whether it was advisable to carry out this commandment, assuming, apparently, that when it comes to wise decisionmaking, one's specific "identity" makes no difference. Aner and Eshkol advised against it. Aner thought it physically risky: to inflict pain upon himself at such an age! And Eshkol counseled against it, for Abraham's enemies might take advantage of his weakened state. Only Mamre brought the matter back to its "interpersonal" context: He saved you from the burning furnace and from hunger and from the (warring) kings, and now that He tells you to circumcise yourself, you will not hearken? (After all He did for you! You would consider not reciprocating His love?)

Choosing Between Courtesy and Caring

The Talmud (*Nedarim* 32), discusses Abram's participation in the war of the kings (Gen. 14:13–24). He mustered 318 young men of his household in order to wage battle to save his nephew Lot, who had been taken captive and, incidentally, to rescue the king of Sodom "and all that was his."

Several of the sages feel that Abram acted improperly here: R. Abahu says in the name of R. El'azar that it was wrong on his part to draft *talmide hakhamim*, "scholars of the Torah" (for, by the terms of the sometimes anachronistic Bible of the Synagogue, could the young men in Abram's household have been less?). Why did he take them away from their study of the Torah for military service? But R. Yohanan has another opinion of what constituted Abram's wrongdoing: "[His sin was that] he kept back people from coming under the wings of the *Shekhinah* [the divine Presence]."

R. Yohanan notes that the victorious Abram brings back many captives to Sodom and also much wealth. He is distressed that Abram responds with noble detachment when the king of Sodom invites him to "take the possessions for yourself" but to "give me the persons," an offer that Abram turns down (Gen. 14:21–24). R. Yohanan feels that Abram should indeed have let the heathen king keep the property but he should not have relinquished the souls, the *nefesh;* he should not have left the persons of his captives to the evil idolater. True, he made a noble and disinterested gesture of justice and he could now justifiably claim that he had gained nothing from the war. But was it the right thing to do?

The French-Israeli Jewish thinker, André Neher, described the situation in the spirit of R. Yohanan:

> The king of Sodom had made him an offer—Give me the persons *[hanefesh]* and take the goods to thyself (Gen. 14:21). How was it, asks the midrash in incredulous indignation, that Abraham could reply that he would take nothing that belonged to the king of Sodom? Surely he ought to have entered into the spirit of the Canaanite's own game, and merely have turned the proposition upside down! Ought he not to have laid claim to the "souls" himself? For more than one decade he had been engaged, together with Sarah, in effecting conversions to the monotheistic faith by means of both teaching and example. Was he now to deny the advantages of that faith to the men of Sodom? . . . Abraham did, no doubt, treat the king of Sodom to an impressive lesson in disinterestedness, but in so doing he missed his messianic rendez vous—he would not take the risk of giving the one and only answer by means of which the Canaanite king would have been not merely edified, but converted.[9]

In having to choose between the justice of the covenant and its demand for engagement, R. Yohanan and his contemporary interpreter, André Neher, declare that Abraham made the wrong choice. He, who together with Sarah steps onto the stage as a soul maker, is here too high-minded to be engaged. Is this a lack of love or commitment? Or is it perhaps a dearth of the reflection that is required when choices must be made?

The Abraham of Yehudah Halevi writes no books, does not "ordain" anyone, and cleaves to God without benefit of philosophy. He knows the distinction between right and wrong and gladly chooses the right, even when it is a burden, because he cannot bear to be deprived of divine love. But to be perfect requires choosing between values and even juggling them; being compassionate and caring, but knowing when justice must be done; being fair and disinterested (sometimes), but without looking away from the other person's face. Is that possible without thinking? Will we, our children, and our pupils be complete human beings without knowing when to "talk back," as Abraham did for the few righteous of Sodom, and when to remain silent, as he did at the *Akedah*, the "binding of Isaac"? And even then to perhaps wonder whether the decision was the right one?

It seems that we ourselves and those we wish to cultivate as disciples of Abraham and Sarah can learn from Yehudah Halevi that sophistication can be inadequate and may even corrupt, blinding the eye to the *nefesh*. But from the Rambam, Maimonides, we may learn that intellectual curiosity, understanding and reflection, if not misused to dissipate love and disparage commitment, enlarge the soul and beautify it. Abraham and Sarah hardly give the new parent, peering into the well, a simple ideal for "what they want for their child."

About Sarah something more must be said. For she represents not merely the ideal ancestor but a distinctive womanly ideal. And our young parent, especially if she is the mother, but, one hopes, the father too, will want to think about that.

The Tent of Sarah:
A Midrashic Conception of Home

I have already mentioned Mother Sarah's tent. It was, says one midrash, overhung by a cloud, a symbol of her righteousness and modesty. The midrash in question describes and discusses Sarah's tent in the context of Eliezer, Abraham's servant, bringing Rebecca to the house of Abraham as a bride for Isaac, after Sarah's death. There the Torah tells us: "Then Isaac brought her *into the tent of his mother* Sarah, and he took Rebecca as his wife, and so he was comforted after his mother's death" (Gen. 24:67). The midrashic commentator judges this verse syntactically difficult. Why does the text not say *ohel Sarah imo* (the tent of Sarah, his mother), rather than *haohelo imo* (to her tent, Sarah his mother)?

Moreover, asks M. A. Mirkin, a modern explicator of *Midrash Rabbah*, was not the tent of Sarah and the tent of Abraham the same? After all, when the angels heard Sarah laughing "in the tent" they were apparently standing next to Abraham's tent! Yet, we cannot imagine that Isaac brought Rebecca to Abraham's tent! Therefore, comments Mirkin, the midrashist understands Isaac to realize that Rebecca is like Sarah; that she is worthy of inheriting her "tent." And what Isaac now saw in Rebecca were the four characteristics of Sarah "in the tent," that marked his mother's mode of life.[10]

> You find that as long as Sarah lived, a cloud hung above her tent. When she died, that cloud disappeared, but when Rebecca came, it returned. As long as Sarah lived, her door was wide open. At her death that openhandedness ceased, but when Rebecca came, it returned. As long as Sarah lived, there was a blessing on her dough and when Rebecca came, it returned. As long as Sarah lived, the lamp used to burn from the evening of the Shabbat until the evening of the following Shabbat. When she died, these ceased, but when Rebecca came, they returned. And so when he saw her following in his mother's footsteps, separating her challah [to give tithes] in purity and handling her dough in purity, [then] straightaway, "and Isaac brought her into the tent of his mother Sarah." (*Genesis Rabbah* 60:16)

The midrash relates Sarah's tent to other biblical tents, using these others as proof texts. Thus, just as a cloud signifying the divine Presence descended on the tent of meeting *(ohel mo'ed)* when Moses approached it (Exod. 33:9), so did it dwell on the life and abode of Mother Sarah. As the tent of Abraham was open so that he could stand at the door of the tent to await visitors (Gen. 18:1), so was Sarah's tent a symbol of hospitality. The midrashic teacher recalls how Abraham rushed to the tent and asked Sarah to prepare dough and cakes for the visitors. The burning lamps evoke the connection between *ohel* and *ya'ahil* (Job 25:5), brightness. Mirkin sums up his understanding of this midrash as follows:

> And all these four things symbolize the Jewish woman: A cloud abides on the door of the tent; here is modesty *(tzniut);* the doors are wide open—there is generosity and compassion [and the proof text is

Proverbs 31:20]: "She stretches out her hand to the poor . . . and to the needy"; the blessing is on her dough [as we find in] *Yebamot* 62b: "Every man who has no wife is left without . . . blessing, and the blessing of dough is the primary blessing in the house." And that "the lamp burns from Shabbat eve to Shabbat eve," reflects diligence [as we find in] Proverbs 31:18: "Her lamp goes not out by night." (Mirkin on *Genesis Rabbah* 60:16)

Of course, the midrash can be understood as saying much more than that! Should the cloud hanging above Sarah's tent, on the basis of the proof text, not be identified with the divine Presence? After all, Sarah's tent is being compared to the tent of meeting!

Clearly we have here a model of feminine living in proximity to this Presence. Sarah is hospitable, though "private"; she provides for family and passersby; her "space" is always illuminated, by the lamp either of industry or of the Sabbath; she is punctilious about the halakhot (laws) of purity and prepares neither priestly tithes nor the family's bread except in (ritual) purity. She even cuts the cakes herself; although constantly in the divine Presence, she considers no menial task as "beneath her."

But this is a different paradigm than that of Abraham, and the division of roles is blatant. She keeps to the tent, even when angels visit; she is "modest." Although she is a princess, she heeds her husband when he requests that she say that she is his sister lest the Egyptians kill him. But it is different in the privacy of her relationship to her husband. Here we find her outspoken regarding the welfare of her family: "Banish this maidservant and her son, for the son of this maidservant will not inherit with my son, Isaac" (Gen. 21:10). And the fate of being childless brings her to bitter laughter.

An Ideal of Womanhood

This model of righteousness delineates a role; it reflects an ideal of "womanhood" that is distinguished from "manhood," as if a separate species. Righteous women remain "in the tent" and "all the glory of the king's daughter is within [the tent]" (Ps. 45:14). Is this the model that the present day Jewish mother will necessarily wish to adopt for her newborn daughter?

No doubt Mother Sarah is a heroine, a prophetic figure, a determined and caring individual. Her tent does bring the divine Presence into the House of Israel and into the world, so that if that singular "tent of the righteous woman" is dismantled, there may well be less divine Presence in the world. And yet, the blatant inequality inherent in the status of "the king's daughter" makes even the praise for Mother Sarah seem patronizing. Are there ways to uphold the gender distinctions that Judaism's classic texts and teachers have taught to be inherently valuable and divinely ordained that yet permit, within the limits of mutual responsibility, maximal individual freedom—for all? That is a cardinal question facing young Jewish parents who hope to bless their daughters that "God may make them like Sarah, Rebecca, Rachel, and Leah" but who wish to see not only feminine caring and compassion in the world but also justice and understanding for the daughters and mothers of Israel.

Nehama Leibowitz, the doyen of Bible teachers in the generation just passed, has pointed to one possible avenue of reinterpretation, based on one line of exegesis on the story of Jacob and Rachel in one late medieval text. Here is the context: Rachel, seeing her sister Leah fertile and herself barren, is overcome with jealousy. She approaches Jacob and declares, "Give me children or else I shall die." Jacob is described as angry with her for this heartfelt outburst. "Can I take the place of God who has denied thee the fruit of the womb?" (Gen. 30:1–2).

Nehama Leibowitz asks why there is this "strange and unfeeling" response. And here she cites the commentary of R. Yitzhak (Isaac) ben Moshe Arama, known as the *Akedat Yitzhak* (also the pen name of the author), of fifteenth-century Spain. In commenting on this verse, Akedat Yitzhak remarks upon the names given to the woman after her creation.

The two names for "woman" (*isha* and "Eve") indicate two purposes. The first teaches that woman was taken from man, stressing that like him [woman] may understand and advance in the intellectual and moral field just as did the matriarchs and many righteous women and prophetesses. . . . The second alludes to the power of childbearing and rearing children, as is indicated by the name Eve *[Hava]*—the mother of all [of the] living. A woman deprived of the power of child-bearing will be deprived of the secondary purpose and [still] be left with the ability to do evil or good [just] like the man who is barren. Of both the barren man and woman Isaiah (66:5) states: "I have given them in My house and within My walls a name that is better than sons and daughters," since the offspring of the righteous is certainly good deeds. Jacob was therefore angry with Rachel when she said, "Give me children or else I die," in order to reprimand her and make her understand this all-important principle, that she was not dead as far as their joint purpose in life because she was childless.

As Leibowitz explains the *Akedat Yitzhak* commentary, Jacob's anger is attributed to Rachel's "forgetting the true and chief purpose of her existence, which is no different from that of her partner, the man's. . . . She, in her yearnings for a child, saw her whole world circumscribed to the second purpose of woman's existence [according to the *Akedat Yitzhak*, the secondary purpose!] to become a mother. . . . This was . . . a flight from her destiny and purpose . . . not in virtue of her being a woman, but in virtue of her being a human being."[11]

An essential question that must be addressed by every parent and teacher is how to demarcate between the chief purpose of each person and his or her secondary one, and what to do when the latter is perceived as impinging on the former. Where this question is not seriously addressed, the thesis of individuality and social role may justly be suspected of being apologetic.

It is a question that will, in one way or another, face every Jewish educator who believes that the language of Torah points both to the uniqueness of each gender ("male and female He made them") and to their having both been made in the divine image. The deep well into which we peer in search of ourselves, and of our first parents, is a fountain upon which we draw. Yet we are drawn to it by its ripples as well as by its depth.

2

TEACHING AT THE
FAMILY TABLE

Teaching and Learning
Within the Family Circle

EVEN CONSCIENTIOUS PARENTS of young children just entering school, after years of hearing why? what? and how? and not always having successfully made the omniscient impression they would have liked, look forward to the lazy luxury of asking, What did you learn in school today? At an early stage, school is expected to take over, to become the place where "education" takes place. There children are to be socialized into the goods of civilization; there they will learn what they must know.

But expressions like socialization, and "learning what one must know," though they have a no-nonsense and self-understood tone to them, are ambiguous. What do they refer to? Socialization into a culture? Into the competitive preacademic life of Grade One? And what must one know? What does it mean "to know"? Certainly much of "socialization" and "what must be known" is not exactly "subject matter." And what must be learned not only begins at home but largely belongs there.

If we are lucky, we have learned around the family table or on the sofa or in the kitchen that what educates us is quite diverse and arises in many different contexts. And we discover that there are

things we are "teaching" and our children are learning that probably never come up in school.

A high point of what can happen educationally in the Jewish
home is the evening of the Passover Seder, during and around the
family reading, singing and study of the Passover Haggadah, which
is a liturgically ordered teaching—a conversation between parents
and children. The Seder meal is paradigmatic in its teaching: of
how we learn, what we transmit, and how families may initiate
young people into a collective memory.

And this is what the modern Jewish thinker, Franz Rosenzweig,
had to say about the bonds he understood to link the generations at
the Seder feast.

> The evening meal of the Passover . . . is the meal of meals. It is the
> only one that from first to last has the character of worship. . . . From
> the very start, the word "freedom" sheds its light upon it. The free-
> dom of this meal at which all are equally free . . . [also] expresses it-
> self in the fact that the youngest child is the one to speak, and what
> the father says at table is adapted to this child's personality and his de-
> gree of maturity. In contrast to all instruction, which is necessarily
> autocratic and never on a basis of equality, the sign of a true and free
> social intercourse is this, that the one who stands—relatively speak-
> ing—nearest the periphery of the circle, gives the cue for the level on
> which the conversation is to be conducted. For this conversation
> must include him. No one who is there in the flesh shall be excluded
> in the spirit. The freedom of a society is always the freedom of every-
> one who belongs to it.[1]

Education, we should note, is transformed in Rosenzweig's description into worship and conversation. Not exactly what they do best
in schools!

Teaching About the Exodus

The way the Passover Haggadah gives liturgical shape to the Seder
as a conversation between generations is by tracing the children

who ask the questions, or who respond or remain silent at the Seder table, back to Scripture itself. The sages cited in the Haggadah give sacred lineage to the conversation they urge upon the generations when they say, "The Torah speaks of four children." Where does the Torah speak of them? In which contexts? How are these children really different from one another?[2] On the face of it, all these children in the Torah located within the text by the sages seem to be asking about the deliverance from Egypt. But a cursory examination suggests that this is not exactly the case, and that not all of the children are actually asking questions.

The first biblical reference cited by the Talmudic masters to an interchange about the Exodus between a child and an adult relates to the commandment to make an offering of a pascal lamb every Pesah, in perpetuity. Even when Israel is settled in the land of their inheritance, states the Torah, "You shall maintain this [sacrificial] service." And when children ask, "What do you mean by this service?" you shall say, "It is the sacrifice of the Lord's Passover, for He passed over the houses of the Israelites in Egypt when He smote the Egyptians, and delivered our houses" (Exod. 12:25–27).

Here then is the original question, and its seemingly innocent context. But the Haggadah, as well as corresponding sources in the Jerusalem Talmud (*Pesahim* 10:4) and in the *Mekhilta*, an early Tannaic midrashic work (Tractate *Pisha* 17), attribute it to "the wicked child," who is assumed to ask mockingly, "What is this service to you?" The source in the Jerusalem *Pesahim* adds a jeering afterthought to the scriptural question, namely, "What is this burdensome thing with which you bother yourselves every year?"

The second biblical reference to teaching the children mentions no question. After having been instructed to refrain from *hametz* (unleavened bread) and to eat matzot for seven days, the Israelites are told to explain to their children: "It is because of what the Lord did for me when I went out from Egypt" (Exod. 13:8). There is some controversy about how this statement should be read. Is the matzah to be eaten because God took Israel out of Egypt? Or did God take them out of Egypt *ba'avur zeh*, "because of that" (that they kept His commandments of the paschal offering and the eating of matzah and *maror*, "bitter herbs")? In any case, here we have an answer without a question. This fact suggests to both the Talmud and the *Mekhilta* texts that we are dealing with a child "who does not know how to ask," a child whose parent must initiate the conversation about the Exodus.

Several verses later, after commanding the Israelites to give first-born animals to the priest and to redeem firstborn Israelite sons, the Torah adds:

> And when in time to come your child will ask you, What is this? you shall say to him/her: It was with a mighty hand that the Lord brought us out of Egypt, the house of bondage. [And the connection is that] when Pharoah stubbornly refused to let us go, the Lord slew every firstborn in the land of Egypt, of man and beast. Therefore I sacrifice to the Lord every male issue of the womb but redeem every firstborn among my sons. (Exod. 13:14–15)

The Haggadah's treatment of this child, although taken basically from the *Mekhilta* text, suggests only the beginning of the Torah's response ("It was with a mighty hand"). And it changes the language of the *Mekhilta* in one detail: rather than calling the child stupid *(tipesh)*, as the *Mekhilta* does, the Haggadah uses an inoffensive appellation, simple *(tam)*.

Finally, in Deuteronomy, we come across our fourth child. This young person is actually asking about something else entirely but is answered in reference to the Exodus. The Torah has just admonished Israel to "diligently keep the commandments, the testimonies and the statutes" of God so that "it will be well with you." And the Torah anticipates that *mahar*, "tomorrow," or "at a time to come," your child will ask you:

> What mean the testimonies and the statutes and the ordinances which the Lord our God has commanded you? And then you shall say to your child: We were slaves to Pharaoh in Egypt and the Lord brought us out of Egypt with a mighty hand. And the Lord wrought signs and wonders upon Egypt, upon Pharaoh and upon all his

household before our eyes, and He brought us out from there in order to bring us in, to give us the land that He swore to our forefathers. And the Lord commanded us to do all these statutes, to fear the Lord our God, for our good always, that He might preserve us alive, as it is this day. (Deut. 6:21)

This child is designated as wise by the Haggadah, the *Mekhilta* (Tractate *Pisha* 18), and the Jerusalem Talmud. He or she, after all, can differentiate between the different types of commandments. He or she can distinguish among the ordinances, the testimonies, and the statutes of the Torah. Both the Jerusalem Talmud and the *Mekhilta* subtly change the Torah's wording and have the child ask about the commandments "that the Lord our God gave us" (rather than *you*).

The response given this child by the Torah is not identical with that of any of our three texts (Talmud, *Mekhilta*, or Haggadah), though the first part, *avadim hayinu l'faro b'mitzraim*, "we were slaves to Pharaoh in Egypt," corresponds to the opening of the answer the Seder leader gives to "the four questions" with which the child begins the Seder's evening of study and "telling." What is offered as a response to the wise child in the *Mekhilta* and the Haggadah is instruction in the laws of Passover *(hilkhot hapesah)*. Some suggest that since it is the very last mishnah of the tractate *Pesahim* that states the law of the *afikoman*, the wise child is to be instructed in all the laws of Passover, up to and including the law of *afikoman*. At the very least, he or she is to be taught the final halakhah of the last mishnah in tractate *Pesahim*, namely, that one may not supplement the paschal meal with an *afikoman*.

What is meant by *afikoman*? Some sages understood it to mean dessert. According to this view, the law is that one should not eat anything on the evening of Pesah following the pascal offering, which represents freedom. In another view, *afikoman* connotes a nightclub, an after-dinner entertainment. Our Talmudic source gives this answer to the *tipesh*, the stupid child, and thus the meaning is, do not move from one circle (of festival celebrants and diners) to another. Stay in the family group.[3]

Being Engaged and Being Curious:
The "Four Children"

Clearly, the masters of the Haggadah wished to impart the lesson that each of these biblical "children" be answered in line with his or her question, or in response to the child's silence. The "wise" child, who demonstrates knowledge of distinctions, should be taught halakhah, law, with all its distinctions; the "wicked" one, who vehemently "takes him/herself out of the community," should be taken out of it; the "simple child" should be given a simple answer; and the one "unable to ask" directed toward the matzah and other objects on the Passover table "for which" God took us out of Egypt. It is hoped that these objects will make some impression and evoke some question or some response.

How are these four children related? How may they be categorized? Asking such questions, we sense that "the wicked child" seems out of place in our Haggadah. For the three others differ only in degrees of wisdom: One is sophisticated, one is simple, and a third is too uneducated to even ask a question. But isn't the wicked child also wise? In fact, it has been argued that the original midrash spoke of only three children: the wise, the foolish, and the one who "cannot ask" and that this original text was then combined with another text that spoke of two children, a wicked one and one who was *tam*, meaning *tamim*, "unblemished, righteous."[4] If that is so, then the original rabbinic passages dealt with differing categories: The first dealt with children with cognitive differences, and the second dealt with moral distinctions. This merger may explain why the *tipesh* is given the answer we would associate with the *hakham*, the "wise child." If the *tipesh* (fool) was originally understood as a *tam*, in the sense of *tamim*, a "righteous person," then he or she would have to be taught the commandments in all their detail. After all, such a *tamim* would already have listened attentively to the opening answer of the Seder. For him or her, as for the Deuteronomic child, knowing that "we were slaves to Pharaoh in Egypt . . . and [that] God took us out" could be expected to lead naturally into "and He commanded us to do all these statutes!" After all, it was *ba'avur zeh*, for this, that God liberated us!

Teaching and Imparting Information

Yet there is another way of classifying these "children." We may see the wise child, and perhaps the wicked one even more so, as passionately involved in their questions. Both of them, then, are asking about themselves, about the way they will live their lives.

In the first case, recall, the (wise) child, in order to observe them properly, wishes to know precisely about the various kinds of commandments that God gave. We have already noted that the Torah text is slightly amended in two of our sources, and the child is led to ask about the commandments "that the Lord our God gave *us*" (rather than *you*). Thus the questioner is presented as unequivocally identified, conversing with a respondent who is happily transmitting the tradition. This child is already a loyal person who wishes to expand his/her knowledge of the Torah and who is being elaborately initiated into it.

In the second case, the questioner is clearly perturbed. There is a scoffing and possibly "wicked" smile here, but perhaps behind it tears as well. What is this service, this work that you impose upon yourselves? Is this a proper way to serve God, all this bother that characterizes the Passover celebration? We seem to hear this child both angry and anxious. And the response is in kind. "You are shutting yourself out? So be it!" As with the wise child, the "question" of the wicked one suggests deep involvement and concern. Moreover, the contemporary reader may suspect that the respondent's involvement is also intense, too much so, for it has shorn him or her of educational perspective and sense. Does not the wicked child's rebellion, because of its obvious concern, perhaps bear hope? Should the child be pushed out of "the circle" so summarily and sternly? Is excommunication the best way to treat a frustrated insider? Is the "wicked" one really just arrogant, or is there anger and disappointment here? Perhaps this child even entertains an inward hope of a redeeming answer, one that will make sense of "this work" for him or her so that he or she can share in it!

Now, let us compare this pair of insiders to the "simple" child and to the "one who does not know how to ask." The simple child asks, *"Ma zot?"* (What is this?) He observes the celebrants at the

Seder busy with special rites, songs, and foods, and his curiosity is aroused. In the Torah, we recall, he asks about the law of the first-born and is given a reasonable and plausible reply: "[Because] Pharaoh stubbornly refused to let us go, the Lord slew every first-born in the land of Egypt, of man and beast. Therefore I sacrifice to the Lord every male issue of the womb but redeem every firstborn among my sons." The biblical child has the matter explained and probably walks away, saying, "I see." Here too, at the Seder, we may well imagine the simple child, after having received an adequate answer, to "simply" acknowledge it, without wishing to be changed, or educated, by it.

As for the child "who does not know how to ask," we may think of him or her as the true sibling and soul mate of the simple one. This non-asker is not necessarily the toddler portrayed in many illustrated editions of the Haggadah. The non-asker is as likely to be a teenager who does not ask because he or she does not know what to ask. This child has never been "into" Jewish things and does not care much about them. He or she observes the proceedings, perhaps for the first time, as a total stranger, bored and bewildered. The adults who are conducting the Seder try to make an impression on this alien who cannot even be bothered to ask, "What is this?" They do so by telling of their experience, of their subsequent commitments ("Because of this has God taken us out . . . ").

From either of these latter children we may expect a response such as "Really! I didn't know that." It might even be, "How interesting!"

Being Informed or Being Engaged

To illuminate the deadly quality of a response like "Really," or "How interesting!" in certain contexts, let us imagine ourselves in the following situation: A friend of ours, a fervent believer in another religion, has long sought to get us to "see the light." We have never considered abandoning our own faith, but are intellectually curious, always anxious to learn new things. One day, in a conversation with our friend about religion, we admit that we really know very little about her faith and would appreciate a good reading list and some help in understanding basic texts of her choosing. The friend is enthusiastic; books are recommended and exchanged and five long sessions of joint study are undertaken. Then, when the minicourse is completed, we thank our friend for helping us to fill a serious gap in our education. And we add, "That was really interesting!"

Our friend is devastated. "Interesting?" she responds, "all you can say is that it's interesting?" The friend, of course, thought that our interest stemmed from an existential problem, that we wished to be instructed on how to live, that she was engaged in "making a soul." She thought she was educating us, only to discover that we wanted objective knowledge. We wished to be *informed* about the other faith, not initiated into it.

The two types of asking and responding I am talking about here are sometimes distinguished as "personal" and "objective" discourse, respectively. Sometimes they are termed *first-order* and *second-order* discourse.[5] In Chapter 1, we saw that Yehudah Halevi referred to them as "knowledge of *Elohim* [God]" and "knowledge of *HaShem* [the Lord]." The *haver*-rabbi, speaking of what we are calling detached, or second-order, discourse, explained to the king of the Kuzars that "the meaning of *Elohim* can be grasped by way of speculation, because a Guide and Manager of the world is a postulate of Reason. Opinions differ on the basis of different speculations but that of the philosophers is the best on the subject."

He distinguishes this knowledge of *Elohim* from first-order speech, which reflects the personal attachment of the individual to his or her knowledge: "The meaning of *HaShem* [the name of God by which He is known to Israel], however, cannot be grasped by speculation, but only by that intuition and prophetic vision which separates man, so to speak, from his kind . . . as it is written: 'You shall be turned into another man,' 'God gave him another heart.'"[6]

The modern reader will perhaps be reminded of Martin Buber's distinction between "I-It" relationships and "I-Thou" experiences respectively.[7] In the latter encounter, we assume that commitment is either anticipated or already present; we speak with each other as insiders; we take as a given that our knowledge makes a difference in the way we live; we are "wrapped up" in a mode of experience. In the former, detached mode, the participants are involved in "speculation," "reason," and philosophy. Anyone can engage in this discourse; all, in principle, are outsiders. Matters are formulated objectively and as communicatively as possible, on the basis of scientific or philosophic rules or methods. One is not required to have experienced it personally in order to understand it.

Let me suggest another example that shows the distinction between the two modes of conversation:

1. When a child in a traditionally Sabbath-observing home asks a parent a question about, say, the laws of "forbidden types of work" on the Sabbath, the parent may suggest that the child "look it up" in some authoritative text. The assumption is that the child is asking because he/she is uncertain about how to act and is seeking knowledge in order to act appropriately. Likewise, a "wise child" may have a moral problem with something in a biblical passage and be referred by the parent or teacher to several midrashic commentaries that "deal with that," or be invited to talk about it. In the first case, the parent is helping the child to act normatively; in the second, the parent is helping the child to resolve a problem that threatens to weaken his/her commitment and to broaden the child's insights into the subject matter of "what we believe."

2. Conversely, imagine someone who has "always been curious" about the laws of the Sabbath or wondered how Jews "make sense of some immoral sentiments of Scripture." This questioner is not seeking normative guidelines for himself or herself or hoping for restored faithfulness to a tradition. The interest is academic, objective, and detached. The difference is like that between being educated in the service of God and being informed about Jewish monotheism and its ritual or "cult."

From What We Know to Who We Are

Of course, we come to detached, nonexperiential second-order discourse with certain funds of first-order experience and commitment. For example, in academic study, we assume the moral and intellectual appropriateness of certain methods of inquiry. We are committed to honesty and integrity; we disdain shoddy arguments. Conversely, first-order discourse, in which there is immediate experience and an insider's stance of conviction (or rebellion!), should not be an excuse for obtuseness or dogmatism. We cannot justify everything by declaring that we believe it or are passionately committed to it, and we may not "brain-wash" in the name of belonging or obligation. Thus, the child's question about the moral problem in the verse is a serious one, and not every midrashic comment will be equally acceptable to a sensitive and wise child.

Thus, first-order thinking is influenced, and properly so, by second-order discourse. All of the things we *know* should have some influence on who we *are*. First-order knowledge, by which people will live their lives, is the heart of education. But to deny the validity of all outside, or objective, knowledge in order to protect or save the first-order truth "we" believe in is indoctrination.

A serious problem in education is that second-order, detached knowledge is more readily communicable than committed "insider" first-order truths. Many people will consider the information conveyed by the former plausible, acceptable, and comprehensible but will not accept teaching that makes demands. Yet the seemingly sensible notion of starting with detached information in order to arrive finally at educated engagement is problematic, for it is very difficult to move from detached, objective, second-order instruction to first-order education. Making something clear, or even plausible, is very different from making it existentially important, intrinsic to a person's identity. Few become committed Jews from exposure to good Jewish public relations. And how often do Jewish studies programs at universities, if indeed they are guided by appropriate academic methods and procedures, make up for inadequate or even traumatic Jewish educational experiences of a decade earlier?

First-order education assumes community and patterns of action that fall within specific frameworks of appropriateness. It involves not so much theological understanding as religious and covenantal relationships. It urges learners to adopt patterns of life, not merely to develop agility in describing and defining. And this urging may seem coercive to those who have never been "inside."

Indeed, the Torah, as a language that provides a key for understanding the world, cannot negate second-order knowledge. The first story of creation (in six days) has many second-order elements. The Torah also states that its laws are "your wisdom and your understanding in the eyes of the nations" (Deut. 4:6). This is certainly an attempt to persuade Israel of the Torah's "objective" excellence, pointing to some "universal" quality of wisdom inherent in the commandments that enables the nations of the world also to identify them as worthy. But as "a tree of life for those who hold fast to it," the Torah clearly wishes children to be initiated into a first-order community.

For this reason, the child who "does not know how to ask" and the simple one too are a problem of a very different kind from the wicked child. The simple child is not read out of the community, but that may be, at least in part, because she or he is not in it! Polite curiosity about redeeming firstborn sons or about matzah may express an alienation greater even than that of the wicked child. That latter child, after all, if answered in true encounter and drawn back into the community, may well become a *hakham* or a *tamim*, a wise or a righteous person.

In our generation, difficulties in discourse between parents and children are perhaps greater than ever before. On the one hand, in the secular-liberal language world, all truth tends to be identified with second-order knowledge, whereas the other kind is relegated to "mere" subjectivity and ascribed to forces of unreason and fanaticism. On the other hand, there does exist, in the very midst of that world and in response to it, blatant fundamentalism. Fundamentalists see only first-order, committed knowledge as pertinent and permissible. And they confuse the categories, insisting that first-order knowledge gives adequate second-order knowledgeability. If, for secular positivists, all character education is suspect and perhaps benighted, for fundamentalists, all real education must be indoctrination.

Being Told—and Telling the Story

Obviously, Torah instruction is fundamentally engaged, normative, first-order. It is designed for a community of covenant. In the first commandment that the Israelite community receives shortly before the Exodus, to sanctify the new moon, Moses and Aaron are told that "this month shall be for you the beginning of the months," about which the sages comment, *"Kaze re'e v'kadesh"* (a new moon such as this shall you see, and sanctify) (Rashi on Exodus 12:2). But many of the children in our schools are outsiders; the expression "for you" does not speak to them. Since we are justifiably worried about preaching at them, we simply tell them about it and hope that they will find it interesting. We do not always face the fact that first-order learning takes place especially at home and that schools, especially achievement-oriented ones, are often not particularly good at it.

Does the tradition of Passover and of the four children suggest ways to move from outside to inside, from information to involvement? The answers given to the various children in the Torah and in the Haggadah are suggestive. In the Torah, all the children who ask, and also the one who does not, are told a *ma'aseh shehayah*, "something that happened." The questions may still be in the future, whenever *mahar* (tomorrow) will be. But the answers are all designed to generate astonishment at what has already happened but is still with us.

We tell the story, but we, the narrators and the listeners, are part of what is being told. We sit in the family circle, eating matzah and bitter herbs, reclining on cushions as freemen did in ancient times. It is today as it was "yesterday." In each generation, we are threatened with enslavement and death, but we celebrate the continuing possibility of liberation. It has happened before so it can—and will—happen again. Today, or at the latest, at a time to come, tomorrow. In the Haggadah, only the wise child, who is already part of the story, moves on from the *story* of the community to the *laws* of the community, to how the community lives. (We recall that when the *tam* was not the simple but the "righteous child," he/she was also told this.) And the law means: Stay with the community. After our celebration of freedom, seek no *afikoman*. Do not look for entertainment outside, a nightclub, or food sweeter than the paschal lamb symbolizing our liberation. Do not move to another circle. Tonight, and always, stay with the family.

Why should even a wise child be prepared to accept this, even if it is a prerequisite for acquiring first-order knowledge (of which one is notoriously ignorant until one has it)? Ultimately, only because he/she has been initiated and has been empowered as a participant and has had the experience of being taken seriously as a participant.

Franz Rosenzweig, in the passage from *The Star of Redemption* with which we began, remarks that the Seder evening is introduced by the child's questions and the parent's answers. But once the frontal learning of the parent's teaching has been concluded, all sing songs of praise together. And, finally, those who began the Seder with questions take the lead, with children's songs. As the Seder, with its anticipation of redemption, of wholeness still to come, draws to a close, the children introduce their parents into ditties of counting and together with them sing an allegory about "a kid that my father bought with two zuzim," a chronicle leading from fire and sticks and ferocious animals to the redemption of "the one kid" by the Holy One. It is a half-understood song of deep meaning, but the atmosphere is all cheer and enjoyment.

Having become part of the community, the children now take their turn leading it. They have been told the story, and they now understand that it also happened to them and that they have something to say within the community. As "children" of the Torah and the Haggadah have always learned, the story becomes theirs when something is going on. There is something being done, at the ancient encampment or sanctuary, or at the table, that symbolizes what is being said, that "explains" it. There is matzah and *maror* (bitter herbs) "for which" God took us out of Egypt and that remind us of it. Being "astonished" by what happened, we reenact it. The story that we are told becomes a story that we must tell, for it is our story!

Remembering Yesterday, Anticipating Tomorrow

Through a structural quirk of the Hebrew calendar, the first day of Pesah always falls on the same day of the week as Tisha B'Av, the anniversary of the destruction of the Temple. A connection I like to make between the two events, of liberation and destruction, passes through a story that a former justice of the Israeli Supreme Court often tells.

This man, in his youth in the 1920s, studied at a famous German university. In those student years, this judge-to-be was punctilious about observing the prescriptions of the *Shulhan Arukh*, the code of Jewish law. Therefore, during the "three weeks" before the fast of Tisha B'Av, he, together with one friend, refrained from shaving, as required by one stringent interpretation of halakhic tradition. There were no other students at that university who walked around the campus unshaven, and the two were well aware of making a slovenly impression.

One day, a professor approached the future jurist and inquired why such generally neat and groomed young men should be un-shaven. "My friend and I are in mourning," the student gravely explained. The professor was genuinely shocked. "Oh, I am so sorry. For whom?" "For our Temple," was the solemn response. The professor was all sympathy. "I didn't know that your Temple had been destroyed," he admitted. "When did this happen?" "Oh," explained the student casually, "about 1,850 years ago." The professor stared at him, wondering whether he was talking to a madman or a fool—or being made a fool of.

Would the student have made matters better or worse by explaining that in his community two millennia made no difference because the mourning was now—and the redemption was anticipated to be tomorrow? That it was "because of this" that Jews were still alive—as children and parents? It is hard to tell. After hearing such an explanation, the professor might have said, "How interesting" and even invited the future judge to speak to his seminar students. Yet that might have been a frustrating experience. In explaining these matters at the professor's seminar, the unshaven young man might have realized that although all first-order matters can, in principle, be partially explained in a second-order fashion to any well-meaning person, it is harder to do so in some cases than in others.

Our own children too have the right to explanations in the open and sophisticated societies in which they live, but explanations may seem incomprehensible or even ludicrous where there is no community, no education about how and where we are situated: between "yesterday" and "tomorrow."

Even good schools are more like seminars than kitchens or living rooms. A seminar room is an important and indispensable place of learning. But it is not a Seder.

3

Holding Hands: Abraham Walks with Isaac

Parents face a serious dilemma when they struggle to make their children into curious and "open" human beings, comfortable with exploration and oriented to encounter with others. "Open" people, so educational psychologists tell us, have learned to believe that the world is basically good. They find it, on the whole, comprehensible. They expect it to be friendly. Their tendency is to trust others and to offer them goodwill and even affection. Conversely, research indicates that those who perceive the world as evil, cruel, and untrustworthy tend to be suspicious and disinclined to enter into relationships, which they have come to see as superfluous and potentially dangerous.

The dilemma arises because "open" parents and teachers wish to present a friendly world to their children so that they too will develop into trusting and affectionate persons. But the adults know that the world is often not friendly and that trust in it, if unjustified, invites disillusionment and often callous indifference to the pain of others. Should parents lie to children in order to foster openness in them? Should they hide what they know and, perhaps, hinder their children from dealing with the world as it really is in order to keep them from mirroring its terrifying and hateful features in their own souls? We want children to be "tender-minded," in William James's intriguing phrase,[1] but reality suggests that "tough-mindedness," despite its price, is more appropriate.

With You in a Time of Trouble

A religious approach that we find in Torah and in some other religious traditions, too, is that although there is much evil in the world, God may be petitioned to give the individual strength to cope with it, to put it into perspective, to overcome it. He is, says the psalmist, "with you [the sufferer] in [your] trouble" (Ps. 91:15). Understanding why there is evil and injustice in the world can be helpful where it is possible, but that does not soothe the hurt and does not necessarily encourage us to be open to encounter. But it is different, intimates this approach, when God, as it were, "holds your hand."

Two insights, not only about God and the suffering human being but also about parents and children, are suggested by this conception of hand holding. One is, as children rather quickly discover, that parents are not able to make everything come right in their world, that sometimes all parents can do is hold your hand. The other is that although holding hands may be built on profound helplessness and disappointment, it may, despite the disillusion that accompanies it, give comfort and point the way to wisdom.

That this approach of holding hands intimates a paradoxical relationship of gratitude and anticipation was succinctly stated by Assaf, a psalmist-poet reputed to have lived in King David's time. In what has come down to us as Psalm 73, Assaf deceptively opens his reflection in apparent contentment: "But God is good to Israel, to the pure of heart." Yet that is rapidly exposed as a problematic credo, for the "but" points to overwhelming troubles. All around him there is evil, the self-aggrandizement of the wicked and the suffering of the innocent. Yet Assaf seems to know about the difficulties of raising children who are open and trusting; he tells of his hesitation to speak forthrightly about the indignities and pain he witnessed lest he "be faithless to the generation of Your children." Perhaps, like devoted educators in every generation, he saw himself charged with the task of making good and loyal members of the faith community out of the young, giving authorized answers to their perplexities, making everything seem all right. Perhaps he toyed with the idea of not probing too much, since he allegedly owed it to himself and his disciples to "keep smiling."

Yet Assaf seems to merit a place in the Psalms not for his (pedagogical) smile but for his honesty. The moral chaos in the world and the silence of Providence troubled him deeply. He tells us that he went to the Temple in Jerusalem, perhaps hoping to have his questions addressed by the educator-priests. It is not implausible that there, in the Temple, our author heard all the answers, all the theodicies with which we are familiar. Possibly the priests, hearing that a prominent teacher was coming to them, seeking solutions to existential problems, organized a "workshop" for him. They may well have explained to our teacher that suffering is a consequence of old and new sins, that society and individuals could, through the proper application of human intelligence, escape the ills that befall the stupid and shortsighted. (Just what we may read now as "post-Holocaust thought.") And apparently he was given some happy anticipations. They include the promise that the wicked will eventually fall and that justice will triumph in the future.

Then he indicates that these answers, true though they may be, are inadequate. Perhaps while still meditating in the Temple, he turns from collective hopes for the future to his personal experience, past and present. And he discovers that God, who inexplicably does not prevent his torments, holds his hand during them, that "the nearness of the Lord is my good." Assaf understands that the words "God is good to Israel" are not only a promise for "the latter days" but also a key to that experience and that potentiality. To be "near" God does not mean to be protected from history or inevitable suffering and death, but to "see," in the midst of these, that "I am continually with You; You hold my right hand." It is those who are distant who shall perish. Those who are near, despite trials and tribulations, "shall tell of God's works."

Yet the Torah describes an episode that makes tender-mindedness and openness appear radically more pathetic than do the human acts of violence and cruelty that Assaf experienced. In this episode (Gen. 22:1–19), God Himself demands an act of cruelty that makes a mockery of nearness and holding hands. The tribulations of human existence that parents cannot prevent or even consistently hold distant could hardly be more sharply signified than by God's commandment to a parent to offer up his child as a burnt offering. It was Abraham, the father, who was to sacrifice his beloved son, Isaac "upon one of the hills that I shall show you" (22:2). And the stark solitude of the matter is unambiguously, yet cryptically, expressed in Abraham's charge to the young men who accompany father and son on their grisly journey, at its terminal point: "Stay you here with the donkey, and I and the boy shall go yonder; and we shall worship and return to you" (22:5).

What do you say to your children on Rosh Hashanah (the New Year), for instance, when the liturgy mandates reading this shattering story? Certainly not that God was holding Abraham's hand!

The *Akedah*, the binding of Isaac, is a never-ending source of wonderment for commentators, masters of liturgy, poetry—and polemics—in our generation, especially polemics. For is the steadfast faith that can countenance such a sacrifice not absurd? Is the very idea of that sacrifice not a monstrous perversion of what parenthood should be?

Living Faithfully in an Uncertain Reality

In thinking about the *Akedah* and the absolutely lonely suffering of the founding parent that it reflects, it is customary to begin where the tradition places it, at the end of a series of trials through which Abraham's faithfulness is verified and demonstrated. Yet the *Akedah*, the tenth trial, not only climaxes Abraham's story but also seems to unravel it. Was it for this conclusion that God sent Abraham and Sarah to an unknown land where they "made souls" for the God of righteousness? Was it for this that He sent them messengers of glad tidings and, having brought the couple safely through the Grar episode (Gen. 20), gave them a son? Was it so that Abraham would have to undergo this ordeal and Sarah, at least according to one midrash, die at the shock of hearing of it?[2]

The entire story of Abraham and Sarah raises many questions but never more than at this climax. Why would God ask such a gift from a person and impose such a test? Is this the way of a moral and merciful God? Why did Abraham, who had previously pleaded so stubbornly for the wicked of Sodom and Gemorrah, simply agree to it? And what made it possible for the patriarch, in the midst of this unbearable ordeal, to promise his young men that he and his son, alive and well, would return? Was that simple fatigue or patronizing falsehood? Was it what the education-minded parent is supposed to do, to put a better face on the horror of his situation? Or was Abraham seeing beyond the trial, enabled by the view "from where he stood" to be tender-minded even in the world as it was?

On Yom Kippur, these Rosh Hashanah questions are, if that is possible, heightened. In the *Selihot* (penitential prayers) of the festive Additional Service *(Mussaf)* of that day, we read about the *asarah harugai malkhut*, the ten sages (tormented to death by the Romans after the Bar Kohba uprising of the second century C.E.). And then, startlingly, the liturgy has us turn to God, beseeching Him, "Look from behind Your veil . . . O God and King Who sits on the seat of mercy!" What mercy?

It is of course possible to maintain that the stories of Abraham and of the martyred sages are not similar at all. Those Talmudic rabbis had no choice: Caesar charged them with the crime of their ancestors who had sold their brother Joseph into slavery. Since one does not choose one's ancestors, they, like the victims of the Holocaust, were, as the liturgy terms them, *likkudim*, "trapped": There was no escape for them. Abraham, it may be said, was not in that position. Why did he not, then, simply refuse?

On the face of it, he could have, and perhaps should have, refused. Perhaps he was simply too trusting, too faithful a servant of God to remember his duty toward that fellow human being for whom his responsibility was greatest, his child. The Israeli philosopher Shmuel Hugo Bergman argues for that position. He declared that had he himself heard such a commandment, he would have affirmed that it could not possibly have come from God.[3] But that is a modern option. I do not think that it was available to Abraham. He did, of course, have a choice, as commanded people always have, but it was a choice between being God's friend and servant and shredding that identity, recoiling from the narrative of his life. Impossible! But loyalty too must have seemed unbearable.

What might be a modern analogy to the plight of Abraham? Consider the case of a military commander of a large force who has decided that a volunteer soldier must be sent on a mission that brings with it certain death. The soldiers from whose ranks the volunteer is to come know only that the mission is dangerous, and there are three brave volunteers, of whom one is chosen by lot. His name and the names of the others are sent in a sealed envelope to the commander (for he may wish to disqualify the marked one and choose one of the others). To his dismay, the commander discovers that the soldier who has volunteered and been chosen is his own son.

The commander can decide to send one of the other two. There are possible ploys. For example, he could send his son on another mission, fraudulently declared to be no less dangerous. The commander could indeed do this, and he is tempted to do so. His son is an only child. The boy means "everything in the world" to his mother. His death may kill her. But he cannot commit this fraud. It will destroy the meaning of his authority, of his decency, of his life, to send to death the son of another mother and father. All he can do without betraying the meaning of his life is to bemoan the absurdity and cruelty of the world in which integrity makes a mockery of love. Abraham, it seems to me, is like that commander. In a sense, this makes the situation of the *asarah harugai malkhut*, in which there is no choice, less brutal than that of the *Akedah*. In either case, where is the God of mercy? Where does He make encounter still meaningful and worthy?

Enter a Biblical Pedagogue

Several years ago, sitting with me in the synagogue during this *Selihot* liturgy of stark death and alleged mercy, my son turned to me with a provocative and pained question: "Just what kind of divine mercy are we talking about here?" And then immediately, as though still musing on that ancient story of the "trapped" sages: "Why did God allow the Holocaust to happen? How can we worship a God of mercy in this terrible world?" And in reference to the *Akedah* too: "Would you trust a *human being*, never mind *a human father*, who acted like that?" My son's question, his shocking, yet honest, reflection, made me realize that he knew of my own frequent helplessness but forgave it, for if God's world was as it seemed to be, who could be blamed? Yet, like all tender-minded parents, I wondered whether there was a way to protect my son, to make it come right, to save him from inevitable bitterness and cynicism. I brought to mind Assaf's psalm, how he begins with "But surely God is good to Israel" and then proceeds to examine whether this assumption is true and what meaning these words may have and what he could do, as a teacher, to keep from "betraying" the generation of the young.

Assaf must have been familiar with questions like my son's. Clearly this poet, Assaf, was a teacher, and in his community he was probably a paragon of propriety and piety, a person who was expected to have the right answers to all awkward questions. Just the man who would open his remarks with references to God's goodness. A teacher and probably a parent! What can we learn from Assaf? A believer in God's goodness, he must have asked, as I did, what is there about the *Akedah* that can help rather than disillusion us, that can allow us to bring up tender-minded children in a world in which there is betrayal and cruelty and torture. The sages who mandated its reading on the High Holidays surely had the same kinds of questions. If they assigned this reading, they must have detected something in the story that they believed penetrated to a deep, albeit elusive, teaching. Let us examine it carefully.

Sharpening the Questions

Abraham, the Bible tells us, was God's friend, His beloved. The nearness of being together "hand in hand," as it were, of which the psalmist speaks, might well be describing Abraham. What will illu-

minate this nearness of Abraham to God, even in a moment of in-
describable sorrow and likely rage? As we read and ask, it becomes
difficult not to think about our own bereavements, the outrages we
suffer, the pain we undergo. What can we say about nearness in the
face of our own experiences of distance?

Philosophies, however profound, have limited usefulness here. It
may indeed be true, as some thinkers posit, that evil and suffering
are largely the consequence of human viciousness. Some of the mis-
ery of human existence may indeed be explained by a kind of divine
"self-limitation" for the sake of human freedom. Perhaps God
Himself is bound to "process" and hence, as the kabbalists tell us, is
hampered *(kivayakhol)*, as it were, by present "fractures" and flaws.
But dealing with our problem only in that way may lead our students to simply, even indifferently, respond with an "I see" of the
"simple child" at the Passover Seder; with the detached comprehension that lacks all passion, that protects against the world but
also seals off real encounter with it. Philosophical solutions may allow them—and us—to reach facile or even comfortable accommodations to distance. If we shun that, then what we need more than
prematurely received solutions, are psalms, *piyutim*, "liturgical poems," and midrashim that sharpen questions and make us see the
point of nearness even when it is distant, that call nearness up for us
and help us to remember our experience of it.

It is in this connection that the following text, which addresses
the commandment of *tzitzit*, the woolen "fringes," which the
Bible commands being placed on four-cornered garments, comes
to mind. The midrashic teacher, as was the style of this pedagogical and homiletic form, opens with a seemingly irrelevant verse
from the biblical "Writings" *(Ketubim):* "Light is sown for the
righteous, and those of upright heart will have joy" (Ps. 97:11).
He continues:

> The Holy One blessed be He . . . left not a thing in the world about
> which He did not charge Israel with some commandment. If an Is-
> raelite goes out to plough, then [she/he is charged with the com-
> mandment]: "You shall not plough with an ox and an ass together"

(Deut. 22:10); to sow: "You shall not sow your vineyard with two kinds of seeds" (22:9); reap: "When you reap your harvest and have forgotten a sheaf . . . you shall not go back to fetch it" (24:19). . . . If she/he builds a house: "You shall make a parapet for your roof (22:8) and then "shall write them [the passages of the *Shema* in the *mezzuzah*] on your doorposts" (6:9); if he wraps himself in a cloak: "Say to them that they make themselves *tzitzit* [fringes]" (Num. 15:37). (*Tanhuma, Shelah Leha* 15)[4]

Further along, the midrash asks:

To what may this be compared? To the case of one who has been thrown into the water. The captain stretches out a rope and says: "Take hold of the rope with your hand and do not let go, for if you do you will lose your life." Similarly, the Holy One blessed be He said to Israel: "As long as you adhere to the commandments then You who cleave to the Lord your God are alive, every one of you to this day" (Deut. 4:4). In the same vein [Scripture] says: "Take fast hold of instruction, let her not go: keep her, for she is your life" (Prov. 4:13). (*Tanhuma, Shelah Lekha* 15)

The imagery here is powerful, paradoxical, and frightening. But here too, we can be prematurely relieved of the terror by philosophizing about it. For example, we can say, with Rabbi J. B. Soloveitchik, that Judaism wisely refrains from demanding explanations for what is beyond human comprehensibility but, rather, systematically addresses the normative demands arising in every situation.[5] Or we can adopt the teaching of Emil Fackenheim that in the excruciating situations in which "the redeeming Presence of God" is clearly absent, we can yet respond to a "commanding Presence" that is indeed perceived to be here.[6] Yet, for such thinkers as Soloveitchik and Fackenheim, the answers surely come only after the hard questions have been asked. These wise teachers would not have offered us solutions unless they had experienced the pain of a precarious faithfulness, of tender-mindedness in a world in which the divine itself appears as the arena of the absurd.

The Tribulations of the Righteous

It is this pain, of being "far" from God, at the very edge of "be-tray[ing] the generation of Your children" (Ps. 73:15) that seems to have wracked the psalmist Assaf and that is here reflected in the teaching of the midrashic sage. Light, the midrashic teachers tell us, is sown for the righteous, and the "straight of heart" shall have joy. What at first glance looks like a pietistic and even sentimental piece about "how many mitzvot (commandments) are waiting to be done" becomes, at its end, a matter of raging waters, ropes, and rescue, a matter of life and death. Reading carefully, we realize that what started with a seemingly comfortable idea is not what it appears to be. The thin and endearing threads of *tzitzit* are, in fact, strong and heavy ropes thrown to those who are shipwrecked in a raging and sinister sea.

But is it true that there is "light for the righteous"? Is the "light sown" here scattered about or buried? And if buried, is it not extinguished? Why, when we see the light buried and extinguished, or even sown about and slowly dying out, ember by ember, a reality we encounter anew with every human atrocity, with every act of injustice and unfairness, should we affirm its reality? If our lives are truly like the lives of those "thrown" into the water, why should we trust the captain who would do that to us in the first place?

Moreover, why think of the commandments as a rope thrown to us so that we do not drown? Does observing them protect us from tragedy and despair and death? Are those who keep them, who adhere to this teaching of faith, really "alive, every one to this day"? (Deut. 4:4). Why, when remembering Abraham in the act of binding his son on the altar or while reciting the saga of the righteous who were tortured to death, should we think of God as sitting on a seat of mercy?

As Abraham takes his son Isaac up to Mount Moriah, what could be going through his mind that makes it possible for him to move, step by step, toward his destination? Why should he obey such an absurd commandment? Why should he trust God? And what was he saying when he said to the young men, "I and the boy shall go yonder; and we shall worship and return to you"? Was he lying? Soothing? Hoping? Or did he know this future with an absolute certainty? Or was he silently conveying a lie when he "walked together" with Isaac to Mount Moriah, holding his hand? Was this a cruel deception? Or did he hold Isaac's hand because someone had to, an act of desperate love in the very midst of betrayal?

And what about all those who sacrificed their children, to Moloch or principles or maniacs—whose children did not "return" with them? What gentle, open, and tender things did their mothers and fathers say to them first? Did they think that made it all right?

Being There for Your Child

The military commander whose son has been chosen for death, and the midrash's captain and Abraham, remind me of a story told by the sociologist Peter L. Berger and a question he addresses to his story:

> A child wakes up at night, perhaps from a bad dream, and finds himself surrounded by darkness, alone, beset by nameless threats. At such a moment the contours of trusted reality are blurred or invisible, and in the terror of incipient chaos the child cries out for his mother. It is hardly an exaggeration to say that, at this moment, the mother is being invoked as the high priestess of protective order. It is she (and in many cases, she alone) who has the power to banish the chaos and to restore the benign shape of the world. And, of course, any good mother will do just that.[7]

The mother, writes Berger, will turn on a lamp that casts reassuring light, she will cradle the child, and perhaps sing or speak to the little one. "And the content of this communication will invariably be the same—'Don't be afraid—everything is in order, everything is all right.'" If all goes well, the child will be reassured, his trust in reality will be recovered, and in this trust he will return to sleep.

Once again, this time with Berger, we must ask: Was the mother lying to the child? On the face of it, nothing is all right! One day, the mother will die, and with her death, her protection and her order-restoring powers will end. Furthermore, Berger reminds us, "The world that the child is being asked to trust is the same world in which he will eventually die."

Berger intimates that unless we have found our way toward a religious understanding of human existence, the ultimate truth about our existence cannot be love or light but is terror and darkness. In that case, "The nightmare of chaos, not the transitory safety of order, would be the final order of the human situation." If there is no truth in the religious interpretation of human existence, the mother is lying, whether deviously or innocently, whether with fervently good intentions or in lazy routine.

Berger suggests that the world is filled with "rumors of angels," intimations of transcendence that invite the choice of faith. There is, for instance, the sense of order and security articulated by the mother of the crying child; there is the determination of the sick and dying to carry out a project or an obligation and to accept death itself as somehow not final. There is humor that puts things into a different and astonishing perspective. The present reality is real enough, but it is not all there is. Speaking biblically and midrashically, light is sown (buried?) in order to give joy. This sounds absurdly paradoxical, but we are asked to recall our experience of it. We are bidden to remember, from the things we have known, the reality of what we believe. And what we remember is taken from our own sense of order, our remembering the right (or wrong) response to the demands made upon us for love and responsibility *as we have seen others respond to such demands*, our persistent urge for more decency, our ability to see things differently as though life makes sense, as though what we do is supremely important. In terms of what I have written above, we are to remember that God is holding our hand or, when He is not, to act *as though* He were, the way we learned to when a parent was holding our hand or when God was—and in anticipation of when He will.

I have written "as though life makes sense, as though . . . ." Then it is, after all, a lie? As we think about it and imagine Abraham "our father" proceeding to Mount Moriah, surely not understanding how the world works completely either, we might return to a second reading of our midrash. Is the captain who is throwing us a rope thereby pulling us out of the water? Hardly, though there is a future promise of happiness that lends itself to such an interpretation. But for now, the commandments that give life are located in murky death-dealing waters. The "captain" is not really providing a way out, but confirming—through the commandments—that the "as though" world is a real one, it is not an illusion at all! It is beyond this world, which we know only too well, but also within it. Those who live in this other "world" are not escaping from real life. To "cleave to God" by way of His commandments, even when He has thrown us into the water, gives life. It *is* life!

And again we are returned to our psalmist. As he looks around at the "obvious" world of the powerful and the wicked, his "flesh and heart fail" (Ps. 73:26). He laments that "all the day have I been plagued and my chastisement came every morning" (Ps. 3:14). Yet, God is "the Rock of my heart" (Ps. 73:26) Despite everything, Assaf can say that "I am continually with Thee" (73:23). He doesn't understand everything and he may be a stranger to systems, but he knows that "the nearness of God is my good; I have made the Lord God my refuge that I may tell of all Your works" (73:28). Note Assaf's words: "*I* have made." This is the teaching that makes Abraham hold Isaac's hand even, especially, at the moment God is not holding his. The parent's teaching of trust, tender-mindedness in the midst of chaos, points to a reality, of light sown for the righteous.

Pointers to a Life of Faith

Perhaps it was Abraham himself, our first teacher, who initially uttered these words, on the three-day journey from his home in Beersheva to Mount Moriah. Abraham, after all, was no stranger to the terrible and the absurd. Before God took him out of Ur and brought him to the Land, so one midrash tells us, he had been cast into a fiery furnace; in the words of another midrash (discussed in Chapter 1), he saw "a burning castle." The sight of that, we recall, led him to a terrible reflection: "Can one say this castle has no master?" When God had looked out of the window of the "burning castle" and said, "I am the guide of the world," Abraham had understood this as a directive: "[Therefore] ... go to the land I shall show you" (Gen. 12:1). In the moment of despair, he was exposed to a world of revelation, both cryptic and commanding. It was his first trial.

Yet how unlike that first trial was to this moment before the consummation of the final trial. For now, everything was going up in flames, and it seemed that God Himself had set that chaotic fire of destruction and delighted in it. We have entertained the thought that the words recorded by Assaf were first spoken by Abraham on the road to Moriah. These words, recalling "nearness" even in the face of death and tragedy, evoked the memory of the voice that had spoken to him out of the burning castle. Perhaps that memory, signifying the beginning of the bond between him and the divine "master of the castle" and "captain," a bond hammered out in subsequent teaching and in trials, made it possible for him to speak to "the young men" as he did, reassuring them, making God his refuge even in His absence. And yet, why should he bother to do so?

Abraham had learned and had taught *tzedek u'mishpat* (what is just and what makes moral sense) to his entire household, including these young men. He knew that they had been morally educated and that the presence of God meant something to them. Yet, they were representatives of the mundane world. Often sad and seared, they turned aside from raging fires; often bored and vaguely desperate, they had no sense of drowning. But, much like his descendant Assaf, who loved the Judaeans of his generation, felt responsibility, toward them, and could not betray them, so Abraham too, felt love and concern for his young men. They were of his household. He felt obliged to explain to them what was happening, to reassure them and bolster their sense that everything was all right. And he had learned in his life with God that whatever happened, there was that world in which, despite burning castles and raging waters, the master could speak and the captain might save. So it would not be a lie to tell the young men that he and Isaac would go and worship and return. It restored their sense of right, though they did not look behind it and did not really understand it.

As he was their mentor, Abraham had to say it, even if it was diffi-cult for him because he did understand it. He knew that the truth of it was "sown" and that he, at the moment of his speaking, stood only at the precarious edge of reassurance, waiting for the nearness of God to be his refuge.

Can we, as teachers and parents, be as faithful and yet honest? Can we help our children to be open, even in the raging sea in which they and we live? Can we, by the way we act and by the ways we react, speak persuasively of our faith that light is sown for the righteous, that tender-mindedness is not an evasion of the world as we know it but a truthful response to it and a pointer to what we should like ourselves to become?

4

Bringing Up a "Problem Child"

Nature or Nurture?

Is character a matter of nature or nurture? Do we get our children—and the baggage we ourselves carry around with us—from genetic endowments? Or is it mainly our upbringing that determines who we are and can become? What we can "make" of our children? And if education is the potent stuff we are often told that it is, are the deficiencies and delinquencies of a generation the fault of its parents and teachers?

A plausible point of departure for thinking about the issue of nature or nurture is in the sad story of Esau, the firstborn twin son of Isaac and Rebecca. Was he born incorrigible, a "bad lot," irredeemable by education? Or is he a classic example of those who, due to miseducation or parental neglect, go wrong?

Esau is a paradigmatic antihero of midrashic tradition, though the Torah, quite nonjudgmentally, simply notes that "when the boys grew up, Esau was one who knew hunting, a man of the field, and Jacob was a quiet man, dwelling in tents" (Gen. 25:27). But he does have qualities that can be interpreted uncharitably, stigmatizing him and setting him off from Jacob, the "good one" of the pair. And midrashic interpretation of the biblical "Esau text" is indeed uncharitable toward him. If the Torah describes Esau as "a man of

the field," whose joy is in hunting and who is uncomfortable in sedate tents, the midrash indicates that Esau is somehow "wild."
Note that when hungry, he will do anything for food.

The sages see him not only as impulsive but also as savage. Unlike Jacob, whose "power is in his (prayerful) voice," Esau's is in his
allegedly violent hands (*Gittin* 57b). Why is there this uncharitable
view of Isaac and Rebecca's firstborn?

It is Esau's historical misfortune to be Edom, the crimson
(bloody?) man who inadvertently gives his name to the hated Roman Empire. Consequently, all that the Romans do wrong is prefigured in him. As those wily Romans seem to have respect for parents, at least for the *pater familias*, so does Esau pretend love for
Isaac; as Romans slyly claim to establish their society upon (twelve
tablets of) law, so does Esau give the impression of concern for law.
But as with his alleged Roman descendants, it is all deviousness.
Esau's "hunting was in [Isaac's] mouth" (Gen. 25:28), meaning, says
one midrash, that "he hunted (laid snares for) his father with his
mouth." For example, he would ask his father questions worthy of
the best rabbinic *bet midrash*, "House of Study," such as what the
halakhah (law) is regarding tithes for straw and salt, knowing that
the Torah exempts both from tithes (*Genesis Rabbah* 63:10). Questions like that made him look halakhically punctilious but it cost
him nothing. Just like the Romans!

Had Esau not been seen as the archetype of Rome, might he have
been judged differently? The text gives us grounds for thinking so.
Esau comes across as a simple and perhaps coarse person, but he
does not lack nobility. Would our father Isaac have loved a person
with no redeeming qualities? Esau reciprocates this love. So when
he sees how upset his parents are at his heathen wives, he marries
his ostensibly more acceptable cousin (Gen. 28:9). Even at the moment when Esau vows to kill Jacob, who deceived him and stole his
blessing, he considerately postpones revenge until after his father's
death (27:41). Later on, at an opportune moment, he seems to simply "forget" to kill his brother. Intriguingly, in the midrashic tradition it is "the angel of Esau" who wrestles with Jacob as the patriarch returns home to Canaan. It is he who finally blesses him and
confers the name Israel on him.

Yet the *literature* of Midrash, dealing with Esau against the backdrop of Roman oppression and duplicity, considers Esau an evil man, the wicked father of an idolatrous and oppressive nation, and that is the way he comes down to us. Even if we have some reservations about it, let us accede to the directive of the rabbinic sages that the way to read the sacred *literature* of the Torah and to get at the *language* is through their own midrashic literature, and ask: How did Esau become that way? Couldn't Isaac and Rebecca, two noble people, have done something to cultivate a finer personality in their older child? Did they, quite simply, fail with him? Or was Esau congenitally the representative of a type, a forerunner and exemplar of all the powerful and evil people we know, the archetype of all who will be judged in "the end of days" when "the kingdom" of the world will become God's (Obad. 21)?

A well-known midrash, cited by Rashi in his commentary on the verse "And the children struggled within her" (Gen. 25:22), takes the second position. The midrash comments: "Whenever [pregnant Rebecca] walked past the doors of the Torah [i.e., the schools of Shem and Eber] Jacob moved convulsively [in his efforts] to be born, but whenever she walked past a pagan temple, Esau struggled to be born" (*Genesis Rabbah* 63:6).

The midrash takes for granted that Shem and Eber, the righteous son and grandson of Noah, ancestors of the Abrahamic line, were teaching Torah even in Rebecca's time, and that Jacob, the tent dweller, received his education in these tents of Torah. It also, less anachronistically, assumes that there were pagan temples available for Esau's perverse devotions. At first sight, then, education could not have changed either of the children much. Esau was a natural pagan; Jacob, from the moment of conception, a lover of Torah. Rebecca wisely recognized this and loved her younger son; Isaac, pathetically unaware of it, allowed his appetite for venison to trap his affections.

Of course, even in this midrashic view of fetuses already naturally good or evil, education might have made a difference. Could not Isaac and Rebecca have devoted efforts to strengthening Jacob's good traits and minimizing or somehow neutralizing Esau's bad ones? Nevertheless, the midrash takes the sting out of educational failure. Parents and teachers can and should do their best, but they are not to blame for the eventual outcome. After all, character is what you are born with. Character is destiny.

The Evil Inclination

But one can give a radically different reading to the determinism of "human nature," a reading that makes good education an absolute necessity and misguided education a travesty—if not a crime. Thus, an important pietistic tendency in Jewish thought declares that the human being can be saved from his/her nature, that is, from him/herself, only by education. According to that school of thought, we are all initially perverse. It is Esau who is the "natural" person in all of us, and only a stringent education in Torah can redeem us. This pietistic tradition goes back to ancient times and is well represented in medieval literature. But even in our century it has its spokesmen, for whom contemporary secularism is synonymous with perennial and natural idolatry, arrogance, and ignorance.

Among the traditionalist writers who have spelled out this educational position are Rabbis Elhanan Bunim Wasserman and Eliyahu Eliezer Dessler, both renowned educational authorities and community leaders in the ultra-Orthodox yeshiva world of the early and mid-twentieth century. Both of them believed that the allegedly fallacious doctrine that teaches the basic goodness of human beings is itself a source of character corruption and social lawlessness. For them virtually all people are inherently and dangerously flawed; unless taught to conquer the evil impulse, they are potentially demonic, a menace to the world. These rabbis take the biblical proclamation that "the tendency of the human being is evil from youth" (Gen. 9:21) to mean that the *yetzer hara*, the "evil impulse," molds human existence and will utterly control it unless a firm education, based on the revealed principles and norms of the Torah, demobilizes it and takes it captive.

Rabbi Wasserman, a disciple of the famed Rabbi Israel Meir Hacohen, known as the Hafetz Haim, finds a startling source on which to base this viewpoint, namely, the verse "And God said, 'Let us make humankind in our image'" (Gen. 1:26). Commentators have traditionally been struck by the oddity of the plural form "us" in this verse, and some have understood it as "the royal plural," analogous to the custom of kings to speak of themselves in the plural (e.g., it is our desire that . . .). Others take it to mean that God consulted with the ministering angels as to whether it would be wise to create such a problematic creature as the human being. Rabbi Wasserman, on the basis of a passage in the Zohar, understands the verse to teach that God invited all already existing creatures to participate in the creation of humans. When humankind was created, therefore, all species and creatures gave him/her something of their attributes and characteristics: Some human qualities were taken from the ox, others from the lion, yet others from the snake. The characteristics of all created beings, including those of the vicious beasts, are incorporated in the human being. And hence, knowing how ferocious each of them is separately, we can deduce that "there is no more wicked beast than [the human being] and furthermore, the human has an instrument of destruction which no animal in the world has, namely, knowledge and speech."[1]

Human beings, therefore, are like beasts, but worse, for they have powers of intelligence and thought with which to carry out their bestial tendencies intelligently, communicatively, and devastatingly. Yet, says Wasserman, God has created a power with which to chain these evil passions: It is *yirat shamayim*, "fear of Heaven." He writes: "Only *[yirat shamayim]* has the power to keep the human from being like a savage beast, and without it no means in the world can keep a person from destructiveness. . . . Even one who is wise and a philosopher like Aristotle [will find] his wisdom insufficient when his impulse 'attacks' him."[2]

From Rabbi Wasserman's perspective, Esau's attachment to pagan temples, even before birth, expressed the base instincts inherent in his own constitution. He, like Amalek his descendent, "did not fear God" (Deut. 25:18). Either Isaac and Rebecca realized in their prophetic wisdom that no teaching of *yirat shamayim* would suffice in his case or they let Esau's (i.e., human) "nature" do its worst with him; they did not infuse him with fear of Heaven. They unwisely "spared the rod."[3]

Rabbi Elijah E. Dessler, a spiritual leader in England and later at the famed Ponovicz Yeshiva in Bnai Brak (Israel), agrees with this position. If the wisest of men, King Solomon, says that he who spares the rod hates the child, then that must be a specific prescription of Torah for education. Not sparing the rod falls into the paradigm of all genuine education, which is primarily intent on breaking the power of the evil impulse. The fear of Heaven arises in the human being only when he or she learns fear. As for those who believe that corporal punishment is unjustified and counterproductive, Dessler states that they have not understood human nature. They would do well to learn it from the Torah, which is the source of all truth about the world, God, and human existence.

> They [i.e., modern and "progressive" educators] think that a person is created without any [innate ethical] traits at all, and that he receives them only from his environment, but this is not so. [And the proof texts are in what God said to Cain:] "Sin lies in wait at the door" (Gen. 4:7) and . . . [even] the embryo has instincts leading to evil, as our Sages said about Esau—that when Rebecca passed houses of idolatry he struggled to get out. . . . [This shows that] the qualities of a person are created with him.[4]

Rabbi Dessler believes that the modern psychological theory that children learn aggressiveness from being punished is based on the erroneous assumptions that children must be guided toward autonomy and that parents and educators should befriend children and pupils. Our tradition, so he insists, teaches us the opposite: aggressiveness is natural to them, and it wells up out of the evil impulse. Hence children's "hearts of stone" must be shattered. In Rabbi Dessler's words:

> They [i.e., modernistic and free-thinking educational theorists] think one has to cultivate independence in children and this is a great mistake. It is not independence [autonomy] that must be developed but submission. [For] even when [the child] is taught humility and submission, he will [by himself] learn pride and killing. But to teach him

[the doctrine of] "Only I [count] and none besides me" is the doctrine of Edom, the doctrine of murder and robbery.[5]

Judaism understands the nature of the human being and prescribes accordingly. An appropriate education neutralizes the evil in the human heart and helps people to conquer it. But the "innovative researchers . . . in their search for novelty and [their desire] to destroy the foundations . . . whose source is God's Torah and the prophets, concocted new inventions [i.e., theories] that turn all the roots upside down and educate impudent little Hitlers."[6]

Through the writings of these ultra-Orthodox *(Haredi)* educators, we might well see Esau as simply natural man. If that "naturalness" seems somehow attractive to us, perhaps we too suffer from the false ideas that underlie the concoctions of modern researchers. Individualism, autonomy, respect for people the way they are, is "the doctrine of Edom." It must be admitted that this view, however startling and even shocking, resonates somewhat differently after the Holocaust than in the earlier age of optimism. The promise of many philosophers, social scientists, and humanists of inevitable and irreversible improvement in the moral quality of life on the basis of our natural intelligence and goodness now sounds no less dogmatic than such pietistic doctrine.

It is indeed a chilling thought that Rabbi Wasserman perished at the hands of the Nazis, children of a cultured nation that certainly, in its academies of learning, "knew Aristotle" but, in town and gown alike, "did not fear God." Nevertheless, the doctrine that sees only a harsh education that violently tames the *yetzer hara* as the solution to every human failing, still seems objectionable, and not only because most contemporary educators, Jewish and others, are under the influence of allegedly free-thinking "innovative researchers." The tradition of Torah itself suggests other, less gloomy, possibilities.

How About the Good Inclination?

Let us look again at the proof text for Rabbi Dessler's endorsement of corporal punishment, namely, the midrash about Esau's prenatal inclinations. Is this midrash only about Esau? Does it not also tell us about Jacob's "inborn" inclination toward "the academies of Shem and Eber"? Isn't being good, then, also a natural option?

A common pietistic measure to counter such benign evidence of good human nature is to place heroic figures so far above the realm of normal humanity that they don't count. Heroes are born without evil inclinations; they are larger than life and beyond our understanding. If we are looking for ourselves, we should be looking, not at giants of the spirit such as Jacob, whose characters we can hardly fathom, but at Esau.[7]

But then how are we to understand the questionable deeds of even the greatest men and women, including patriarchs and matriarchs? Why does the medieval commentator Rabbi Moshe ben Nahman (Nachmanides, known by the acronym Ramban) declare that Abraham sinned at the court of Avimelech by saying that Sarah was his sister (Gen. 20:12)? Why did Rachel steal the *teraphim*, "household idols" from her father, Laban? Why was Isaac "blind" to Esau's paganism? What about Jacob's acts of deception? Miriam's gossip against her brother Moses? Moses' striking the rock in anger? And what are we to make of the favorable traits that the Bible itself finds in Esau? Perhaps, despite certain natural inclinations, Esau did learn something from his parents? Perhaps, just as there is a natural inclination to bad qualities and deeds, there is also a natural potential for good. Perhaps we would expect people to be influenced by their environment and their mentors. Surely Sarah feared the influence Ishmael was exerting on her Isaac! Why would it not have been "natural" for Esau to have learned something from his good environment?

One sage, R. Yitzhak, seems to hold that view, for he praises those who decline the evil influence in their environments and censures those who refuse to learn from good ones. Offering a reason why Obadiah, a prophet of King Ahab's time, should have been sent to prophesy against Edom, he suggests: "The Holy One, blessed be He, said, let Obadiah, who dwelt between two wicked people [Ahab and Jezebel] and did not learn from their deeds, prophesy against

Esau, who dwelt among two righteous people [Isaac and Rebecca] and did not learn from their deeds" (*Sanhedrin* 39b).

But perhaps, once again, education was insignificant. Perhaps Obadiah was naturally good and impervious to bad influence, as Esau was naturally bad.

Recognizing our Children's Individuality and Diversity

Rabbi Samson Raphael Hirsch, the nineteenth-century founder of neo-Orthodoxy, in his commentary on the Torah, takes another approach. He does not deny that "nature" is important but insists that education does make the essential difference in the final analysis. People do bring natural tendencies into the world with them but it is precisely these tendencies that parents and teachers are to educate, to channel, rather than to obliterate. They are to be drawn out and mobilized in the service of the ideals that, when actualized, mark the educated person.

In his commentary on the verse "When the boys grew up, Esau was one who knew hunting, a man of the field, and Jacob was a quiet man, dwelling in tents" (Gen. 25:27), Hirsch criticizes Isaac and Rebecca for raising both boys without regard to the differences in their temperaments. The parents forgot "the fundamental law of education," which is to "educate each child according to its own way" (Prov. 22:6). Isaac and Rebecca wished for both Jacob and Esau to be "good Jews," walking in the paths of justice and righteousness. That was the educational ideal. But they seemed to ignore what Jacob, in his varied blessings to his twelve sons, would keep clearly in mind, namely, that this task is entrusted to a diversified nation—of priests and farmers, merchants, scholars, and soldiers. And where there is "natural" diversity, there must be educational consideration for different temperaments. Precisely because there are certain things that all should be educated to share, each child must be brought up "according to his way." For Hirsch, the common goal is the life of mitzvot, of commandments; yet, if that goal is meant to be common to all, it must be achievable by more than one type of person. Says Hirsch:

> To try to bring up a Jacob and an Esau in the same college, make them have the same habits and hobbies, to want to teach and educate them in the same way for some studious, sedate, meditative life is the surest way to court disaster. . . .
>
> Had Isaac and Rebecca studied Esau's nature and character early enough, and asked themselves how even an Esau . . . [and] all the strength and energy, agility and courage . . . slumbering in this child, might be won over for use in the service of God . . . then Jacob and Esau with their totally different natures could still have remained twin-brothers in spirit and life. . . . But as it was, *vayigdilu hane'arim,* only when the boys had grown into men, one was surprised to see . . . despite their having had exactly the same care, training and schooling, two such different persons emerge.[8]

Hirsch's criticism is that Isaac and Rebecca thought that only a tent dweller could be a noble Jewish character. Consequently, they educated Esau as though he ought to have Jacob's tent-dwelling nature. They forgot that the Torah is given to an entire people and hence must be suited to every temperament. No parent or teacher should forget or ignore this: His or her task is set by the athletic and perhaps brusque child no less than by the bookish and perhaps introverted one. The nature of the child is not something to be broken nor is it a predetermined fate, of good or bad character.

Children have diverse natures. These do not make education superfluous, but challenge it to diversity. Each kind of character invites an examination of how educational ideals, rooted in the revealed *language* of the Torah, may be applied by and for differently inclined individuals. In good education, neither the child nor the ideal is to be sacrificed.

No One is a "Bad Seed"

The Talmudic sages debated whether the character of people was determined by *mazzalot* (lucky or unlucky days, ruled by beneficent or malevolent stars). Some were of the opinion that *ain mazal leYis-rael* (Israel is not subservient to the stars) and that, hence, astrological data have no influence on Israel. Others disagreed. For example one view had it that a person born under the sign of Mars *(Ma'adim)* will be a shedder of blood. Once again, the "redness"— *odem*—of blood, of Edom! On this view, Rav Nahman ben Yitzhak commented, "Such a person might be a blood letter, a ritual slaughterer *(shohet)* or a circumciser *(mohel)*" *(Shabbat* 156a).

In Rav Nahman ben Yitzhak's view, a "shedder of blood" need not be a murderer or expected to become one. There are, he said, other, beneficial, and even commanded ways of shedding blood! Clearly, this sage, like Hirsch many centuries after him, believed that education can work with nature and shape it. He apparently felt that the Torah is more concerned with people and their diverse natures than with the fixed curricula of certain "tents." There must indeed be centers of the spirit and of study, but if Torah is for everyone, it must be found "in the field," and in field people, as well.

"Field people" can only approach Torah in their own ways. Yet they are routinely told by their studious and sedate brothers and sisters and elders that brutal Esau is their archetype and that the field is appropriate only for savages. If, as parents and teachers, we do not want every Esau to become an Edom, we might beware of encouraging such sentiments or voicing them. We too might rather learn to appreciate the smells, the beauties, and the riches of human experience, in fields as well as elsewhere, and to teach appreciation of them.

This need not lead to a pagan contempt for the tent. Where such contempt is fostered, the field is transformed into an arena of "noble" violence, threatening to release all the primordial energies of the *yetzer hara* from the bonds of decency. We have seen it happen in the twentieth century. The children of a cultured nation were turned, with dizzying speed, into the spiritual seed of Esau-Edom.

Human beings come into the world with innate qualities, perhaps even personalities. Certainly, too, some children present, because of organic problems, sometimes insurmountable difficulties of growth and development. Yet ethical monotheists, who believe in the unity of the moral order no matter how difficult its achievement in human life, and for whom R. Nahman ben Yitzhak is a teacher, must declare that all persons can be brought up to decency and toward an inner nobility, that no one is a "bad seed." All parents may hope that on the basis of what their children have brought with them into the world, they may come to exemplify, each in his or her own way, a life of Torah.

5

LEARNING TO
MAKE DECISIONS

How We Think

THE PREVIOUS CHAPTERS, especially Chapter 2, seem to place education into a severely normative mold. Though children are invited to participate in the life of society and even "sing their own songs," for example at the Seder, this participation may well seem like a "song and dance," a way of getting them inside "first order" knowledge. That knowledge, after all, is about identity and caring. It is a story to be *re*told, a way of life that precedes the child, that restrains as it enriches.

And the following question may be polemically posed: Is good education merely, or mainly, a way to bring children into a set of memories, roles, rules, and expectations? Or is it primarily the art of guiding them through experiences that will enable them to face new problems and that will make them eager and able to devise sound solutions to these problems? Perhaps *that* is what we should see as the essence of real education, so that parents and teachers should open young minds for intelligent deliberation rather than clutter them with decrepit furnishings of traditional virtues.

This way of presenting the issue may be tendentious, but it makes things quite clear. Stated this way, the issue whether education inculcates norms or is primarily about clear thinking and competent problem solving appears very much in line with its formulation by the American philosopher and educational thinker John Dewey. In a famous passage, he presents the matter as follows:

> A man travelling in an unfamiliar region comes to a branching of the road. Having no sure knowledge to fall back on, he is brought to a standstill of hesitation and suspense. Which road is right? And how shall his perplexity be resolved? There are but two alternatives: he must either blindly and arbitrarily take his course, trusting to luck for the outcome, or he must discover grounds for the conclusion that a given road is right.[1]

This parable appears in a work entitled *How We Think*. Dewey's intention here is not merely to describe the thinking process, which he understands as primarily a response to concrete and pressing problems. He seems also to be demanding that we recognize how radically different our age is from former ones; it is itself "an unfamiliar region." This reality, Dewey argues, summons us to intellectual courage. We are called upon to engage in new ways of thinking, in fresh deliberation.

Clearly, Dewey's image of "the branching of the road" intimates a polemic against the traditionalist way of thinking that presumes to solve all new problems in old, rule-bound ways. This time-honored way of thinking, and learning too, suggests that when any problem arises, we need merely look up the right answer in a sacred or classical source and then proceed to act on the basis of eternal verities. This approach, it can be argued, is rule directed, not open to fresh ways of perceiving and thinking. Caged in by allegedly perennial truths, rule-bound or normative persons fail to solve, or even to see, new problems and thus are kept from dealing reasonably and responsibly with them. Habituated to associating reason with the most abstract and unearthly theorizing, they are incapable of using it to review past situations, tackle present tasks, or theoretically anticipate future problems.

Viewing the Dewey passage as a polemic against normative thinking, teachers quite naturally use it for purposes of juxtaposition: between tradition and inquiry, between eternally valid values and deliberation, between stultifying "holy texts" and new thinking that proceeds not from ancient insights but from present needs. However, polarizing the two approaches is not always appropriate. Even an authoritative and normative tradition such as Judaism, which identifies "language" with revelation itself and makes the story of God's redemptive acts in Egypt paradigmatic of all possible saving acts, will also, as though from within a pragmatic or experimentalist worldview, describe people in unfamiliar territory, sometimes showing them at a loss for ways to deal with new situations.

True, the narratives of Torah and the midrashic "literature" on these narratives will not generally leave people to stand alone at "the branching of the road" but will describe leaders and teachers helping them to find their way at the crossroads and will recall the ancient stories of how it happened "then." Yet in its own normative way, such a tradition seeks to teach people how to think afresh. It may even demand, from within a sacred tradition, that people understand *how* they think and to recognize occasions that require rethinking on their part.

The First Crisis of Freedom:
Having to Choose

The Torah itself describes the Exodus from Egypt as a prime example of a new situation beset by new and unfamiliar problems, of perplexity arising out of inexperience. And throughout the Torah's epic of liberation, from the Exodus until the moment that Israel stands at the gateway to the Promised Land, there are crises. We read of fear, uncertainty, anger, wishful thinking, evasion, and occasional bravado. Sometimes these upheavals become organized as mutiny, as in the case of Korah (Num. 16). At other times, as in the story of the twelve spies who "brought back an evil report of the land," there is a mass failure of nerve, which the Torah identifies as lack of faith (Num. 13–14). In that particular case, the failure to know "which road to take" is followed by an ill-considered assault on the Canaanites at Arad, which ends in an ignoble defeat. Moses had told the Israelites not to do it, but they are panicky, not listening, not trusting, not thinking.

At the very beginning of the great liberation from Egypt, the Israelites do trust Moses, a man guided by God, therefore one presumed to know about problems and their solutions. But we may assume that they do not have any working conception of what a problem is, at least in their divinely redeemed situation. The first crisis follows freedom almost immediately, within days. Pharaoh and his six hundred chosen chariots are pursuing the Israelites, approaching from behind, and the Red Sea, obviously impassible, is in front of them. No one told them it would be like this. They do not know what to do. A midrash relates that at this unanticipated juncture the Israelites were divided into four groups: "One group said: Let us throw ourselves into the sea. One said: Let us return to Egypt. One said: Let us fight them; and one said, Let us cry out against them [i.e., pray]" (*Mekhilta*, Tractate *Beshallah* 3).

Here, then, are four solutions that came to the minds of the Israelites who, as slaves, had never before faced such a problem. The first proposed solution is suicide. If we stand still, waiting for the assault, we shall surely be killed. So let us move ahead, even to certain death. The second group attempts to solve the unfamiliar problem by tacitly denying that there is one! Why did we leave Egypt? In the face of present ills, past problems look softer and are revised. Did we not sit by the fleshpots there? Later, in another instance of panic and evasion, they recall the cucumbers and other delicacies that they ostensibly ate in Egypt (Num. 11:5). In order to deny more completely that there ever was a problem in Egypt, they may even feel guilty about being free. Why did we impudently disobey our masters? If we are contrite now, perhaps they will not kill us. Perhaps they will forgive us and allow us to come back to our homes, to our fleshpots—and labors. The third group, opting for military action, seems to have courage and a realistic understanding of the situation, but the courage is really no more than ignorant bravado. The Israelites have never engaged in warfare, and we may assume that they have not the slightest idea of how to wage war. They are like children who have heard adults sagely devising policies to be pursued and are now mouthing "grown-up" conversation.

The fourth group chooses prayer. This activity, the *Mekhilta* tells us in another place, is something they indeed know how to do. It is, in the words of the midrash, "the occupation of the fathers." Abraham, Isaac, and Jacob all did this well; in the case of Jacob, a midrash earlier in *Beshallah* 3 says that even when he claims to have used "his sword and his bow" (Gen. 48:22), this warrior-like act refers (only) to prayer. But the Torah—and God—are ambivalent about this prayer solution. The Midrash sometimes finds God to be pleased by the prayers of the Israelites but also imagines His getting annoyed by overly long prayers or by prayer at the wrong time. From the text of the Torah itself, we know that God is particularly impatient with Moses: "Why do you cry out to Me? Speak to the children of Israel; so that they move forward [into the sea]" (Exod. 14:15).

Moses is supposed to stretch out his rod to split the sea, not to engage in lengthy prayer at a time of danger. There is a time for prayer and a time for action. The Israelites have experience only with prayer, but at that moment, prayer's highest achievement would be to bring God into conversation with Moses, to have Him tell Moses what must be done. But, in fact, that conversation is taking place and God is telling him what to do. Moses is to act, to go forward. Prayers here are superfluous, evasive, a distraction.

So Moses himself must learn something about praying. And then he must teach the people the uses and abuses, in their new situation, of the one "occupation" they know well.

The Children of Israel: Children?

How does Moses respond to the Israelites' various solutions? What does he answer? We return to our midrash:

> The one that said, "Let us throw ourselves into the sea," was told "Stand still and see the salvation of the Lord." The one that said: "Let us return to Egypt," was told: "For as you have seen the Egyp-

tians today, you shall never see them again." The one that said, "Let us fight them" was told: "The Lord will fight for you." The one that said, "Let us cry out against them," was told: "And you shall hold your peace."

And on the words "The Lord will fight for you," the midrash adds, strangely enough for those who experienced, if not the Holocaust, then the Roman legions: "Not only at this time, but at all times will He fight against your enemies" (*Mekhilta*, Tractate *Beshallah* 3).

The answer that Moses gives to the confused and complaining Israelites (Exod. 14:13–14) is divided into four parts, corresponding to the midrash's four groups. And each group is both soothed and offered guidance. Moses understands the distress of his charges. He treats them as the children that they are, but anticipates their "growing up." And so, wherever possible, but not in every case, he intimates how it will be eventually be.

First, there is the group that wishes to throw itself into the sea. These people are desperate, but they seem to understand that there is no going back. They have no solution to the problem, but they will not pretend that the problem is not there. Moses explains to them that their sense of moving forward is right but that they need not interpret this new situation as crippling or hopeless. Would God have taken them out of Egypt only to have them confront, alone, a problem that is too great for them?

Moses speaks similarly to those who suggest waging war. Without insulting them by putting them in their place as inexperienced "children," he finds a way to teach them that although their idea is praiseworthy, it is also premature. For now, like any good parent, God, will take care of them and fight for them. Like any good parent, God will seem "able to do anything." You, this group is told, will not be expected to solve a problem for which you have no training, for which you are unprepared.

Moses knows that this miraculously shielding providence is only temporary. But just as a teacher in the first years of elementary school refrains from telling pupils that "the great time we're having and the interesting things we're learning" lead sooner or later to serious challenges and expectations, so does Moses refrain from dwelling on the Israelites' future responsibilities. Indeed, he might now tell them that God will nourish them with manna throughout the trek to the Land, and that they will live on a diet of miracles. Yet Moses knows that this miraculous existence is only for the world of their childhood and that it will pass once they have learned to stand on their own feet.

So, for the moment, Moses tells them that God will fight for them; they are not expected to wage war. Shortly thereafter, the Israelites, untrained for war and inexperienced, are to be further reassured. When Amalek attacks them, Moses holds up his hands so that the war may be miraculously won. Afterward, the Torah will promise the people that a miraculous hornet or wild bee *(zir'ah)*, will instantaneously defeat their enemies for them (Exod. 23:28) by spitting venom and blinding them (Rashi).[2] At the Red Sea it was not the time to tell them that when they become adults they will have to wage their own wars and grow their own food, that when they cross the Jordan the manna will cease, and that the reassuring and fantastical hornet will not "cross the Jordan" with them; it will remain a mythic memory, a symbol of God's protection *(Sotah* 36a).[3] Certainly, it was not the time to tell them that God will seem, in dark days far in the future, to have utterly deserted them.[4] Moreover, Moses makes no mention of "the real world" of adults who must face adult realities. For now, the Israelites must learn to trust, to be assured that growing up is not to be feared. Teachers and God are there with them so that they can eventually become adults.

As for those who wished to return to Egypt, like children who have angered their arbitrary but powerful elders and now want to appease them, Moses informs them that after the events about to transpire they will see the Egyptians differently, they will gain a different perspective. You now see them, Moses seems to be saying, the way only God should be seen. These chariot-people are not all-powerful; one should neither fear them nor trust them. And to the group of those who opt for prayer, Moses says that there is a time for silence. Or as the midrash would have it, it is now time to praise "him in whose hands are the fortunes of war," not pray (*Mekhilta*, Tractate *Beshallah*).

Why praise? Why not prayer? Prayer is the occupation the Israelites have learned from tradition. In the face of an uncertain future, why should they not pray? Yet Moses seems intent on weaning the Israelites from too much prayer, from doing something simply because they know how to do it. His argument is that now that the coming salvation is assured, the people may consider it to have already happened, as past. One does not pray for the past. The past cannot be changed. "If only it had happened differently" is a vain prayer, useless, a seemingly religious way of evading reality. At times, prayer itself may be a way of evading responsibility. Nevertheless, Moses teaches them, this aspect of prayer does not signify distancing themselves from God. On the contrary, now that the (coming) salvation is certain, the time has come for praise, for gratitude, for the self-confidence that gives strength but shuns the arrogance of ascribing victory to their own prowess.

Moses teaches his people how to have faith and hence how to act in their present state. They need to learn trust; they should not think that moving forward brings death or that moving ahead requires them to shoulder tasks that are as yet beyond their powers. They can gain a perspective that allows them to trust and fear only God, not mortal despots. They can distinguish between hope for the future, expressed in prayer, and gratitude for what has been, expressed in praise. And they must leave behind them the childish wish to undo the past. The people of Israel will have to choose a road in unfamiliar territory, but they won't have to do it alone. Moses leads them on to a road of deliberation, but he gives them a religious orientation for their uses of intelligence. This orientation teaches that they are not on the road alone, not at that moment and not after they have reached the stage of responsibility. Albeit without mythical hornets, God will be with them. "Not only at this time, but at all times will He fight against your enemies."

Only later will they learn, when the manna has ceased and the battles for the land begin, that God's promise is conditional. The defeat of the Israelites in the battle for Ai (Josh. 7) intimates that

God's "protecting" them and being with them depends on their obedience to His laws and, concomitantly, on good strategic thinking. According to Joshua 7:2–5, it appears that the war was undertaken on the basis of faulty intelligence, which, in turn, may have been a consequence of the demoralization caused by the taking of spoils at Jericho by Akhan of the tribe of Judah (Josh. 7:1).[5]

The Midrash Presents an Educational Ideal

After their lesson "at the branching of the roads," what happens to Israel next? Having been eased through the intersection in the road so that they can face future "branchings" more confidently and competently, they must now do what the situation requires, namely, go into the sea. But practice regarding the unanticipated requires at least as much courage as coming to grips with the idea of the unfamiliar. And on the verse "And the children of Israel went into the midst of the sea" (Exod. 14:22), the *Mekhilta* records a complex controversy between Rabbi Meir and Rabbi Yehudah. Here is part of it:

> R. Meir says: When the tribes of Israel stood by the sea, one said, "I will go down to the sea first," and the other said: "[No you won't!], I will go down to the sea first." While they were standing there wrangling with one another, the tribe of Benjamin jumped up and went down to the sea first. . . . [And] what reward did the tribe of Benjamin receive for going down to the sea first? The *Shekhinah* [divine Presence] rested in his portion [at the Temple site].
>
> R. Yehudah says, When the Israelites stood at the sea, one said, "I do not want to go down to the sea first," and the other said, "I do not want to go down to the sea first." . . . While they were standing there deliberating, Nahshon the son of Amminadav [of the tribe of Judah] jumped up first and fell into the waves. . . . The Holy One, blessed be He said [to Moses]: "Moses, My friend [Nahshon] is sinking in the water. . . . Lift up thy rod." Now, what did Israel say then at the sea? "The Lord shall reign forever and ever" (Exod. 15:18). The Holy One, blessed be He therefore said: "He who was the cause of My be-

ing proclaimed king at the sea, him will I make king over Israel."
(*Mekhilta*, Tractate *Beshallah* 6)

If we understand R. Meir in the light of our discussion above, we
may picture the tribes to be like children in a classroom who feel
assured that the environment is friendly. (That, in fact, is exactly
what Moses did assure them!) So every time the teacher asks a
question, they all frenetically raise their hands. (Which elementary
school teacher hasn't seen this?) But having learned the lesson of
trust, that they are in good hands and need not fear, they do not
know what to do with that lesson. They do not understand that
they have to do *something* with it. (Picture that classroom situation:
Many of those energetically volunteering to answer wilt when actually called upon.) So too the tribes of Israel. They know that they
may expect to see the salvation of God, but they misunderstand that
to mean that they do not really have to participate in the events.
God will do all the acting necessary. They see Moses' promises, not
as a space in which the inexperienced may grow, but as an excuse to
be infantile. They argue about who shall go down to the sea first,
but none of them actually do it. (Nehama Leibowitz once remarked
that their behavior would make sense only if there were a narrow
doorway leading to the sea, in front of which one might jostle for
position.) They think it is enough to raise their hands wildly. This
show of enthusiasm testifies to their feeling of security, but they
think that such feelings are a substitute for comprehension and
courage. But the reassurances were given to them so that they could
develop those traits!

Only the tribe of Benjamin has learned from the encounter. Benjamin went down to the sea, after which the others are presumed to
have followed. Benjamin understands that the protected *are* protected in order to cultivate their intelligence and maturity: to make
them capable of reasoning "at the forks in the road." The life of the
spirit is lived "under the wings of the *Shekhinah*," but that is no escape from real situations. Hence, the Temple, the sanctuary of
spirit and the dwelling place of the *Shekhinah*, will be built within
the territory of Benjamin.

R. Yehudah understands the situation differently. He sees the tribes playing it safe. They do not really believe Moses' reassurance. Though childishly afraid, they are worldly-wise. They think they have seen through Moses' solution to the problem, but they have forgotten what the problem is, and they really have only a faint notion of how the solution is to work. Here we are not dealing with spiritual prowess, but with being "smart" without benefit of courage or intelligence. This worldly-wise stance looks temporarily plausible: Let someone else figure out the problem, and then worry about what the genuine alternatives are.

Nahshon breaks the spell of clever evasion, but when the Judaean jumps into the water, the smart prudence of the others seems vindicated, for he appears to be drowning. And Moses has to be pulled from his prayers to save God's "friend": "Lift up thy rod."

Once the resolution of the problem has been presented as dependent upon God's salvation, suddenly and paradoxically everything seems to depend on intelligent analysis and timely action. Nahshon's tribe merits leadership. Like the Maccabees, many centuries later, whose daring leadership may have inspired this midrash, Nahshon knows that "God helps those who help themselves." In fact, that one must act as though, without the human endeavor, God's help may come too late. It certainly looked like that here. Nahshon, declares the midrash, was up to his nose in water before the sea split.

Nahshon is a hero in the Jewish tradition, the eponym for those who "go first," who "dive in" and disdain the false safety of doing nothing. It is interesting that the midrashic view of Nahshon not only celebrates his courage and initiative but also affirms that such a one well represents God's view of leadership, and His plan. The Judaean descendants of Nahshon are to be kings of Israel.

The midrash argues, then, that norms and intelligence are not in conflict quite as Dewey, in a much later generation, is to portray matters. Nahshon and hence his tribe merit leadership. When prayer is inappropriate, Nahshon does not pray simply because that's what he knows how to do. He does not shirk responsibility despite the reassuring promises of Moses that God would protect

Israel. Only Nahshon (according to Rabbi Yehudah) draws the conclusion that the beneficent powerful world of Providence and adult leadership, parents, teachers, and counselors, is "there for you" so that the protected and trusting child can become a friend.

For God, a friend is one who will proclaim His kingdom, which, in a significant sense, will not be there unless so proclaimed and acted out. For human beings, a friend is one who will know when to act and when to pray, who has been taught that the Torah is not only the warmth of identity and of the certain and stated norm but also a challenge "at the crossroads." And, as we learn from Moses, an adult to be trusted extends a guiding hand that educates the young person at whatever stage he or she is.

Educated children, like the Benjaminites and Nahshon of the tribe of Judah, have been taught trust by those who seem to know what they are doing and who do not confuse faith with passivity or panic. Having learned trust, these children may themselves become trustworthy adults. They may be trusted not only when they impress upon their own children the Torah's norms, ever reinterpreted, yet symbolizing stability and order in the world, but also at the branching of the road, when they decide how to present problems to their children while holding their hands. They are sympathetic with the inexperience of the young, but they do not romanticize it or otherwise manipulate it. The parent and the teacher want children to grow up.

The believing parent and teacher do indeed teach the child to pray that God will be there with him or her at the branching of the road. But these mentors may also teach that this Presence itself sometimes comes in unfamiliar forms, and that, where action is demanded, God may be impatient with prayer.

PART 2

The Community:
From the Home to the School

Rav Yehudah said: There was one [in the latter years of the Second Commonwealth] who should be remembered for good, and his name was Yehoshua ben Gamla. But for him, Torah would have been forgotten by [the people of] Israel. [Why?] Before his time, those who had parents would be taught by them and those who didn't, would [simply] not learn. That practice was based on [on an interpretation of Deuteronomy 11:19]: And you shall teach them [otam], as though it read, "And you yourselves [atem] shall teach," ... till Yehoshua ben Gamla legislated that teachers of children would be placed in every province and every town, and children would be brought [to these teachers] at the age of six or seven.

—Baba Batra 21b

I HAVE ALWAYS WONDERED WHY, when three have eaten together, they initiate the blessing after the meal with the declaration: "Let us bless Him of whose bounty we have partaken," whereas where *ten* have eaten, they say, "Let us bless *our God* of whose bounty we have partaken" *(Daily Prayer Book)*. What does that suggest about the view of religion as "what the human being does with his or her solitude"? What does it tell us about the status of community in an educated life of faith?

6

THE COMMUNITY
TEACHES THE
NARRATIVE OF
BEGINNINGS

THE STATUS OF THE SCHOOL in Jewish education has always been problematic. If it is the parent who should educate the child, why turn to teachers? And if teachers are indeed necessary, as surrogates or as more accomplished scholars, why not in a tutorial, more individualized manner, so that education is recognized, even by the young, as a form of conversation?

The Talmudic passage that opens Part 2, about Yehoshua (Joshua) ben Gamla, the celebrated founder of municipal schooling, pinpoints the problem. Was that community leader building a dike against the torrents of ignorance or putting his finger into one? Was there, until his time, indifference to teaching as such, so that he single-handedly created a renaissance of community education, or was there a calamitous neglect of orphans and other unfortunates who had no parents to teach them? Was there a decline in parental competence to teach, so that the community had to tactfully insist that "children would be brought" to teachers? And what kind of responsibility did schools actually take? What did they teach?

This historical question, heavily laden with ideological controversy, leads readily to a consideration of the supplementary Jewish
school in our time, the so-called Hebrew school, which is still the
community's fare for those parents who want a modicum of social
initiation into Judaism for their children. Whether because it reflects a flight from parental instruction or whether it is all that can
be imposed on largely unwilling children, it has not been a particularly successful venture, and no one is much surprised by surveys
and studies that report that most children in afternoon or "Hebrew" schools claim to be bored by what goes on there. In the
words of one preteenager: "Most of what they talk about there is
Bible stories. And I don't believe them."

In not believing "them," this particular youngster probably has
both the texts and the teachers in mind. Most likely, this unwilling
pupil, unlike the youthful nonbelievers of previous generations,
does not even bother to ask, provoke, or argue. He or she just sits
through it, with disdain. And being "turned off" ancient myths, the
saga of Adam and Eve, the first Bible story, may be expected to
leave the child especially bored and cold. After all, there never were
such people, and even if there were, why would they concern
present–day children? As a contemporary scholar of Jewish
thought, Norbert Samuelson, once wrote, a proven way *not* to find
someone you are looking for, and even to deduce that she or he
does not exist, is to have the wrong description of that person
and/or faulty directions as to where or how to look for him or her.[1]

In practice, for correct descriptions and understandings of formative events, of foundational people, of God, of themselves, Jews
have traditionally relied on the texts of Torah, and by way of these
descriptions and these understandings they have traditionally initiated the young, in the home and within the community's institutions of education. But it has never been simple to determine where
exactly to look and how to decipher what one finds, if and when one
does. It is a complicated affair, and there has been a never-ending
exegetical discussion among scholars and students about where to
look and how to read the descriptions. Let us look at a small segment of this discussion and see whether our young Hebrew school

sufferer has been given a good description of what he did not find, or "believe."

Looking for Adam: Finding Ourselves

In trying to discover where teachers and their communities might profitably look, we can begin with a place suggested by Martin Buber in the story that opens his essay "The Way of Man According to the Teaching of Hasidism":

> Rabbi Shneur Zalman, the rav [rabbi] of Northern White Russia (died 1813) was put in jail in Petersburg, because the *mitnagdim* [the opponents of the *hasidic* movement] had denounced [him] . . . to the government. He was awaiting trial when the chief of the gendarmes entered his cell. . . . He began to converse with his prisoner. . . . Finally he asked, "How are we to understand that God, the all-knowing, said to Adam, 'Where art thou?'"
>
> "Do you believe," answered the rav, "that the Scriptures are eternal and that every era, every generation and every man is included in them?" "I believe this," said the other. "Well, then," said the *tzaddik* [righteous person], "in every era God calls to every man, 'Where are you in your world? So many years and days of those allotted to you have passed, and how far have you gotten in your world?' God says something like this: 'You have lived forty-six years. How far along are you?'"
>
> When the chief of the gendarmes heard his age mentioned, he pulled himself together, laid his hand on the rav's shoulder, and cried: "Bravo." But his heart trembled.[2]

The chief of the gendarmes trembled because he suddenly understood that the story of Adam was truly about *himself*, that the place to look for its meaning was in his own soul. The rabbi could teach the man that lesson because he made him realize that every person "is included" in Scripture. The Gentile police officer had found Adam! Unlike the young Hebrew school pupil, he had found someone to help him discover what he was looking for. The rabbi was distant enough to instruct, yet, as a righteous man, close enough to teach.

To whom, then, may we send our bored Hebrew school child? How do we get him into a "curriculum"? Tradition suggests that we first send him to the eleventh-century commentator who has classically been the doyen of describers and exponents, Rabbi Shlomo Yitzhaki (son of Isaac), known by the acronym Rashi. Many people who have "learned Torah" since Rashi's time have stated categorically that you cannot really understand it without Rashi. In schoolrooms, at Friday evening tables, and wherever teachers and parents have "talked Torah" with children or with their peers, one of the first questions with regard to any "difficulty" in a word or verse of Torah has traditionally been, "And what does Rashi say?" Though our pupil may not "get" Rashi at first, living at some distance from the midrashic and exegetical world the savant took for granted, at least those who deign to teach the child might do well to start with him.

Rashi's First Commentary

Immediately, however, in Rashi's opening commentary to the Torah, we find a "difficulty" that itself needs deciphering. There Rashi elaborates a midrashic passage (*Genesis Rabbah* 1:2) that seems irrelevant and incongruous. Says Rashi on the very first words of the Torah, "In the beginning [God created the heaven and the earth]":

> Rabbi Isaac said: "The Torah should have commenced with [the verse] (Exod. 12:1) 'This month shall be the first of the months to you' which is the first commandment given to Israel. What is the reason, then, that it commences with the Creation? Because of [the thought expressed in another] . . . text which reads (Ps. 111:6): 'He declared to His people the strength of His works [i.e., He gave an account of the Creation] in order that He might give them the heritage of the nations.' For should the peoples of the world say to Israel, 'You are robbers, because you took by force the land of the seven nations

[of Canaan],' Israel may reply to them 'All the earth belongs to the Holy One, blessed be He; He created it and gave it to whom He pleased. When He willed, He gave it to them, and when He willed He took it from them and gave it to us.'"

This commentary of Rashi is extremely, some would say overly, popular in religious schools, especially Israeli ones, in which the right of the Jewish people to the land is here supplied with a theological proof text in sometimes too casual and cavalier a fashion. No doubt it also pinpoints a central historical reality, much noted and explicated in Genesis and beyond, namely, that the people of Israel came upon the historical scene when the territories of the known world had already been allocated to the various nations; Israel was a latecomer and its land had to be "promised" to it because the land was already occupied (by the Amorites). It is also clear that Rashi directs our attention to the character of pre-Abrahamic narrative. It is Torah: It is, as Buber's Rabbi Shneur Zalman taught the chief of the gendarmes, instruction about and for ourselves, not merely a chronicle of prehistory.

Nevertheless, there seems to be something problematic about Rashi's remark. What does this proclamation of national (Jewish) rights have to do with the creation of the world? And why does Rashi maintain that, on the face of it, the Torah should have begun with the twelfth chapter of Exodus?

Abraham Joshua Heschel, the renowned twentieth-century philosopher of Judaism, once attributed Rashi's remark to what he called the pan-halakhic attitude of some Jewish sages, scholars, and thinkers, those who posit the essence of Torah and Judaism as legal commandment. According to them, "If it isn't halakhah it isn't (Jewishly) important."[3] Rashi is depicted as such a pan-halakhist, one who wonders why an entire book of the Torah, allegedly bereft of halakhah, should be in the Torah altogether.

I find it hard to conceive of Rashi as a pan-halakhist. "Pan-halakhism" is mainly a modern way of thinking about Judaism that is congenial to acculturated traditionalists. Pan-halakhism makes ample room for general culture in Jewish life by claiming that if it isn't halakhah, it can't be (Jewishly) relevant—so it's all right (to do other general things). Moreover, even the strictest halakhist would agree that the story of Creation and of our first parents lays the foundations and teaches the fundamental language of halakhah, that it provides the framework within which the halakhah finds its context and makes sense. Here, in the *parashah* (portion) of *Bereshit,* "The Beginning," is the creation of the Sabbath, completing a seven-day cycle. Here we are introduced to the Jewish week and made sensitive to the number seven in the Jewish scheme of things. Around this number, seven, we shall later find the peculiar holiness of the seventh day and the special status of the seventh month of the Jewish calendar (Tishre), the seventh Sabbatical year, and the (seven times seven) Jubilee year. In this *parashah* we find humans commanded to procreate. Already here, we come upon sacrifice and the requirement that it be accompanied by a sincere intention on the part of the person bringing the offering.

Perhaps most focally, we are introduced here to the doctrine that the relationship between humans and God is largely dependent on obedience to the divine commandment. The commandment, it is taught, is the source of human and, as it were, divine "knowledge" of good and evil. Human beings, we learn, are distinguished by their ability to choose good or evil and by God's demand that they do so. The first "nonrational" commandment of the Torah is paradigmatic of all those still to come; it revolves around a "tree of good and evil," establishing relationships between God and human beings, between people, and between human beings and their environment. It poses the question, Will the ambiance of human life be one of trust, obedience, love, and at-homeness in the world, or will there be rebellion, recrimination, anger, and exile?

As for the Tree of Life, which enables people to "live forever," we find it later amalgamated with the Tree of Knowledge, that is, with the Torah that confronts us with the choice of good (the acceptance of God's commandment) and evil (its rejection). This Tree of Knowledge is symbolic of the Torah and its commandments as a whole, but Torah, in its attribute of wisdom, is also "*a tree of life* for those who cleave to it." It is this "tree" through which, as the blessing recited upon reading the Torah has it, God "has planted eternal life in our midst."

Thus, to imagine the Torah beginning with the first (concrete) commandment given to Israel in Exodus is to forgo the cultural-spiritual language and the worldview in which the commandments and their halakhic particulars are spoken. It is to make them arbitrary and incomprehensible. Could Rashi have meant that?

Genesis Asks Ultimate Questions

I will state the issue more forcefully and universally: The sacred character of the story of creation and Genesis does not rest only on its practical—legal or halakhic—elements. What is essential to any sacred book and actually defines it as sacred is that, in one way or another, it raises ultimate questions and makes its readers view these questions as "deep." These deep questions include:

1. Who am I, really?
2. What is and what should be most important to me?
3. How should I live my life, with myself and with others?
4. What can I know?
5. And what is most important to know?
6. Where did it all start?
7. And where is it all going?
8. Or, as the White Russian police officer learned to ask: *Where am I in my life?*

Every sacred book, in some fashion, gives guidance for keeping such deep or "ultimate" questions in mind. Every such book helps us to understand the profound possibilities of meaning concealed within these questions. Through the sacred book or teaching we are invited to live with these problems and, if possible, to deal with them. How the problems are to be seen and how we may grapple and live with them constitute the specific and particular teaching of the "story" that the book is telling. Torah, of course, is such a teaching. And *Bereshit* (Genesis) sets the stage and initiates the story.

Writing the Book of Me

How are ultimate questions different from those that deal with simple facts? The distinction is not always clear, and it is sometimes tempting to confuse profound questions with the (also) challenging ones that scientific inquiry seeks to answer. Yet they are fundamentally different.

For example, Who am I? is easily answered and reduced to psychosociological or biophysiological references and explanations of how I am constructed or how I function, but that does not answer the same question. "Who I am" is an existential issue, inviting reflection about "who I may become." Similarly, beginnings are irreducible to what happened at the moment of the Big Bang or the meeting of procreative cells. And discussions about destinations are not exhausted by descriptions of the burial and the disintegration of dead bodies or the apparently inevitable freezing of the cosmos.

To understand why this is so, let us follow a line of thinking suggested by the educational philosopher, Philip Phenix.[4] Imagine a couple, ten or twenty years after marriage, looking around the breakfast table where originally only the two of them sat and where they now see two or three or five others. In a reflective moment, perhaps of contentment or worry or perplexity, this couple may ask such questions as: Where did they come from? meaning, How did we become parents of these? Why does each of these individuals legitimately expect us to love him or her and to love her and him more than other children? Why do we have to buy them shoes (with money we could spend on a new car)? Where did their "personalities," their diverse smiles, quirks, hopes, and abilities, come from? How did they become part of our story? Are we helping them to write the first chapters of their own stories, by teaching, by setting an example, and, conversely, by giving them space? Why is all this? Why do we feel ourselves obliged? thankful? concerned? The parents surely know where these children "came from" biologically. But that is not what they are asking.

Or we look in the mirror, experience our aging, know that we, like everyone else, will die. Of course, objectively, we know about dying, burial, organic disintegration. But that does not keep us from asking about humankind, about society, and ourselves: Where are we going? Will the "book" of our lives be preserved in any way? How? If not, why are we so concerned about writing it well? If yes, how should we act? How does our understanding of beginnings and ends affect the way we live now? How do we live meaningfully? These are not inherently scientific questions, though it is possible to believe that scientific inquiry is the most reliable source of answers to such ultimate questions or even the only one available to us. (Those who believe that to be the case are often said to have a secular faith.)

Such questions and the answers to them are the "plot" of the story that I, together with others, am inexplicably forced to write. In the Jewish religious tradition, the book is often portrayed and viewed as a matter of life and death in an almost literal sense. For it is portrayed as open to the Judge of who we really are. God is pictured asking Russian gendarmes as well as hasidic masters where they are, now, today. He is seen as writing a "book of life" and a "book of forgiveness and atonement" in which we desire to be "inscribed," parallel to the ones we are writing.

Until I write a good deal of my "book," I may never know who I really am. And I write in fits and starts, though perhaps most copiously in situations in which I must make decisions. In such situations I may take counsel, and refuge, in "objective" (for example, psychological) wisdom, or seek guidance in previous chapters of my book, and/or be "taught of the Lord," through the book that is Torah.

Tracing Beginnings and Imagining Ends

The three foci of ultimate questioning: beginnings (from where?), destinations (to where?) and the way through life (how?), are all raised and responded to in the first chapters, the first portion, of the Torah. The answer given there to the ultimate question of beginnings is called creation. About ends, we are taught through a story of transgression about death. And between beginnings and death, the human being, who has free choice, must decide, after realizing that she or he is free, how to live a life in which there is wandering but, nevertheless, an elusive but ever-present Providence that shows a way, yet is usually as light-handed as "the wind among the trees of the garden" that Adam and Eve heard (Gen. 3:8). The Teaching is that all three foci of ultimate questions, taken together, offer a model of human relationship with God.

The existential answers, however, are not closed or exhaustive. Even after learning about creation as an "answer" to the question of why there is a world, we may still wonder, along with the sages of the Talmud and the Midrash, why God would want to create such a world and what possibilities of meaning it contains. We do not learn exactly what death is, or what death is meant to teach. Adam and Eve do not actually die on the day of their sin, as God had threatened originally. And we cannot know, from the tale of their expulsion from Eden and their being sent on a thorny way, what human possibilities of alienation and reconciliation, of transgression and repentance, still await them. But those who seek instruction from this story, engage in "learning Torah." Like the rabbinic teachers who gave us rich stores of Midrash, contemporary learners, too, seek to recognize the questions and explore the answers of Torah. To this learning, Jewish education is classically seen as an introduction. It begins at home and continues in schools, camps, retreats, community centers, and wherever Jewish civilization makes its (communal) home.

The human possibilities exposed to view here involve both imagination and action. Knowing that one is created makes it possible to imagine beginnings and, in some sense, to begin again. Knowing "where we are going," having the uniquely human awareness of our inevitable deaths, makes us either despair or become accountable—or perhaps both. And the realization that we must write the text of our lives invites us to autonomy, sometimes creativity, always a measure of responsibility, but also, paradoxically, it evokes a desire for guidance, for limits, and for "instruction." Torah makes us free and responsible, yet disciplines and teaches us.

Biblical Stories as Paradigms

And now, we may return to Rashi's strange commentary about the Land of Israel and the nations. What does he say that this story prefigures? What does he consider its halakhic and existential pedagogy?

Stories of biblical happenings are often paradigms. For example, God's pity on the unintentional killer, Cain (for how could he know that his blow would deal death?) was a paradigm: As God had mercy on Cain, so would He, in later days, have mercy on those who committed accidental acts of wrongdoing, by legislating "cities of refuge" for them (Exod. 21:13). Similarly, God clothed our first parents, whose disobedience made them ashamed of their nakedness, at the beginning of the Torah, and He buried Moses at its end (*Sotah* 14a). These acts prefigure the halakhic-moral demand that we clothe the naked and bury the dead. God's resting on the seventh day is pure paradigm: He who "neither sleeps nor slumbers" and needs no rest wishes the Sabbath to be holy to us, and for us to rest on that day.

What is puzzling about Rashi's comment is that the Land, Eretz Yisrael, and the particular visions and worries of Israel with regard to its land, seem incongruent with what is being prefigured in this story. For the stories of Creation and human beginnings are not about Israel at all! In speaking of these stories, our sages say, "the deeds of the parents are signs for their children" (*ma'ase avot siman l'banim*). But Adam and Eve are the parents of all humanity! Shouldn't what we are taught here, in "ultimate" terms, reflect universal concerns? Shouldn't we be asking what, in the tradition of Torah, actually corresponds to the beginnings, destinations, and the "way" between these poles for humanity? Isn't the real issue here what the universal questions are and how Judaism, a monotheistic faith, responds to them and how they are given halakhic-paradigmatic expression in Judaism? Isn't that which is prefigured here? Why, then, does this universalistic story suggest to Rashi the particular Jewish problem of the right of the Jewish people to the Land of Israel?

A Jewish Model of Universalism: The Festivals of Tishre

In thinking of a paradigmatic expression of the teaching of (universal) beginnings, ways and ends within Judaism, what may plausibly come to mind are the month of Tishre and its festivals: Rosh Hashanah, Yom Kippur, and Sukkot (Tabernacles). These festivals seem very different from one another, yet they may well be seen as distinct themes or facets of one spiritual composition. They are the celebration of the seventh month, which, in the language of the seven days of the created world, is the holy one, that is, the one that most lucidly and urgently raises the "ultimate" questions and gives guidance for answering them.

Rosh Hashanah is, quite obviously, the festival of beginnings. It is, in the words of the liturgical poet, "the birthday of the world" and the first day of the year. But it is also the day for new beginnings, the day of re-turning, of *teshuvah*, and of envisioning a new world in which all nations "shall make one union to do Your will" and on which "the Lord will be one, and His name one." As Yom Hazikaron, "Day of Remembrance," Rosh Hashanah turns us back to origins so that we may imagine ends differently.

This festival is followed by Yom Kippur, the Day of Atonement, surely an explicit confrontation with ends. Yom Kippur is a prolonged moment of abstinence and abject creatureliness. Jonah the prophet, sitting in the belly of a whale, in abeyance between life and death, is an appropriate representation of the human condition that the day evokes. Not by chance does the tradition suggest the wearing of a shroud (*kittel*) on Yom Kippur, for it is the day on which one is invited to experience, albeit symbolically, death and judgment after death. Unlike Rosh Hashanah, which stirs one to noble feelings of regeneration by way of scriptural readings about noble men and women (Abraham, Sarah, Isaac, Samuel, and Rachel), the Yom Kippur readings are about the less sublime, even threatening, aspects of our existence. We are directed to mysterious priestly rites and hapless scapegoats—and warned that illicit sexual relations will cause the land to "vomit you out" (Lev. 18:25). Yom Kippur is about the death that follows sin. It hangs on the thread of hope that God will "open the gate at the time of the closing of the gate," the hope of divine forgiveness. For although all are mortal, "knowing good and evil," the hope of Yom Kippur is that all may partake of the Tree of Life, through Torah. Hence, "You who cleave to the

Lord your God are, all of you, alive this day" (Deut. 4:4), awaiting not the "end" of final death but messianic days to come.

And Sukkot, a festival of temporary abodes, recalls the tabernacles God provided for our ancestors in the wilderness. It points both to a wandering existence and to providential care. Indeed, this festival is rich in specific commandments (mitzvot), for "the way" of this wandering existence is the way of Torah. But Sukkot, the time in which seventy sacrifices were offered in the Temple on behalf of the seventy nations of the world, is also the festival in which we await "the end," the final pre-messianic conflict of Gog and Magog, and then, the redemption of the world.

Here, then, is a halakhic translation of a primordial and universal paradigm. Three festivals that are one, teaching that the human being who recalls beginnings is also the one who dreads death. It is she or he who may learn to rejoice at the divine care experienced in the temporary abode that is our mortal existence and to look ahead to the redemptive destination that was "foreseen from the beginning." Tishre is truly congenial to the story of Genesis! Yet Rashi, introducing his commentary on "the beginning," seems to evoke the contemporary festivals of the spring month of Iyar, Yom HaAtzma'ut and Yom Yerushalayim, Israel's Independence Day and Jerusalem Day. That is truly a "difficulty," requiring some in-depth search and some creative conjecture.

Theology, Experience, and Education: Yehudah Halevi Comments

The month of Tishre, like Creation and the Garden of Eden, is about existential categories of existence. But how are such existential categories known, and how may they be transmitted? How are they really experienced? These questions will bring us back to Rashi. And they appear to have preoccupied that great poet of the Jewish medieval theological tradition, Yehudah Halevi, in *The Kuzari* dialogue already referred to, between a *haver*-rabbi and a pagan king who seeks the truth about how to live his life.[5] Having turned first to a philosopher, a Moslem, and a Christian and being dissatisfied with their responses, the king finally asks a rabbi about the principles of his faith. The rabbi replies:

> I believe in the God of Abraham, Isaac and Israel, who led the children of Israel out of Egypt with signs and miracles; who fed them in the desert and gave them the land, after having made them traverse the sea and the Jordan in a miraculous way; who sent Moses with His law, and subsequently thousands of prophets who confirmed His law by promises to the obedient and threats to the disobedient. Our belief is comprised in the Torah—a very large domain.

The king expresses his disappointment with what he perceives to be an unphilosophical and even crude explication of belief. He asks why the rabbi could not overcome such "narrow-minded views": "Now shouldst thou, O Jew, not have said that thou believest in the Creator of the world, its Governor and Guide, and in Him who created and keeps thee, and such attributes which serve as evidence for every believer, and for the sake of which he pursues justice in order to resemble the Creator in His wisdom and justice?"

Here, the Kuzar king directs the rabbi-teacher back to the answers appropriate to universal and ultimate questions. When we are speaking of God, humanity, and the world—of beginnings, the paths of wise life, and ends, isn't the place to look in Genesis? Isn't that, rather than the nationalist and particularistic memories of Exodus and conquest, the place to look?

Indeed, what the king is saying sounds a good deal like what I said when I wondered whether Rashi's comment was incongruent with the themes of the Creation! To this query, the rabbi gives a commonsense and basically educational answer:

> That which thou dost express is religion based on speculation and system, the research of thought, but open to many doubts. Now ask the philosophers, and thou wilt find that they do not agree on one action or one principle, since some doctrines can be established by arguments which are only partially satisfactory, and still much less capable of being proved.

The rabbi intimates that we have not really experienced the Creation. True, we do have experiences of wonder at "creation," that is, the world. We do occasionally experience a sense of creativity and an urge to re-create in our own lives. But to trace these experiences back to divine Creation is a theological construction, "the research of thought, but open to many doubts." In other words, in our experience, there are indeed ultimate questions, but there is no agreement among human beings about "the one action or one principle" that is the completely satisfactory or the proven answer or doctrine. The cogency of a particular set of answers and guidelines has to be founded on something more experiential than "speculation and system."

Yehudah Halevi finds this "something," certainly for Jews, in the religious life of the Jewish people, its memories of commandment, and salvation. About these things we know, he argues, because they have happened to us, and each generation passes on these memories and this knowledge through the initiation of the young into the life of the community. In the community, one learns the "language" and becomes empowered to speak it. Once one has learned that "God took us out of Egypt and gave us the Torah and the Land," with all that this implies and requires for the moral and religious life of the nation, then one can perceive the connection between inner search and the "beginning." Then all individuals can hear the question, Where art thou? addressed to them, as to Adam and Eve, in a voice that specifically addresses them, that speaks their language.

Experience Begins at Home:
The Teaching of Shmini Atzeret

And so we may now come back to Rashi and the comment he attributes to Rabbi Isaac. True, the story of our first human parents is not about Israel and the nations or about Israel and its land. But Rashi seems to be suggesting that experience begins at home. The way to existential instruction by that Genesis story leads through the concrete experiences of the family, the group, the people, with what the national religious community has seen with its own eyes. This experience begins with the "creation" of that people in Egypt. Children should therefore be taught to "have been there." In the words of the Passover Haggadah:

> In each and every generation it is a person's duty to regard him/herself as having gone out of Egypt, as it is said, "And you shall tell your child on that day, It is because of that which the Lord did for *me* when I came forth from Egypt." Not only our ancestors did the Holy One, blessed be He, redeem then, but us too He redeemed with them, as it is said, "And He brought us out from there, that He might bring us in, to give us the Land which He swore to our forbears."

And now we may recall that Shmini Atzeret (the Eighth Day of Assembly), called the Concluding Festival of Tishre, is interpreted by Talmudic sages as a national festival. The sacrifices offered on that day, unlike those of Sukkot, are on behalf of Israel only: "R. El'azar said: Those seventy bullocks [offered on Sukkot], for whom are they? For the seventy nations. [Yet] The single bullock [offered on Shmini Atzeret], is for the single nation" (*Sukkah* 55b). On the festival of the Eighth Day of Assembly, which follows Sukkot, God turns to Israel and requests that they make him a small and intimate banquet, not like the large one they had made on behalf of the nations.

Not accidentally did the second (exilic) day of Shmini Atzeret *(Yom Tov sheni shel Galuyot)* become Simhat Torah (the Rejoicing of the Torah), the occasion for concluding—and starting afresh—the annual cycle of Torah reading. The universal, but potentially speculative, event of beginnings and ends, was made into a graphic and concrete experience of the Jewish people. It was their experience, one in which children participated from an early age, that a new year had not truly begun until the Torah was literally rolled back, from its "end" to its "beginning." The universal year was given tangible shape by being provided with its Jewish way. No wonder children, from earliest childhood, love Simhat Torah but are often initially bored by the solemnity of Rosh Hashanah and Yom Kippur.

No wonder they associate Sukkot with adventure and decorations rather than with wanderings and impermanence. After all, children are initiated into a story and enjoy becoming part of it before they realize that they too must write one! Rashi puts them squarely within the story.

If so, why is the way his commentary is used in some schools offensive? Perhaps for the same reason that the "national" Shmini Atzeret must find its context in Tishre. It is a conclusion to the "universal" festival of Sukkot. Rashi's commentary requires the universal biblical story that it mediates. When it does mediate it, then we see that the Rosh Hashanah–Yom Kippur–Sukkot spirit is not compromised by Shmini Atzeret but is completed by it. But Shmini Atzeret alone is not what the story is all about. The one bullock of Shmini Atzeret is meaningful because it follows the seventy bullocks of Sukkot.

Why this conclusion and completion? Simply because we do not *really* remember the Creation, and we have not *really* experienced our own deaths or completed the possibly surprising "way" of our stories and lives. But we clearly remember being invited, at the end of the festive season, to "stay one more day," to sing and dance and to roll the Torah back to its beginning. Through such memories and experiences, Yehudah Halevi suggests, Judaism and its communities approach ultimate questions and get young people into the "language." That is the way they educate.

An Afterthought: As My Father Used to Say . . .

It is the opinion of many Rashi scholars that the Rabbi Isaac referred to by Rashi in his opening commentary was his own father. Yehudah Halevi lived almost a century before Rashi, but he would surely have appreciated Rashi's intimation that the way to begin teaching Torah is by recalling what one's immediate parents and teachers "used to say." Yehudah Halevi would have had no trouble understanding what Rashi was teaching when he began his biblical commentary with something his own father had said.

7

PRIESTLY GARMENTS AND ALL THAT: STILL SPLENDID?

WE MAY NOW ASK WHETHER the young person with whom we began, having been shown what Rashi's commentary on the first verse of the Bible can teach us about the "large questions," will still be bored by Bible stories. He will probably be more respectful, but we cannot be certain that he will become engaged. It may seem to him that the large questions that drew our attention can be found throughout his cultural environment in various formulations, most of them easier to identify and to handle than the text of the Torah, and requiring no Rashi and no Hebrew school.

Whether Jewish education can cultivate specific and singular types of educated persons comes down to the following issue: Can the patterns, narratives, and normative expectations of a social and religious system situated in Levitical law no less than in the narratives of "the beginning" still incorporate and embody the large questions that we found in the first "portion" of Genesis? In Chapter 6, I approached this cardinal educational question of contemporary Judaism from the bright side of universal concerns. But no conception of Jewish teaching can be complete without addressing

the issue from its other, institutional, particularistic, and "ritual" aspect, not as a pedagogic ploy, but as an essential feature of Jewish
teaching as it dwells within the specific historic community of Judaism. That more murky and perhaps embarrassing aspect of educating a Jewish child is the subject in the following two chapters.

I begin with an incident that perturbed me for a considerable
time. It happened when I was teaching at the Jerusalem Institute
for Youth Leaders from Abroad, then widely known by its Hebrew
name, the Machon l'Madrichai Chutz l'Aretz. "The Machon," then
as now, conducted a yearlong training program for young leaders of
Jewish, mostly Zionist, youth movements from around the world.

Those were the days when the Shah still ruled over his various
provinces and peoples, and there were often students from Iran at
the Machon. One of these, on the last day of his stay in Jerusalem,
informed me confidentially, almost conspiratorially, that another
member of his movement who was coming to the course the following year needed to be treated with respect. "Why?" I asked, "is
he the head of your movement?" "No," he answered quite
solemnly, "in fact the fellow that's coming is quite shy and not
very knowledgeable. But he is special. You see, he's a *kohen* (a
priest)."

Though I felt like making a joke of it, it was clearly no laughing
matter to my student. I said, "Oh, I see," with all the solemnity I
could muster, thinking that the shy and not very knowledgeable
young man being sent, priest or not, was probably not very bright.
Then I caught myself and thought again. Wasn't it reasonable to assume that that young *kohen* blessed my present pupil in the synagogue in Teheran on every festival, in the name of God? So why
should I think it funny for his friend to describe him as special? And
yet, there was something peculiar about his remark that I could not
put my finger on; some problem at the juncture where tradition and
modernity were supposed to meet for me.

Thinking now about this episode, I am struck by the image of
the *kohen*, the priest, in the Bible and what is left of priesthood in
contemporary Judaism. How were priests "special"? Is it feasible
to still see them, or anyone else, as special, simply as a matter of

birth? How does one approach such features of the tradition in a world wherein children, like adults, think that specialness depends on ability and character and not on caste. What, if anything, is the large question here with which educators wish to confront children?

Grandeur? Or Inauthenticity?

The *parashat hashavua* (portion of the week) that is the centerpiece of the discussion here, *Tetsavveh* (Exod. 27:20–30:10), has a number of peculiar features. One is that it is the only *parashah*, after the book of Genesis of course, in which the name of Moses is never mentioned. Although God repeatedly turns to him with commandments and instructions, God addresses him throughout only in the second person, you. Another is that Moses here finds himself preparing his brother and his brother's sons for their priestly tasks. These are tasks that Moses originally performed and that he must now turn over to them. These two characteristics of *Parashat Tetsavveh* may be related, for they both suggest a kind of self-effacement on the part of Moses, a stepping into the shadows, at least momentarily and symbolically.

Moreover, they may be linked to a third peculiar characteristic of the *parashah*, namely, that virtually an entire chapter, forty verses in all, is devoted to describing the garments of the High Priest, in addition to two additional verses describing the clothing of the lesser priests. We learn that the High Priest is to wear no less than eight prescribed articles of clothing; the lesser priests, four. These high-priestly garments are lavish and unique. There is an abundance of gold in them, and there are bells attached. One not only sees the *kohen gadol*, "High Priest," approaching but hears him too. Who can fail to be impressed by such grandeur?

A candid answer would be, most modern people. So what are Jewish children, who are modern people, to make of this wardrobe of honor and adornment *(kavod* and *tiferet)*, that the Torah details with such perplexing solemnity? Why can't the priestly functions be carried out without special and ornamental clothes? Why must the High Priest not dare approach the Holy Place without his special garments "that he not die"?

Once these questions are raised, others follow in their wake: Why should there be priestly functions at all? Why should some people be born priests? By what right are they traditionally called to the reading of the Torah first so as not to "insult" them? Are these people any better than others? Can any person be considered better or more deserving than another simply because of a family connection or an inherited status? And while we are speaking of hereditary elites, why the formal distinction between Israel and the nations? And why does Jewish law distinguish between the rights and obligations of women and men?

Yet other distinctions come to mind. Why is one day of the week, the Sabbath, special? Why not celebrate transcendence when one is in the mood? Why wear Shabbat clothes? Why should it be "insulting" to the Sabbath if we greeted the day without putting on special clothes? Also, Why repent of sins specifically on Rosh Hashanah and Yom Kippur? The witticism that compares Purim to "Yom Hakippurim" is pithy in pointing out the likeness between the days. On both, people wear masks; on Purim they play act as clowns and on Yom Hakippurim, the Day of Atonement, they pretend to be righteous. Why pretend?

Doesn't this humorous comment point to the sham in all institutional religion? For, in asking these seemingly rhetorical questions, we appear to have undercut the foundations of the entire tradition. If it is odd to think of a student at a leadership institute, or on a football team for that matter, as special because he is a *kohen*, isn't it also laughable to honor a parchment on the doorpost or a fallen sacred book by kissing them? Or to show respect to the old just because they are in the special category of old? Or to honor parents and, for example, not to sit in their accustomed seats? What is all this for? Aren't they—and we—people like everyone else? So the *parashah* seems to have it all wrong, to exemplify, in fact, inauthentic human existence as such, as though the value of a person were in clothing, in appearance, in being superficially impressive.

The House of Aaron—and Moses

Yet we should bear in mind that even in the *parashah* of *Tetsavveh*, the external grandeur of the priests and the rich detail of prescription and description is set off for us in the figure of Moses, father of prophets, God's confidant. But he seems to step into anonymity here, to become nameless. After being informed of all the High Priest's grand apparel, we may realize that we have been told nothing of Moses' clothing. For all the Torah seems to care, he may have worn a simple shepherd's cloak and sandals. When Moses speaks to God, he is far from the public eye, on a mountain, under a cloud, hidden in the cleft of a rock. Once, indeed, on "the day of assembly," God revealed His commandments in the sight of the entire people. But the impression that made was momentary; the tablets brought down in colorful pageantry had to be broken after the people, bored by the waiting and fearful, built their Golden Calf. It all had to be done again, new tablets had to be fashioned, this time quietly, without fanfare.

Aaron and the historic House of Aaron indeed "wear" holiness and celebrate it. The Yom Kippur service of the High Priest, described in *Parashat Aharei Mot* (Lev. 6), is still recited with great fervor in traditional synagogues during the *Mussaf* service of that day, accompanied by poetic descriptions of how beautiful the appearance of the High Priest was "when he emerged from the Holy of Holies unscathed *(b'li pega)*."

An ancient writer describes the occasion. On the evening of the conclusion of Yom Kippur, he reports, when the High Priest had concluded his service:

> all the people in Jerusalem would pass before him, many with torches
> . . . all dressed in white clothing, and all windows decorated with lace
> and filled with candles. And the priests told me that in many years the
> High Priest could not get to his home before midnight because,
> though all were fasting, they wouldn't go to their homes till they had
> [tried to] . . . approach the priest and kiss his hand.

And the following day, he would make a great feast for his friends and relations, and would make the day a holiday because he had come out from the Holy of Holies "in peace," unscathed. Then he would order a goldsmith to make him a tablet of gold and engrave on it the following: I, [so and so], High Priest, son of [so and so] the Priest, officiated as High Priest in the great and holy House to serve Him who caused His name to dwell there, and this was in the [particular] year after the Creation. May He who favored and allowed me to perform this service, merit my son to do so after me, to stand in office before the Lord.[1]

This description is touching but self-congratulatory. It is very unlike anything in the life of a prophet. No one ever celebrated him or her, not even Moses, the chief of prophets. Even though it was he who brought the essential message of Yom Kippur back from Mount Sinai: "*Salahti*, I, [God] have forgiven," for it was Moses who obtained atonement for the sin of the Golden Calf, a sin in which Aaron had a hand! Perhaps we would be justified therefore in placing all the priestly pomp and circumstance in historical perspective and at a historical distance—together with all those institutional features of the Torah and "religion" that endow people and artifacts with make-believe stature, that discriminate and impose arbitrary obligations and restrictions. Perhaps we are justified in laughing at priests and priestly robes, at ceremonial roles and regulations.

Debunking Honor in the Name of Dignity

The problem we have with *Parashat Tetsavveh* and with many other matters that are staples of "how the community educates" is well analyzed by Peter Berger, Brigette Berger, and Hansfried Kellner in their study, *The Homeless Mind*. The authors differentiate there between two concepts: honor and dignity. Let us examine their distinction.

Honor, as they explain the term, refers to a sense one has of oneself in society and what that sense demands socially.[2] It has to do with knights in armor, with proper patterns of behavior vis-à-vis social inferiors (and superiors), with the "right thing to do" and the shame associated with not doing it. It is honor that obliges people to be offended by an intended slight and even to risk their lives and "save their honor" by dueling.

The authors posit that the modern sense of *dignity* was born when the social concept of honor was debunked; when the disguises behind which we hid our common humanity were removed, we discovered our freedom and our rights "irrespective of race, creed, and color" or of gender or social status. The sociological message of dignity is that all biological or historical distinctions between human beings are "either simply unreal or essentially irrelevant." The anthropological message is that "the real self" is located "over and beyond all these differentiations." Whereas honor "implies that identity is essentially and . . . importantly linked to institutional roles, the modern concept of dignity implies that identity is essentially independent of them."[3]

Where dignity reigns, honor is decried as inauthentic. The champion of undiluted dignity declares that the individual can discover his or her true identity only by emancipating her/himself from socially imposed roles. Those are only masks, entangling the individual in illusion, alienation, and "bad faith." Whereas in a world of honor, the individual discovers his or her true identity in roles to be played, it is radically otherwise in the world of dignity. There one is taught to see seemingly obliging historical traditions and "proud" consciousness of succession as mystifications and manipulations and, therefore, as instruments of enslavement.

Where there is honor, there are institutions through which honor is articulated. Institutions assign roles, create social expectations, enable people to place themselves in a social world. In terms of the discussion above, the High Priest knew who he was through his clothes. He knew that the solemn fast of Yom Kippur "meant" hunger, trepidation, and solitude, that it was the one day of the year he had to take off his gold-laid vestments and come into the Holy of Holies in garments of linen alone, so as not to "remind" God on that sacred occasion that His people had fashioned a Golden Calf.

But he also knew that the next day was naturally a *yom tov*, a "festive occasion," for him, a day for feasting and fellowship, a day for gold. His fondest hope was that his sons after him would continue within this reality, just as he continued the world of his father, the priest. It would have been dishonorable for the High Priest to act outside this social reality, a badge of shame for him. As for the people of Jerusalem, they knew that the night after Yom Kippur was the time for rejoicing, candles, torches, and milling around the *kohen gadol*. That was fitting and was associated with the religious sense of things and thanksgiving for the meanings they had been given. Hence, their cry, still recorded and proclaimed in the *Avodah* liturgy that commemorates the high-priestly service on Yom Kippur: "Happy is the people who have it so, happy the people whose God is the Lord" (Ps. 144:15).

Where dignity has conquered and reigns supreme, institutions have lost their power. Yet without institutions, what really happens to identity? Berger, Berger, and Kellner point out that when institutions become fragile, unstable, and even "unreal," then "the individual is thrown back on himself, on his own subjectivity, from which he must dredge up the meaning and the stability that he requires to exist."[4] This state of affairs is problematic, for we are social beings. Hence, a life of undiluted dignity is likely to bring Erich Fromm's well-known "Escape from Freedom" in its wake. Having given up the institutions of society and the honorable patterns that maintain them, people are likely to run away from their solitude, to seek release from the solitary search for meaning in totalitarian movements and states. In such states, the only impressive institution is the dictator and the only honorable roles are mindless ceremony and blind obedience. The highest reality there is the ability to impose pain and the fate of bearing it.

In short, Berger, Berger, and Kellner claim that without honor people cannot live in society. But there is a paradox here: One must be liberated from honor in order to have the inner freedom of a dignified existence, and at the same time, one needs honor and the reality of being somehow enveloped in it. For just as there is no modern freedom and authenticity without dignity, so is there no bearable freedom without the structures that honor provides.

But is there not a vicious circle here? Is the yearning for honor not romantic and reactionary? Can we really have both dignity and honor? Can honor be restored without artificiality? Or does it always entail the loss of the inner freedom of dignity?

Dignity, Honor, and Torah

Parashat Tetsavveh relates explicitly and implicitly to the issues of honor and dignity. We have here the explicitly enumerated and described vestments of honor, and we have the priest himself personifying an institution and subject to its seemingly artificial but impressive rules. Yet the institution itself is initiated by the most uninstitutionalized of people, the prophet. The prophet relativizes the institution, for he declares that it is worthy of respect and that it authorizes honorable behavior only because God commanded it. And the prophet, the messenger of God, supervises it, in his simple cloak and sandals. He is the authority. He knows that honor is vital and often exhilarating but insists that it be limited to what God legislates.

The prophet teaches that only God knows how much "honor" is needed by human beings. Having made them creatures of meaning, God instructs them, through the prophet, as to what they shall see to be truly significant. Because they have agreed to constitute a holy society, they are open to transcendent meaning. Despite the vulnerability and frailty of human beings, they are invited, even bidden, to live by a teaching that translates ultimate meaning into social reality. But having learned to see themselves as finite creatures, as being "before God," they know that they cannot invent ultimate meaning. Therefore they understand that the institutions of honor in a covenantal society are Torah. But beyond all that, there is the simplicity of dignity and majesty that is not put on with clothes. It is the dignity that flows from within, like the rays on Moses' forehead.

Where in this *parashah* of honor, of clothes and sacrificial ceremony, does the Torah deal with dignity? Let us recall once again that throughout these proceedings Moses is addressed only as "you." The fact that his name is not mentioned may be seen, as I noted, as self-effacing or perhaps as suggesting that he stepped aside from honor in favor of his brother. R. Moshe Alschech, a sixteenth-century commentator in Safed, sees another side to it. Alschech imagines Moses as disappointed and frustrated that God, the source of all real honor, turned the building of the Tabernacle and the divine service over to others, to Bezalel the artisan and Aaron the priest, respectively. Says Alschech:

> To comfort him and redress the balance God said: *Ve'attah* (You yourself), i.e., you in person [shall command it]. The accent on the word [*ve'attah* in the traditional cantillation of the Torah] in all three cases [*gershayim, pazer, revi'a,* i.e., three musical notes of cantillation] represent a louder pitch or rising intonation, as if to say: Listen, Moses, don't worry. It's all really you. . . . All fulfill themselves through you. Through the commandments that you have transmitted to Israel including that of the taking of the oil, they are enabled "to cause the lamp to burn continually"—symbolizing the spiritual illumination of eternity that they would never achieve without you. This goes for the Jewish people as a whole. Similarly . . . the priestly role of Aaron and his sons. . . . Their achievement of this status is all your doing. "You yourself *(Ve'attah)* bring Aaron near to thee." Through your bringing near they will become worthy. Even the garments have no power to consecrate them as priests except through you. . . . You yourself shall speak. . . . [It is all] only through the fact that the command came through you.[5]

Moses, the person of dignity who forgoes honor, "places" it. He prophetically testifies to its limitations and yet establishes its domain.

Teaching Honor with Dignity

It is difficult to imagine a Jewish upbringing or a formal education without initiation into the life of the Jewish people, without teaching the categories of honor. Without Shabbat, without rules and roles, without conceptions of the sacred and profane, there can be no societal norms of holiness and no holy people. In educating toward that, we are swimming against the stream of modern culture, which considers "standing before God" a myth and therefore insists that it is undignified for human beings not to make their own meanings. Our children, the pupils in our schools, and we ourselves are modern, so we naturally experience difficulty with notions of honor. Sometimes it seems to us that the logical thing is to choose between benighted honor and emancipating dignity. But is that really the choice placed before us?

The traditional Torah reading for the afternoon of Yom Kippur declares, "You shall observe My statutes and My ordinances, which, if a person do them, she/he will live by them" (Lev. 18:5). To this R. Meir comments: "From whence do we know that even an idolater who occupies himself with Torah is like a High Priest? Scripture teaches: A *person* shall do them. Priests, Levites and Israelites is not said, but a person" (*Baba Kamma* 38a). And a later midrash asks why, when Pinhas the son of El'azar (grandson of Aaron) was still serving Israel, Deborah was needed to "judge Israel at that time" (Judg. 4:4). Who needed a simple Israelite woman to rule Israel when there was a High Priest doing it? One midrash finds an answer to this question in Deborah's deeds, not in her status: "I call heaven and earth to witness that whether it be heathen or Jew, whether it be man or woman, a manservant or a maidservant, the holy spirit will suffuse each of them according to his or her deeds" (*Debe Eliyahu Rabbah* 48).

As children, our pupils are likely to understand the "glorious appearance of the High Priest as he emerged from the Holy of Holies" before they fathom the "dignified" teaching of R. Meir and the midrash.[6] But as moderns, they quickly learn that they should have no patience with formal splendor and that only R. Meir and that midrash represent the "spiritual side of Judaism." What will reconcile them, as moderns, to the honor-oriented dimensions of our tradition, which teaches them to grow into adulthood within a society that makes demands upon them and protects them and that offers them a realm of meaning? Let us recall: In the world of

Moses, there is no pomp and circumstance; his sons will not be prophets, and no one engraves his name in gold. Only if that is remembered, even as we teach about the garments of Aaron and his sons, can the concepts of *kavod* (honor) and *tiferet* (adornment) be placed in their cultural and spiritual contexts. The grandeur of the High Priest and his garments all depend on Moses. Honor, certainly for modern people, where there is no dignity, threatens to become a sham.

Clothing, Once Again

Our sages, who were not modern, and who related to the honor-bound side of human existence with utmost seriousness,[7] carefully juxtaposed the Torah reading of Yom Kippur morning, which relates the service of the High Priest for that day, with a prophetic passage from Isaiah. In this haftorah, the prophet rebukes and mocks those who come to the Temple to carry out their "service," beating their breasts in ritualized remorse, fasting and swaying as they go through the forms of prayer. The prophet has these honor-minded people turning to God with the question, Why have you not seen our fasting and "afflicting of soul"? And this question deserves an answer:

> Behold, you fast for strife and contention, and to smite with the fist of wickedness; you fast not this day to make your voice heard on high. Is such the fast I have chosen? . . . Is it [for each] to bow down his head as a bulrush, and to spread sackcloth and ashes under him? Will you call this a fast, an acceptable day to the Lord? [Rather] is this not the fast I have chosen? To loose the fetters of wickedness . . . to deal your bread to the hungry [and to] . . . bring the poor that are cast out to your house? When you see the naked, that you cover him? (Isa. 58:3–7)

For the second time on Yom Kippur, then, the sages who assigned these scriptural readings draw our attention to clothing. But here it is to remind us that the ordered solemnity of the Yom Kippur rite is "not heard" where there is deafness to the cry—and to the dignity—of the hungry and the poor who have no garments with which to cover themselves.

Between the insight of R. Meir and the ordered and ordained world of my Iranian student at the Institute for Youth Leaders from Abroad, stands the prophet and also the teacher. It is he or she who, through the mitzvah of educating, puts the ordered world into place. The teacher also belongs to this ordered and commanded world, and he or she teaches that a reflective participation in its splendors is Torah. But again like the prophet, he or she also represents another teaching, namely, that in addition to holy garments, there must be a holy spirit to attune each individual to hear those who need to be clothed.

On Yom Kippur, shortly after celebrating the service of the High Priest in all its "honorable" pageantry, with its joyful message of atonement "for the entire community of Israel," the liturgy returns us to the *Selihot*, the penitential prayers. At that moment, it is as though no social institution could help us. We are still alone with our fragile dignity, still burdened with our failings. There, in the *Selihot* of the *Mussaf* service, each of us, woman and man, *kohen* and simple Israelite, confronts the prayer that we have already said twice that day, that we are now to say as though no Temple pageant, no *Avodah*, had intervened: "Do not cast us out from Your Presence, and do not take Your holy Spirit from us."[8]

The teacher is charged with bringing children into a world in which Presence and holy Spirit suggest a wealth of meanings and obligations. It is the teacher who, together with parents, may guide the child into a cultural and spiritual reality of order and spontaneity, freedom, and continuity, dignity and honor.

8

JEWISH LAW AND
HUMAN NATURE:
EDUCATIONAL
MODELS

Educational Ideals

IN CHAPTER 7, I DEALT WITH the fact of Judaism's specificity and the educational problem of initiating children into the particular religious culture, into the specific narratives, idioms, and associations of the Jewish tradition. This I did by composing, with the help of a sociological thesis of Berger, Berger, and Kellner, what might be called "a midrash on clothing." In the manner of what, with Petuchowski, I have been calling the Bible of the Synagogue," I constructed the midrash on the foundations of an "unlikely" text describing priestly pageantry. This was done on the assumption that Jewish acculturation transmits not only a certain kind of ethical sensitivity and existential awareness but also the "language" and life patterns of a people that, throughout its historical crises, bears a singular religious vision.

More specifically, the discussion in the previous chapter viewed the irremediable dissonance between "honorable" priestly rites and the "dignity" of the individual person as illustrative of a tension inherent in human life. This discussion was built on a fundamental religious and educational assumption, namely, that educated Jewish persons and publics do well to seek and place themselves in relationship to an ethical and religious system founded on an ideal of law and lawfulness, and that this relationship is not a subversion of the religious spirit or an inauthentic substitute for it but, rather, a sublime expression of spirituality. Here I shall try to show not only how Jewish law, the halakhah, draws the commandments of the Torah into the concrete circumstances of life, but also how the law's internal controversies reflect diverse philosophical and educational positions.

I shall look at several focal questions that concern philosophers of education from one corner of the halakhic world of faith. To get into the subject more readily, I cite statements of two twentieth-century scholars. At the end of my brief investigation, I offer a thought about a question I should have asked my grandmother, but did not.

The first of my two observations comes from a philosopher of Jewish law, Ze'ev Falk. The second is that of Leo Strauss, a political philosopher.

Falk posits that law and religion cannot guide human behavior unless they have a working conception, or "image," of the average as well as of the ideal person. He writes:

> [Such an image] is derived from observation and reason as well as from culture and belief. There can be no effective guidance in legal or religious matters without knowledge of the common man; on the other hand, any normative system aspires to the ideal, which means that there must also be an image of the ideal person. Moreover, both law and religion deal with offenses against their norms, which means that they have to create also a corresponding image of the criminal.[1]

Similarly, Strauss argues for a philosophical conception of worthiness in social and political life: "All political action," he writes, "aims at either preservation or change. When desiring to preserve, we wish to prevent a change for the worse; when desiring to change, we wish to bring about something better. All political action is then guided by some thought of better and worse. But thought of better or worse implies thought of the good."[2]

Success and Failure in Education

Neither Falk's nor Strauss's statement is specifically directed at society's *educational* concerns, yet both might well have been. For as every reflective teacher and parent knows, we cannot hope to educate human beings unless we have a principled and defensible idea of how people normally are and what potential they have for being changed and becoming different, if becoming different is, indeed, desirable. Principled ideas and convictions, then, are the foundations of our educational, no less than of our social and political, visions, and they inform our approaches to understanding what we want and evaluating what we are doing.

Since we generally do wish to effect desirable changes in our pupils or children, we consider evidence of such change educational success. Conversely, an inability to move the young in what we consider worthy directions, we call failure. Conversely, we may believe that it is good to preserve in children their native insights, talents, and innocence. In that case, we shall see many changes as being for the worse. We shall then envision children who have not been corrupted by too much culture. If that is the vision, failure for us will be synonymous with changing them by miseducating them, drawing them away from their true selves!

In short, thinking about education involves deciding what characterizes people as they are, with due respect for the variety among them. It means discussing and determining, on the basis of some ideal or vision, whether those characteristics, as a whole or in part, should be encouraged and cultivated or whether some or all of them should be changed. And then, together with those who know the appropriate theories and those who have the requisite experience, educators must consider how best to achieve the changes that have been judged desirable.

Of course, it cannot be assumed that what someone considers an ideal change can actually be realized through education or to what extent. Legitimate educational effort is not indoctrination: It is not the case that anything goes, especially not manipulations that deny the learner's dignity. Furthermore, human beings, even children, are partly what they are or adamantly wish to be. Thus, parents and teachers who believe that education involves changing what there is into something better must always ask themselves which compromises they may legitimately make between the ideal "ought" and the human reality as it is. If one believes that not everything is permissible and that situations and human beings are partly intractable, some accommodations seem to be sensible compromises, whereas others will be considered unacceptable. Conversely, educators and parents who want to preserve what they consider the "natural good(ness)" in young people will generally admit that some accommodation to society is legitimate. After all, children who have been empowered to function in the social world as it (unfortunately) is without undue vulnerability are better off than those who cannot function within it. They are probably also more capable of changing that social world for the better.

Since the communities of culture and belief in the world are diverse, there is no universal agreement regarding such questions as: Who is the ideal human being? and What is virtue in human beings? That which traditional Jews consider virtuous is decried as repressive by orthodox Freudians; what humanists and democrats cultivate as an ideal has been condemned as criminal and degenerate by Nazis and lesser totalitarians. The platform of progressive educators is founded on the belief that what is innate in the child is basically good and must be thoughtfully but unabashedly developed. Conversely, "essentialist" educators believe that children learn to leave their natural wildness behind, and that they become fully human only through exposure to a (mainly literary) heritage. Those educators anticipate that this heritage will "in-form" them (i.e., give them form), make them "cultured." The issue that underlies these questions, whether human beings are innately good or "evil from early youth" (Gen. 8:21) or even before that, is perhaps the most fundamental one facing shapers of educational policies.

Even those who defend the view that people are naturally good admit, at least on the basis of observation, that human beings are often corrupted by pathological conditions and influences. However, proponents of human goodness insist that evil is a social and existential problem that can be solved; it is a sickness to be healed. This optimistic view characterizes ancient Socratic thinkers as well as modern philosophers of the Enlightenment such as Immanuel Kant. The contemporary moral philosopher John Kekes, has noted that people who believe in the basic goodness of humankind tend to "psychologize" wrongdoing, to find some (extrinsic) reason for it, but they refrain from psychologizing good deeds. That is because they assume that bad deeds require an explanation but not the good ones, which come naturally.[3] (Admittedly some people are better at being good than others, but that is attributed by the optimists to a maximal cultivation of their natural endowments.)

This doctrine of natural goodness has always had its critics. For example, the Greek, medieval, and modern dramatists who represent the tragic tradition maintain that the evil around and within us, which the optimist confidently dismisses as an aberration or a repair to be made, should be viewed as a dominant feature of our own natures. The flaws in our souls inevitably control us; they not only cause our problems, but they also poison and pervert our proposed solutions. Therefore, evil will always prevail, and we ourselves, even when we mean well, will always inflict harm upon ourselves and others. This evil is generally greater than we intend or our victims "deserve," but it is what we should expect in a world pervaded by tragic flaws, within and around us.

There is a third possibility. It is that "the heart of the human being is (indeed) evil from early youth" (Gen. 8:21), but that we can be brought, by wise reflection and prudent instruction, to a maximal control of evil, for we also have the resources to control the "evil impulse." In this view, there is within us, in addition to the evil impulse, a potential for goodwill, intelligence, and benevolence. Yet that potential must be drawn out by wise education, which ought itself to be based on wise laws, standards and social expectations.

In modern rationalistic and pragmatic Jewish thought, there has been a tendency not only to negate totally the tragic view, but also to espouse the optimistic one. With much passion, religious liberals and pragmatists argue that, on basic theological grounds, Judaism is opposed to the tragic conception of life, for in the world of tragedy, there cannot be a benevolent Creator. The tragic cosmos is either ruled by sinister forces or is absolutely devoid of meaning. The optimistic view, of innate human goodness, is supported by such features of Jewish doctrine as "the image of God" inherent in human beings, God's willingness to relate to flesh and blood, and even His need, as it were, for humans to "complete the Creation" and to bring holiness into the world. A prominent proof text for theological optimism is the opening of a meditation at the beginning of the morning prayer: "O my God, the soul that You have given me is pure."

Since traditional Jewish education assumes that initiation of the young into the world of halakhah is part of what characterizes the educational enterprise, and most liberal Jewish education argues for considering halakhic discourse significant, even if not necessarily normative, in Jewish education, reflective Jewish teaching will have to examine its various approaches to this corpus of law on the basis of some conception of human nature. This nature, we recall, is one that education may try to change for the better and/or to preserve in its fine traits. And in conjunction with that general philosophical issue, the nature of covenant and Jewish religious life will necessarily arise.

If one makes the optimistic assumption of innate goodness (possibly) corrupted by too little knowledge, bad habits, and pathological ambitions and interests, then it may well make sense to view the commandments of the Torah and the halakhic laws that establish its legal patterns and parameters as aiming to maintain this goodness, to curb corruption, and to foster what is morally natural. In that case, the halakhah must have been ordained by the divine Legislator or, as others might say, inspired legislators, with respect to innate and legitimate human needs and spelled out by generations of human interpreters on the basis of "natural" understanding and intuition.

That is one way to make sense of the halakhah. But the human being can also be conceived as inherently delinquent or congenitally flawed, as always being under the influence of the evil impulse or even, tragically, enslaved to it. In that case, the laws of the Torah may be seen as liberating him or her from the dominion of the evil impulse. If there is a tragic, or at least highly problematic, element in the human soul, the Torah, "given from Heaven" and thus unaffected by human corruptibility, must educate people away from their natures. It must give them a new perspective on what real needs are, as against the seductive and false ones with which the *yetzer hara*, "the evil impulse," has seduced them. In the tragic view, the status of Torah as divine fiat, even when inexplicably so, becomes the plausible position. Human beings, since they are flawed, are not capable of solving the problem of their own existence. Only divine "grace" *(hesed)*, can do this.

Which view best grasps the "life of Torah," toward which the halakhah educates? Which is the way to go and what is its point of departure?

Clearly, the assumption of Torah learners throughout the generations has been that God, the Educator, knows the hearts of His children-pupils and legislates, at least in principle, for every human eventuality. There are laws, halakhot, for instances of homicide, replete with court procedures; there are halakhic directives and sanctions for cases of theft. In God's Torah, Jews have maintained, He established laws that symbolically express His relationship with humans and remind us of what is expected of His covenanted people: For example, we are bidden not to eat "torn" *(terefah)* meat, for "you shall be holy people unto Me" (Exod. 22:30).

But what is the divine Educator's point of departure and legislative intention? Is He concerned that murder and theft be properly dealt with lest the *aberration* of crime corrupt all society and infect it with the criminal's sickness of soul? Or is the Torah's legislation based upon divine knowledge of natural murderous tendencies that must be uprooted, so that people will be enabled, through lawful lives, to go beyond their bestial "natures"? Is it teaching us that the cruelty associated with torn meat will pervert people's natural kindness or that cruelty itself is natural, but not holy? And that being holy people and a holy nation is a new and "unnatural" higher stage of existence for human beings? What a particular philosophy of Jewish education will mandate and envision largely depends on the answers to these questions.

Locating the Heart of Halakhah

In order to clarify this ultimately educational issue, we may now look in on several rooms in the mansion of the Halkhah. A good place to begin is a passage (Exod. 15:22–26) in the *parashah* of *Beshallah* and several interpretive comments upon it. Immediately after they cross the Red Sea, we are told, the Israelites come to Marah, where the waters, as the name of the place leads us to expect, are bitter. They complain to Moses, who turns to God. The Lord shows him a tree (or log), which Moses throws into the waters, sweetening them. The Torah continues: "There He gave them a statute and an ordinance *(hok u'mishpat)* and there He tested them. And He said, 'If you will diligently hearken to the Lord your God, doing what is right in His sight, giving ear to His commandments and keeping all His statutes, then I will not bring upon you any of the diseases I brought upon the Egyptians, for I the Lord am your physician'" (Exod. 15:25–26).

Which statute He gave them on this occasion of murmuring, and which ordinance, is a matter of controversy among the rabbis of the Midrash. In the midrashic collection entitled *Mekhilta* (Tractate *Vayassa* 1), Rabbi Yehoshua states that the statute *(hok)* is the law of the Sabbath and the ordinance *(mishpat)* is the law of honoring parents. In the opinion of R. Eleazer of Modi'im the statute alluded to is the law against incest, and ordinance refers to laws about robbery, fines, and injuries. Rashi (on v. 25) opines (with *Seder Eliyahu Zuta* 84) that God also gave the statute of the red heifer *(parah adumah)*, whose ashes purify the (ritually) impure (Num. 19).

To make sense of this controversy, let us explain ordinances (*mishpatim*) as commentators have done, namely, as the ethical and evidently right thing to do.[4] As for statutes, they are classically understood to be inexplicable divine decrees (Rashi on Numbers 19:2). If *mishpat* and *hok* are to be understood in this manner, we seem to have a discussion here of whether the Sabbath and the prohibition against incest should be viewed as "unreasonable" statute-decrees of this kind, unlike such understandable and reasonable social laws (*mishpatim*) as honoring parents and establishing codes of civil law. We may even conjecture that optimists will always be inclined to center their halakhic consciousness on *ordinances*, while *statutes* will be focal for those who presuppose the insufficiency of human sentiment and reason. Thus pessimists may consider even the laws of the Sabbath to be a statute, characterized mainly by its "difficult" and seemingly unreasonable restrictions.

The distinction between optimists and pessimists with regard to statutes and ordinances in rabbinic exegesis also touches upon the question, What precisely does God promise at Marah? Recall: His laws will prevent "the diseases I brought upon the Egyptians." He is the "physician" of Israel. He knows, in the Torah's metaphor here, what is healthy and prevents disease. "Health" might be the consequence of obeying the laws proscribing theft and mandating the honor of parents, two natural ways of guarding against such existential and social corruptions or inclinations as greed or ingratitude. But "health" might also be conceived as cleansing the impure by way of the ashes of the red heifer (*parah adumah*). Here, surely, is an incomprehensible statute that protects from disease in a way that only the "physician" understands. And here, Rashi's comment is illuminating: "'. . . because I am the Lord your physician': . . . And its literal meaning is, for I am the Lord who heals you and teaches you the Law and commandments so that you may be saved from [these diseases. It is] like a physician who says to a person, Do not eat this thing lest it bring you into danger from this disease. So too it is stated: (Prov. 3:8), 'Obedience will be wholesome to your body.'"

The thirteenth-century Nachmanides (Ramban) cites Rashi's explanation in his commentary on this verse in order to take issue with it, but his citation from the Rashi text indicates that the Rashi commentary he used varied slightly from our own. ". . . and its literal meaning is, like a physician who says to a person not to eat things *that bring him back to his illness.*"

These two readings of Rashi, the one we find in our present-day editions of the Torah and the one Nachmanides used, suggest two possibilities. One possibility is that God, the "physician," keeps people from illness through His commandments, that is, He keeps them healthy. In accordance with their true (good) nature, God gave them laws that "will be wholesome to [the] body." Ignoring these laws will make them susceptible to (natural) illness. On this premise, Israel's relationship to God is based on the conviction that He is a sound and reliable protector of spiritual health. The Torah is accepted by people because it understands them; hence, Israel's obedience is (also) an act of good sense. They trust "the physician" to keep them healthy. If the ordinances are so reasonable and wise in the eyes of their recipients, then trust may even seem to be no more than simple prudence. Nevertheless, there is an element of faith, even here. Being convinced by the eminent reasonableness of the ordinances, the "patients," that is, those who have accepted the Torah, trust "the physician" even with regard to *hukim*, the inexplicable statutes, even though they can't even "read the prescription." The commandments of the Torah, the mitzvot, are accepted as a design for "right living," even though a few of those commandments, such as the law of the *parah adumah*, demand blind obedience. Even the "naturally good" are aware that there is debilitating sickness in the world and that "the doctor knows best" how to prevent it.

Nachmanides' reading opens up a second possibility, namely, that God offered, in His covenantal gesture, to bestow health on Israel, to save Israel from the fate of tragic existence. Here, trust precedes good sense. This trust arises in an encounter of God and Israel wherein the people become aware of their present state as unhealthy, albeit natural. They wish to be redeemed and believe that the commandments will let them put their state of illness behind them. Having undertaken to trust the physician, they are given the commandments, which constitute a prescription for change, for living differently, in order to become healthy. In this approach, the *hukim*, the laws that cannot be understood, are the key to a new understanding. Only the physician knows what is good for us. But through that change, the powers of decency, sense, and benevolence within us are drawn out, so that we can "see," at some stage, how wise the ordinances are. Through this new "sight," occasioned by the pristine trust of those who accepted the Torah, its "way" is vindicated.

A Set Table: Halakhah as
Nourishment or as Table Manners

Once we become aware that the halakhah can be seen as either answering to the needs of people by maintaining them in their innate goodness, or as redeeming them from the "evil impulse" and giving them the tools to conquer it, we find ambiguity in places where formerly we may have assumed doctrinal certainties. Let us look, for example, at Rashi's commentary on the first verse of *Parashat Mishpatim* (Exod. 21:1): "And these are the ordinances that you shall set before them." On the latter part of the verse, Rashi paraphrases a midrash from the *Mekhilta*:

> ". . . that you shall set before them": the Holy One, blessed be He, said to Moses: "You shall not think, I shall teach them the chapter and the *halakhah* two or three times until they can repeat it properly, but I shall not bother to get them to understand the reasons for the matter and its interpretation." Therefore it is said, "that you shall set before them," as a set table *(shulhan arukh)* ready for people to [sit down at and] eat from. *(Mekhilta,* Tractate *Nezikin* 1)

The expression "a set table" *(shulhan arukh)* suggests that everything has been readied; the teacher must simply get everyone to sit down and eat. For this to happen, "for their own good," they must be drilled to "repeat . . . properly" the various *halakhot* that will govern their behavior in all matters, upon all requisite occasions.

Presumably they would not know them, were the people not drilled; for these laws do not conform to natural human tendencies or whims. Moreover, because of the obstinacy of human nature, it is a tedious task to train the people; the laws must be repeated a number of times. Moses, our teacher, can be seen as initiating his people into a regimen that will change them, for the better, of course.

But Rashi's comment does not confine itself to drill. For God warns Moses not to think that he simply has to "socialize" the people into the commandments. He also has to teach them "to understand the reasons for the matter and its interpretation." Certainly, then, he has to address their intelligence. And here the question arises: Is the sought-for understanding already "educated" by the (previously drilled and performed) commandments or does it precede it? Is it something people have learned while gaining a new perspective informed by the Torah, or is it innate in them?

The analogy to a set table "ready . . . to eat from" can be understood either way. On the one hand, it may suggest that these laws serve a natural need of people, much as food does. To know, understand, and observe these laws is in tune with the "nature" of people and will satiate their normal appetites. They are invited to sit down at a "set table." Since they trust the Torah, they know that what they will find there is wholesome, that it will safeguard their natures from corruption, it will "keep them healthy." On the other hand, it is possible that Moses is to set the table and drill the people so that they will get used to other, healthier foods than those they are used to. Perhaps they will learn new ways of eating, even new table manners, because they are naturally ignorant and wild! And once they have learned to "behave" and have been removed from their former illness, they will understand differently.

Let us look at the features of Rashi's prescription with an eye on educational practice. What is required is that the teacher both repeat the laws until they are correctly memorized and that he or she gets people to understand them. Of course, to get people "to repeat [the laws] properly" is, in principle, not so difficult. Any child can learn to do it. Furthermore, like anything learned by drill, it re-

quires no individuation but merely overt and socially correct behavior. In their externals, everybody can learn to see him/herself
commanded to carry out these laws and to do so in more or less the
same way, and frequently, together. Plumbers, teachers, philosophers, and athletes are not distinguishable in the way they are to
shake a *lulav* (palm branch) or to make a blessing over food, or to
treat the poor or the downtrodden.

But that does not apply to understanding. In teaching people to
"understand the reasons for the matter," Moses, the teacher, must
differentiate between people of different temperaments and endowments. Individuals do understand things differently. Surely
Rashi is not suggesting that there is one "right" understanding that
is to be taught in a properly repeatable way to everyone. For that
would mean that certain people, who do not fit into such a strait-
jacket, will fail to understand God's commandments. The metaphor
of the "set table" does not seem appropriate here, unless we say that
God instructed Moses to entice everyone to this particular table,
through understandings and interpretations that correspond to
what he or she is.

Or perhaps, that is precisely what is being demanded? Is every
person to be changed by the practices of the Torah into one who
can share understandings with all other pious practitioners? Won't
those understandings be incomprehensible to those not shaped by
the "healing" laws of the Torah?

That brings us back to our former question: Must the particular
natures of individuals, with their particular sensibilities and insights, be preserved and enhanced through the commandments, or
changed? Should normativeness take on an existential dimension,
of personal decisionmaking, when it comes to individual appropria-
tion of the mitzvot? Or is there a normative or even uniform ideal
of a person who, having been redeemed from tragic existence, has
learned "how to think about it properly?"

The ambiguity we have come upon seems reflected also in the
following comments of R. Ishmael and Issa b. Akiva on the verse
"You shall be holy people unto Me" (22:30): "R. Ishmael says: 'If
you are holy, then you are Mine.' Issa b. Akiva says, 'With every

new commandment that God issues to Israel He adds holiness to them'" (*Mekhilta*, Tractate *Kaspa* 2).

R. Ishmael is perhaps suggesting that the urge to holiness is natural ("if you are holy") and must simply be cultivated. If so, perhaps the commandments clearly refer back to the creation of humans "in God's image" and translate this abstract idea into social and existential practice. Conversely, perhaps the commandments re-create human beings so that they can truly grow into holiness, as we may understand Issa b. Akiva to suggest when he says that God's laws *add* holiness to us!

Educationally, we seem to have distinct prescriptions here, based on conflicting diagnoses. On the one hand, we may be hearing that humans are naturally wild, cruel, bestial. They take delight in tearing limbs from animals or tearing them as sport. God, then, through the Torah, redeems people from the illness of their natures. On the other hand, one may understand what we have learned here as assuming that such inclinations are deviant, an "illness." The Torah, then, strengthens what is best in us and keeps us from slipping into perversion and disease. In this view, people have natural sympathy for sentient creatures and empathy with their suffering.

We Shall Do and We Shall Hear:
Habit Precedes Reason

Those who take the view that humans are naturally wild tend to be conservative in their educational approach. They fear that they will spoil the child if they (literally or figuratively) spare the rod. They are always fighting an uphill battle, dragging the young toward an ultimate, but only partially attainable, ideal, which seeks to remake them according to a preconceived and sometimes rigid mold. They set a halakhic table with foods that are highly medicinal, but seldom tasty. Conversely, adherents of the opposite view are generally progressive, championing more open forms of education. They trust children and distrust prescriptions for their betterment that are external to them and imposed upon them. They look to "set a table" of Torah for children geared to where children are and in line with what they like. But there is always the risk that in order to entice the children to the table, those people will supply mainly junk food.

Are the two views of human nature inimical to each other, or can they be reconciled? An additional halakhic narrative may clarify the matter: After the promulgation of its various laws following the public revelation on Mount Sinai, the Torah describes the ratification of the covenant.

> And Moses came and told the people all the words of the Lord, and all the ordinances, and the whole people answered with one voice, and said, "All the words that the Lord has spoken we will do." And Moses wrote all the words of the Lord and [after the offering of sacrifices] . . . he took the book of the covenant and read it to the people and they said, "All that the Lord has spoken, we shall do, and we shall hear." (Exod. 24:3–7)

How did they dare undertake a commitment ("do") that they did not yet understand ("hear")? Wasn't that a self-destructive act of blind subservience, inimical to their natural selves, which were free of *halakhot*? (see Rashi on Numbers 11:5). Had they, as the "conservatives" might suggest, already been educated and "changed" at Marah, where, owing to thirst, a prominent feature of the abject human predicament, they had had no choice but to accept God's commandments?[5] Or did they sense, just the way they were, that order is better than chaos, and that it is as vital to the human being as nourishment? Did they sense that law is not necessarily the enemy of freedom but can be its complement and even its guarantor? Or perhaps they had the intimation that the Torah is a "set table" that *both* feeds the hungry *and* removes people from natural but bestial appetites. In that case, we may learn from their response of "we shall do, and we shall hear," that the conservative-progressive dichotomy is not a choice of alternatives, but an inherent tension within life and law and education that must be negotiated.

Recall that we have mentioned a third approach, neither sanguine nor tragic. This approach recognizes that there is evil within us but argues that goodwill, good habits, and intelligence enable us, with the guidance of God's Torah, to control and restrain this evil. According to this model, children are indeed socialized into the law. They first learn to do, and that, thanks to childish desire to be part of the group and conformism, they tend to learn quite naturally. However, with increasing maturity they rightfully, and naturally, demand to understand.

Here the tension arises between seeing the law as an expression and embodiment of authoritative value, imposed upon us, essentially statute *(hok)*, and seeing our inherent values helping us understand and interpret the law, to set priorities, and to resolve dilemmas that arise in "the life of the law." Because we have been educated to doing before understanding, we expect that the law will shape our deliberation. We pray that it will have made us more than we were before there was a Torah, before we were educated and changed by it. We believe that Torah continues to supply us with values and to nourish the way we think valuatively. It "makes us healthy." But the way we are, simply as human beings, must be considered in the way we understand and interpret. That is because the Torah was given to human beings who have to understand it, and in order to understand they have to make use of their intelligence. After all, would they have accepted the Torah before they understood it if they had been too sick to recognize its wisdom? There must have been some good sense that drew them to the "set table," and in committing themselves blindly to eating these new foods, they must have recognized that they needed medical help.

An aphorism of Abraham Joshua Heschel seems helpful in pinpointing this dialectic. The Torah, says Heschel, is "from Heaven." And what is written in this Torah? "That it is not in Heaven" (Deut. 30:12).[6]

In Praise of Order—and an Irreverent Shrug

My maternal grandmother, a woman both enlightened and pious, once recommended that I carefully consider the expression in the *Mussaf* service of the Sabbath in which we promise God that, after the restoration of the Temple in Jerusalem, we shall make the sacrifices obligatory upon us. We speak there of *temidim k'sidram u'mussafim k'hilkhatam* (the perpetual [daily] offerings according to their order and additional [special] sacrifices according to the prescriptions), the halakhot, that govern the manner of their offering. Grandmother believed that the phrase *k'sidram . . . k'hilkhatam* was close to the heart of Judaism: a relationship with God governed by "their [i.e., the sacrifices'] routine order and their halakhot." That struck a deep chord in her: of what was in tune with real human needs, what kept important things in focus, what was nourishment for the soul, a "set table." "But," she added with an irreverent shrug, "that doesn't mean I feel comfortable with sacrifices *(korbanot).*"

Now for my question: Did she mean that when the Messiah came, she would "do" even before "understanding," because she trusted the order established by the Torah as inherently sensible and wise, even natural? Or that with the doing (i.e., sacrifices offered in the Temple) so far denied us, the commandment itself, in the practice, would change her so that she would realize that her former understanding was flawed, reflecting a sickness attendant on the human condition when bereft of Torah? Or perhaps she meant to say that she insisted on her right to her own search for understanding and interpretation, because an understanding that did not reflect that search seemed like a mere catechism to her, a set table without an explanatory menu that the divine Chef had prepared with her in mind. Did she wish to say that a set table, completely oblivious to her tastes, could not reflect who she was and (therefore) could not "change" her?

Now I'm sorry I never asked her.

9

LEARNING AND
LEADERSHIP:
HILLEL AND
MENAHEM

How HOMES AND SCHOOLS can initiate children into the framework of spiritual belonging has been the subject of the preceding chapters. I have illustrated how that might be done by making children conversant with *literatures* that grow out of the *language* of Judaism. Now, in the final chapter of Part 2, we may consider what educational thinkers call end aims for Jewish education. Taking off from a somewhat odd passage in Deuteronomy, we may raise the following question: On the basis of discrete dispositions transmitted, memories shared, moral sensibilities cultivated, and abilities fostered, what can we say about the person we would recognize as a success story in Jewish education? What might the person who has internalized given "end aims" look and be like? What is the face of his or her society?

There are no simple answers to these questions, for goals and community visions have their own contexts, which qualify them. (The discussion of these contexts, for the most part, still lies ahead of us.) Moreover, the assumption that educational "products" are achieved by parents and mentors is usually simplistic, for it presupposes that these people are not only devoted and capable but that their efforts are not informed—or marred—by problems of their own. But in fact, not all people have the unusually good fortune of living in a good time and in a good place. Not all actually empathize with the children they educate or even genuinely like them; and not all educators are blessed with both vision and competence.

The formulators of end goals in education also tend to forget, as we have seen Hirsch point out with regard to the education of Esau, that children are diversely endowed. It seems, therefore, more than questionable that even end aims be identical for all. At least in nontotalitarian societies, commonalities must be circumscribed and diversities given respected space.

Finally, it is worth keeping in mind that educational and social ideals are not only societal and psychological but also historical, ideological, and spiritual. End aims themselves are the subject of controversy, even within specific traditions. Hence this chapter is not simply about an ideal, but about an argument, a sometimes acrimonious one. It is, as we so often find in the tradition of Torah, an argument about what is *really* meant by a teaching of the Bible that seems, at first blush, straightforward and simple. Such arguments are part of the "language" itself, though they may generate suspicion and fear in those critical moments of history when unity seems especially essential.

Hence, the discussion of end aims too has a context, even though it seems to be concerned merely with two biblical verses and their simple and "eternal" meaning. The context is that of a perennial argument about the highest ideals and demands of Jewish education. Here, the context is also a conversation overheard on one of the early and dark days of the Yom Kippur War of 1973, a conversation that beautifully reflects that perennial argument.

To bring that situation back to mind: The proud defense forces of Israel were in retreat; the combat planes of its air force diminished daily. Hundreds of young Israelis were falling in action. The country was in shock and mounting grief.

Not yet having been called up for army service, I found myself on the eve of the festival of Sukkot in the ultra-Orthodox Jerusalem quarter of Meah Shearim, to buy a set of the Four Species for our family. The mood was not congenial to this "season of our rejoicing" but the commandment to thankfully bless God with an *etrog*, "citron," and *lulav* (palm branch) with myrtle branches and willows in hand, is sometimes experienced as strangely impervious to mood.

While standing at a Meah Shearim bus stop on the way home, I overheard two black-suited young men, who clearly had not seen each other for a while, engaged in warm greeting. "How are things?" the one asked. *"Baruch HaShem* (thank God), very well," said the other. "What are you learning this year?" the first asked. "[The tractate] *Kedushin* [dealing mainly with the laws of marriage], and I'm learning with Rabbi _____ at the _____ Yeshiva," the other replied. "That's great," said the first one, "no wonder you're happy. My learning is also going well, thank God. Nu, have a great year and have a *gut yontef* (a happy holiday)."

I remember not knowing whether to laugh or weep at these young men who lived in a Jewish world where there was no Jewish war going on, no fear, and no pain, and who were serenely happy because of that. Was their attitude sublime or obtuse? Was it the secret of Jewish survival or a key to Jewish misfortune? Did these young men represent a legitimate aristocracy in Jewish life, a coterie of leaders who are paradoxically spared many problems that beset the "other" people? Does a particular kind of knowledge confer a status that protects and empowers?

This chapter is about these questions. It addresses the issue of what might constitute "success" in Jewish education, but not in Jewish education alone. It asks the question whether social or other distinctions must indeed be built into educational thinking. It asks what character education is and how it is related to both creativity and accommodation. In the idiom of this book, character education is certainly about the Tree of Knowledge, which restrains human beings, points to their identity, and "places" them in the social scheme of things. But it is also about the Tree of Life, which empowers them and enhances their lives.

Who is to be given access to this magic tree of self-realization? For whom is inner discipline and nobility and good character, which we may associate with the Tree of Knowledge, enough? Or is the distinction itself, which puts some "in their place" and others at the pinnacle of human existence, itself outrageous and perverse?

What Does God Ask of You But . . . ?
A Conception of "The Good Life"

The textual focus of my reflection is a passage of the Torah that explicitly declares "what God asks of you." This passage raises crucial educational issues, for God's "request" is, in fact, a statement about what constitutes the good life and what should be done to achieve it. It is about issues that parents and teachers must always address, for example, What knowledge is worth most? Who is an, or *the*, ideal human being?

The text, opening the fifth "reading" of the *Ekev* portion in the yearly cycle of Torah reading, is succinct but, upon careful study, difficult and even odd: "And now, O Israel, what does the Lord your God ask of you but that you fear the Lord your God, to walk in all of His ways, to love Him and to serve the Lord your God with all your heart and all your soul. And to keep the commandments of the Lord and His statutes which I command you this day for your good" (Deut. 10:12–13).

What is obvious and clear about this two-verse statement is that it deals with a conception of the "good life," which, unlike many contemporary statements on the subject, is defined in the light of an unambiguously religious assumption, of a desirable and normative divine-human relationship. The good life is a commanded one, built upon the specific, perhaps contradictory, foundations of "fear" and "love" of God. Yet it is, despite the emphasis on service, not a contract of servitude: It is not a master's conception of the good life for the slave. Rather, it justifies its ideal as being "for your good"; not divine self-aggrandizement, but human self-understanding and self-realization are intended.

The difficulties become immediately apparent. Can everyone achieve this ideal, and are those who cannot achieve it fundamentally unworthy, though they can hardly be blamed for not reaching the required heights? Moreover, is perhaps the goal itself unrealizable and thus no more than a recipe for frustration and guilty conscience?

The passage, as I said, is odd, though it seems simple and straightforward. God appears to be asking for a great deal, one might even say, for everything possible. That makes some obvious sense, for it seems plausible that the good life is not to be conceived as an extracurricular activity that enhances leisure moments or merely provides peak experiences. But then, why introduce it by "but," a qualifying preposition, "What does the Lord your God ask of you *but* . . . " as though it were a mere trifle to fear Him and love Him (whatever that means), to serve Him wholeheartedly (whatever we are to understand by that), and to keep all His commandments. Is this tongue in cheek? A mere rhetorical bit of divine musing?

The sages of the Midrash suggest various approaches to the problem of the seemingly ironic "but . . . ." I shall mention two of the many approaches within the annals of classic commentary. Then I shall discuss a third view that brings into view a central, yet problematic, thread in the fabric of Jewish conceptions of the ideal life and of appropriate Jewish education.

Is the Ideal Unachievable?

One approach is to see the divine request, introduced by the intriguing "but," as expressing an *almost* unrealizable ideal. In the idiom of the Talmud, "As far as Moses was concerned it was a small matter" (*Berakhot* 33b). For the sage who suggests this solution, the entire life of Moses represents the ideal; it was wholly focused on the fear, love, and will of God. So to Moses it seemed that God was not asking for much. But in communicating the divine message to his people, the leader, as it were, "forgot" that no one else was on his spiritual level. That which was "a small matter" for him was overwhelming to others. Yet Rabbi Hanina, the Talmudic sage who offers this explanation, certainly believes that the ideal remains as a guidepost and a challenge. The challenge may be formulated as, How close can you get to Moses, for whom all this was a "small matter"?

Nevertheless, one may ask our sage whether, or why, everyone, including those with endowments and inclinations very different from those of Moses, should be like him. The story of the hasidic Rabbi Zusya of Hanipol, made accessible to contemporary readers by Martin Buber in his *Tales of the Hasidim*,[1] suggests a very different orientation. Of Rabbi Zusya it is related that his disciples found him on his deathbed in a state of great trepidation. When they asked him what was agitating him so much, he replied: "In the world-to-come to which I am now being called, I will perhaps be asked why I wasn't like Abraham or Moses. I am not afraid of such questions and have an answer at hand, namely, 'I am neither Abraham nor Moses.' The question I dread is: 'Why weren't you Zusya, why weren't you all you could have been?' And to that, I have no answer."

All Education Is Character Education

A second line of interpretation suggests that the word "but" limits God's demand of the commanded human being to the moral and religious life, to the fear and love of God, and to the fulfillment of the commandments. "But" for those moral and religious choices, everything (else) is outside the realm of human control and therefore not worthy of excessive concern or effort, and for that matter, it is of minor educational importance. That is the point of a midrashic passage describing the creation of the human being:

> Before the creation of the embryo in its mother's womb, the Holy One, blessed be He, decrees what is in store for it: whether male or female, whether weak or strong, whether poor or rich, whether short or tall, whether ugly or handsome . . . and also, all that will happen to it, but whether it will become a righteous or a wicked individual is not determined—but rather, that matter He puts in the hands of the human being alone.[2]

And as a parallel midrashic text puts it, "Everything is in the hands of Heaven except for the Fear of Heaven."[3]

For these midrashic teachers, God really is not demanding too much. After all, God does not ask of anyone to improve his or her appearance, to make a fortune, or to make undue efforts toward achieving an emotionally pleasant, materially comfortable, or even particularly "creative" life. These things, it is posited in this blatantly pietistic view, are really not in our hands. God actually requires nothing of Israel "but" that they fear, love, and serve Him "for your good." The assumption seems to be that every soul has to make this choice and every soul is capable of making it.

The Merchant and the Scholar:
An Organic Approach

The assumption that every soul can make that choice is severely qualified by a third approach, which relates not so much to the individual and the demands made upon him or her, but to the social organism as a whole. This orientation views the individual as part of the group to which all belong. The social organism offers him or her protection and belongingness but also assigns to each person, as a member of some social subgrouping, a specific role in the life of the collective. This approach is well articulated in the rationale given by the (male) director of the ultra-Orthodox Beth Yaakov girls' schools in pre–World War II Poland for the absence of Talmud in the curriculum, which was based on the ultra-Orthodox halakhic ruling that the study of Talmud is indeed out of bounds for women. "There is a division of labor within the Jewish people and if one accepts the notion of the essential unity of Israel . . . then one accepts this division as natural and positive. It isn't important who puts on phylacteries *(tefillin)*, sits in the Sukkah, or studies Gemara (Talmud), as long as these commandments are, in the end performed by someone."[4]

What is perhaps the classic expression of this approach is found in the Midrash *(Tanhuma)* and summarized by Rashi. We find it in the context of Jacob's blessings to his sons before his death. Jacob's blessing to his son Zevulun is that "Zevulun shall dwell at the shore of the sea, and he shall be a shore for ships" (Gen. 49:13). On this Rashi comments:

> He will constantly be at the haven for ships—the port—where the ships bring merchandise. For Zevulun was engaged in business and provided food for the tribe of Issachar while these engaged in the study of the Torah. It is to this that Moses alludes (in his blessing, Deuteronomy 33:18), "Rejoice Zevulun in your going out and Issachar in your tents" [which Rashi explains in his commentary on Genesis 25:27 as "tents of Torah."].

The tribe of Issachar, in the words of Jacob's blessing, "inclined his shoulder to receive the burden and became a servant unto tribute" (Gen. 49:14). This rather undistinguished blessing is transfigured by the organic orientation: Rashi teaches that Issachar's inclining of the "shoulder to receive the burden" relates to "the burden of teaching the Torah," and his servitude means that he served Israel by teaching Torah and "deciding points of law for them."

Those who adopt this organic approach will declare that the passage in Deuteronomy 10 and its complex commandment, about what God asks of us, is addressed to the entire community, with various segments charged with diverse aspects of the commandment, and with specific groups carrying it out in diverse ways, all of which are vital for society. For each group, then, the "but" suggests the limits of its members' specific obligations and the parameters of their education. If they are to reside and work in the tents of Torah, then that is what they must be prepared for and what they must do; if they are to engage in commerce, they must learn how to do that well while resting assured that the "burden" of Torah is being shouldered by others.

The organic approach is deeply embedded in Jewish tradition. In its open and pluralistic form, it looks upon the other, whether Zevulun or Issachar, as equally blessed. But this approach, especially in politically and socially precarious situations, quickly becomes hierarchical. It readily learns to view the few as leading inherently worthy lives and the many as lesser beings, "respectable" only to the extent they serve the common good. As students and scholars of Jewish social history have shown, rabbinic literature itself at times sharply criticizes the tendency of scholars to see in the life of the academy the entire purpose and the sole goal of significant life and to cultivate an aristocratic aloofness and disdain with regard to the "others." Rabbinic literature criticizes this tendency, for every Jewish person is obliged to engage in the study of Torah whether or not that person will be a scholar.[5] But truth to tell, rabbinic literature also reflects that tendency. We shall return to this tension.

An Organic Hierarchy: The Scholar and the Housewife

An explicit formulation of this hierarchical position as an explanation of the passage from Deuteronomy is found in the Torah commentary of Rabbi Naftali Zvi Berlin, known in the world of Jewish learning by the acronym Netziv. Rabbi Berlin, a nineteenth-century scholar, was head of the famed Volozhin Yeshiva of White Russia. Though not indifferent to the modern world and himself drawn to the proto-Zionist Hovevai Zion (Lovers of Zion) movement, he was also unswervingly loyal to the Talmudic and halakhic tradition and was an outstanding and erudite spokesman for this (then as now) embattled point of view. This traditionalism founded its fortresses in the consciously elitist yeshiva world of Eastern Europe. For Netziv, as for other leaders of the yeshiva world, the *talmid hakham*, "scholar of the Torah," was the ideal type of Jew, the authentic embodiment of saintliness. Rabbi Berlin's vision made room for nobility among community and national leaders as well. Yet it was the *talmid hakham* who defined their role and obligations.

Rabbi Berlin explains his view in some detail in his commentary on the Torah, entitled *Ha'amek Davar*, with specific reference to our passage. First, he presents the problem. It is implausible, he says, that the love of God, which is achievable only through the Temple service and the study of Torah, should be demanded of every Israelite; after all, God does not ask of people what they cannot achieve. Not everyone can be a *talmid hakham*! Therefore, he suggests, we should understand this complex commandment as a set of discrete demands made on different sectors of the people. As in the description of the initiation of Israel into the covenant (Deut. 29:9–11), our text assumes everyone to be "standing before the Lord: heads (political leaders) and magistrates, elders, all the men of Israel, and women, servants and your little ones." Each is part of the covenant, but each is diversely commanded. "What the Holy One asks of one, He does not ask of the other."

Rabbi Berlin elaborates. "The heads of tribes are the leaders of any particular generation who must provide for the needs of the public." Were these leaders to turn their minds and hearts to inward religious zeal, to the love of God, their attention to their civic tasks would become deficient. (Keep in mind that, in the view of Netziv, such love and attachment can be achieved only through study of the Torah or a halakhic understanding of the sacrificial cult in the Temple.) Community leaders are to learn proper behavior from Abraham, who, when about to converse with God, found himself visited by three men and immediately turned his attention to them (Gen. 18:1–3). Abraham understood that receiving guests took priority even over "receiving the divine Presence." Rabbi Berlin clinches his argument by noting that the halakhah frees one who is engaged in public service from reciting the *Shema* at its appointed times, morning and evening. That particular halakhah teaches us that the mitzvah of serving the public has the power to exempt the public servant from preoccupation with the love of God, for which the recitation of the *Shema* is a symbolic expression.

What, then, does our text specifically instruct civic leaders? From them, Rabbi Berlin declares, we learn that the Torah demands fear of God, which alone will save them from self-importance, self-aggrandizement, and, ultimately, corruption. The public leader must always be aware of who is above him. Through fear of God, the leader comes to recognize his responsibilities and his limitations.

It is otherwise with the elders of each generation, the scholars of the Torah. They are commanded to love God and to cultivate attachment to Him by study of Torah, teaching it to disciples, carrying out His commandments with great exactitude and zeal, and by emulating God's moral attributes such as compassion and justice. Torah scholars are to be different from other people, even in the ways they eat, walk, and speak. They embody the religious ideal.

Moreover, like the priests and Levites of the Temple itself (who were also "elders"), scholars enjoy a special status in the order of things. Just as the Temple was outside and above the natural order, assuring Israel of miraculous divine Providence, so too is it with scholars in their Houses of Study, in their yeshivot: it is all miraculous, outside "the stable foundations that every nation enjoys on its own soil." The life of Torah upheld by the "elders," by *talmide hakhamim*, is not based on economic or political factors or calculations and may not be influenced by them. This form of life embodies the very miracle of Jewish existence, even, or perhaps especially, in the dispersed condition of Israel, bereft of the Temple. The "but" of the scholar is in his liberation from worldly concerns. "All" that God asks of him is study of Torah.

These concerns, for livelihood and material well-being, fall mainly on the shoulders of the masses of Jews who work for their bread. God's demand of them is that they take heed lest the burdens of professional or commercial life make them forget their share in the covenant, which is "to observe His commandments and statutes." From them the Torah does not demand love or even excessive fear, but "only" lives of steady piety, through observance.

Netziv considers women, children, and servants to play an instrumental role in the covenant. For what does the Holy One ask of them but to be beneficial to the community and to its social requirements and norms? "And as our sages say, who is a worthy woman? She who does the will of her husband." Rabbi Berlin reminds us of the Talmudic teaching (*Berakhot* 17a): "A woman achieves merit by bringing her children to school, sending her husband to the House of Study, to the *bet midrash*, and waiting for him with supper," or even granting him permission to spend time studying Torah away from home. As for servants, they are to do what is beneficial for their masters, and children are to obey their parents.

Rabbi Berlin believes that these several requests were spoken together because the entire covenantal agreement was made in the presence of all its members; all are included, though each is differently obliged. This seems to solve the problem of the troublesome "What does God ask of you *but* . . . ." Something is demanded of each group included in the covenant, but each group is responsible only for what is reasonable, for what is within its power. In the sense that all are included in the covenant, all are equal, and all exercise the power that their roles dictate. Note that women, whom Rabbi Berlin treats with what a contemporary reader must consider overt disdain, yet have the power to give, or to deny, their husbands permission to maximize their Torah study, even though for a potential or actual "elder," that is defined as the very purpose of his life before God.

But like the social classes in Plato's *Republic*, some are clearly more equal than others. The *talmid hakham* is indeed a philosopher-king, and the men of practical wisdom, the community leaders, also enjoy great, albeit lesser, esteem. After all, organizing the life of society in the natural world is less sublime than living in a supernatural sphere, and fear is secondary to love. As for all the others, they are providers and managers. From the respectable and diligently pious householder *(ba'al habayit)* to the worthy woman of valor, they keep the wheels turning, as breadwinners or housekeepers.

The organic approach articulated here by Rabbi Berlin makes it possible for everyone to belong but for only the few to excel significantly. It explains sending some children to vocational schools early in their schooling and others to a yeshiva, "for their good." It sets forth a clear hierarchy of what is ideal, and at the pinnacle, it places a single ideal, significantly superior to the practical one of civic leadership and far removed from the instrumental ambiance that envelops the others. The yeshiva world alone is wrapped in providential grace. We should not be surprised if, to others, it sometimes seems to be aloof and vaguely contemptuous.

That, then, is one way of interpreting our text. It reflects one strand in the tradition. Especially when political conditions are stormy, spiritual leaders often decide that the best policy is to lie low—to withdraw from the fray and to strengthen internal foundations. Unsettled and floundering social mores or revolutionary social circumstances make the orderly and disciplined ways, where everything has its place and everyone knows where she or he belongs, seem most protective and most conducive to social morality, most restorative of the world as it ought to be.

Yet these paradigms of social cohesion, especially when too readily identified with "the love of God" and with sublime religious truths, tend to become sanctified, indivisible from the constituent elements of faith itself. Then they appear to be what "we have always believed and done" and what we must continue to believe and do even when situations and sensibilities have changed. Educationally and theologically, therefore, there is value in demonstrating that an organic approach is not the only one possible for understanding the Jewish social and educational tradition and that organic approaches may themselves be moved in the direction of empathy for those who are different, toward respect for diversity.

The Status of Scholars: Two Approaches

The following teaching has come down to us as a creed of the masters of Yavne, the leaders of Israel in the generation after the great destruction of 70 C.E.:

> I am a creature [of God] and my fellow is a creature [of God]. My work is in the city and his is in the field. I rise early to go to my work and he rises early to go to his work. As he does not deign to do my work, I do not deign to do his. But should you think: I do much [Rashi: in the study of Torah] and he does little, we have learned: "Do more, do less, it matters not, so long as one's heart is turned toward Heaven." (*Berakhot* 17a)

Applying this teaching to our text, we may understand it as a divine demand that each person, regardless of vocation, bring a faith orientation, a "love of God," to his or her work. Although for the sages who expressed this sentiment, the study of Torah was a supreme good, they agreed that society needed the work of the "field" no less than that of the "city," that workers in both could justly feel comfortable and worthy, and that all could live in the consciousness of a common humanity: "I am a creature and my fellow is a creature"! If, then, the turning of the heart toward Heaven is feasible for all and inherently required of all, it is the litmus test of individuals and of society as a whole. The "but" introducing God's demand might then be said to refer to the parameters of each person's life and deeds, the way he or she performs specific vocations in the social world and the existential "place" in which each finds him/herself. One may be a great pianist, a devoted farmer, a merchant, a scholar, or a family provider or maintainer, but the point is to do what one does "faithfully," imbued with a commanded religious vision of human existence. Here, fear and love are specific activities only insofar as they inform the practice of the divine commandments; beyond that, they are a direction, illuminated by (much or little) study of Torah.

The sages of Yavne certainly believed that their "work" was eminently dignified and that it served as a model for all others in the study of Torah. Indeed, the "doing more or less" of which they spoke was Torah study. There can be no doubt that they considered the scholar, the *talmid hakham* to be a heroic and excellent type. But their credo does not suggest that they had a rigid hierarchical conception. Had they had one, they would not only have been proud of their calling but would have looked down on others and their various vocations even while admitting to their necessity for society. The sages' concern was not mainly with the good of society but with the good soul. "It matters not" what one does, they said, but how one does it.

Scholars of rabbinic history and literature have recorded two kinds of relationship between the scholars and the community that must be examined by educators who seek philosophical guidelines for their work and their standards of achievement. On the one hand, there is the ideal of the *talmid hakham*, one who is sensitive to the needs of his community and identified with it, seeing all Israelites as "royalty" (*Baba Metzia* 113b), and making halakhic rulings that are sensitive to their needs. On the other hand, there was what can also now be found: exclusivity, disregard, and disdain for what is not germane to the world of scholarship, and hence, suspicion of, and even apathy about, the providers and managers of Jewish life.

Hillel on the Roof:
Is There a Place for the Poor?

A pivotal Talmudic story that both illustrates and implicitly criticizes the ideal of aloof aristocracy and its attendant lack of sensitivity is about the young man Hillel, an anonymous and poor immigrant to the Land of Israel, having come from Babylonia, who thirsts for learning but cannot afford it. This young man of the final pre-Christian century is, of course, Hillel "the Elder," who is later to become a model of learning and leadership.

The Talmud tells the story in the context of the importance of study for everyone. It says that if on the day of judgment a person claims that he was too poor to engage in Torah, they of the heavenly court will say to him, "Were you poorer than Hillel?" As for the story itself:

> They related about Hillel the Elder that every day he would work and earn a *tropaik* [a meager amount of money]. Half of it he gave to the doorkeeper of the *Bet Hamidrash* [the House of Study] and half was for his and his family's livelihood. Once he found no work, and the doorkeeper did not let him enter. He climbed up [to the roof] and hung over the skylight and sat on it in order to hear the words of the living God from the mouths of Shemayah and Avtalyon [the outstanding scholars of the generation].
>
> They [who told the story] said: "That day was the eve of the Sabbath [Friday], and it was the season of Tevet [winter], and snow fell upon him from the heavens. And when dawn came up, [on the Sabbath morning] Shemaya said to Avtalyon: 'Avtalyon my brother, every day the house is lit up and today it is dark. Perhaps it is a cloudy day?' They looked up and saw the form of a person on the skylight. They went up and found three cubits of snow covering him. They brushed

him off, washed him, rubbed oil on him, and sat him down in front of
the stove. They said, 'This one deserves having the Sabbath desecrated for him.'" (*Yoma* 35b)

On the foundations laid by the prominent scholar of rabbinic
literature, Yonah Frankel, we may read this story carefully. Hillel
cannot enter the House of Study without padding the pockets of
the doorkeeper. Probably, says Frankel, that was an unprecedented and singular practice of which the masters were not
aware.[6] We learn that Hillel works part of the day to earn a paltry
sum. Did he earn such a meager amount because he was unskilled
or because he looked for part-time employment so as to spend
most of his time in the *bet midrash*? In any case, after the doorkeeper was paid, only half remained for his food and the upkeep
of his household. If Hillel could not enter the *bet midrash* on that
day, we can also assume that he could not eat that day or provide
for his family—on the eve of the Sabbath! But Hillel's overriding
concern was to hear "the words of the living God"! He climbed
onto the roof and remained there, notwithstanding a heavy snow-
fall (three cubits, more than three feet, highly unusual in
Jerusalem) throughout Friday night. He did not spend the Sabbath evening with his family, and it must be noted, the scholars
seem not to have done so either!

In the morning, the scholars Shemayah and Avtalyon, sitting
comfortably in the house, notice that it is darker than usual. The
outside world, which generally provides light, now does not. Perhaps it is a cloudy day? Evidently, the sages have been oblivious to
the unusually inclement weather. They are in the House of Study;
there is a warm stove; and they are engaged in Torah study. What
can interest them or even draw their attention in the outside world?
Only the unusual appearance of the morning leads them to look up
and go up to the roof. They find a young man who, to "hear the
words of the living God," endangered his life and failed to provide
for his and his family's livelihood. Despite Sabbath restrictions on
anointing the body, the scholars have no compunctions: "This one
deserves having the Sabbath desecrated for him."

The scholars, until they noticed that the house was dark, apparently did not pay attention to the absence of the intense young man, Hillel. Perhaps they now realize, as Frankel suggests, that the light with which the "house is lit up each day" radiates from the anonymous learner who paid half his earnings to sit there and study the words of the living God. Perhaps they now realize that "the people out there," even if the demands of making a living allows them only a little Torah learning, also have their hearts turned toward Heaven, that they are also "brothers" as Shemayah and Avtalyon are. Do they suddenly understand why, in an emergency, one may desecrate the Sabbath for every Jew, even those coming from outside? Or is it only that they feel that the heretofore unknown young man is worthy of being counted among the brothers, that for such a one as he, one may desecrate the Sabbath, for without him the *bet midrash* will be dark? Both seem plausible interpretations.

Angering the "Gentle" Hillel

In years to come, Hillel is to become president of the highest and most authoritative institution of Torah study and jurisdiction, the Sanhedrin in Jerusalem, previously headed by Shemayah and Avtalyon. Like his predecessors going back four generations, Hillel, as president of the Sanhedrin, had a deputy president who himself enjoyed high rank, known as the head of the court *(av bet din)*. But although the president and his deputy were appointed for life, a mishnah in tractate *Hagigah* relates that, quite unconventionally, Hillel's colleague Menahem left his position as head of the court and was replaced by the renowned Shammai. In discussing a complex halakhic controversy about whether one who brings a sacrifice on a festival "lays his hands" upon it, the mishnah relates that all the previous *zugot*, "pairs" (of president and head of the court) had disagreed about this question. The mishnah continues: "Hillel and Menahem did not differ [about the laying of hands], but Menahem went forth and Shammai entered [his position]" *(Hagigah 2:2)*.

In the Gemara's discussion of the mishnah in question, it is stated in the name of the sage, Abaye, that Menahem went forth *(yatzah)*

from the ways of God and become degenerate in character and deeds.
Furthermore, Rava states and a supporting (Tannaic) *braita* elaborates: "He went forth to the service of the king, and eighty pairs of
disciples went with him, dressed in garments of royalty" (*Hagigah*
16:6).[7] The Palestinian (Jerusalem) Talmud relates that Menahem
"changed his attributes," perhaps, his ideological orientation. The
Palestinian Talmud adds that the remaining sages ferociously de-
nounced Menahem and the others who had left, accusing them of
abandoning the God of Israel as the Hellenists of Maccabean times
had done.

Historian Ben-Zion Luria, in an interesting study entitled "Who
Is Menahem?" examines this episode against the backdrop of the
national and political events of the time.[8] It was the period of
Herod, the evil prince who was attempting, with Roman help, to
usurp the crown of the last of the priestly Hasmonean line,
Antigonus.[9] The latter was apparently not a skillful diplomat or a
tactful man and had once managed, while serving as high priest, to
anger Shemayah and Avtalyon at the close of the Yom Kippur service by referring disparagingly to their Gentile origins. In any case,
both they and Hillel, in the tormenting events of their time, caught
up in the conflict between the unsavory Herod and Antony, his Roman patron, on the one hand, and Antigonus and his Partian sup-
porters, on the other, had apparently decided that all political involvement was mistaken. A plague on all their houses! Only the
"world of Torah" should be cultivated.

Luria presents the thesis that wherever the number eighty appears in records of people and description of events, the reference is
to military activity. His conclusion is that Menahem became convinced that the hour had come for military enlistment in the cause
of Antigonus. Moreover, Menahem convinced many disciples that
the military defense of this last scion of Hasmonean royalty was indeed the call of the hour. The "garments of royalty," then, may perhaps be understood as uniforms! This decision of Menahem and
the disciples greatly diminished the ranks of Torah scholars. No
wonder that those who favored letting Herod be, who demanded
that the spiritual leadership of Israel look inward and cultivate the

teachings of the Torah, fumed and accused Menahem of *tarbut ra'ah*, of "having come to a bad end," irreligion, apostasy, and playing up to one of the arrogant leaders who strutted across the bloody historical stage.

In a renowned mishnah in *Pirke Avot (The Ethics of the Fathers)*, Hillel pours contempt on those who leave the study of Torah, who reject the quietism of the *bet midrash*. In earlier days of that unsettled period, Hillel's own teachers had warned the scholars about that outside world. Shemayah had inveighed against "positions of lordship" and intimacy with the ruling authorities, and Avtalyon had instructed the disciples to "be careful with your words lest you incur the penalty of exile" (*Avot* 1:11–12). In the following mishnah, we find the proverbially gentle Hillel bitterly deprecating those who leave the study of Torah for other things: "One who seeks a name loses one's name, one who does not increase knowledge decreases it, one who does not study deserves to die, and one who makes use of the crown will die" (*Avot* 1:13).

Could Hillel be addressing himself here to Menahem and the disciples who, in Luria's thesis, believed that there was a time for study and also a time for action? Was Hillel suggesting that God requires nothing "but" the religious and moral virtues accessible through study alone? Were his pronouncements that "one who does not study deserves to die, and one who makes use of the crown will die" simply angry hyperbole? Or is that an attitude that expects nothing of the outside world but that it not disturb the scholars? The insufferable Herod had once as a youth been on the verge of contempt of court in the Sanhedrin. But now, as political leader, he was expected to leave the scholars alone and pay occasional lip service to the virtues of Torah study. Did Hillel see that as enough, as all that could be expected from a corrupt government and a base leader?

We cannot tell. We do not really know who Menahem was, what he did in the service of the king, and even whom he served. According to another historical thesis, it was Herod whom he served, the Herod who, according to Josephus Flavius, had himself pushed for his appointment to the Sanhedrin's second highest post. Nor is it certain that the "fanatical" Menahem in our narrative is not being

confused with another man of the same name who fought stubbornly in the ill-fated War of Independence in the years 67–70 C.E.
And we do not know why or under what circumstances Hillel chose
to lash out at those who desert the study of Torah.

The historical data are sparse and the historical theses of histori-
ans of the period are perhaps much like the midrashim they interpret. But let us for a moment reflect on Luria's thesis and wonder
whether even the tolerant and humane Hillel, in a situation that
tempted spiritual leaders to close themselves off from tempestuous
events, lost his understanding for other ideals in the city and the
field, and "knew" that there was only one right way. Was there, in
Hillel's words, merely a heated expression of his love of learning
and pride in his exalted calling? Or was there a total social conception in which anything, even continued national independence, was
necessarily trivial in comparison to study of Torah, so that those
who took such matters seriously and believed that love of God
could be expressed in such pursuits as well were fools or, if onetime
scholars, traitors who deserved to die?

What Hillel really meant by his tirade and what Menahem,
whose opinion is not recorded, himself had to say about his leaving
the Sanhedrin, is something to think about in trying times. Does
the worth of one educational ideal necessarily put all others "in
their place"? Should we be educating for various options of the inherently worthy life or is there a "best" (way) designed only for the
best (people)? Does the religious ideal of fear and love set up barri-
ers and predetermined roles, or can it unify through a shared vision, variously understood and diversely implemented? Is the "but"
of God's request a sanction for placing people in socially valued
roles? Or is it an invitation to existential awareness of the individual
"for your good," to discover who she or he is, to perceive the potential accompanying him or her in a specific time and place? Is
part of being an educated person to recognize different contexts
and to hear what they demand, or is that the way to perdition in
troubled times? What is the minimum of an educational "end goal"
and when do formulations become too "heavy" and thus discriminatory and unjust?

When thinking about these questions, I sometimes remember those two yeshiva boys who were having "a great year" in Jerusalem, while outside their Houses of Study, it was dark and the storm of the Yom Kippur war was raging. I have my doubts about the educational ideal that helped make them so happy and thus, perhaps forgetful of "the brothers." Yet I suppose that I can understand, in this post-Holocaust generation, where they were coming from.

PART 3

Inside Out:
Learning About Ourselves and Others

If someone says to you that there is wisdom among the nations [of the World], believe it [but] if someone says to you that there is Torah among the nations, don't believe it.

— *Lamentations Rabbah 2*

"You shall observe My statutes and My ordinances, which, if a person do them, s/he will live by them . . . " (Lev. 18:5). *To this R. Meir comments: "From whence do we know that even an idolater who occupies himself with Torah is like a High Priest? Scripture teaches: a person shall do them. Priests, Levites and Israelites is not said, but a person . . . ."*

— *Baba Kamma 38a*

in a highly pluralistic world in which commons and sect are separated by walls of one sort or another, the health of the commons depends on the possibility of strong sectarian education. At the same time, the bare possibility of strong sectarian education depends for its continued existence upon maintaining the viability of the commons. Yet it occurs to me—more as conjecture than conviction—that the necessary elements of any moral education may be discoverable only in the context of sectarian education, that is to say, it will be understood only by examining education in a setting where adults are able to say to youth with confidence, with clarity and for a very long time, "This is who we are and this is why we do these things." Any awkward hesitation or apology in this presentation, either on the grounds that it is too complex a story for children to grasp or that there are alternatives among which an eventual choice must be made—any such hesitation will spell disaster for attempts at moral education. Such a context for education is paradigmatically a community of text and liturgy, even when the text is a constitution and the liturgy is found in a variety of civic rites.

—Thomas F. Green
Voices: The Educational Formation of Moral Conscience

10

JACOB AND ESAU: STRATEGIES FOR COEXISTENCE

I RETURN NOW TO MY maternal grandmother, first mentioned in Chapter 8, and the question I did not ask her, about the sacrificial offerings for whose restoration she prayed even while feeling uncomfortable with the idea of animal sacrifice. Where did the rich, complex, and seemingly untidy culture that was the world of my grandmother come from?

She was, as I said, both pious and a *maskilah*, "enlightened one." She read the weekly portion of the Torah reading carefully and regularly and admitted to having written a commentary "of sorts" on Genesis. But she was also perfectly at home in the poems of Pushkin and in the stories and plays of Chekhov. Grandmother was a fervent Zionist who spoke Hebrew and avidly read Hebrew poetry long before the Nazis turned her adopted German homeland into a criminal state and her into a subhuman non-Aryan. Hitler hastened her departure for the Land of Israel, but her Zionism arose from sympathy with iconoclastic Hebrew writers like Joseph Haim Brenner and conflicted ones like Haim Nahman Bialik. She was fascinated by the spiritual upheavals in the souls of such people, though she, a halakhically observant Jew, entertained their notions but could never adopt them as her own.

Much later, when these questions became cardinal in my own life and in my educational concerns, I asked myself, Where and how did my grandmother become a humanist as well as a faithful Jew of the early twentieth century? How did she come to fervent love of Western and Russian culture while holding to quite realistic notions of the distance between them and her? How did she manage both to learn from these cultures and to share in them, and at the same time, to put a distance, even physically, between them and herself? What was it, in her education and in her experience, that made her both devout and open to truth wherever she found it, both particularistic and universalistic, at home in lecture halls of science and secure in her own Jewish identity?

I do not really know the answers to these questions; however, as a person of theory, I have some educated guesses. But they are no more than guesses. I got to know my grandmother very late in her life, when I came to live in Israel in the mid-1950s. After that, I came often to her small Tel Aviv apartment, once a bold pioneering structure on sand dunes, by the time of my arrival, merely a shabby house. The place then already breathed the ambiance of untidiness and temporality that often characterizes the homes of the very old, whose vision is too impaired to see dust and whose thoughts dwell more on where they have been and where and when they are going than to where they are. It was not an environment for asking such questions, and in any case, I did not know how to ask clearly and succinctly, How did you learn about putting sacrifices "in their right order," together with Pushkin? Where did you get your love of worldly wisdom and culture together with the good and unsentimental sense to leave "them" when their writers, together with their streets, became vicious? How does this love of scientific inquiry exist together with the "order" of the innocent religious life?

In the following chapters, these questions will take center stage and I shall explore some possible lines of inquiry that touch upon education for identity, for commitment, and for openness. In Chapter 10 I look at possible paradigms of relationship between the people of Israel and the nations of the world. Is enmity between Jacob and Esau an iron-clad law of human history, or can they be brothers and friends, sharing human experience and stores of wisdom? In Chapter 11, I move to a consideration of Jewish life as exile and dispersion, wherein duality of identity seems to lead inevitably toward persecution or assimilation. Is it indeed so? In Chapter 12, the inside ("we") and outside ("you") conception is examined as a theological issue, and I wonder whether the distinction is indeed inherently confrontational. Finally, in Chapter 13, I explore the vulnerability of the world of faith (ours) vis-à-vis the world of scientific inquiry (everyone's, so really the world's). And I allow myself to wonder whether inside-outside is an adequate conception for understanding everything we need to know about the identity—or rather, identities—into which we seek to educate young people. I dedicate these explorations to the grandmother whose educated Jewish personality I hardly got to know.

Maimonides Depicts a Dire Picture

When we are looking for an expansive view of identity and self-understanding, it seems safe to turn to Moses Maimonides, medieval Jewry's most renowned philosopher and a champion of universal and rational truths. Yet in his *Epistle to Yemen*, in which he urged his fellow Jews to remain steadfast in their faith in the face of Islamic pressure to convert, Rambam expressed a dour view of Israel's vulnerability among the nations.

> Ever since the time of Revelation, every despot or slave that has attained to power . . . has made it his first aim and his final purpose to destroy our law and vitiate our religion, by means of the sword, by violence, or by brute force. . . . This is one of two classes which attempt to foil the divine will. The second class consists of the most intelligent and educated among the nations. . . . These also endeavor to demolish our law and to vitiate it by means of arguments which they invent and by means of controversies which they institute. They seek to render the Torah ineffectual and to wipe out every trace thereof by

means of their polemical writings, just as the despots plan to do with the sword.[1]

Let us recall the midrashic pronouncement that seems to underlie the epistle even of the worldly, wise, and rational Maimonides: Esau hates Jacob. This sharply segregationist statement is a good entry point into the issue of "Israel and the Nations" from the perspective of the Bible of the Synagogue. And since Esau is the historical and perennial villain of the piece, we might well look at the issue by way of an episode in the story of Jacob and Esau. For the sages of the Midrash, they are the "brothers" who prefigure it all.

A Strange and Dramatic Episode

But first, a personal confession. Most autumns, when the portion of the week Genesis 32:4–36:43 *(Parashat Vayishlah)* is read, I am troubled by the promise Jacob made to Esau, during their encounter on the edge of Eretz Yisrael. Our patriarch Jacob said he would follow his brother to Esau's home on Mount Seir, but he meant to do no such thing. And our oft-mentioned doyen of commentators, Rashi, in defending Jacob's integrity, adds insult to injury: "When will Jacob [really] do so [go to Seir]? At the end of days, as it is written (Obad., v. 21), 'And saviours will go up to Mount Zion to judge the mount of Edom, and the kingdom will be the Lord's.'" Not only will Father Jacob never visit Esau, even though he promised to do so, but he will judge him. That the promise not be falsified, Rashi, basing his twist on a midrash, of course, converts it into a threat! How shall we understand it? Is this the behavior of an exemplary person, a patriarch?

The account of the meeting between Jacob and Esau is truly one of the strange and dramatic episodes in the Torah. Jacob is returning to his homeland after twenty years of exile. He had left at the behest of his mother, Rebecca, who feared that Esau wished to kill him for his—and her—act of deception. Now Jacob hears that Esau is approaching, with four hundred men! His past, heavily armed, seems to be rushing toward him, truly with a vengeance. He does not know what to expect, but it is reasonable to expect the worst. There are premonitions that confirm his fears, but the signals are mixed.

In the process of moving his family to the Land of Israel Jacob struggles throughout the night with a man who seeks to overcome him, who wounds him and then, at dawn, blesses him. Given Jacob's preoccupation with the brother-enemy whom he must encounter the following day, we cannot be surprised that our sages identified the man as "the angel of Esau," who attempts to overcome Jacob even before they meet. Indeed, Jacob will later tell his brother that "to see your face is like seeing the face of God" (Gen. 33:10).

Jacob's preparations for the meeting suggest that he does not know precisely what to expect or to do. In addition to praying and sending large gifts to Esau, he prepares for war. He divides his camp into two, so that if Esau attacks the one, the other may escape.

War? Well, not exactly, for this is a strategy for survival, not victory. The sages of the Midrash have already intimated that Jacob, the tent dweller, is more of a survivor than a warrior. They tell us that when Jacob fled to the home of his Uncle Laban, Esau had his son Eliphaz pursue Jacob to kill him, but Jacob talked Eliphaz out of it. He casuistically made his case to Eliphaz by arguing that Eliphaz could carry out his father's instructions "to the letter" simply by taking all Jacob's possessions, in accordance with the Talmudic principle that "a poor person is accounted as dead" (*Rashi* on Genesis 29:11). In other words, Jacob's weapon on that occasion was a halakhic nicety. We get the sense that young Eliphaz had a soft spot in his heart for his uncle. We do not know whether he considered him pitiful or mad.

Getting Rid of Esau

Now it is twenty years later, but there is reason to believe that Esau's memory of slight and injury is fresh and potent. Yet, astoundingly, when Esau arrives on the scene he is all love and kisses.

Jacob is no doubt relieved but finds the situation discomforting. He is perhaps appalled to find that Esau thinks that they are the best of friends, and that he seems to assume that Jacob is on the way to his, Esau's, fortress-home at Mount Seir. Esau not only extends a cordial invitation but actually offers to go with him, at whatever leisurely pace Jacob's flocks and children require. Jacob can now think of nothing but how to rid himself of this brother-stranger. He makes up excuses; he promises to come, but slowly, and later. He brushes off Esau's offer to leave men with him to escort him. Rabbi Naftali Zvi Berlin is on firm ground in commenting (in *Ha'amek Davar*, on Genesis 33:15) that Esau must have departed in some anger, realizing that Jacob wanted nothing to do with him. The Torah tells us of only one more meeting between the two, at the funeral of their father Isaac.

Thomas Mann, in the first of his Joseph novels, *The Tales of Jacob*,[2] has a profound and thoroughly "midrashic" description of the scene. He depicts Esau arriving on the scene of meeting in exuberance and heavy sentimentality: "He danced and sprang across the open meadow towards his brother and his brother's train; blowing [pipes], becking, laughing and weeping, until Jacob, between shame and scorn, and pity and disgust, could only think for himself something like 'For Heaven's sake'!" Esau's attitude is friendly, patronizing, effusively forgiving. Yet every expression of forgiveness on Esau's lips insinuates Jacob's former "mischief" and "knavishness" anew. Therefore, when Esau suggests that they live the rest of their lives together at Seir, "like twins before the Lord," Jacob will have none of it.

"Thanks very much" was Jacob's thought to himself. "Go to Edom, shall I, and be a piping he-goat like thee and live forever with thee, thou fool? But that is not the meaning of God nor of my soul. All that thou speakest is but empty and idle words in my ear, for that which happened between us will not be buried, thou thyself bringest it into every word that thou utterest. . . . " Aloud he said: "The words of my lord are an enchantment and each one singly has hearkened to the innermost wishes of his servant's heart. But . . . "

At that point Jacob mentions the half-grown children, and little Joseph, "a weakling on a journey," and the suckling calves and lambs. He will come slowly and "softly" to "my lord at Seir to dwell fondly together." Mann writes:

> It was a polite refusal, and Esau, rather gloweringly, understood it as such. He made, indeed, another trial, suggesting to his brother that he should leave some of his people with him to lead the train and to cover its rear. But Jacob thanked him and said there was no need, if only he found grace in the sight of his lord—so that the emptiness of his words stood revealed. Esau shrugged his shaggy shoulders, turned his back on the fine and false one, and went hence into his mountains with cattle and train. Jacob, behind him, lingered a little, then at the first turning took another way and disappeared.

A Missed Opportunity for Reconciliation?

Why does Jacob behave this way? That question seems to have troubled R. Huna, who, in the name of R. Abba the priest of Badillya, connects it to Dinah, daughter of Jacob and Leah, whose tragic tale is the subject of Genesis 34.

> It is written (Job 6:14) "One who is in despair [literally, 'melting'] should be treated with kindness *[hesed]*." You [Jacob] held back kindness from your brother. [So] she [Dinah eventually] married Job who was neither a proselyte nor circumcised. You did not wish her to marry a circumcised man, so she married an uncircumcised one; you did not wish her to marry in a permissible manner, so she married in a prohibited manner. This is what is written, "And Dinah went out . . . " (Gen. 34:1). (*Genesis Rabbah* 80:4)

R. Huna and R. Abba refer here to the fact that Jacob apparently hid his daughter Dinah during Esau's visit. (After all, she is not mentioned among those in the "two camps" whom Esau meets.) They suggest that Jacob did so because he feared Esau might wish to marry her. Sometime thereafter, the Torah tells us, Dinah "went out to see among the daughters of the land," and was raped by Shechem, who only then asked for her hand in marriage. This wild and wily episode led to the deception wherein her brothers agreed to the marriage on the condition that all the men of Shechem be circumcised. Simon and Levi, on the third day after the Shechemites' circumcision, "when they were in pain," massacred all of them for having defiled their sister. Dinah, according to the particular rabbinic tradition of our midrash, later married Job. Truly a fitting match: a woman of sorrow brought together with a man of suffering.

These rabbis, playing on the word *hesed*, which means kindness, even in the sense of betrothal and marriage (Jer. 2:2), but also, a shameful sexual act (Lev. 20:17), find cause to criticize Jacob. He did not want his daughter to marry Esau, who, as a son of Isaac, was circumcised and would certainly have agreed to a proper marriage. Perhaps, too, a still-innocent Dinah, not yet burdened by violence done to her and to others for the sake of her "honor," would have been able to do for Esau what Jacob was incapable of—bring him back to the family of the covenant!

But why? Why the withdrawals, the evasions, the flight from everything that seems inordinately to threaten all that is "not the meaning of God nor of my soul"? Why couldn't Jacob continue the tradition of Abraham who actively "made souls," befriended Gentiles, bravely waged war, and negotiated magnanimous peace?

An Ideology of Self-Segregation

A key to our problem may be found in the following tale of R. Yehoshua ben Hananyah, a prominent sage of the first postdestruction generation, in the first century of the Common Era. R. Yehoshua, we are told, once stood in the presence of the "Caesar" (Hadrian) when a heretic who was also present made a gesture signifying that God has turned His face from Israel. R. Yehoshua gestured in reply, "His [protecting] arm is [still] stretched over us." When the emperor asked R. Yehoshua what the heretic had shown him by pantomime, he answered: [He said, "Israel is] a people whose Lord has turned His face from them," and I answered him, "His hand is [still] stretched over us."

> [The emperor] said to the heretic: "What did you show him?" [He replied: "They are] a people whose Lord has turned His face from them." [The Emperor:] "And what did he show you?" [The heretic replied]: "I do not know." They [the emperor's court] said, "A man who does not understand what he is being shown by pantomime should hold converse before the king?" They led him forth and slew him. (*Hagigah* 5b)

After relating this example of R. Yehoshua's pantomimic prowess in the battle against nonbelievers and slanderers, the Talmud continues:

> When R. Yehoshua was about to die, the Sages said to him: "How will we stand up against the heretics when we have no sage like you to answer them?" He said to them [citing Jeremiah 49:7]: "Counsel is perished from the children. Their wisdom vanished." [This] should be interpreted to mean, when wisdom is departed from the sons [the Jews], then wisdom will vanish among the nations of the world. And if you wish, learn [this idea from Genesis 33:12], "[Esau said:] 'Let us start on our journey and I shall travel at your pace' [i.e., the nations, "Esau," rise and fall together with Israel, that is, proceed at their pace]." (*Hagigah* 5b)

R. Yehoshua b. Hananyah appears to be comforting the sages by saying that with the demise of such masters of confrontation as he, who can understand the others without being understood, the wise of the nations will also cease. This is his homily on the cited verse from Jeremiah. The second proof text may be making the identical point, but perhaps it suggested to R. Yehoshua a strategy of nonconfrontation. If we are not wise to them, then they will lose their wisdom toward us and leave us alone. If we cannot be wise, let us make their wisdom vanish for us. Let us not take them on or even hear what they are saying so we will not have to deal with them and their "wisdom."

The verse from our Jacob-Esau narrative is used not only to proclaim a new reality but also to suggest a new normative paradigm:
Keep away from them. Do not walk with them and do not let them
walk with you. All "debates" foisted upon us by those who would
lead us to Seir are programmed for us to lose. This is a new historical situation, in which the enemies of Israel, from ecclesiastical and
royal thrones, cite Israel's Scripture against it.

If that is indeed what R. Yehoshua ben Hananyah was suggesting,
it must have been difficult for him to give this "comfort." If one
possesses the truth, why not engage in confrontation? But in the
situation of exile, given the might of the nations and the precariousness of Jewish existence, all spiritual dialogue and fellowship can
lead only to defeat and humiliation.

This is indeed a new reality; it was not always so. Ecclesiastes,
who is identified by the Talmudic sages with King Solomon, took
on the Gentile world and was immersed in it. He emerges sophisticated but unscathed. After uninhibited exploration of the goods of
the world "under the sun," he concludes that to "fear God and keep
His commandments . . . is the entire human being." Despite the
Greek wisdom in it, the sages admitted *Kohelet* (Ecclesiastes) into
the canon because "its first and its last words are Torah" (*Shabbat*
30b). Similarly, Hillel had no hesitation in conversing with hea-
thens who wished to know about Torah: He converted them and
taught them (*Shabbat* 31a). Even in the last generation of the Temple, Rabban Yohanan ben Zakkai engaged in apparently good-natured conversation with a heathen about the meaning of the mysterious law of the *parah adumah*, "red heifer."[3]

But once the Temple was destroyed, even a wise man like R.
Yehoshua, who "knows how to answer the heretics," had to engage
in the sport of pantomime debate before the king of the oppressors.
Did he anticipate that soon, it would be the Jew, and not the heretic
or Gentile, who would be executed for "impudence"?

The story of Jacob intimates the paradigm of a powerless Jewish
life. Jacob, in the eyes of the midrashic masters, seems an apt representative of that life. He is an inward person, seeking refuge in the
tent of Torah and introspection from the turmoil of a stormy tale of

which he is the hero, but in which he sometimes looks ridiculous. He spends two decades in Aramaean exile and earns distrust for his successes, thereby prefiguring the tribulations of his son Joseph in Egyptian service. No doubt he is a spiritual titan; after all, he sees angels ascending and descending on a ladder to Heaven! But would he have reached that moment of revelation had he not calmly endured the humiliation imposed upon him by the child Eliphaz? He builds his hopes on having one camp escape the oppressor who blithely strikes at the other. His unwavering goal, until the day of the final judgment of Esau, is of a righteous, or at least surviving, remnant. And he has no illusions about that stranger, his brother. No matter how good-natured, friendly, and hospitable Esau sometimes is, Jacob senses that behind the smile there are huge appetites, maliciously nurtured memories, and unruly impulses: something menacing, accusing, and destructive. It is best to keep away.

As we see from the counsel of R. Yehoshua ben Hananyah, the paradigm perceived and then elaborated by the sages in the Jacob story is not only about the threat of physical destruction. From the meeting with Esau one can also learn to keep away from sharing, or comparing, wisdom. For if they start arguing, what can you say? Should you try to answer "arguments which they invent" and engage in "controversies which they institute" they will only press you into a corner. If you attempt to make the spiritual heritage of Jacob lucid and comprehensible, you must adopt their conceptual patterns, speak their language. In that case, they will declare you redundant, holding on, with tribal loyalty, to a mere instance of universal truth and morality (at best). Should you insist on speaking your own language, using the idiomatic and conceptual equipment of Jewish tradition, you sacrifice relevance for authenticity. Then they will say that you are obscure and stubbornly archaic. What happens to those who explain everything and "talk too much"? Don't they tend to disappear? In contrast, those who refuse to talk at all are praised in this paradigm as uncompromisingly faithful. Even if, in many historical situations—ancient, medieval, and especially modern—they seem narrow and fanatical, those who keep their own counsel somehow survive even when cruelly decimated.

The realities of "life with Esau" seem to justify this paradigm. The most one can hope for in *galut*, "exile," is a Purim-like salvation, which converts a near disaster into a miraculous deliverance. Even then it is best to remain anonymous, to celebrate bemasked, and then to slip once again into the shadows.

Three Models of Israel in the World

Our father Jacob is brave and competent but also beleaguered and, therefore, deviously evasive. But the tradition has other models to offer besides Jacob, the determined yet dreamy man of the spirit wondering how to handle his brother. For example, there is our first patriarch, Abraham, the vigorous pioneer who made proselytes. He walked with kings even as he walked before God. We recall from an earlier chapter that he even dared to consult with his Gentile friends about whether to carry out God's commandment of circumcision! Nevertheless, his universalism is not only in his social intercourse and concern for others, but in his passion to teach others his "universal" monotheistic truth and yet to maintain warm relationships with those who do not accept it. Abraham is not so much interested in the wisdom of others; for that he speaks to God! Rather, he is bound to them by human sympathy, well represented by his proverbial hospitality.[4]

And there is a third model. It is represented in the teachings of R. Yohanan, the famed third-century sage: "Everyone who speaks a word of wisdom among the nations of the world is called wise" (*Megillah* 16a); and "Gentiles outside of the Land of Israel are not idolaters but simply follow the ways of their fathers [i.e., their traditions]" (*Hullin* 13b). Biblically, we may term these teachings the Solomonic model, for it stands behind the books attributed to that wise king: Song of Songs, Proverbs, and Ecclesiastes. This model recognizes the fact that although there is no Torah among the nations, "there is wisdom among them" (*Lamentations Rabbah* 2), and that the nations can recognize the wisdom of Israel (Deut. 4:6). It begins with Torah and ends with it, but it does not shrink from dialogue and reveres sagacity wherever it finds it. And it does not shirk from romantic imagery to depict loving relationships, even between God and the community of Israel. In the Solomonic model, great art and a good movie and a good theory can be appreciated as well as critiqued: A fine university education can coexist fruitfully with a life whose "beginning and end is Torah" and immeasurably enrich it.

The Solomonic model is not without its own complexities. The rabbis strenuously debated whether Ecclesiastes could be admitted into the canon, and the same R. Yohanan who appreciates wisdom from everywhere also states, "A Gentile who studies the Torah is deserving of the death penalty" (*Sanhedrin* 39a). This shocking statement reflects an awareness that a new faith is abroad that is attempting to undermine Jewish faith by its own citations of Scripture. Some things must be (ruthlessly?) protected. Not everything can be learned from—or even discussed with—the wise of the nations. For R. Yohanan, too, the "Jacob paradigm" has its place.

R. Abraham Isaac Kook, the first chief rabbi of the modern Jewish community *(yishuv)* in the Land of Israel, spoke of these complexities at the opening ceremony of the Hebrew University in Jerusalem in 1925.[5] In this address, he gives expression to his joy at the establishment of the university, a beacon of wisdom, a harbinger of ingathering and redemption.

But he admits to fear as well. As Israel, in its own land, takes the wisdom of the world into its inner sanctuary, will it use it to enrich its own spirit, or will this universal knowledge erode and destroy that spirit? Will Jerusalem be Hellenized by worldly wisdom or will it be enriched through it?

In his view, the nascent Hebrew University will bring blessing to Israel only if the "houses of (Torah) study" remain vital and carry out their function of maintaining the inner spirit of Israel. To be part of a dialectically balanced redemption, Israel must take in all the wisdom studied academically, and simultaneously, it must anticipate the rebuilding of the Temple "to which all the nations will flow, to take Torah from Zion and the word of the Lord from

Jerusalem." The taking (of worldly wisdom) and the giving (of Torah) are part of the same messianic process.

Shoshana and Her Doll:
Signs of Paradigm Change?

Rabbi Kook, as a loyal son of Jacob, remains fearful. Yet he realizes that the Jacob paradigm can no longer be upheld unchanged in the new situation of national renaissance. In his letter of congratulation upon the founding of the Bezalel Academy of Arts and Design in Jerusalem (1907),[6] he speaks metaphorically of "a pleasant and beloved child, after a long and forlorn illness," who is on the way to recovery. The sign of her recovery is her asking her mother for the doll she has not seen for all the long time she was too ill to think of playing.

> Little Shoshana is asking for the doll! Thank God, a sign for the good, surely the fever has gone. . . . Now there is hope that Shoshana will live. She will grow and become beautiful, and she will be a woman among women. . . . Her spirit and body will grow stronger and she will ask for medicine, for soup, for bread and meat . . . and then for teachers, pens, books, work and much more.

The analogy is to Jerusalem: ". . . this precious daughter . . . [was] afflicted with the bitter disease of Exile, prolonged and stormy. . . . Now a life-giving stream has gently shaken the depressed sickly bones and she demands beauty and works of art."

Although R. Kook pleads with the leadership of Bezalel to adhere to halakhic restrictions pertaining to (pagan) works of art, he recognizes in the institution dedicated to "beauty and works of art" a return to health and vigor. Surely a bow in the direction of the Solomonic view of wisdom and beauty.

In this generation, the reexamination or modification of the Jacob paradigm may appear even more problematic than in Rav Kook's time. He, after all, walked with British high commissioners in Mandatory Palestine, in an hour that seemed so clearly to be "the beginning of redemption." He died before the seemingly more friendly than ever and enlightened Esau carried out his most ruthless and unspeakable campaign of annihilation against the House of Jacob. Nor was Rav Kook witness to the present-day cultural victories of those Maimonides calls "the most intelligent and educated among the nations," those who seek to render the Torah ineffectual and to wipe out every trace of it with soft-spoken polemics.

New Realities and Fresh Orientations

Nevertheless, the Jacob paradigm must be reexamined and modified. It is not functioning well, and Jewish life and education are blessed with numerous cultural associations, images, and memories that are available to us and that draw on different sources. Should we refuse to explore them and to draw diverse paradigms into new normative patterns, we may find ourselves unable to deal with new situations. If we are unable to balance different paradigms in terms of new needs, old patterns may become a burden and even, a spiritual liability. Unreflectively grafting old paradigms onto new challenges and tasks can lead to confusions, distortions, and caricatures. Why?

There is no doubt that the Jacob paradigm is a vital source and support of Jewish spirituality, but it is founded on intuitions and responses that are theologically and politically passive. (Recall Jacob and his nephew Eliphaz.) Most Jews perceive the mind-set that is most congenial to this paradigm and what it prescribes as incongruous and inappropriate in the restored active life of Israel in its own land and even in the freely functioning Jewish communities of the democratic world.

For example, "Cast your anger upon the nations that do not know You," a prayer recited on the evening of the Passover Seder, was touching, in the passivity of exile, and it stands as a testimony to a spiritual culture that leaves vengeance to God. (One interpretation of the custom of opening the door at the Seder before reciting this prayer I learned from my father. It is that the Gentile neighbors, who suspect mysterious and sinister ceremonies at the Seder, are here candidly shown what they are ostensibly afraid of—a curse on evildoers. The door is opened to show them that the prayer is not directed against them if they, through their religious faiths, are among the "knowers" of God.) And yet, in the State of Israel, this prayer, if not reinterpreted and placed in historical perspective, can readily be (mis)understood as a military policy. Similarly, the wish "May God avenge the blood" of martyrs looks towards the Providential righting of historical wrongs, but it all too readily become a battle cry.

Those who maintain the Jacob paradigm without balancing it with the Abrahamic model and the Solomonic one tend to become self-segregating, self-righteous, and even manipulative onlookers in contemporary Jewish life. In Israel, they declare themselves disgusted by the arrogant activism and "false messianism" of "the Zionists," but they generally are happy to receive monetary support from them. A reverse tendency within the Jacob paradigm, of having nothing to do with Esau while actively hating him, is also possible. Especially in Israel, it can be expressed through a "proud" and premature messianism whose adherents infer that God is redeeming us now from the humiliating passivity and silence of the past and all that we must do is cooperate with him "against Esau." The ultratraditionalists, for the most part, have the virtue of admitting that their model is one of withdrawal and not confrontation; the premature messianists speak and sometimes attempt to act like prophets armed.

Despite the Holocaust, there is room in our education and our community for the Abrahamic model and the Solomonic one. To maintain a healthy suspicion of the wily Esau is no less than historical and social realism. But the models that suggest ways to learn wisdom from all without sacrificing our own particularity deserve reexploration. Keeping both our "first and last words" anchored to Torah while speaking to others and exploring all that is "under the sun" need not lead to catastrophe, though we are often warned that it will. The wise Ecclesiastes might, in our situation, have suggested that the contrary is true: In a society (like his and ours) where every question and all options appear legitimate, the way to make Torah accessible, with its teaching of what is "the whole person," is to put many paradigms to work in the religious and spiritual life of the Jewish people. It is to make room and create space for more who wish to remain—or become—Jews!

In a society in which Jewish marriages and Jewish continuity are perceived as choices, we may, of course, return to self-segregation. There are many who choose this way and urge it upon others. They are not concerned with being irrelevant, and there is heroism in that. But is all heroism wise?

Jacob was a man of many parts, and perhaps Esau, too, was a character of diverse potentialities. Let us return, for a moment, to "the man" with whom Jacob wrestled. That man-angel of Esau wounded Jacob but could not overcome him. At dawn, the surprisingly valiant and victorious Jacob demanded that "the man" bless him. Through that blessing, a new name, "Israel," was added to his identity, although the name Jacob was not abandoned.

Does that point to a different blend of paradigms? Is there a messianic hope in the fact that it was Esau, his brother, who (finally) blessed him? And that Jacob wanted to be blessed by him?

11

THE CURRICULUM OF JEWISH LIFE— GOSHEN AND THE LAND OF ISRAEL

THE LAND OF ISRAEL has been inseparable from Judaism and Jewish identity from the beginning, from the moment that God told Abraham to "go to the land that I shall show you, and I shall make you a great nation and all the families of the earth will be blessed in you" (Gen. 12:1). What is this strange connection? And what educational difficulties does it raise for Jews who live happily outside its borders and who plausibly wonder what Eretz Yisrael represents in the curriculum of Jewish life?

How Is This Land Holy?

What has distinguished the Land of Israel for Jews throughout the ages is not its natural beauty, however much that is lauded in rabbinic literature. Rather, the "Land" takes on its significance by being a central institution of Judaism, part and parcel of its national-religious existence.

Indeed, one can hardly read anything within the tradition of Torah without encountering the Land. It is the place that God chose for the family of Abraham; it is the goal of forty years of wandering in the desert after Egyptian bondage. And it is the "Lord's inheritance," dear to God and to the nation that is covenanted to Him. It is the site of God's Temple, the focus of pilgrimage, from the far corners of the Land and even from the wide-flung Diaspora.

Three representative rabbinic texts articulate well the special status of Eretz Yisrael; the first speaks of the covenant in personal, almost romantic terms: ""Said the Holy One to Moses: The Land [of Israel] is dear to me and [the people of] Israel is dear to me. I will bring Israel that is dear to me into the land that is dear to me" (*Numbers Rabbah* 23:7).

God will bring his bride into the chambers He has thoughtfully chosen for her. Yet the recurring biblical motif of impending exile for Israel's (mainly social) transgressions makes it clear that the romantic and the moral themes are interlocked. For the holy land has been apportioned to Israel so that Israel can there live a holy, covenantal life, so that Israel can be a nation that constitutes a different model of nationalism, characterized by a relationship with God, the "king" who commands a moral understanding of what it means to be a true people.

Yet the divine commandments that are the contents of the covenant are not limited to moral codes and behavior. Even the ritual and symbolic commandments require the Land for their implementation. For the holiness of the Land lies in the divine decree that only there may various commandments be carried out. It is in the social entity commanded upon the Jewish people, and in the presence of its King, that the theopolitical phenomenon entitled Judaism may be fully realized: "There are ten degrees of holiness. Eretz Yisrael is holier than any other land. Wherein lies its holiness? In that from it they may bring the Omer, the First Fruits and the Two Loaves which they may not bring from any other land" (*Kelim* 1:6).[1]

This sensibility, of the land that is an inheritance to enable the fulfillment of the covenant, is attributed to Moses himself. Moses pleads to God to revoke his decree and to permit him to cross the Jordan into the Promised Land, but God does not relent. The midrashic teachers asked themselves why Moses was so eager to do so, even at the age of one hundred and twenty: "Why did Moses our teacher yearn to enter Eretz Yisrael? Did he need to eat of its fruits or to be satiated by its abundant goodness? [Obviously not!] But this is what Moses said: Israel has been given many commandments that are to be fulfilled only in the Land of Israel [and I yearn for the opportunity to fulfill them]" (*Sotah* 14b).

Through the centuries of exile the Land remained inherent to what Jewish faith and commitment were; all Jews "remembered" that Judaism's holiest place, the Temple on Mount Moriah, had been built there because Abraham was prepared to sacrifice his son there, in accordance with the inexplicable divine will. Every Jew wished to have a packet of soil from Eretz Yisrael scattered in the earth where he or she was buried, for who did not wish to be buried, even symbolically, in Eretz Yisrael, the first locus of the final resurrection of the dead? Who, after the dispersion of Israel in Roman times, did not pray three times a day for the return of Israel to its land? And those fortunate enough to eat three meals a day enjoyed another three opportunities to recite the prayer that God "build Jerusalem, the holy city, speedily and in our days." Jerusalem was mentioned at every circumcision, for the blessing bestowed on the tender child was that he be worthy to ascend to Jerusalem and the Temple as a pilgrim, three times a year. Every bride and groom were sent on their way with the blessing that they be among those ingathered within Jerusalem and Eretz Yisrael "in joy," and the groom broke a glass under the wedding canopy in memory of destroyed Jerusalem. Maimonides in legal, yet powerful, rhetoric summarizes the anticipation of Israel for restoration to its land and the significance of this return for a life of pristine Torah:

> King Messiah will arise and restore the kingdom of David to its former state and original sovereignty. He will rebuild the Sanctuary and gather the dispersed of Israel. All the ancient laws will be reinstituted in his days; sacrifices will again be offered; the Sabbatical and Jubilee

years will again be observed in accordance with the commandments set forth in the Torah.[2]

But even the jurist is overwhelmed by the existential and emotional underpinnings of his halakhic pronouncement:

> He who does not believe in a restoration or does not look forward to the coming of the Messiah denies not only the teachings of the prophets but also those of the Torah and Moses, our teacher, for Scripture affirms the rehabilitation of Israel, as it is said, "Then the Lord your God will turn your captivity and have compassion upon you and will return and gather you . . . and the Lord your God will bring you into the land which your forefathers possessed (Deut. 30: 3–5).[3]

A Paradox of Contemporary Jewish Life:
Israel and Diaspora

The State of Israel represents an unprecedented historical "return," a messianic enterprise of Jews who, for the most part, no longer expected a miraculous redemption in the Land of Israel and who were quite certain that the ancient laws of the Torah no longer had a normative call on their loyalties. But they too, though they often disclaimed belief in supernatural events and insisted that they themselves were effecting the "miracle," often admitted to experiencing the events, in however secularized a fashion, as somehow miraculous.

Eretz Yisrael is still a central feature of the "informal curriculum" of Jewish education, namely, that curriculum that explicitly cultivates commitments, expands cultural associations through practice, and shapes identity by pointing the young in the direction of selected features of the social and cultural landscape. And yet this feature, which speaks for the significance of a generally distant territory within a universal faith community, raises difficult questions for contemporary Jews and for the education that is to foster commitments, values, and hopes. Most Jews in our time live in societies with which they can identify, which are experienced as liberal, culturally enhancing, and pluralistic. In the world of the modern Jew, the connection between Judaism and Eretz Yisrael is in many ways incongruent. It suggests that Judaism has a specific geography, that its memories and myths have a particular and continuing historical and cultural context, that Jews have a land, and that they are a nation. Can the modern Jew believe that? And if so, in which sense?

There is a paradox here: On the one hand, Eretz Yisrael and the state of the Jews there are meaningful to identified Jews. Some, from all the lands of Jewish settlement, have "gone up," to make their homes there. Others among the most Jewishly committed recall, or look forward to, some "Israel experience": study, agricultural or other professional work, "total immersion" courses in Hebrew language, or archeological digs. For those who come to Israel to tour, it can be an eye-opening experience: of Jewish life not necessarily defined religiously, of a place where the public sphere is Jewish, however sloppy the definitions or chaotic the confrontations. Not a few Jews open the newspaper or turn to newscasts to find out "what's new" in Israel, unfortunately always in the news.

On the other hand, at this juncture in history, most Jews feel at home in the "lands of their dispersion," and sometimes even wince when their communities are referred to as the Diaspora. To the extent that their sense of Jewish commitment and identity is significant, they are happy to live in the times of a restored Jewish commonwealth and they wish to educate others for the building of cultural and religious ties to it, yet they are happy where they are. Are the concern with Israel in schools, the mourning on Tisha B'Av in summer camps to mark the destruction of the Temple, the Hebrew, and the songs simply features of fixation, or do they point to something in the nature of the Jewish experience that those who have devised the "informal curriculum" of almost all Jewish educational frameworks understand but have difficulty in articulating? What can we learn about this problem from Torah study?

The Israeli novelist A. B. Yehoshua, who ideologically negates the Diaspora as a "neurotic" phenomenon in Jewish history, likes to look to Torah for insights. Sardonically, he suggests that Jews outside of Eretz Israel have biblical and midrashic precedents for their attachment to "exilic" life. His favorite proof text is the descent of Abraham from Canaan, very shortly after his arrival, because "there was a famine in the land" (Gen. 12:10). We are not to imagine, notes Yehoshua, that the Canaanites also left their homes and went down to Egypt to escape the famine. They, he scoffingly conjectures, simply ate less. Abraham, in contrast, could not distinguish "between a homeland and a five-star hotel."

What Yehoshua would do with the second part of the following midrashic sermon leaves little to the imagination. The midrashic teacher notes that no blank space is left in the scroll of the Torah between the end of the portion of *Vayiggash* (Gen. 47:27) and the beginning of the following one, *Vayehi* (47:28), as is usual between portions of the Torah. He suggests two possible meanings for this anomaly:

> "And Jacob lived in the land of Egypt seventeen years" (Gen. 47:28). Why is this section more "closed" than all others in the Torah [i.e., no blank space is left between its beginning and the ending of the last section]? Because as soon as our father Jacob died, the Egyptian servitude began for Israel [and this "closed" their hearts with suffering and despair]. . . . Another reason: Because all the troubles of the world were now "closed" to him [i.e., Jacob was completely happy in Egypt]. (*Genesis Rabbah* 96:1)

What was the nature of Jacob's happiness? Was it anything like what Jews experience today throughout the Western world? Let us examine some midrashic musings on that first dispersion and see whether they may illuminate anything in contemporary Jewish experience.

Joseph's Family in Egypt: A Dual Identity

In the story of Joseph and of his family in Egypt, there is a strange duality. An episode in which that is particularly clear is the encounter between Joseph and his sons at the sickbed of Jacob. Joseph, having been told, "Your father is ill" (Gen. 48:1), takes his sons, Manasseh and Ephraim, to visit him. Jacob first ignores Joseph's sons and speaks of other things. Finally, he "sees" or "notices" them and asks: "'Who are these?' And Joseph said to his father, 'These are my sons whom God has given me in this place'" (Gen. 48:8–9).

Did Jacob not know these young men? One can hardly imagine that Joseph would have kept them hidden from his father for seventeen years! If he had, would Jacob have blessed them, not in a perfunctory gesture, but in an explicit act of adopting them as his own sons, full-fledged tribes in the family federation of "Israel"? Would he have known that Ephraim, the younger, had covenantal priority over the first-born Manasseh? Or was there something peculiar, alien, about these children that Jacob, with his fading eyesight, could not place? Perhaps they looked too Egyptian in dress and hairstyle; perhaps they were so clean-shaven that Jacob became uncertain or critical. That would explain why Joseph found it necessary to remind his father that God had given him these sons "in this place." As if to say: They are after all, children of this place, father. You can't expect them to look different from their friends. But you need not worry. They are still my sons.

Why would Joseph, "the righteous one," so calmly accept such assimilative tendencies in his sons? Judging from some of his own actions, we might say that he had no choice, for they were merely following in his footsteps! The biblical scholar Nahum Sarna posits that indeed Joseph saw no difficulty in adopting the appearance of the Egyptians. But xenophobia, or even anti-Semitism, put a brake on his acculturation. Says Sarna:

> Attention must . . . be drawn to two tendencies that our narrative has very delicately opposed one against the other. On the one hand, the foreign origins of Joseph are constantly emphasized. The Egyptians with whom he comes into contact are always aware of them. Potiphar's wife sneeringly calls him "a Hebrew" . . . the cupbearer describes Joseph to Pharaoh as "a Hebrew youth," the Egyptians did not eat with Joseph because their particularistic religion forbade them to dine with Hebrews. Against this external counter-pressure to

assimilation is opposed an inner drive towards Egyptianization on the part of Joseph. His outer garb, his changed name, his marriage to the daughter of a high priest of Re and his mastery of the Egyptian language, were all calculated to make him outwardly indistinguishable from his fellow-Egyptians, and though they could not accept Joseph wholeheartedly as their equal, he was yet, apparently, so thoroughly satisfied with his situation that he preferred not to be reminded of his past.[4]

Sarna sees the duality of the story as juxtaposing internal inclinations and external xenophobic pressures. And yet even the internal inclinations are, paradoxically, described as pointing outward. It seems that Joseph himself, is inwardly dual.

On the one hand, Joseph appears as a loyal "Hebrew." His speech is replete with invocations of God and references to Him. Joseph resists the temptation to be sexually intimate with Potiphar's wife, for that, he explicitly says, would be a sin. A midrash tells us that on the day of her attempted seduction of him, Joseph was alone in the house because everyone had gone to an Egyptian festival (*Tanhuma, Vayeshev* 9). From this we may learn that he did not take part in such festivities. No less important, he resists the temptation to appear as autonomously wise or magically endowed: He tells the king, as he had told the royal cupbearer and baker previously, that dreams and their interpretations are from God.

Later, as viceroy, Joseph tests his brothers harshly, but when he finds that they are solicitous of Benjamin and thus genuinely repentant, he sends everybody (Egyptian!) out of the hall and tearfully makes himself known to them. Joseph then arranges for his family to live in Goshen. That is a place far removed from the center; there they can pursue their vocation and continue as Hebrew shepherds. And now, hearing that his father is ill, Joseph rushes to him, then brings his sons to be blessed as distinct tribes of "Israel," with individual inheritances after the anticipated return to the Promised Land. Moreover, despite the political embarrassment it may cause, he pledges to bury his father in Canaan. Thereafter, together with his brothers and the entire "House of Joseph," he goes up to the patriarchal burial cave in Hebron for the funeral. And on his own deathbed, Joseph's last request of his family is that, when "God will remember you and bring you up from this land to the Land He promised [to the fathers]," they take his bones "up [to the Land] from here" (Gen. 50:24–25).

This testament is, perhaps ironically, positioned adjacent to the final verse of Genesis: ". . . and he was embalmed and placed in a coffin in Egypt." For, on the other hand, Joseph looks and acts like an Egyptian. Moreover, he speaks (fluently) like one, for his brothers do not recognize him when they meet and they speak "with an interpreter between them" (Gen. 42:23). Joseph accepts an Egyptian name and marries the daughter of an Egyptian priest. And when he dies, he is embalmed, as befits an Egyptian of exalted rank.

The Comfort of Exile in Egypt

Not only Joseph has a dual identity, but Jacob in his "Egyptian period" does as well. Jacob is clearly thankful for spending his last years in Egypt, close to his beloved son. He says, "I never expected to see your face again, and now God has shown me your children too" (Gen. 48:10). Jacob, in Egypt, is "closed off" from all troubles or unhappiness. Nevertheless, he pleads not to be buried in Egypt. Rabbi Samson R. Hirsch, himself a consciously proud Jew but deeply immersed in German culture, comments: "Jacob had lived seventeen years with his family in Egypt [and] could have noticed what a powerful influence the 'becoming rooted in it' *(he'ahez ba)* (47:27) was beginning to have on his descendants, how they already began to see the Jordan in the Nile and to find their stay in Egypt no *Galut* (exile)" (commentary on 47:29). If that is indeed Jacob's sentiment, how shall we explain Jacob's not telling his people to leave exile, to give up the Nile for the Jordan? For that matter, why did R. Hirsch himself not leave the River Main in Frankfurt?

Let us picture the family of Jacob "going up" to Canaan to bury their father. What memories did this land and this landscape bring back to the brothers, who had left it only seventeen years before, but whose formative years were spent, for most of them, in Haran, at the home of their granduncle, Laban? What memories did it evoke for Joseph, who did grow up there, not happily? Why, at this time, long after the years of famine, didn't they just stay in their land? Had the decision to do with Joseph's credibility vis-à-vis Pharaoh, to whom he had promised to return, and who had given him permission to bury his father in Hebron? Or perhaps, with the Amorites still in the land, the family found it convenient to be passive actors in a play written by God? For "the covenant of the parts" set the script: generations of slavery in Egypt still to come, followed by a glorious redemption!

But is there not an element of evasion in this passivity? Can human beings not affect and even change God's script through their actions and decisions? That it can be done, in one direction or another, is taught by the midrashic teachers of Eretz Yisrael, who declare: "Had Israel ascended [to the Land of Israel] en masse [lit., as a wall] from the Dispersion of Babylonia [at the start of the Second Commonwealth], the Temple would never have been destroyed again" (*Song of Songs Rabbah* 8:10). Is it simply as Hirsch suggests—that they had learned to love it there in Egypt?

In Hiding: A Mode of Survival in Exile

There is something disingenuous, an element of hiding, in this story. Joseph hides his survival from his father for twenty years, and then he hides his identity from his brothers; he wears the mask of kingship. Later, we find him introducing only some of his brothers to Pharaoh. In the opinion of our sages, he did not wish "to give the wrong impression" that his brothers were strong men who could endanger Pharaoh and Egypt; at the same time, he did not want to tempt Pharaoh into mobilizing them as his warriors (*Genesis Rabbah* 94:4). Then Joseph keeps his family hidden in Goshen; their shepherding is, after all, "an abomination to Egypt" (Gen. 46:34). Joseph looks like a real Egyptian, but he obviously has another life as well. The tribes of Israel are his brothers; he is part of Jacob's story and part of his blessing. Yet he lives elsewhere and, perhaps, differently. Pharaoh needs him and he promises to "come right back" from his father's funeral, but he hides his other side from Pharaoh, the side that sees Egypt as a temporary abode, that awaits God's promise to "remember" his family and "bring them up" to the land of Canaan.

The Book of Esther relates a similar story, also of *galut*. There, hiding is an explicit theme. Esther, whose name suggests her own hiddenness (the meaning of the word *hester*), does not reveal her "nation." Her name, Esther, is a study in "hiddenness" in another sense as well: It has not only midrashic connotations but also Persian ones, reminding us of the goddess Ishtar. Esther hides her intentions from the king and from Haman. There is uncertainty, danger, and intrigue everywhere. She cannot visit her royal husband without permission; therefore, the Jews must pray and fast for her safety as she approaches him without being called, on behalf of her "real" people.

A midrash (*Esther Rabbah* 8:7) tells us that even the days of fasting Esther ordained for the Jews of Shushan to aid her in making her daring appearance before the king raised a halakhic dilemma. It turned out that one of those three days was the first day of Passover, a fact—and a problem—to which the larger society was obviously indifferent and oblivious. Mordecai and Esther had to deliberate about what was to take precedence that year: mourning and supplication for a miracle or the observance of Passover. Esther's argument, that "if there are no Jews, there will be no Passover," won the day. Surely an insider's problem, too weird to tell the others about, reminiscent of questions and responsa from Holocaust Europe some two and one-half millennia later.

And when salvation is granted, we remember and celebrate it by being, for a day, what we are not. We playact and hide behind masks, putting on false faces. We are joyful but still uncertain, for Ahashverus, that thoughtless and foolish despot, is still on his throne. And so we strengthen our inner moral and social cohesion, which is never absolutely secure, by giving gifts to the poor, and sending *mannot*, "portions," of fruit and cake, to our friends.

Just as the sages discover a model or paradigm of "walking alone" in the story of Jacob and Esau (see Chapter 10), they find a paradigm of *galut* in the story of Joseph. Throughout the story, the midrashic sages and medieval commentators detect and effect a mirroring cultural dynamic; they locate elements in the story that repeat themselves throughout millennia of exile, and they project features of later exiles onto the story. There is physical segregation in Goshen, which was situated at a distance from the center, but also cultural self-segregation. The Talmud, projecting its own insights and institutions upon the patriarch, informs us that Jacob sat and taught in a yeshiva in Goshen (*Yoma* 28b). Just as the "dweller of tents" had "learned Torah" in the "tent" (i.e., yeshiva) of Shem and Eber, a son and grandson of Noah, so Jacob now taught the future generations of Israel in his own "tent." That is one dimension of the paradigm of *galut*.

There is a reverse side to it too, a sense of having "made it" in Egypt. Jacob, we are told in another midrashic comment, did not wish to be buried in Egypt lest his grave become an (Egyptian) shrine. And indeed, the Torah informs us that "Egypt wept for [Jacob for] seventy days" (Gen. 50:3). The requirements of the *galut* situation, and perhaps the hope of "making it," mandate some accommodation to the surrounding culture, yet when accommodation seems to border on assimilation, we are "reassured" that it is only external, a kind of mask. "These are my sons, [even if they look Egyptian]." And much of the accommodation is no doubt a kind of compartmentalization. Joseph is a Jew at home and a man— or at least, an Egyptian—on the street. But he cannot be certain whether the Egyptians, among themselves, do not mock the exalted minister of state as "that Hebrew." Does that make him angry? Or does he only pretend to be angry? Or pretend not to be? We do not know.

A Midrash on Commitment

There is an additional element in this paradigm, one entirely straightforward, innocent, and open. On the verse "Assemble and hearken, sons of Jacob, hearken to Israel your father" (Gen. 49:1), a midrash teaches:

R. El'azar b. Achu said: At the time Jacob was about to depart from the world, he called his twelve sons to him and said, "Listen! Is the God of Israel [i.e., my God] your Father? [Or] do you perhaps have some reservations about the Holy One, blessed be He?" They said to him (Deut. 6:4), "'Hear O Israel'. . . Our father, as there is no desire in your heart to break away from the Holy One blessed be He, so there is none in our hearts, but rather, 'the Lord is our God, the Lord is one.'" Whereupon he uttered the words, "May the name of His glorious kingdom be forever blessed."

R. Berechya and R. Helbo said in the name of R. Shmuel: This is why [the people of] Israel [early] each morning and each evening say, *Shema Yisrael*, Hear O Israel, our father [buried] in the *Ma'arat Hamakhpelah*, the Double Cave. That which you commanded us is still our way, [to declare] "the Lord is our God, the Lord is One." (*Genesis Rabbah* 98:3)

The midrash understands the verse "Hear O Israel" to be a declaration of faith *by the sons to the father.* Israel is the name given to Jacob by the angel who wrestled with him and then, by God Himself. Thus, Israel here is Jacob himself. His children are gathered together, a family in exile. With their father on his deathbed and a foreboding future looming, they await to hear what will happen when God "remembers" them. They want to know who will be their king when they are restored to their land and how each of them will fare there. But Jacob wishes first to know whether his God, that is, the God of "Israel-Jacob," is their "father." To this they respond: Hear O Israel (you, Jacob, our earthly father), He (the Holy One) is indeed our God. Even in exile, we remain strong in faith, and our faith will resound even to your grave, throughout the generations. Our daily recitation of the *Shema* is really a constantly renewed and affirmative answer to your question: Do you remain faithful to "Israel's father"?

In composite, this paradigm, "discovered" in the Torah, dictated the patterns of Jewish life for many centuries of exile, and generations of Jewish children were raised upon it. There was passive waiting in it, and in the meantime, wherever possible, much accommodation, but only "on the outside," make believe, a "Purim shpiel [play]". Sometimes Jews "made it" but knew, or were reminded, that their success was only temporary. There was segregation in ghettos, for the heretical Hebrew presence was feared and despised in the outside society, but there was also self-segregation—in the community, in the home, in the tents of teaching. There was foreboding, fear, uncertainty, and a kind of hiding but also an uninhibited unity of faith and certainty about a messianic ingathering to come. Father Jacob, "from the grave," knew that there was nothing to worry about, that the blessing was in good hands.

As already noted, most Jews in the contemporary Diaspora do not live by this model. They do not live in anticipation of being restored to their land. Disdaining segregation and secretiveness, which they identify with shame, they build synagogues on main thoroughfares, even though, in some lands, these synagogues need to be routinely protected by police. And many of Jacob's children have wearied of synagogues; their only faith is what Marshal Sklare, citing Rabbi Henry Cohen, has called "academic commitment": "[its] method is scientific . . . its morality, the ideals of humanism rooted in finite human experience, its messianic hope that man, through understanding the consequences of his actions, can build a better world."[5]

The situation in which the Joseph-Esther paradigm readily explained almost everything has changed. The great oppression is a raw memory for us, not a fatalistic expectation. Astoundingly, there is Jewish rule in the Land of Israel, although our forefathers could hardly have anticipated that Jews, possessing unprecedented power, would yet need to accommodate themselves to sharing the land with another people and to ruling in less than all of it. Our medieval forebears did not conceive of a miraculous return without a Messiah and without unreserved faith in "Israel's father." So can we still raise and educate our children on the Joseph-Esther paradigm? Is Jewish life in exile still a Purim shpiel, a game of cultural hide-and-seek? Is the Land of Israel still the focus of longing?

The Limits of Cultural and
Educational Paradigms

Paradigms are a comfort. Once solidified, they present themselves as lucid portraits of perennial reality that can domesticate or neutralize all seemingly new and bewildering situations.

Educators have a particular affinity for using paradigms. They present their students with something already known (it was always this way) and then use the already known to set before their pupils the new and as-yet unknown. This method facilitates comprehension. Children learn to "place" things more easily when everything that happens or must be done "belongs" somewhere. New things are learned more easily and they appear less threatening when there is really "nothing new under the sun."

Even in times of great upheaval, parents and educators who wish to defend a cultural tradition will understandably attempt to stay with it uncritically. They can then claim, with some justice, that their children and pupils are secure, certain, and untroubled. But in doing so, the parents and educators may lose sight of the fact that every living faith has diverse paradigms, and present theirs as synonymous with faith and tradition. They may forget that paradigms that are never reexamined or placed in perspective may also betray, blind, and incapacitate us. Remaining stubbornly with a paradigm may make us incapable of clearly apprehending new circumstances with which we must deal—or new opportunities and responsibilities. Equally serious, the equation of a partially outworn or irrelevant paradigm with the faith and culture that provide it with its context and its basic words and pictures may alienate people from the faith and culture themselves.

The scholar Ephraim Urbach has given us, in one historical study, an enlightening example of how paradigms work and (then) become worn, with particular reference to the centrality of Eretz Yisrael and the authority of its sages in the era of the Second Commonwealth.[6] This paradigm, replete with proof texts, was axiomatically held as self-evident Jewish teaching throughout the Second

Commonwealth and even in the Mishnaic period. It was part of being an identified Jew to be taxed half a shekel for the maintenance of the Temple service, for the Temple was sacred and Jerusalem was the "mother city" even of Hellenized Jews.

And yet, as Urbach demonstrates, this once self-evident paradigm of the centrality of Eretz Yisrael could not be maintained intact after the destruction of the Temple and became increasingly fractured. The sages of Babylonia recognized that the authority that had once rested on Jerusalem and then shifted to Yavne and the Galilee had moved to the land of the Euphrates. In opposition to the sages of Eretz Yisrael, who insisted that "dwelling in Eretz Yisrael weighs as much as all the other commandments [together]" and that "Israelites living outside of the Land [are to be considered] worshippers of idols," the sages of Babylonia went as far as to say, "One who goes up to Eretz Yisrael from Babylonia transgresses a positive commandment" and "as it is forbidden to go from Eretz Yisrael to Babylonia, so is it forbidden to leave Babylonia for another land." And Rashi explains why they said that. It was, he states, "because there are Yeshivot there [in Babylonia] from which Torah comes forth continually." Under the new circumstances of Jewish national powerlessness, the Babylonian sages were giving the new exilic centers of learning their spiritual and national due and insisting that their status be recognized.

Urbach's thesis is that when the spiritual and political power of the Jewish polity in Eretz Yisrael ceased, the rabbis here cited reexamined the paradigm of Eretz Yisrael's Jewish centrality, which had been based largely on that power. That they found adequate proof texts for their reexamination demonstrates that the tradition encompasses more than any one paradigm.

Yet it is noteworthy that they recognized the link between each paradigm and the totality of the Torah tradition. They made a culturally loyal effort to maintain the integrity and sanctity even of the previous, now reexamined, paradigm. They assumed that there was surely much to be learned from it in every situation, for it was, or had become, an aspect of Torah. That is perhaps the source of the stricture against going from Eretz Yisrael to another land. They taught us that paradigms, as aspects of Torah, are not to be dropped but, rather, reexamined and gently, with the aid of other paradigms, put into a new perspective.

Two Epistles: From the Land of Israel
to the Diaspora—and Back

Israeli and Diaspora Jews of this generation are not in hiding, but some things, if they wish to survive, need to remain a private agenda. Not all Jews in the Diaspora intend to be "remembered" for a personal return to the Land of Israel. Yet without loss of integrity they may share an assumption of Philo, the first-century Alexandrian founder of "the philosophy of Judaism." Philo wrote that though Jews are at home in many places, Jerusalem is "their mother city." It is interesting that in making this point parenthetically, Philo, intentionally or not, increases its force. It is so casually remarked that it appears as self-understood. In his words:

> They [the Jews] settle in many of the most prosperous countries in Europe and Asia, and while they hold the Holy City where stands the sacred Temple of the most high God to be their mother city, yet those [cities in the Diaspora] which are theirs by inheritance from their fathers, grandfathers, and ancestors even farther back, are in each case accounted by them to be their fatherlands in which they were born and reared.[7]

After the Holocaust, it is unlikely that Jews will see religious or moral sense in passively following a prewritten plot of history. Rather, even the traditionalists may gently move the Joseph paradigm aside to make room for the halakhic one that considers bold and unprecedented action, even on a wide historical canvas, as a mitzvah dictated by the specific time. That was certainly the position of religious Zionism, whose adherents were ready to partially abandon some paradigms and patterns that were previously self-evident, such as not speaking Hebrew and not "defying the nations" by ascending to the Land of Israel, in order to protect and preserve the faith and the people of Israel. Other paradigms have come (back) into view, such as that of (present) restoration of the Jewish people in its land and that of an open and accommodating Judaism in free societies "in which [Jews] . . . were born and reared."

Yet, even at a time of reverent, yet critical, reexamination of the Joseph-Esther paradigm, two features of it seem to remain relevant and crucial. Those are its assumptions that Jewish life cannot be lived or transmitted if there is no particularity in it, and that Jews are always walking on a bridge between their collective memory and their future.

The Second Book of Maccabees begins with an epistle from Jerusalem "to the brethren, the Jews of Egypt," demanding that they celebrate the victory and redemption of Hanukkah with "the brethren in Jerusalem and throughout the land of Judaea":

> The brethren, the Jews in Jerusalem and throughout the land of Judaea, wish you perfect peace; may God do good unto you, and remember His covenant with Abraham and Isaac and Jacob . . . may He give you an open heart for His law and for His statutes, and make peace, and hearken to your supplications, may He be reconciled to you and not forsake you in times of evil. . . . In the reign of Demetrius, in the hundred threescore and ninth year we the Jews have already written unto you in the extreme tribulation that came upon us in these years . . . but we besought the Lord and were heard; we offered sacrifice and made the meal offering, we lighted the lamps and set forth the showbread. *See [to it] that ye keep the Feast of Tabernacles in the month of Kislev.*

The Jews of Egypt, previously informed of the tribulations that had befallen their Jerusalem brethren, are now notified of the deliverance that followed: that they had "besought the Lord and were heard." The Diaspora community is instructed to observe the eight-day feast of Hanukkah, which during that year was also to be celebrated as Sukkot.[8]

The Jerusalem Jews are well aware that if those Jews living among the Gentiles had heard the story at all, it was most likely with a different slant. Yet wherever Jews are living, even with "perfect peace," they are assumed ready to live within their history and to observe its fasts and feasts.

Although we seem to have here merely the model of "the centrality of the Land of Israel," that is not precisely so. For in the Book of Esther, we have a similar, earlier, "epistle," this one from Mordecai, written in (exilic) "Shushan, the capital" of Persia to all Jews everywhere, to observe "these days of Purim from year to year," and we find that, there too, all Jewish communities "established and took upon themselves, and upon their children and all who joined themselves to them . . . that these days of Purim would not cease from among the Jews." (Esther 9:27).

The link between all Jewish "brethren," as between memory and future, cannot, in this historical age, bypass the State of Israel. Israel is preeminently founded on a paradigm different from the Joseph-Esther one and is engaged in a spiritual struggle not to discard the "baby" of historical Judaism with the "bath water" of *galut* habits and models. Yet Joseph was certainly expressing the core faith of Judaism, not merely a paradigm, when he connected the future redemptive "remembrance" of God with the patriarchs of the past—those whom God first brought to the Land and to whom He was faithful.

Jerusalem and Jewish Learning

What will not bypassing the State of Israel mean for contemporary Jews, living in differing circumstances, facing discrete challenges? How will young Jews be educated to remain one people and to see rebuilt Jerusalem as their "mother city"? That is a question for Israeli and Diaspora leaders and educators, bearing diverse insights, to confront together.

In one of its midrashic interpretations, the story of Joseph and Jacob in Egypt suggests a fruitful insight. In Goshen, we recall, "the family" was not held together only by looking different from the Egyptians or by anticipating the future. As we have speculated, the sons of Joseph, though being the fathers of two tribes of Israel, did not "look different" at all and all the tribes learned to take root in Egypt. But in Goshen, our sages anachronistically say, there was a yeshiva where Jacob taught his family. And we may imagine that after Jacob's death, Judah and the others who continued to teach brought memories and insights to the "yeshiva" that were not exactly what Jacob had remembered from the yeshiva "of Shem and Eber." After all, they had studied in a different yeshiva than had their father; surely their own lives were reflected in the Torah that they taught, even as they remained the faithful sons of Israel, their father.

If a "yeshiva" brought and held the family together in Goshen, why should Jewish learning in Jerusalem and throughout its land not bring the family together in our time? Now that Eretz Yisrael has regained a certain centrality through Jewish sovereignty, Torah, diversely understood and taught, can, to paraphrase Rashi, come forth from its Yeshivot continually. Jewish learning in the Land of Israel can give "the brethren in Egypt" and everywhere common landscapes to which they may return again and again, a common language in which they learn to recognize one another as brothers and sisters, a language that gives them a stake in Torah, variously interpreted and applied. Can Jerusalem and its land remain the "mother city" if it is not a "tent" of learning for all Jews, in their diverse ways? And if it does not, will Jews retain one cultural language, to pray or hope, together, that "God [may] do good unto [us]," throughout the lands of our dispersion and in Jerusalem?

12

CHILDREN OF
TWO COVENANTS

THREE CENTRAL FIGURES in the Torah, neither Jewish nor Gentile, represent humankind as such: Adam, Eve, and Noah. Noah, who has a portion the Torah named for him, is unique in that God makes a covenant of moral law with humankind through him. This covenant binds all people to a moral code, but it binds God as well. As explicated by the Talmudic teachers (*Sanhedrin* 56), this covenant is the basis for an ethical and religious relationship between God and all the children of Noah. It is meant to set things straight in the world.

But if so, what need is there for the covenant of Abraham and Sinai? Doesn't this second, specifically Jewish, covenant reflect a superfluous and potentially pernicious apartness? That is one of the most perturbing questions of contemporary Jewish life in societies of freedom and basic "Noahide" morality. It is constantly there, in what may be called the informal curriculum of Jewish education— that which conveys attitudes, commitments, and moral inclinations most explicitly. The presentation of two covenants in Jewish life, one universal and the other particular, seems to invite young people to question the need for Jewish identity and commitment, on the one hand, or to disparage those who are not of the family of Abraham, on the other.

No philosophy of Jewish education that takes the theological dimensions of particularism and universalism seriously can ignore this problem. And a good place to begin examining it through the prism of Torah is by way of the Bible's epic drama of Noah.

Starting Anew: What Did God Intend?

At first glance, the Torah's story of Noah and the Flood seems simple and straightforward. God found humankind to have become unbearably evil and decided to destroy it because He regretted having made humans. Corruption and consequent violence led to the complete destruction of the human and even the animal world, "with the earth."

But then why are we, Noah's children, here to tell the tale? Why was the destruction not complete? The ancient Mesopotamian flood stories, unlike the biblical one, had a simple answer to this. As Nahum Sarna reminds us, these pagan tales assume that humanity was indeed to be utterly destroyed, so that "the rescue of the hero occurs inadvertently, by dint of the perfidy and subterfuge of one of the gods acting against the intent of the others."[1] But in the Torah's narrative, God Himself works to sabotage His own plan. "Noah," we are told even before the story begins, making the tale almost anticlimactic, "found favor with the Lord" (Gen. 6:8).

In saving Noah's whole family, God brought the situation back to square one, to the first "beginning." As in the story of Adam and Eve, here once again was a family with three sons, one of whom was a man of unbridled passions. Once more, one sees human hubris, represented in the postdiluvian age by the arrogant builders of the Tower of Babel. As for Noah himself, though he "walked with God" and was "righteous in his generation," his righteousness, according to one much supported Talmudic-midrashic opinion, was of mediocre quality, praiseworthy in his debased generation, but hardly sterling. Unlike Abraham, he did not "stand before God," pleading for the wicked. He was passive and, finally, escaped from reality—and dignity—through drink. He walked with God but, unlike Abraham, not *before* Him.

The Flood: Simply Punitive Justice?

Destroying all creatures "with the earth" seems like a terrible act of vengeance, at best, the act of a fierce deity bent on ruthless justice. So it is strange that the story of Noah and his ark shows up in Jewish liturgy as an occasion of Providence, as an archetype of divine compassion and "remembering." In the *Mussaf* service of Rosh Hashanah, in the section entitled "rememberings," we, as it were, remind God of His own "remembering," which is meant to evoke our remembering of Him. And there Noah makes an appearance:

> Happy is the one who does not forget You and the person who strengthens him/herself in You: for they who seek You shall never stumble, neither shall those who trust You be put to shame. For the remembrance of all works comes before You and You inquire into all their doings. Of Noah You were also mindful and You gave him a promise of deliverance and mercy, when You brought the waters of the flood to destroy all creatures because of their evil deeds . . . as it is written in Your Torah: "And God remembered Noah, and every living thing and all the cattle that were with him in the ark and God made a wind to pass over the earth and the waters subsided."

The imagery here, on Rosh Hashanah, is reminiscent of the story of Jonah, recited during the *Minhah* (afternoon) service of Yom Kippur. There, the wicked people of Nineveh deserve destruction, yet God has mercy and spares them, not only because they have repented, at least for the moment, but also because they are, to the Creator, pitiful in their creaturely vulnerability. And then there are the children! "Shall I not have pity," God asks Jonah rhetorically, "on that great city, in which there are more than six score thousand persons that cannot discern between their right and their left hand, and also much cattle?" (Jon. 4:11).

The biblical description of God's "remembering" Noah presents a picture that must also arouse pity, ours and His: of a family, together with representatives of all the living things, afloat on the waters that cover a dead world. Tossed about in a limbo, they must have wondered when the illusion of safety in an ark would end and they too would sink helplessly into the deep. Yet, in the previous paragraph of the *Mussaf* meditation, we learn that Noah and his family did not despair but "strengthened themselves in Him." And the Torah itself tells us that God, as in the primordial creation, fashioned a wind that blew away the earth's watery mantle and again established a place for human habitation by making a division between the upper and the lower waters.

The Seven Noahide Commandments

What exactly are we to make of this complicated story? Can we really associate mercy with it? What happened to God's "regret" about creating humanity? Did God change His mind? Doesn't the Bible declare emphatically, "He is not human that He should change His mind"? (1 Sam. 15:29).

Moreover, if God wanted to make a clean sweep so that there would be a humankind that would "serve Him with a perfect heart," why did He lower His standards after the Flood? Why were the Noahides permitted to kill animals for food while antediluvian humankind was not? The explanation of the Torah is that God "realized" that "the heart of man is evil from earliest youth" (Gen. 8:21). Now, after God destroyed the world without solving the problem, His pristine vision of perfect peace among all creatures is seemingly shattered. He says to Noah: "The fear and the dread of you shall be upon all the beasts of the field and all the birds of the sky . . . and upon the fish of the sea. . . . Every creature that lives shall be yours to eat" (Gen. 9:2–3).

God no longer demands what people seem incapable of doing, and He makes a covenant with humankind as it is, with the human heart as He finds it. The symbol of this covenant is the rainbow, which has been interpreted to represent an inverted bow.[2] With its sides pointing down, it poses no threat of arrows being shot to earth from the heavens; rather, it is a mark of divine benignity. God has made a covenant of peace; He has inverted His bow. He will no longer threaten the world. His promise is never again to disturb the order of nature and its seasons.

Yet the covenant and its promise of peace obliges humanity as well. The human obligation is in the norms of behavior that the Talmud calls the seven Noahide commandments; they constitute what the sages understand to be the universal laws of morality that make human existence possible. According to many sages and commentators, most of these commandments were given to Adam. Yet one of the Talmudic sages, Rabbi Yehudah, holds that Adam received only one commandment, namely, not to worship other gods. In Rabbi Yehudah's view, all the others were first given to Noah (*Sanhedrin* 56b).

In the generally accepted enumeration of the Noahide commandments, they consist of six prohibitions and one positive commandment, and together, they confer the same moral status on Gentiles (*bene Noah*) as the more numerous mitzvot of the Torah do on Jews. Hence, according to R. Meir, any non-Jew who "engages in [the] Torah" that obligates him or her as a Noahide is like a High Priest (*Sanhedrin* 59a), and those who observe the Noahide commandments as divine commandments are "the righteous of the nations,"[3] who have "a share in the world to come."

Imagining Creation: Two Midrashic Passages

Behind all the factors that make a seemingly simple story complicated, there lies a fundamental question that has perennially agitated all reflective people who believe in the creation of the world and of humankind by a free and benevolent God: Why did God create a world in which there is so much suffering and evil? Why did He create humans, who rebel against God with seeming impunity? Wouldn't it have been better for the world not to have been created? A famous midrash on the verse "Let us make the human in our image" (Gen. 1:26) poses this question well. The author understands the plural ("us") in this verse to suggest that God consulted with the angels before the creation of the human being.

> The ministering angels formed groups, some of which said, "Let him be created," while others said, "Let him not be created." . . . Kindness said, "Let him be created for he does kind acts." And truth said, "Let

him not be created for he is all lies." Righteousness said, "Let him be created for he does acts of righteousness." Peace said, "Let him not be created for he is all strife." What did the Holy One do? He seized Truth and threw her to the ground. . . . While the angels were busy arguing among themselves, the Holy One created the human. He said to them, "What are you arguing about? I have already created [the human being]." (*Genesis Rabbah* 8:5)

The angels, presented here as abstract ideals ("righteousness," "truth," and so on) cannot agree that the human, to be endowed with an evil inclination and with free will, is worthy of creation. Perhaps they have noticed that it is only regarding humans that the Torah does not declare the creation to be "good." While they are arguing, God, apparently tiring of their abstract discussion, creates the human being, after having "thrown Truth to the ground." As Ephraim Urbach explains it, Truth was overtly disqualified to judge the matter, having said that "he is all lies." This, God knew, was not the truth.[4] Humans lie, but they are not *all* lies. Even Truth, as a mere angel—and abstraction—could not be trusted to tell the whole truth!

Yet this midrash merely poses the question and reiterates what we already know: that God "decided" to create the world and humankind. But why? Another rabbinic discussion proposes an almost "systematic" answer:

Six things preceded the creation of the world. Some of these were created [before the world] and some of them arose in God's mind to be created [later]. The Torah and the seat of [divine] glory were created [before the world] . . . the patriarchs and Israel and the Temple and the name of the Messiah arose in God's mind to be created. R. Z'aira says, Also repentance. (*Genesis Rabbah* 1:4)

The answer of this midrash to our question is that God did not arbitrarily decide to create the world. Rather, having already created the Torah and the seat of glory, God had, as it were, no choice but to create the world, and with human beings. Why? The Torah is meaningless unless there are moral agents to carry it out. "Love thy neighbor as thyself" remains a dead letter where there is no neighbor, no "other." Likewise, the "seat of glory" established God's sovereignty. But where there is a sovereign, must there not be subjects?

In other words, God, having created a purpose for the world, had to create a world. The world's ultimate purpose, our midrash declares, is the realization of the Torah in the human world and the establishment of God's sovereignty. Creation looks toward the final (messianic) redemption. Once that messianic blueprint was drawn up, creation became inevitable. However, since humans have free will, there is no assurance that they will either live by the Torah or accept God's kingship. They can thwart the purposes of Creation. They have the capacity to be corrupt and violent; they can decide to ignore Torah and the "seat of glory."

To give the plan of creation that explains and justifies it some hope of consummation, God, as it were, "thinks ahead" toward elements of the created human world that can be expected to comprehend, accept, and work toward the achievement of His purpose. Hence there are the patriarchs, who broadcast God's name and teach their households righteousness and justice, namely, that "the world is God's" and that it "makes sense" only through Torah. Hence there is Israel, the nation that was instructed to see itself as bound by Torah and a harbinger of God's kingdom. Similarly, God envisioned the Temple in which humans might atone for their transgressions and thus return to the paths of righteousness. Finally, the Messiah, under whose guidance humankind would accept the Torah and God's kingdom, was also "planned." Quite realistically, however, R. Z'aira points out that as long as humans are humans, they will have free will and will sin; a world without repentance, therefore, cannot become what it was created to be.

It makes sense to say that this idyllic world in which God's sovereignty is acknowledged is what God intended for Eden. He commanded the humans not to eat of the Tree of the Knowledge of Good and Evil for no other reason than to establish His kingship, and He created the male and female to live by the primordial

Torah, in truth and love. They were to act together, as people, as parents, as custodians of a natural world that would also be beneficent and perfect. After all, Torah and the "throne of glory" are to lead all creatures to harmony and friendship. Moreover, according to Rabbi Yehudah, who holds that the other Noahide commandments were not given to Adam, God did command even that first couple not to serve idols, perhaps hoping that no more was needed to prevent disobedience, bloodshed, alienation, and pain.

But apparently that one commandment alone did not suffice, as more concrete and specific laws might have, to distinguish between right and wrong. Therefore, the perfect world God had envisioned, where all creatures could live in friendship and wherein none would harm the other, did not come about. Not possessing norms of appropriate behavior, God's creatures misunderstood friendship as random interbreeding and thereby destroyed the integrity of the species He had created. At the same time, paradoxically, all fell upon all in random violence. Every creature acted arbitrarily; the "kingdom" became the domain of the "sons of God," the powerful who did whatever they pleased.[5]

The Noahide commandments of human morality, whether first promulgated after the Flood or only then reiterated within a framework of covenant, are more focused. They forbid arbitrariness, self-aggrandizement, and self-glorification. More specifically, by mandating the establishment of courts of law, these commandments prohibit arbitrary rule. They forbid idolatry, that is, the worship of whatever is undeserving of ultimate concern or adulation, be it "power," "nature" or "honor." They forbid blasphemy, the expression of enmity to a moral monotheism that sets limits to one's right to do whatever one wants at any price. They forbid bloodshed, which is the consequence of disregard for the human person and his/her dignity, viewing people as expendable objects and bereft of sacredness. The Noahide commandments proscribe sexual immorality, that is, behavior resting on the axiom that natural desires are inalienable goods regardless of how the exercise of these desires affects others, an axiom indifferent to the establishment of responsible relationships. Theft is forbidden, for the fact of power should not authorize the despoliation and victimization of the weak. Finally, Noahides may not tear limbs from living animals for food, for such behavior is cruel and teaches the vicious assumption that the imposition of suffering upon sentient beings is natural or unimportant in the cosmic scheme of things.

A Midrash on Decency:
The King of Katzia Sits in Judgment

God's plan for the creation of humanity is represented by "Torah and the seat of glory." The achievement of this purpose fulfills a religious and moral vision of perfection. But in the absence of basic laws of decent human behavior, this vision is quickly corrupted, for it may itself countenance less than moral means to achieve it. The Noahide laws are more modest in scope: They enable human beings to exist, to manage all that is evil and weak in them. Where there are no such laws of basic decency, human life becomes unbearable and, finally, impossible. Not all people have the right to demand from all others the same view of "Torah and the seat of glory," but all should understand that without the Noahide laws, there will be no humaneness and, ultimately, no humankind. Religiously speaking, we have the right to hope for the maintenance of the natural world as God promised in the covenant so that a moral human existence, as demanded by the covenant, will be possible.

A midrashic teacher relates that once Alexander the Great paid a visit to a certain king in the land of Katzia because he wished to see how that king "at the ends of the earth" dispensed justice.[6] On the particular day of Alexander's visit, two people came before the king to present their dispute for adjudication. One had sold a dunghill to his neighbor; the other had bought it and found a treasure within it.

The buyer said: "I bought a dunghill, not a treasure," whereas the seller declared, "I sold a dunghill and whatever is within it." The king asked one of the two: "Do you have a son?" He answered him, "Yes." He asked the other one, "Do you have a daughter?" He answered,

"Yes." [The king] said to them, "Let them be married to each other and the treasure will be theirs."

Alexander watched the proceedings, bemused. When the king of Katzia asked Alexander how he would have judged such a case, he replied:

We would have killed both [the men] and taken the treasure for ourselves. He [the king] asked: "Does it rain in your country? . . . Does the sun shine there?" He [Alexander] said, "Yes." He asked, "Do you have domesticated goats and sheep *(behemah dakka)* in your country?" He said, "Yes." [The king of Katzia] said to him, "May [you] be blasted *(tipah ruho shel oto ish)*. Not by your merit does it rain in your country, or does the sun shine there but for the sake of the animals, as it is written, 'Man and beast You save, O Lord' (Ps. 36:7); You save humans for the sake of the beasts." (*Genesis Rabbah* 33:1)

For all we know, the king of Katzia may have had no vision of the ultimate purpose and significance of human life. Yet he knew that there is a relationship between human morality and the very physical maintenance of human existence, symbolized by rainfall and sunshine. The Noahide covenant promises that, and perhaps it is enough for him. His solutions to problems may not articulate the highest potential of Torah; for though as a righteous Noahide, he believes that God's commandment underlies moral judgment, he does not make decisions "in the name of God." Perhaps he has no idea of how the world could be perfected. He deals with matters as they arise.

Two Covenants:
A Paradox of Religious Jewish Education

A religiously oriented Jewish education is informed by a biblical-midrashic vision of the purpose and significance of human life. But there seem to be two visions rather than one.

On the one hand, Judaism teaches that Israel "arose in God's mind" to be created from the beginning, as the nation that chooses this vision and is prepared to live by it. The laws of the Torah are to translate this vision into practice, and the messianic hope points toward its consummation. It looks further than to the rainbow of nonbelligerence and sees humankind ascending to the mountain of God, calling Him by name and cleaving to Him. But on the other hand, without the Noahide assumptions of decency, themselves understood as integral foundations of Torah, the vision readily becomes skewed, detached from human realities, open to parochial fanaticism and sectarian absurdities.

Here paradoxes and educational dilemmas arise. To begin with, in the worldview of Torah, only the covenant of Adam, restored to the world by Abraham and Sarah and their household, is redemptive; only that covenant can ultimately explain why God decided to create the world. That covenant contains a picture of the potential of human life, of what is yet to be created as it "arose in God's mind." When Jews teach that the faith of Judaism is a true one, they are teaching that.

Yet our experience is that ideologies of perfection can endanger the real world. Utopias seem all too willing to sacrifice decency on the altar of the dream. In the Jewish tradition there is an awareness of that; hence the tradition's abhorrence of idolatries, which are falsely redemptive. Hence its reliance on both revelation and human interpretation. Hence, too, its culture of *mahloket*, of controversy and debate "for the sake of Heaven." For where there is only one true and narrow opinion of how God's kingdom is reached and how it functions, there is theocracy and clericalism but no holiness, no ongoing discussion between "the ministering angels" of Righteousness and Kindness. In such a utopian situation, even Truth falsifies. But as we know from experience, the problem—and the danger—remain. How shall we teach a vision that requires, on the one hand, great commitment and cultural self-esteem but, on the other hand, also a measure of ambiguity, some uncertainty, and much discussion and even self-criticism?

Our sages teach that the Noahide covenant is spiritually significant; it, too, is a revelation. For Judaism, it constitutes the substance of righteous human life for all. It teaches all peoples that, given the "evil inclination" within all of us, there must be decency before there can be perfection. In our epoch, stained by horrendous visions of perfection, by a "kingdom of Satan" that wished to obliterate Israel as a centerpiece of its war against Torah and "the seat of glory," we have much reason to respect and love loyal Noahides throughout the human family. And that must include even those who, unlike the lovable king of Katzia, do not recognize the religious character of their commitments, who perhaps adhere to no rite. So, what shall we say to those of our children and pupils who declare that the Noahide covenant suffices? What shall we say to those who think that the covenant of Torah and "God's throne" is superfluous or even dangerous? To those who want to quit the world of Jewish language and literature and who know that there is life after that too?

One solution to the paradoxical demand of cultivating particularistic loyalty and love together with broad universal sharing and sensibility is to deny the paradox by downgrading the Noahide covenant. This solution is to declare that Jews "walk before God," leading the way to redemption, and to leave the Noahide norms to "the nations of the world." That solves the theological problem because it means that we have the whole truth, after all, and need not emphasize controversy or neurotically engage in self-criticism. It solves the educational dilemma by dogmatically locating those who have only the Noahide covenant on a different and lower plane, on a different moral planet.

But there is a second approach, one that does not obliterate the paradoxes and dilemmas, but candidly states them. In this approach, the Noahide covenant is an integral aspect of the Abrahamic as well as the Adamic one. Although the Talmudic tradition formally identifies Noahides as non-Jews (because they are bound by no more than seven commandments), we and our children are essentially also Noahides, for the universal covenant of morality binds us all, and must learn what that means. In addition to living a response to the question, Why did God make this world and what does He demand of me, as a member of the community of Israel? we, with all Noahides, must address the questions: What is required of human beings to maintain the world? Who are our allies in that? How may we take in the world and trust it, despite the pain of our history? How, despite our open wounds and our own frailties, may we ourselves be understanding and compassionate?

Life—even before it is a dream of God of what we may become and what is yet to be, through Israel, the Temple, and the Messiah—is a communal human reality to be managed, necessarily with some sense of comradeship, one hopes with a measure of joy. But it is Israel's covenant of Torah that informs us what an uncertain affair the covenant of decency is, that it depends on God's promise and compassion, and that it requires universal adherence to God's (Noahide) commandments. It is the covenant of Abraham that educates us to understand that the Noahide code is also a covenant; our own tradition gives us, as Jews, a language to articulate that. Other faiths too will, in their diverse ways, express that truth, namely, that decency must ultimately be anchored in a transcendent, even a messianic, narrative.[7] Certainly, educated Jews, through the Torah that is addressed to Israel alone, may learn to appreciate the moral and religious imagination of a king of Katzia. They may share his understanding about what makes God "remember," why and when He "shall save man and beast."

In an era in which Jews live freely in the midst of the nations and have been restored to membership in the family of nations in their own land, we should consciously and conscientiously teach about the king of Katzia. We should do so not because we wish to show our humanistic credentials or prove that we deserve to be loved, but because the king of Katzia represents the covenant of Noah. As such, he is part of the narrative of compassion and justice that Jews call Torah.

13

A Tale of
Two Tents:
Scholarship and
Faith

Throughout this section of our study, I have been concerned with the relationship between Judaism and the Jewish people and non-Jewish "languages"; I have been asking what is inside and what is outside for educated Jews. I have also frequently noted that contemporary Jews speak several languages fluently and, largely, as insiders, so that all talk of "Jewish insider language" constantly skirts a thin line between self-understanding and preaching.

There are various aspects of the insider-outsider problem in Jewish education. One is to choose a paradigm of "us and them" that protects Jewish life and identity against assimilation and disappearance yet does so without parochial narrowing or corrosive fanaticism. The discussion of Jacob and Esau (Chapter 10) attempted to place that paradigm, and other possible ones, in historical, cultural, and moral context. Another dimension of the problem of "we" and "you" is the complex web of relationship between Israel and the Jewish Diaspora (Chapter 11). Our discussion then moved to a third feature of identity involving the covenant that gives theological grounds to Jewish particularism. I suggested an educational handle on the apparent dichotomy between Jewish particularism and universalism by exploring a biblical narrative that teaches an educational approach wherein universalism is not only "them" but also "us." This educational approach was located in the Noahide covenant of morality and common decency as the Bible of the Synagogue presents it to us.

A dimension of insider-outsider relationships and realities that I have left for last is the domain of scientific research. Contemporary Western theology has worked steadily throughout the centuries of modernity to make room, even in the mansion of traditional culture, for science, both theoretical and applied, so that for most Jews too, the insider-outsider conception appears irrelevant to scientific research. And though segregationists, who are wary of all significant contact with "the others," are alarmed by the erosive and secular influence of modern science on traditional culture, all others, in a matter-of-fact fashion, make ample room for it. Thus, even Orthodox Jewish schools assume that "secular subjects" will serenely coexist with "religious" ones and that scientific knowledge will threaten religious faith only when one of the two is "misunderstood," that is, not appropriately negotiated from a theological perspective.

Nevertheless, the matter is blatantly more problematic when scientific research takes on the fortress of faith itself—the Bible or other holy literature. In one sense, the most acute intellectual problem, at least for traditional Jewish education, is the challenge to sacred beliefs and texts on the basis of scientific inquiry, inquiry that allegedly exposes their true origins and, armed with a rhetoric of suspicion, debunks their supposedly spurious claims to revealed truth.

For educators who were always wary of the dangers of secular science, the so-called fundamentalists, there is actually no problem. They never suffered any illusions about scientific research, biblical or other. To them, scientific inquiry, with the exception of that which is oriented to technology, is fashioned in the image of the (idolatrous or heretical) views of the researchers.

But the cognitive "negotiator" who proceeds from the philosophical approach that everything known calls for a measure of integration does not have this option. She has two degrees from a reputable university and has learned those scientific ways of thinking that she uses to advantage, by habit and conviction. It would not be useful for her to consign such thinking, even when it touches upon fundamental doctrines and commitments of Judaism, to the wily ways of the cognitive majority, as Maimonides could in his *Epistle to Yemen* (see Chapter 10). Yet, at the same time, she/he will not countenance the world of Jewish faith, value, and sense being portrayed and perceived as mere fable or ancient fabrication. For were that to be accepted, there would be no Jewish "language" to defend and amplify and thus, little sense even in cultural negotiation. How, then, to proceed?

Is Scientific Inquiry Inimical to Faith?

Traditional Jews and teachers of Bible in all but outspokenly secular schools often express antipathy to biblical research or criticism, at least to its use in teaching. Yet the question, Does that lead them to shun some kinds of knowledge, to shut themselves off from an avenue of truth seeking? must be asked. And if it does so, what does that mean for the quality of traditional Jewish piety in our time and for the integrity of religious teaching in our schools?

The distaste of Orthodox believers for the academic study of Bible is easily understood. In their view, such scholarship is heretical, a secular or Protestant plot to discredit the "Old Testament" and to undermine the faith of the faithful who know it as Torah. But it seems that the non-Orthodox religious teacher also favors a holistic approach. In Moshe Greenberg's felicitous words, that teacher "seeks to reconstitute the perception of the text by an ideal reader living at a time when it had reached its present disposition." This "ideal reader" is "a personified realization of the possibilities inherent in the text at that moment."[1] The text to be studied and taken seriously, then, is the one that has reached us and is now before us. And tradition-oriented secular teachers, especially in Israel, tend to agree with religiously oriented ones that initiation into Jewish culture is achieved, primarily, by placing this foundational work in front of children and showing them how Jews have lived with and struggled with this book, interpreting it and reconciling it with other texts and other truths.

All three groups of educators, the ultratradionalists, the religiously oriented ones, and even the tradition-oriented nonreligious ones, argue that laying cultural and spiritual foundations by way of Bible study requires approaching it without a rhetoric of suspicion. They agree, although perhaps with differing degrees of fervor and angst, that academic research of the Bible "cuts Torah down to size," taking the holiness and mystery out of it. Higher biblical criticism makes the Bible into a corpus of historical, literary, and philological artifacts. Its inherent difficulties to be fathomed are transformed into "mere" documents to be compared, words that await emendation, gaps to be filled or verses to be rearranged. In the hands of the "critical" scientific Bible scholar, the text is reduced to historical and philological artifacts to be dissected, something not to be seen from within but to be "seen through." Most teachers are content to place all that at the edge of consciousness or even beyond the pale.

Yet the matter is not simple. We wish our children to become truthful human beings, and for the most part we expect them to study at universities. It is true that academically educated contemporary readers of the Bible do tend to discover difficulties in their Bible reading that arise from scientific and other modern ways of seeing things, from contemporary "habits of the heart." This intellectual inclination of modern readers engenders an interest in how things are put together and why, and nourishes the habit of reading simply out of curiosity. It is not an inclination with which traditional teachers of Torah are comfortable, and the questions raised by scientific thinking about the Bible are not ones that preoccupy these traditional teachers of Torah.

Is the choice, then, between a truth made accessible through the universal mode of science and a self-deceiving particularism that is to be described at best as quaint, and at worst, as untruthful? Only if the worlds of research and classical commentary are always or automatically at loggerheads is inquiry a clear and present danger to religious life and education. But when the scientist is drawn to his or her subject by a conviction that the Bible must be studied with the best tools at our disposal in order for contemporary Jews to reappropriate it with religious integrity and theological plausibility, there may indeed be an intriguing continuum between classic and contemporary reading. Then, the worlds of "criticism" and classical commentary may meet to yield fresh approaches that expose to view perennial questions for new reflection and commentary.

The possibility of this continuum has been discerningly pointed to by Peter Ochs, when he argues that rabbinic and ecclesiastical traditions of interpretation should be given both the benefit of the doubt and the benefit of doubt:

> the former by assuming that there are dimensions of scriptural meaning *which are disclosed only by way of the hermeneutical practices of believing communities and believing traditions of Jews and Christians* [emphasis added]; the latter by assuming, in the spirit of post-Spinozistic criticism, that these dimensions may be clarified through the disciplined practice of philological, historical, and textual/rhetorical criticism. . . . [Many scholars practice a] . . . hermeneutic claiming that the *text . . . has its meaning . . . for a normative community* rather than identifying the meaning of the text with some historical or cognitive "sense" that is available to any reader.[2]

Moshe Greenberg has pointed out that most Christian Bible scholars cultivate a "midrashic" approach to the Bible and to the New Testament in particular. He writes, "They regard themselves as a link in a continuing chain of interpreters of the message of the Bible to their brothers." His explanation is that these scholars are generally members of religious communities that are themselves part of a religiously educated and Bible-interpretative public. Most Jewish Bible scholars are not members of religious communities; they take on Old Testament studies without recourse to the Jewish interpretative community that, of course, looks to the Old Testa-

ment, the *Tanakh*, much as the Christian one does to the New Testament.[3]

A Case in Point: The Tabernacle Narrative

If understanding Torah is indeed related to membership in a believing community, I shall here speak as such a member, hoping to discover a way of speaking about Torah that will be generally communicable. That way of speaking, nevertheless, should express
"internal" scriptural meanings for educators who, though they live
in the contemporary world, also wish to teach Torah as, what our
sages called, a "unique treasure" bestowed upon Israel.

I am not a biblical scholar but an academic teacher of educators.
Though a university person, I try not to approach Torah with a
rhetoric of suspicion; my intention is to learn it and learn from it.
Nevertheless, I often find myself, especially while following the
weekly Torah reading on a Shabbat morning in the synagogue, facing some "critical" questions, in addition to some of the Rashi-type
questions we have already explored in this book.

For example, I have wondered about the discrepancies in the descriptions of the Holy Place, the Tabernacle, erected in the desert
by our ancestors by divine command. We find this Holy Place variously known as *ohel mo'ed*, "tent of meeting," and *mikdash*, "sanctuary," or *mishkan*, "dwelling for the divine Presence." Is it at the center of the camp or at a remove from it? Is it, as indicated by some
texts, the domain of priests and Levites or guarded only by Joshua,
Moses' disciple, as other texts have it? Does God speak to Moses—
and in some cases, others—from the Holy of Holies, "between the
cherubim," or outside the tent, from within a pillar of cloud at the
door of the tent? One can find instances of both, and the discrepancies are not explained or even noted by the text.

Formulating the issues that way, I have entered a universe of discourse that raises questions not quite traditional in format—or
even, in expectation. Making use of this vocabulary ("traditions,"
"discrepancies," and so on), I come upon, not simply difficulties to
be ultimately resolved, but a line of "critical" exploration: I am led

by my questions to a query that sounds detached, academic, and estranged, namely, Are there two narrative traditions here?

I often read about such narrative traditions with a certain practiced equanimity, but I admit to feeling uncomfortable with them if the scholarship in question is not somehow echoed in the tradition. Like many readers who live in a Jewish religious community, I want to learn something from the problems uncovered by contemporary scholars, and at the same time, however oddly and atavistically, I want to know whether Rashi (or someone else from within the tradition) "has already asked the same question."

For people like myself who live in interpretative communities, the question of the "tent" is particularly striking, and the problem particularly acute on the Sabbath on which the episode of the Golden Calf and its aftermath appears in the Torah reading, in Exodus 30:11–34:35 (the portion of *Ki Tissa*). Here we learn how Moses responds to God's distancing Himself from Israel after that transgression by seeming to do the same, perhaps in wrath, perhaps the better to plead his people's case:

> And Moses took the Tent and pitched it outside the camp, at some distance from the camp. And he called it the Tent of Meeting *(ohel mo'ed)* and whoever sought the Lord would go out to the Tent of Meeting which was outside the camp. And whenever Moses went out to the Tent, all the people would rise and stand, each at the entrance of his tent. And when Moses entered the Tent, the pillar of cloud would descend and stand at the entrance of the Tent while He spoke with Moses. And when all the people saw the cloud poised at the entrance of the Tent, all the people would rise and bow low, each at the entrance of his tent. The Lord would speak to Moses face to face as does one person with another. And [Moses] would then return to the camp; but his attendant, Joshua son of Nun, a youth, would not stir out of the Tent. (Exod. 33:7–11)

The committed student of Torah generally looks first to Rashi and other classic commentators for expansion of the issues raised in the text. In this instance, it seems clear that Rashi as well as all those who follow him and the dominant midrashic tradition on which he draws—which enlists the sympathies even of such moderns as Samson Raphael Hirsch, M. D. Cassuto, and Benno Jacob—insist that there was only one sanctuary tent. The tent described in this passage, we are told, is simply the tent of Moses himself. Moses withdraws from the camp as an act of identification with the divine Presence that has withdrawn from Israel.

Why then is it called a *tent of meeting*? That is because God, who refused to come within the camp after the sin of the Golden Calf, met there with Moses, as evidenced by the pillar of cloud. Benno Jacob suggests that until the real tent of meeting *(ohel mo'ed)* could be built, this one served as a substitute. He follows the midrashic school of thought according to which Moses' tent "outside the camp" was maintained only from the time of the transgression, during the summer after the Exodus, until the first of the month of Nissan the following spring, when the Tabernacle, the true tent of meeting, was completed. From then on, God spoke to Moses there. When the divine Presence returned to the community, Moses, with his tent, also returned.

But there are difficulties. If this tent was Moses' private dwelling, how was it that any Israelite could go to this tent, which was also, by virtue of the pillar of cloud that enveloped it, a holy place? There are of course homiletic answers: It is to teach us that a person who goes to the home of his or her teacher is like one who is meeting the divine Presence. For those who went to Moses' home to "learn Torah" from him, it was as though they were received by God Himself. Also, we may learn that even when God withdraws from the collective of Israel, He is always accessible to the individual who seeks Him. But these are homiletic answers, and the question remains.

For there are also further difficulties and questions. Why did seventy leaders, who received of Moses' spirit in order to share in the burden of leadership, go to the *tent* that was apparently outside the camp, unlike the other two elders, Eldad and Maidad, who stayed "within the camp" (Num. 11:24–26)? After all, at the time of that episode, the real tent of meeting, the *mishkan*, had already been constructed, and it was in the center of the camp, not outside it! Why did God scold Aaron and Miriam for their slander of Moses in the tent that God ordered them to go *out to* (Num. 12:4)? Why was Moses told to transfer leadership to Joshua in the tent where the pillar of cloud appeared and also stood over the *door* of the tent (Deut. 31:14–15)?

While looking into the subject one Shabbat morning, I perused Jacob Milgrom's scientific exegesis to the book of Numbers in the Jewish Publication Society's series of Torah cum commentary. On the *ohel mo'ed*, Milgrom writes in an excursus to Numbers:

> That there are two traditions concerning the *ohel mo'ed*, "The Tent of Meeting," is clear merely from its two loci: According to the priestly tradition it is located in the very center of the camp (e.g., 2:17; 3:38), and according to the epic tradition it is located outside the camp (e.g., 11:24–27; 12:4–5). Do they refer to the same Tent? Some scholars say yes. There is, however, a rabbinic source that speaks of two tents, one inside the camp for cultic purposes, the other outside the camp for oracular purposes (*Exodus Rabbah* 51:2; *Tanh. Pekudai* 5; *Tanh. B. Exodus*, 127; *Yal.* 1.737). Indeed, most moderns follow this rabbinic tradition.[4]

In the Name of the "First Speaker"; Two Scholars Suggest an Approach

Milgrom's thesis, as well as his style, gave me great satisfaction. As already said, I, like most traditional teachers, am not naturally comfortable with the conjectures and conclusions of biblical scholars. I am, however unjustifiably, put off by the scientific jargon in contemporary Bible studies, even by such anthropological terms as *cultic, oracular, priestly*. That is not because I am certain that academic study of religious texts is theologically shattering. On one level, I try to convince myself that these studies are not even, at least in principle, threatening. Just as biological descriptions of the reproductive processes in humans need not undermine the belief that human beings are "children of God" and created in God's image, so should understanding of historical processes not touch upon the sacred "way" taught by Scripture. My theology on the subject is very close to that expressed so succinctly by Franz Rosenzweig. In a letter to an Orthodox leader, Jacob Rosenheim, he sets the terms for his understanding of the Bible as teaching and distinguishes it from the conventionally traditional one:

> We too translate the Bible as the one and unique book; for us too it is the creation of one spirit. . . . Among us we signify him (this final formulator of the Bible) with the same code letter as that of the critical scientist. . . . In line with the hypothesis of this science, they call him R (redactor). But we understand this code letter (R) not as "redactor" but as "*rabbainu*" (our teacher) . . . he is our teacher and his theology is our doctrine.[5]

Yet elsewhere, Rosenzweig declares:

> None of . . . [the nations] knows at birth just what it is to be; their faces are not molded while they are still in nature's lap.
>
> But our people, the only one that did not originate from the womb of nature that bears nations, but—and this is unheard of—was led forth "a nation from the midst of another nation" (Deut. 4:34)—our people was decreed a different fate. Its very birth became the great moment of its life, its mere being already harbored its destiny. Even "before it was formed" it was "known," like Jeremiah its prophet. And so only he who remembers this determining origin can belong to it; while he who no longer can or will utter the new word he has to say "in the name of the original speaker," who refuses to be a link in the golden chain, no longer belongs to his people. And that is why this people must learn what is knowable as a condition for learning what is unknown, for making it his own.[6]

This passage is astounding. The same Rosenzweig who has "deprived" Moses of the authorship of the Torah now subtly, and with almost ultra-Orthodox zealousness, returns it to him. For the moment of Israel's creation is the moment that God "knows" it and determines the meaning of its existence. Everything is contained in this origin: all that will happen and all that can be said. Hence, the foundation of Jewish creativity is to refer everything back to the original speaker. The "new word" is just commentary!

It seems to me that Rosenzweig is implying that it is indeed the prophecy of Moses that has come down to us through the redactor-*rabbainu* but also that the Torah is divine instruction for us. This unknown R-*rabbainu* prophet-teacher may be seen as having radically applied the principle that became so normative for Jewish commentary, that all is said in the name of the original speaker. It is all the Torah of Moses, our teacher; and Moses' Torah, which forms Israel as a nation and for which Israel was taken out "a nation from the midst of another nation," is from Heaven, for it is God who formed us and found us in Egypt.

Moreover, if the Torah is the word of God, then historical and literary scholarship has the uniquely modern capacity to examine the historical process by which the word of God came to us. This process itself, pursued with a zeal for truth, has enormous exegetical value. Why is that? Isn't the Torah, for believing Jews, closed, in that it always refers back to what was already asked and already "given"? Yes. But it is equally true that Torah always remains open, for each generation must ask the questions again. And on the basis of what it knows, as well as in the light of the questions that have already been asked and answered—each generation must learn what was, until now, unknown.

Then, what disturbs me about biblical criticism? It is, I think, the mode of scholarship that dismisses the old questions, that punctuates its work with the assumptions and convictions of another, unacknowledged, faith that competes for the loyalty of my students with a religious Jewish one. I refer to the studies conducted under the aegis of certain positivist schools of non-Jewish scholarship that put the "Old Testament" in its place, that claim that only scholars of that positivistic faith deserve to be considered true scientists, that only they are serious scholars. So, I was happy to see Professor Milgrom, on behalf of a (Jewish) faith we shared, noting that midrashic sources that had never come to my attention "asked the same question" about the text that he does; a question he might never have asked himself but for "most moderns," scholars who, lo and behold, are described as following in the footsteps of some important "first speakers," sages of the rabbinic tradition!

In fact, there do not seem to be many such sources; the tendency of rabbinic tradition is to explain the Tabernacle as one. It is not difficult to understand why that should be so. Medieval commentators can declare that the Torah nowhere speaks of two institutions termed *ohel mo'ed*. The people built only one, and the references to the other place two thousand cubits removed from the camp can be explained as Moses' own tent. Perhaps the predisposition to reject the notion of two tents is even more pronounced in traditionally minded moderns, who wish to hold the fort against positivism and what they perceive to be an anti-Semitic undercurrent among orthodox adherents of the documentary thesis, that the Bible evolved as a composite of the work of four schools or authors.

These modern Jewish commentators know their "critical" customers. They are acquainted with theories concerning two tents. They know the culturally biased conjectures and theories of juxtaposition: about primitive versus more elaborate "cultic" worship, about prophetic simplicity versus priestly and institutional embellishments. They know that the "two tent theory" invites scholars to assume that nomadic tribes became sedentary and (literally!) put simple, pure, and prophetic religion in a box (the Ark) and hid it in the recesses of a sanctuary of gold and precious stones, guarded by a secretive clergy.

Drawing the Scientific Community into Theological Conversation

Shortly after reading Milgrom's excursus, I came upon a book of Torah commentary on the portions of the week by the late Israeli Chief Rabbi Shlomo Goren, a man well known in Israel for his outstanding halakhic and philosophical scholarship. Rabbi Goren, though, was never an ivory tower savant. Throughout his life, he was always where the action was. He was chief rabbi of the Israeli

Defense Forces for many years; he dared to make radical halakhic decisions on questions that he considered pressing and he brooked no halfway solutions. Also, he never hesitated to adopt political and social positions with great fervor but questionable finesse. Taking the bull by its horns—whatever the bull happened to be and however menacing the horns—was his trademark. Consequently, he was exorbitantly admired by some and heartily disliked by others.

In his book on the Torah portions, Rabbi Goren devotes two chapters to the problem of the tent. This Orthodox scholar, unlike, for example, the liberal Benno Jacob, states categorically that there were indeed two tents. He brings to our attention a midrash *(Sifra Zura)* that comments on Numbers 18:4: "They [the Levites] shall be attached to you [the priests] and discharge the duties of the Tent of Meeting, all the service of the Tent." On this, the fact that the verse twice mentions "tent," "Rabbi Shimon said: Here we have learned that there were two tents, the tent of [sacrificial] worship and the tent of speaking."[7]

Rabbi Goren finds this notion of two tents elaborated in the midrashic *Yalkut Shimoni*, in a comment on Numbers 11:24. The people have complained that they have no meat to eat, whereupon God promises that He will provide and tells Moses to bring seventy elders to the tent where He will "draw upon the spirit that is within you and put it upon them: they shall share the burden of the people with you and you shall not bear it alone" (v. 17). Whereupon, "Moses went out and reported the words of the Lord to the people and he gathered seventy of the elders of the people and stationed them around the tent" (v. 24). To this, the midrash comments: "This was at the *Tent of Speaking* that is outside the camp. And the outside tent had the same dimensions as the inside one and the Levites served in both with wagons [to carry them and their vessels during the travels of the Israelites] . . . for we find it written: 'And he gathered seventy of the elders of the people and stationed them around the tent.'"

It is this tent, of "speaking," that R. Goren identifies with the one Moses pitched at a distance of two thousand cubits from the camp. That is the place in which God spoke to Moses "face to face, as does one person with another." And though R. Goren notes Rashi's opinion that the outer tent was dismantled after the construction of the Tabernacle, he remarks that "one doesn't have to interpret as Rashi does." Rather, when the Torah states that Moses pitched a tent at a distance from the camp and called it Tent of Meeting, this refers to the second tent, the "tent of speaking," which was maintained together with the Tabernacle, the tent of sacrificial worship, throughout the wanderings in the desert.[8]

An additional proof text, mentioned by both Professor Milgrom and Rabbi Goren,[9] is a midrashic commentary on Exodus 38:21: "These are the accounts of the Tabernacle, even the tabernacle of testimony."

> When Moses came to Bezalel [the chief architect of the Tabernacle] and saw the amount of material left after the Tabernacle had been constructed, he said to God: "Master of the Universe! We have now made the Tabernacle and we have material left over. What shall we do with the remainder?" [The reply was:] "Make with it a tabernacle for the testimony." Moses went and did so and when afterwards he came to give the details of the expenditure involved, he told the Israelites: "So much we spent on the Tabernacle and with the remainder constructed a tabernacle for the testimony." This is the meaning of: "These are the accounts of the Tabernacle, even the tabernacle of the testimony." (*Exodus Rabbah* 51:2)

This midrash is ambiguous. Is the second tent an additional shelter or separation within the Holy of Holies for the Ark, which contains the divine commandments that *testify* to the covenant? Or does the "tabernacle of testimony" here refer to the place where people testify to their "seeking of God" and desire to speak to Him? In any case, Rabbi Goren finds in these sources evidence that the rabbinic tradition, too, speaks of two tents. In the first tent, the priests officiated and God revealed parts of the Torah that had not been "said" at Mount Sinai to Moses. In the second tent, the tent of speaking, Moses taught Torah to the people and spoke to God "outside the framework of the revelation of Torah."[10] As long as

Moses was leader of the people, he would receive the Torah in the Tabernacle at the center of the camp. God would speak to him from "between the cherubim" on the golden lid *(kapporet)* of the Ark, which symbolized the place of God's Presence. Moses would then go to the "other" tent, outside the camp, to teach the Torah to the people. In this second tent God imparted His holy spirit to the elders. Here he rebuked Aaron and Miriam and gave of His spirit to Joshua. When Moses lost his leadership, he could no longer enter the central Tabernacle to receive the Torah; he could only go the to outer one, to teach and to bless. Thus does Rabbi Goren understand the final "going" of Moses: "And Moses went and spoke all these words, [of song and of blessing] unto all Israel" (Deut. 31:1).

The differences symbolized by these two tents are significant. One tent is in the midst of the people, if they deserve it; the other, at a distance. The central one, within the community, is attended by a priesthood that serves the community; in the other, there sits alone the servant of Moses, preparing himself for his future leadership. In the first, there is a teaching imposed: God dictates His Torah. In the other, there is speaking in intimacy and fellowship. Moses speaks to God, and he speaks to his people. The Torah he teaches there is imbued with his personality and with the personal "speaking" that is an integral part of all true meeting between teacher and learner. However, the inner sanctuary, the Holy of Holies, is closed to all but Moses and, on Yom Kippur, Aaron, who enters it on that day to gain atonement for Israel. Yet even he must bring incense into the Holy of Holies to create a barrier between himself and the divine Presence (Lev. 16:12). To sum up, in the community sanctuary, only the representatives of society may offer sacrifices and atone for the community; the outer tent is for all who seek God's presence.

This seeking is not a simple undertaking: One must remove oneself by two thousand cubits, a considerable distance, from the community to do so. Moreover, in the outer tent, the divine Presence is not symbolized by shelter. God does not appear inside the tent of speaking; His cloud of Presence stands at the door, outside. Those inside, as though wishing to take shelter from His presence, are called out. They must confront Him without benefit of institutional protection.[11] They may come to hear the voice of God, but they cannot know if they will be asked to speak.

The two tents represent two aspects of religious life. On the one hand, there are the norms and symbols that make it possible for God to dwell in the midst of the community; on the other hand, there stands the individual who needs to hear God's voice, out in the open. This one may also wish to be heard and may, even while being taught Torah, speak.

The Two Tents—And My "Commentary"

I admit to a special interest in what the notion of two tents suggests. Some years ago, I wrote a book that argued for a distinction between what I called explicit religion and implicit religiosity as poles of religious life and education.[12] I suggested that "explicit" religion represents the imposed, doctrinal, and obliging elements in religion, mediated by the covenanted society, whereas "implicit religiosity" represents the individual and his or her unique personhood and approach to transcendence. I suggested there that human beings cannot live in faith if either the normative and prosaic or the poetic and existential dimensions of religious life are not fostered in education. My thesis there, which is reiterated in much of this book, was that the two need to be integrated in the personality of the teacher and that both must be adequately represented in subject matter; there must be halakhah and aggadah, Leviticus and Job. I argued that children must be helped to live under the sometimes heavy and mysterious, yet affirming and reassuring, "yoke" of commandments and also within a sphere of spiritual concern and even vulnerability and uncertainty. When I saw Milgrom's discussion, I could not help wondering whether the two tents did not, perhaps, represent these two poles of "meeting."

If this comment of Milgrom so strongly spoke to me and raised these theological reflections for me, it is probably because, like Franz Rosenzweig and most traditional Jews, I am attuned to the cultural bias, or theological conviction, that Jewish exposition is never really new and that it is best and most authentic when it is a series of glossaries or notes to the "text." Gershom Scholem once said this better than I can: "Originality is not a value highly considered by the great religions. They do not think that truth has still to be discovered. It is there, in Revelation, for all to see. . . . There is still immense room for the exercise of originality—but of an originality that does not acknowledge itself as such. Rather does it hide behind the unassuming name of commentary."[13]

I suspect that I hoped, surreptitiously, that my philosophical work in Jewish education could be shown to be "merely" a commentary on the Torah, in other words, something original within the tradition. That would mean that the issues I had raised about religion and religious education were questions that the midrash "already asks" and that there were answers that two (or more) sages had already discussed and, probably, resolved on the basis of something said by "the first speaker."

Along the same lines, I wonder why Rabbi Goren came down so decisively on the side of the scattered and, as he himself intimates, not necessarily congruent rabbinic commentaries that argue for the "two tents" approach. I conjecture that it is because modern biblical scholars have argued for this position and he wished to place the issue where he felt it belonged, with those who "had already asked that question," much as Professor Milgrom did.

But if I am right, Rabbi Goren was also saying that he might not have hit upon this problem and taken it on if the question had not "already been asked" by those modern biblical scholars and that they too had to be considered. If they stood outside the tradition and within another one, Rabbi Goren would surely have "answered" them, simply and bitingly. But perhaps he envisioned a conversation with them, based on "learning Torah," of saying original and illuminating things within a tradition of commentary and, hence, of figuratively moving from tent to tent.

PART 4

Learning About Ourselves:
Jewish Self-Education

Every Israelite is obligated to study Torah, whether he is rich or poor, in sound health or ailing, in the vigor of youth or very old and feeble . . .

. . . Until what period in life ought one to study Torah? Until the day of one's death, as it is said (Deut. 4:9) "And lest they (the commandments) depart from your heart all the days of your life."

—*Maimonides*, **Mishneh Torah,**
"**Laws of Torah Study**"

I OFTEN CITE THE FOLLOWING STORY, told to me by the late historian Uriel Tal: A hasidic young man wished to ask his *rebbe* (rabbi-mentor) how to act in a particular matter. He went to the *rebbe's* house, knocked on the door and heard the *rebbe* asking from within, "Who's there?" "Yankele," said the hasid. The response of the *rebbe* was silence; Yankele was not invited in. Assuming the rebbe to be indisposed, Yankele left and returned the following day. Again Yankele knocked, introduced himself and found himself uninvited to the *rebbe's* room.

Then he went home and thought about it. Upon coming the next day, knocking on the door and hearing the *rebbe* ask "Who's there," Yankele remained silent. Now the *rebbe's* voice came through the door loud and clear. "Come in!" And then he explained to Yankele what the young man had already worked out for himself. "Yankele," said the *rebbe*, "a person who knows who he is doesn't need a *rebbe*."

14

A QUESTION OF CHARACTER: THE CASE OF JOSEPH

WE HAVE FOLLOWED the Jewish child's education in the home and the community, through the prism of some study of Torah. We now find the young person at the portals of the university, about to face the challenges to the "language" of Judaism that await her or him there, for example, in the scientific study of sacred sources. What happens next? Anything?

Let us entertain the large assumption that a good number of the children we have in mind have received what philosophers and practitioners may consider an adequate Jewish education. They have been to Jewish schools, have had positive experiences in Jewish summer camps, and have had the benefit of homes that exemplified what schools, community centers, youth movements, and camps have presented as Jewish life patterns and values. Is their education now complete? Will there be anything that may be called Jewish self-education?

University students are likely to realize, especially on campuses where the study of liberal arts is still an option or even a requirement, that self-actualization within any cultural world requires more knowledge, understanding, and competence than anyone learns as a child. The education given to the young is only a basis on which the consenting and choosing adult builds modes of action, participation, and mastery. University study, especially in "civilization" courses and throughout the liberal arts, makes that absolutely clear with respect to Western life and letters. And what about the "language" of Judaism? Is it deemed worthy of pursuing in adult life, and does it have anything to say about self-actualization? Are there Jewish educational philosophies of individuation and finding oneself, or is it all no more than socialization, ultimately somewhat hapless within the cognitive constructions of the West or within the global village? Here we shall explore the question What is Jewish self-education? and what is a possible conceptual framework for it? by way of the story of Joseph, a onetime spoiled brat who became, through his own efforts, a paradigm of righteousness.

Maimonides Discusses
Two Types of Well-Being

A plausible place to begin this investigation is "Education for Mitzvot," an essay written by the late Isaiah Leibowitz, one of Israel's most notable savants. Leibowitz's rhetoric seems to confirm the notion that Jewish education is, and should be, zealously oriented toward narrow socialization. With regard to Judaism, he argues that it must be defined as a social and publicly recognizable phenomenon, as a lifestyle determined by the halakhah. As for Jewish education, to be continuous with the consciousness of the particular historical entity called "the Jews," it must be halakhic religious education. Hence, Jewish education is an institutional and even monolithic enterprise: It is education for the observance of the mitzvot! It is an initiation into specific patterns of community and individual behavior. In formulating the matter in this way, Leibowitz, as was his wont, unequivocally dismissed not only all secularly oriented Jewish educators (in Israel, the majority) but also religiously oriented ones who conceive religious education to be an invitation to (largely) individual encounters of the young with transcendence and the cultivation of their religious sensibilities. But one need not read to the end to understand that the matter is not so simple. For Leibowitz's references tell us that his position is based on an interpretation of Moses Maimonides' political-religious and educational philosophy.[1]

In his philosophical opus *Guide to the Perplexed*, Maimonides draws a distinction between what he considers the two objectives of the Torah: *tikkun hagoof*, the "well-being of the body," and *tikkun hanefesh*, the "well-being of the soul." The former, he states, "is established by a proper management of the relations in which we live one to another" and is attained in two ways: "first by removing all violence from our midst; that is to say, that we do not do everyone as he pleases, desires and is able to do; but everyone does that which contributes towards the common welfare; secondly, by teaching every one of us such good morals as must produce a good social state." Maimonides explains that the well-being of the body is the object of the law (the halakhah), which treats of both the negative and the positive aspects "most carefully and most minutely, because the well-being of the soul can only be obtained after that of the body has been secured."[2]

From that explanation we readily understand, as Maimonides himself explicitly states, that the well-being of the soul is the end aim of the Torah, whereas the "well-being of the body," that is, the proper and moral organization of society, is a means to that end. As for that well-being of the soul, it cannot be achieved by the simple in the philosophical manner we may anticipate that it can by the sophisticated. For the simple, it is the sum of "correct opinions communicated to [them] according to their capacity," often in metaphoric or allegoric forms so that even they will have at least an inkling of metaphysical truth, the knowledge of which distinguishes the human from the beast. But for those who are endowed with wisdom or are ready to make strenuous efforts, the second end [the well-being of the soul] envisions [the person's] becoming an "actually intelligent being; he knows about the things in existence all that a person perfectly developed is capable of knowing." The achievement of this end, states Maimonides, "does not include any action or good conduct, but only knowledge, which is arrived at by speculation, or established by research."

We would seem to have a clear contradistinction between the social end (of the "body"), both in its negative aspect of "removing all
violence from our midst" and in its positive aspect of "teaching
good morals that must produce a good social state," and the individual end, which is concerned with knowing the truth, on either a
popular or a pristinely philosophical level. And the latter, so we
seem to hear Maimonides saying, is indifferent to "any action or
good conduct." But that, as we shall see, presents a deceptive dichotomy. For "knowing the truth" is ultimately synonymous with
knowing and "loving" God, and that love mandates practice. How
so?

In the final chapter of *Guide to the Perplexed*,[3] Maimonides distinguishes among four conceptions of human perfection. First, there is
the totally unworthy and trivial "perfection" of property, "the possession of money, garments, furniture, servants, land and the like."
This perfection is completely "external" and often transient. The
second perfection, concerned with health, strength, and physical
well-being, is always relative: Man possesses it (temporarily), together with the lowest of the animals. The third perfection is
higher and is, indeed, the aim of most of the precepts (of the
Torah). Here is found moral perfection and excellence of character.
However, "even this kind is only a preparation for another perfection, and this [moral perfection] is not sought for its own sake."
The reason for that is that "all moral principles concern the relations of people to one another," but true and ultimate perfection of
a person is within him or herself. It is in no way external. It is not
dependent on the presence of others who are the objects of morality but is exclusively the possession of the individual who has
achieved it.[4]

Hence, following Aristotle, Maimonides posits a fourth and
"true" perfection: the achievement of the highest intellectual faculties, "the possession of such notions which lead to true metaphysical opinions as regards God. With this perfection man has attained
his final object; it gives him true human perfection; it remains to
him alone; it gives him immortality, and on its account he is called
man."[5]

However, that (Aristotelian) conclusion is not where matters end for Maimonides. He finds the proof text for the true dimensions of the fourth perfection in Jeremiah 9:22–23, which begins: "Thus says the Lord, let not the wise man glory in his wisdom, nor let the mighty man glory in his might, let not the rich man glory in his riches; but let him that glories glory in this, that he understands and knows Me."[6]

Maimonides reads the prophetic statement not only as a philosopher but also as a midrashic teacher. Thus he finds in it, first of all, the negation or qualification of the first three perfections. The "rich man," the mighty man (of strong body), and even the wise man, the one of good moral principles, should refrain from "glorying" in their achievements. Only the one who "understands and knows Me" deserves to do that. However, "understanding" and "knowing" have to be properly conceived, and for that we need the text in its entirety:

> The prophet does not content himself with explaining that the knowledge of God is the highest kind of perfection; for if this only had been his intention, he would have said, "But in this let him who glories glory, that he understands and knows Me" and stopped there. . . . But [he concludes with the words, "I am the Lord who exercises mercy, justice and righteousness in the world, for in these things I delight, says the Lord]." We are thus told in this passage that the divine acts that ought to be known and ought to serve as a guide for our actions are, *hesed*, loving kindness, *mishpat*, judgement, and *tzedakah*, righteousness. . . . The object of the above passage is therefore to declare that the perfection in which man can truly glory is attained by him when he has acquired—as far as this is possible for man—the knowledge of God, which is incomplete without the knowledge of His providence. . . . Having acquired this knowledge he will then be determined always to seek loving kindness, judgement and righteousness, and thus to imitate the ways of God.[7]

Thus, perfection of the soul is reached through philosophical inquiry that brings a person to the knowledge of God and therefore to a knowledge of God's moral attributes, those that the spiritually perfect person understands as attributes to be emulated. Without this emulation, God is not really "known." The morality that flows from this knowledge is different than that of the third perfection insofar as it derives from a philosophical comprehension: It is a characteristic of the self-achieved religious personality, rather than mere social conscience, established within the confines of a social contract that enables societies to protect themselves from violence and anarchy. The morality of the fourth perfection is built on the firm basis of wisdom, which, in turn, is understood by the wise as demanding appropriate sensibilities and action. As Hartman states: For the perfected individual, "theoretical knowledge of God affects practice."[8]

Now we may return to Leibowitz and his seeming obsession with socialization, that is, the imparting of the method and patterns of "the well-being of the body." But a close and more extensive reading demonstrates that what our thinker really says is that education for the observance of the mitzvot is the sum total of externally imposed education, that is, education that is societal and institutional. All that society and its institutions are capable of is to teach social proprieties and usages and fundamental doctrines. To entrust society with more is useless, for each person must embark on the high road to *tikkun hanefesh*, "perfection of the soul," alone. It is also spiritually dangerous to incorporate individuation into the curriculum, for the learner may be led on the road to spiritual maturity by teachers who take the name of wisdom in vain. Hence, the purpose of the seemingly arid and conventional education for mitzvot, is to lay the groundwork for the individual to find his or her way to perfection of the soul, which is achievable only by way of the commandments.

[Although] religious education is aught but the imposition of the yoke of Torah and commandments upon the person, nevertheless it is clear and obvious to us that study of Torah and observance of the commandments do not exhaust what Torah [means]. Within the Torah itself . . . there are elements that are means to an end and elements that are ultimate ends . . . the being and essence of [Jewish] religion is conveyed by "And you shall love [the Lord your God with all your heart and all your soul and might]," yet it is impossible to include in religious education anything but the instruments of religion—the practical commandments, and no education in the world can give a person more than preparation towards the end goal [of his or her life]. What is above and beyond that is not within the domain of educational influence but is given over to the personal and inner decision-making of the individual after having received educational training. Religious education is not the imparting of values but training for their attainment. Religious values cannot be imparted! "Education is naught but a method [for the ultimate education that individuals must give themselves] and [one] may not give [young people] anything beyond these methodological tools."[9]

Leibowitz is here interpreting not only the Maimonidean conception of the two end goals (of the body and of the soul) and the means of their realization but also, albeit with paradoxical elaboration, the classic rabbinic assumption that the "education" of the child is a kind of training for the observance of the mitzvot that becomes obligatory at the advent of adulthood (age twelve for girls, thirteen for boys) and remains obligatory upon the individual throughout life. This obligation applies with special force to the commandment of Torah study. The child, as it were, is trained to observance and then, as an adult, must continually deepen his or her understanding of what the observance means, what it encompasses, how it enables the individual to become what he or she may become, on the basis of a philosophical understanding of the Torah. Real education, in this conception, begins after training in the mitzvot and never ends, because the learner is called upon to perpetually deepen his discernment of Torah and the world in order to arrive at the philosophical, yet active, "love of God." In other words, the individual is initiated into the community, its patterns of practice, and its normative expectations and must then choose a path to perfection of the soul, through the channel of "learning" Torah. It is hoped that this person will stay within the community, cleave to its patterns of "perfection of the body," and teach young members of the community to ascend the lower rungs of the ladder set firmly upon the earth and reaching Heaven. Rather than being an extracurricular activity, adult education is the goal of what should be termed childhood training. Education, that is, the learning of Torah, is the way individuals draw themselves out and strive for their potential, and this potential comes fully into its own only in adulthood.

The import of this orientation to "education" has been well expressed in existential terms by Van Cleve Morris. Morris describes the moment when "the individual first discovers himself as existing," when he realizes that he cannot simply be coerced. Paradoxically, this realization marks the beginning of true responsibility. The young person discovers an "existential moment," which, in Maimonidean terms, may be described as the entrance into the portals of "perfection of the soul." It may begin, suggests Morris, with parents tongue-lashing their child for some misdemeanor and with the child sullenly responding, "Well, I didn't ask to be born, y'know."[10]

That, what Morris calls "the child's first complete existential thought," is shot through with irony. For though the remark is "overpoweringly true," it means "absolutely nothing. We consider such a remark idiotic and ridiculous . . . it has the fatal flaw of total irrelevance." "So you did not ask to be born: what a remarkable insight. But you have spoken a vacuous verity. For whether you asked to come or not, *here you are!* Here you are in the world, responsible for yourself."[11]

Leibowitz might well translate Morris's insight into Jewish terms as follows: Having been "socialized" through training in the observance of the mitzvot but without being responsible because you were only being "trained," you are now free because you have understood that "you didn't ask to be born." But now you are responsible. To whom? That depends on you, but certainly to yourself, to the kind of person you wish to be. From now on you will be the educator of yourself, and this education will be "for its own sake," that is, for the sake of who you want to be, in the presence of whomever you will see yourself responsible to. The religious educators of the community have taught you to direct your sense of responsibility to God. They hope that in the course of your advance toward "perfection of the soul," you will grasp what they meant by that responsibility and arrive at it by your own understanding through your own spiritual (i.e., philosophical) search. The greatest tragedy signaling the failure of education, then, is to be incapable of "learning," of self-education, of moving toward perfection of the soul, perhaps because no adequate "training" preceded the existential moment at which self-education begins.

Can we trace these ideas, of Maimonides and his interpreters, as well as of educational philosophers, to the Torah itself? More to the point of this book, what can the Torah, through its laws and narratives, tell us about education as self-education, as moving the individual in the direction of the fourth perfection, of the soul?

And Now, to Joseph

Only one personage in the entire Torah is, in rabbinic literature, called the righteous one: Joseph, son of Jacob. It should therefore be a good text and context to explore the processes of self-education, of moving toward the perfection that Maimonides finds in the ninth chapter of Jeremiah.

When we meet Joseph in Genesis 37, he impresses us as an unpleasant adolescent. He tells tales about his brothers to his father. Jacob, in turn, apparently seeing in him a reflection of his beloved and prematurely deceased Rachel, favors and pampers him. Joseph dreams of domination over his brothers and cannot wait to tell everyone all about it. He is self-centered and insensitive. Not unnaturally, his brothers cordially hate him and cannot "speak peaceably with him." Finally, when the opportunity arises, the brothers sell him into slavery, at Judah's demand "doing him the favor" of not simply killing him. How could such a person come to deserve the appellation "the righteous one"? How did he change?

This question cannot be answered by reference to his successes. The man evidently knew how to run a high-class household like

Potiphar's and, finally, Egypt itself; he clearly had the knack of dealing with the rich and powerful. Though once betrayed by the master and mistress of the house (Potiphar and his wife), he bounced back: He learned how to make himself at home in their world. This shows him to be resourceful. But righteous? He was, so the midrashic teacher would have it, also inordinately interested in the second of the four perfections of the self, that of bodily health and well-being. That raised eyebrows among the midrashic masters. On the verse "and Joseph was of beautiful form and fair to look at" (Gen. 39:6), the Midrash states:

> Seeing himself as a ruler [in the house of Potiphar] he began eating and drinking and curling his hair. Said the Holy One: "Your father is in mourning [for you] and you curl your hair? I shall incite the bear [Potiphar's wife] against you." And so [v. 7] immediately thereafter, [his master's wife cast her eyes upon Joseph and she said, "Lie with me."]. (*Tanhuma*, *Vayeshev* 8)

Once again, where is the "righteousness" of Joseph?

The story of Joseph, perhaps the most dramatic short story in the Torah, has many points to make. But it is unclear about a very central issue, namely, Whose story is this? Is God telling us about Joseph, so that we have the unfolding of divine Providence, or is it Joseph's story, about himself and about God?

Thomas Mann, in *Joseph the Provider*, the fourth novel of his tetralogy, describes the final reconciliation between Joseph and his brothers, after Jacob's death, and indirectly ponders this crucial question:

> "But brothers, my dear old brothers!" he answered, and bent down to them with his arms stretched out. "What you are saying, as though you were afraid—you talk as though you were and want me to forgive you! Am I then as God? Down in Egypt they say I am as Pharaoh and he is called god; but he is just a sweet pathetic thing. When you talk to me about forgiveness it seems to me you have missed the whole

point of the story we are in. I do not blame you for that. One can easily be in a story and not understand it."[12]

What the point of the story is and how it should be understood as a story of Torah that we are "in," is a subject that has preoccupied commentators and teachers and students of literature for millennia. Here, then, is one more brief attempt to understand the story.

The Torah Tells the Story of Joseph

I shall emphasize several points to begin the exploration. The first is that the Joseph story is, indeed, a story. There is plot and character development; there are climaxes and a "resolution." The second point is that the question, Whose story is being told? is crucial. Is Moses recording God's story of Joseph, or is this God's story of the *brit ben habetarim*, the "covenant of the parts," that destined the Israelites to bondage in Egypt? Or, perhaps, it is the story of God's "search" for the one of the tribes who deserved to become the leader of Israel? Or is it perhaps, as Thomas Mann suggests at the very end of his tetralogy, also Joseph's story of God, telling us what Joseph thought God wanted Joseph to "narrate" about Him? To put these questions in our specific terms of reference: Is this a story of Joseph's self-education as he tries to understand God, or is it God's education of him, which he only slowly identifies as such (as "the story he's in")?

In either case, this story is clearly a bildungsroman, a novella of "personal development," the story of an education. Ultimately, it is a success story. We follow the fortunes of a pampered and unpleasant young man who grows up to become wise and, eventually, righteous. To the reader who is inspired by it, because it shows what a person can do or what God can do for a person, it demonstrates the possibilities in a life. For the not yet old, it rekindles hopes that may have prematurely faded. For those who look back on most of their lives, it is, in Erik H. Erikson's fine phrase, an invitation to choose "ego integrity" in place of despair.[13]

The third point is that the story is replete with things that are not what they seem to be. The hero is in hiding and we are "in on it" together with him and, if he is also hiding from himself, even more than he. We wonder when the other characters will find out, catch on, so that all can "live happily ever after." Reading the Joseph story, we are reminded that in our own lives too much is playacting, and much takes place in a suspense of waiting. Few of us reflect, as Joseph seems to have done, that God is "behind" the whole story that he is "in," but that possibility may enter our minds at times.

The fourth point: What happens in the story has a rich and complex background, and the tale is leading to a climax that is weighty with half-hidden significances. Why did the brothers hate Joseph so much? Could it have been only because of the "coat of many colors" and some childish dreams? Was it indeed simply "causeless hatred" that here and in later history led inextricably to exile? What are the tangled relationships here, and why are they so fractured? The story is filled with intimations of mystery that the reader, certainly the midrashic one, examines carefully for clues. When is Joseph called son, and when is he called brother, and by whom? When is Jacob referred to as our father, thy servant? When does Jacob plead, when give in? When is he dependent on his sons, and when does he exercise authority? What does he suspect and what does he know?

Fifth, there are features of the story that seem all wrong. And yet we know they make the story what it is, and we expect that these matters will eventually be explained to us. Why does Joseph torment his brothers with harshness and remoteness, with imprisonment, accusations, and frame-ups? Most amazing, why does the young man, as the overseer in Potiphar's house and as Pharaoh's vizier, never, in all of twenty-two years, contact his father? After all, he knows that the old man back in Canaan believes his most beloved son to be dead! Doesn't his father's love count for anything? Doesn't he want to ease his pain? Why not a letter sent with some caravan? How can that omission be justified? How can such a person be called righteous? There must be something we, and perhaps Joseph too, do not see—or understand—yet. Or perhaps, does he think that such heartlessness is part of God's plot and that he is therefore free to ignore his father as he does?

The sixth point is that because it is a story, in the midst of the incomprehensible, mysterious, and outrageous, there are elements we recognize, that make "story sense." Some are even the staples of fairy tales, as Bettleheim in his already classic *The Uses of Enchantment*,[14] has delineated them. There is the young son, an outcast among his brothers, seemingly a "dummy," an impractical dreamer. Joseph is the beloved son, yet the father sends him inexplicably off on a mission that leaves him on his own, that marks the beginning of his growing up. For the first time, the boy experiences the always-protecting and doting father as remote, seemingly indifferent, perhaps helpless, but easily imagined as betraying his beloved child.

Joseph finds himself suddenly at the center of a new story. The once-pampered boy finds himself in one pit after another. He has to extricate himself and find himself. He is the hero who must struggle toward maturity, facing sexual temptation and assaults on his ego on the way to the fulfillment of his destiny. He is the one who eventually becomes "king," with a "magic cup." He is in a position to judge his brothers and exact retribution from them. They, of course, cannot imagine that the hero on whose mercy their lives now depend is the "dummy," but they will eventually recognize his greatness. But because this is Torah and not a fairy tale, such as "The Three Feathers" or "The Goose Girl" or "Cinderella," we wonder how it happened that Jacob wasn't in on it all; why he didn't know or act? And why did Joseph follow the plot (of God?) rather than his conscience. Or could it indeed be, as Maurice Samuel suggests in his critical portrait of Joseph, that he did not have a conscience?[15]

Naturally, having read the story many times, we know that it will all turn out well. But that is also true of character development novels and fairy tales. We know that in the bildungsroman, the trials of reaching adulthood and maturity are indispensable and that the hero is often carrying too much "baggage" to be concerned with others in attaining his or her identity. But do the tribulations attending growth justify what happens here, what Joseph does? Is

Joseph simply a maturing adolescent? Can all that he puts his father Jacob through be explained as necessary for Joseph's growing
up?

This central problem, why Joseph did not inform his father that
he was alive, much perturbed students and masters of the Torah.
Likewise, they asked why, when his brothers came to Egypt to buy
grain in the years of famine, Joseph did not immediately make himself known to them. One prominent answer is that of the thirteenth-century Nahmanides, generally referred to by the acronym
Ramban. Ramban links the two problems, suggesting a common
motivation. Joseph, he says, in his first dream of domination, had
seen eleven sheaves, representing his brothers, bowing down to his
sheaf (i.e., to him!). This dream could only be realized if Benjamin,
who had been left at home with Father Jacob, would be brought to
him as well. Hence he demanded that the brothers leave Simon as a
hostage, to be thrown into a prison "pit" (an apt act of retributive
justice),[16] and that they go home and bring Benjamin back with
them. Thereafter, he could have his father come too, so that the
second dream, of "the sun, the moon and the stars" bowing down
to him, would also be realized.[17]

Nehama Leibowitz Expresses Concern
About Joseph's Action

Nehama Leibowitz, in her *Studies in Bereshit* [Genesis], and in her
teaching, dealt extensively with the Joseph stories. She is not happy
with Nahmanides' solution, which seems ruthless and inappropriate for one who is ostensibly a righteous person. She cites the cri-
tique of R. Yitzhak Arama, the fifteenth-century Spanish sage
whose commentary is known as *Akedat Yitzhak*, the "Binding of
Isaac": "What did this [making sure his dreams came true] benefit
Joseph? And even if it profited him, he should not have sinned
against his father. As for the dreams, leave it to Him Who sends
them to make them come true. It seems infinitely foolish for a man
to strive to fulfill his dreams, which are matters beyond his control."[18]

Yet Leibowitz cannot agree with the approach of the *Akedat Yitzhak* either. She insists that "leaving everything to God" and seeing "dreams" as out of human control is not the biblical way.

> Gideon (Judg. 7:14–15) did not leave it to Providence to fulfill the dream that foretold that he would deliver Midian into the hands of Israel. Rather he immediately made practical preparations to further the success of Israel's armies. Similarly, though Jeremiah foretold that God would restore the Jewish people to their land after seventy years of exile in Babylonia, the leaders of the Babylonian exile did not wait for it to come to pass. But before the seventy years were up Zerrubavel and Jeshua the son of Jozadak [their leaders] went up to the land with forty two thousand three hundred and three score of their fellow Jews (Ezra 2).[19]

We should note that the *Akedat Yitzhak*, no less than Nahmanides, is assuming that Joseph's dreams are prophetic harbingers of what is to come, of Joseph's redemptive role in the history of his family, and of hungry nations. They view the story as God's, and Joseph as only "in" it. But a moral-philosophical problem arises: Is the person playing a role in God's story justified in thinking he or she "has no choice"? Or is acting on that deterministic belief also a choice? The *Akedat Yitzhak*, it would seem, is morally troubled by the choice Joseph makes. Because Joseph may be assuming that he has no choice, for "the dream must be fulfilled," he considers himself free to act ruthlessly and manipulatively, even toward his own father! R. Yitzhak Arama suggests that a person can and must make moral choices despite divinely established destiny. Although historical "process" may be left to God, we are commanded to moral sensitivity and action.

Leibowitz stands between these two positions. In her view, human beings indeed have much choice and are to be praised for initiative, as long as they move themselves and events in the direction of destiny. But this choice, though also "moving history along" as prophetically envisioned, may never be devoid of moral considerations. Hence her question: "Could not Joseph have accomplished

the realization of his dream without making his brothers and his father suffer?" Even when a given action is seen as necessary, we expect moral people to consider the consequences of their ways, to
look for the most ethical possible way of acting. Joseph seems
delinquent in that regard. He still appears as aiming merely for the
superficial perfection, of power.

N. Leibowitz proposes another thesis. Perhaps Joseph did not reveal himself to his brothers, thus causing his family anguish, not because he was concerned with his own role in making the dreams
come true, but rather because he wished to determine whether his
brothers, who had sinned against him, had truly repented. If that is
the reason for his harshness, then, within our conceptual framework, we may see him as having moved from the first perfection of
the self, of power and riches, to the third rung on the ladder of self-
perfection, that of moral rectitude.

This solution to the problem of Joseph's apparent heartlessness is
based on Maimonides' halakhic model of the process of *teshuvah*,
"repentance." According to Rambam, repentance consists of four
stages: The first three are that the sinner (1) becomes aware of
his/her sin; (2) expresses remorse; and (3) confesses to having
sinned. But consciousness of sin, regret, and verbal remorse are not
sufficient for *teshuvah gemurah*, "complete repentance." That is
achieved only when the former transgressor finds him/herself once
more "confronted by the identical thing wherein he or she trans-
gressed, within a situation that allows for the possibility of committing the transgression." If truly repentant, the (former) sinner does
not succumb again but instead resists the temptation, motivated
only by repentance and not by fear or weakness. Rambam gives an
example of such *teshuvah gemurah*. "If [a man] . . . had relations
with a woman forbidden to him and he was subsequently alone with
her, still in the full possession of his passion for her and his virility
unabated and in the country where the transgression took place; if
he [nevertheless] abstained and did not sin, this is a true penitent"
(*Mishneh Torah, Hilkhot Teshuvah* 2:1).

Joseph, according to this approach, both spurred his brothers to
teshuvah and tested them to see whether they were "completely re-

pentant." He made the brothers aware of their sin, got them to verbalize their guilt and to express remorse (e.g., Gen. 42:21), and he then placed Benjamin in a situation that was almost identical with the one in which the brothers had sold and betrayed him, Joseph, two decades before. Joseph must have suspected that Jacob would favor the "surviving" son of Rachel, his beloved wife, and would fear for the life of this young man more than, say, the life of Simon. Also, Joseph now pampered Benjamin as Father Jacob had pampered him. He made it easy for the brothers to "sell" him into slavery. All they had to do was to agree that Benjamin deserved it for having stolen Joseph's divining cup. The brothers, by categorically refusing to abandon Benjamin, despite the pain his preferred treatment by both father and the "Egyptian" vizier must have caused them, demonstrated true and complete penitence. Since they had learned to be true brothers, Joseph could then reveal himself to them, as a brother.

But even this solution does not appear to meet Leibowitz's requirement, that Joseph not make his brothers and father suffer. True, the agonized reactions of the brothers to the trials and tribulations engineered by Joseph make the story deeply moving. The brothers recall how they had been deaf to his pleas and realize, because of the strange things happening to them, that "God has found out" their (previous) iniquity. But is Joseph justified in putting them through all of that? Can he do it without "making his brothers and his father suffer"? Hardly. And the unease we feel is articulated with startling frankness by Rabbi Naftali Zvi Berlin, in his commentary, *Ha'amek Davar*. Rabbi Berlin wonders why Joseph, when the brothers appear before him for the second time, having now brought Benjamin with them, asks about the well-being of their father: "And he asked them of their welfare, and said, 'Is your father well, the old man of whom you spoke? Is he yet alive?'" (Gen. 43:27).

Ha'amek Davar suggests that various thoughts were passing through Joseph's mind: "Now that the first dream is fulfilled [with all eleven brothers here] how about the second? . . . Perhaps the gift sent by Father suffices for the fulfillment of the second dream as well? . . . But no, if I keep Benjamin here, Father is sure to come as well [and then] the second dream, [of the sun and moon and of eleven stars bowing down to me] will be really fulfilled." Rabbi Berlin finds that had Judah not mentioned in his plea to Joseph for mercy that the captivity of Benjamin would drive their father to his grave (Gen. 44:34), Joseph would have gone through with his plan to frame and imprison Benjamin. But Judah's speech is still to come. Hence, the reason for Joseph's asking about the father's welfare is that he "had to know whether [Jacob] was in really good health and it would not harm him that Benjamin be detained. And they [the brothers] did not understand [his motivation] and thought he asked for reasons of affection and love."

As *Ha'amek Davar* describes him here, Joseph is hardly a sage teacher of *teshuvah*; he seems more a benign and calculating inquisitor! The brothers, who touchingly "thought that Joseph acted out of affection and love" in inquiring about the welfare of their father, seem far nobler than he. Of course Joseph could have claimed that the dreams, the penitence, and the reunion of the family are "all the same story," elements of God's plan. But would that have made it better? Doesn't the *teshuvah* theory lose its luster when put together with Joseph's wish to see his dreams fulfilled? Can the *teshuvah* element be used to "protect" Joseph from the charge of inflicting pain on his brothers and his father? Is it by virtue of this trial that Joseph should be considered a *tzaddik*, "righteous person"? Is this the end-product of the (self-)education described in the Torah's bildungsroman of Joseph? That is hard to believe.

Perhaps the "*teshuvah* teaching" approach, that Joseph was just testing the authenticity of their repentance, needs to be reexamined. True, in many character development stories, some wise and saintly individual, like Reb Saunders in Chaim Potok's novel *The Chosen*, is putting some young person (in that case, his insensitive son Daniel) through an ordeal "for his own good." But what is more frequently the case is that a far from perfect person vents unconscious rage or weakness by inflicting pain, which is rationalized as "educational," for the victim's alleged benefit. Which description better fits Joseph as the brothers stood before him as the accused?

The fact that the Torah here chooses to teach us by way of a story may suggest that we look at Bettleheim once again to learn something more about stories. Perhaps he can help us to decipher the rich background and the half-hidden significances in the tale.

And so we recall: Joseph has a history. His father "loved him too much." The contemporary Bible scholar Uriel Simon once suggested that the father (Jacob), who was insufficiently loved by his own father, was determined that "his Joseph" would not suffer as he had. In this context, Simon pointed out that no one can protect his or her children from having to live their own lives. As Bettleheim would say, the hero, in order to actualize his potential(!) heroism, must be "sent out into the world." Joseph was much sinned against by the brothers, but he also provoked them mercilessly. Moreover, his father seemed to have deserted him. Perhaps Joseph, in not contacting the old man for twenty-two years, was acting out his anger. Indeed, his behavior reminds us how Jacob behaved when, upon returning home from Laban's house, he tarried at Sukkot for many months before going on to Hebron to rejoin his father!

We can understand Joseph and his less than perfect behavior as we follow him toward the fulfillment of his dreams and/or, of God's plans. But is he the person who may inflict suffering on others, to "redeem" them by making them understand their own wrongdoing? Does he even understand his own motives sufficiently to make him the teacher of his brothers *and of his father*, and to cause them suffering "for their own good"?

Joseph's Path to Righteousness

If he does not understand his own motives, when does Joseph truly deserve the appellation, *Yosef Ha-tzaddik*, "Joseph the righteous one"? Where is the real denouement of this character development story that teaches us the fourth perfection of the self through the (ultimately) righteous personality of Joseph?

Actually, we are shown several self-educative stations on the way to Joseph's attainment of these heights. He withstood temptation when Potiphar's wife attempted to seduce him. At that moment, says a midrash, "he saw the image of his father appearing before him" (*Genesis Rabbah* 87:7). At the last moment, he took seriously the voice of conscience that asked, "What would Father say?" He had then already acquired "character," defined by the ability and strength to distinguish between right and wrong, between the permitted and the forbidden, even, and especially, "when no one is looking." The education for mitzvot received from Father Jacob set limits to the permissible, allowing Joseph to proceed toward the goal and the meaning of the commandments on his own. When he is in prison, we find his former arrogance mellowed into a self-confidence tempered by religious humility. He invites Pharaoh's butler and baker to relate their dreams and offers to interpret them: "Are not interpretations from God?" (Gen. 40:8). We find him wise in counsel and firm in administration. And then, after testing his brothers so cleverly, he is reconciled to them and to his father.

But we have found this "testing" problematic. It is moral, but narrowly so, appropriate perhaps for the third perfection of the self of which Maimonides speaks. But there is little *hesed*, "loving-kindness," in it. Therefore, it may be that we should look for the full realization of Joseph's righteousness not at the moment the brothers stand before him but only much later, after the death of Jacob. It was then, the Torah tells us, that the brothers, fearful that Joseph would now take revenge on them for having sold him, send him a message:

> Your father commanded before his death, "So shall you say to Joseph: Forgive, I pray, the transgression of the servants of the God of your father." And Joseph wept when they spoke to him. And his brothers also went and fell down before him and said, "Behold we are your bondsmen." And Joseph said to them, "Fear not, for am I in place of God?" (Gen. 50:16–19)

We might imagine Joseph happy at this moment. His dreams of lordship over his brothers have been completely fulfilled. The brothers are terrified, and he has absolute power over them. And yet Joseph weeps. He is certain that the brothers have told their father nothing of the sale of Joseph and of their lying to him about finding the bloody coat of many colors in some distant field. So at this moment they are also lying because they are frightened. At that, Joseph weeps and says to them, in the identical words used by Jacob to rebuke Rachel for pleading that he "give" her children, "Am I in place of God?" (Gen. 30:2). But now, as Thomas Mann well intimates, the words are not harsh and insensitive and there is no rebuke in them. What Joseph means by them is, Why do you think that I have the right to punish you? Do not be impressed with the external perfections of power.

Joseph has, with this exclamation, redeemed the harsh words of his father to his mother. He has reconciled himself to his brothers. And, perhaps most important, he now understands why he himself, as our sages tell us, never told his father that his brothers had sold him.[20] He now realizes what he must have intuited seventeen years before, when his father came down to Egypt, namely, that divulging that secret to the old father, however morally justified, was not the way to the fourth perfection of the self.

15

LEARNING TO COPE
WITH WHAT WE
REMEMBER

EVERYONE OF US WAS RAISED by parents or others who mentored us. Sometimes these people were inspiring and often admirable. But alas, as we get older, we look back and think about what they did not only *for* us but also *to* us, and sometimes their failings have left us resentful and scarred. We all remember some teachers fondly but others, less so. The latter we would prefer to forget, and we wonder why we did not have the will or the courage to say to them, "I didn't ask to be born," or "Let me be."

What has the tradition of Torah to teach us about understanding our parents and mentors and dealing with our experiences of them so that we not remain "stuck," unable to educate ourselves? I shall try to approach this question as the Midrash itself often does, from a context that hardly seems relevant, beginning in what seems to be "out in left field." And in the midrash we shall be studying, the subject of this chapter, though not treated directly in the text, will eventually come into view.

Living Responsibly:
"A Psychology of Daytime"

We begin with a commentary of Rabbi Samson Raphael Hirsch, an already-mentioned leader of early modern Orthodoxy. In a discussion of "symbolism" in the commandments, Rabbi Hirsch offers an explanation of why such acts as the blowing of the shofar, circumcision, and rendering legal judgments must be carried out in daylight hours and are invalid when performed at night. His thesis is that these are acts that seem to impose themselves authoritatively on human consciousness and will; something about them is mysterious and intimidating. Were they to be performed at night, they would inculcate a "psychology of night." They would convey the message that human beings are puny, rightfully cowering in the face of overwhelming cosmic forces. The "psychology of night," he says, bespeaks dependence, fear and insecurity.[1]

Hirsch contrasts this "psychology of night" with a "psychology of daytime." During the day, he argues, people take control over their lives, regain a confidence that they can cope with reality and live responsibly. Therefore, the mitzvot that seem as though they might educate the soul to mindless subservience, that suggest *night*, must be carried out during the daylight hours, when people feel free of the insecurities and trepidations of the night, when they feel themselves to be in charge—of themselves and of their world. Hirsch declares that Jews are bidden to find God where they find themselves, where they are active and responsible. They are not to run away from themselves into "nighttime" in order to find God.

Educating for Life

Hirsch's insight stands in sharp contrast to at least one feature of George Orwell's well-known allegorical novel of Communist totalitarianism, *Animal Farm*. In this parable there is a shady and socially peripheral character named Moses the Raven. At first, after the revolution of the animals that overthrows human oppression, Moses is banished from the revolutionary society of Animal Farm, but when things become bleak there, he is allowed to come back and to rehearse his clichéd promises of eternally green pastures, of plentiful hay and sugar, to the weary and forlorn beasts.

Detractors of Jewish and other religious beliefs and educational credos have often described them as variations on the theme of Moses the Raven, preaching and promising "pie in the sky" to the lean and hungry in a grim and sparse world. Hirsch is, of course, taking conscious issue with that "pie in the sky" orientation. Religious sensibilities, convictions, and loyalties, he is saying, are not an escape from real life. They are not an alternative option to courage, responsibility, or reality. We may expect him to agree that success in Jewish education is reflected wherever Jewish action, learning, and "being in the world" are not viewed as alongside and in contrast to the other, real, matters in our lives. Within a "psychology of daytime," we wish for Jewish language and literature to be a framework for seeing the totality of life, dealing with it, dwelling within it, even though it is complicated and even when it is unpleasant. In Hirsch's terms, acts of faith that may appear to suggest dependence and passivity should be imbued with "the psychology of daytime," when we know what we are doing and feel capable of coping with the complexities of life. Education should be a daytime activity; otherwise it will stultify the self-education that is intended as its purpose and "perfection."

The entire Torah, and Genesis in particular, may be viewed as establishing "daytime" foundations for spiritual life. There we are taught to view religion, that is, the meeting of God and people and what they do when they meet, as paradoxical, ironic, and often painful. In the Torah men and women never "live happily ever after" as a consequence of, or as a reward for, seeking God or serving Him. Genesis may be said to be primarily about genuine *yirat shamayim*, "fear of Heaven." That is, it teaches by (positive and negative) example how people may learn to be both creaturely and reliable, responsible and dependent. It describes how, when a choice between dependence and responsibility must be made, they are called upon to decide which is appropriate.[2] Not surprisingly, therefore, decisions are constantly being made in its tales about what is suitable and just, and questions addressed to these decisions are a staple of Torah study: Should Abraham have banished Ishmael to save Isaac from his influence? Should he have agreed to offer his son as a burnt offering? Should Rebecca have deceived Isaac to assure the blessing for the one she knew to be the right son? Should Rachel have stolen her father's gods? Should Joseph have tested his brothers?

Genesis is a book that describes these tensions, and not unexpectedly, it has its share of quarreling, family conflicts, and people doing their best under the circumstances. There are blessings there but also aroused passions, hopes, and occasional bitterness. There are promises and dreams, but there is also much waiting, often in agonizing patience, for their consummation. God is there, in the midst of the lives of its heroes and heroines, but that sometimes highlights the problems. Rarely does God's presence simply make problems go away.

The Torah Describes Three Reconciliations

As there are misunderstandings and conflicts in Genesis, so are there reconciliations. These ostensibly begin with Cain. A midrash teaches that when Adam and Cain once met, after the expulsion from Eden and the killing of Abel, Cain told his father, "I repented and am reconciled." Whereupon Adam, astounded that divine atonement might be bestowed even for fratricide, decided that he too might be accepted as a penitent. Anticipating his descendant, the psalmist, he declared: "A song for the Sabbath day: It is good to make confession *(lehodot)* unto the Lord" (*Genesis Rabbah*: 22:13 on *Psalms* 42:1).[3] In addition, perhaps in the wake of this new awareness, Adam and Eve also became reconciled after more than a century of recriminations: One hundred and thirty years after the episode of the apple and the alienation in Eden, "Adam knew his wife Eve."

The most extended dramatic, yet leisurely, tale of reconciliation is without doubt that of Joseph and his brothers. But within the confines of that story, the midrash suggests two other stories of reconciliation: first, between Jacob and Joseph, and, then, between Jacob and the memory of his father, Isaac. We have already discussed the relations between Jacob and Joseph and here I shall only add a few points that place Joseph's feelings into the context of reconciliation.

Jacob, indeed, did "everything" for this son of his. But apparently such discriminatory affection toward one child, culminating in the gift of a coat of many colors (Gen. 37:3–4), was not a good way for Jacob to mourn Rachel or to make up for the insufficiency of his own father's love for him. Nor did it serve Joseph well. Didn't that conspicuous affection contribute to the seventeen year old's insufferable conceits? Didn't it make him the object of sibling hatred so violent that his brothers could not bear to speak to him, could not stand the sight of him? There are indications that, along with the love, there must have been much anger and guilt between the father and the son. We have already asked why Joseph refrained from contacting his father, even once, in his first twenty-odd years in Egypt. Why did he let Jacob stew in anguish? Moreover, we find Joseph listening quite calmly as his brothers describe their (mutual) father to him as "thy servant, our father"; the sages see a measure of conscious disrespect in his equanimity (*Sotah* 13a).

One midrash seems to spell out the problem of anger that keeps people from self-educative development. The midrash comments on the verse, "And [Joseph's brothers] told [Jacob] all the words of Joseph which he had said to them, and when [Jacob] saw the wagons *(agalot)* which Joseph had sent to carry him, the spirit of Jacob their father revived" (Gen. 45:27).

> Rabbi Levi said in the name of Rabbi Yohanan ben Shaul: [Joseph] had told them: If [Jacob] believes you [that I am Joseph], it is well; but if not, say to him [in my name]: When I left you, was I not engaged in studying the matter of the *eglah arufah* (the beheaded heifer)? Hence it says, "When he saw the *agalot* . . . the spirit of Jacob their father revived." (*Genesis Rabbah* 94:3)

What is that all about?

First we should note that Rabbi Levi is punning: *agalah*, "wagon," is suggestive of *eglah*, "heifer." We must also keep in mind that the teachers of the Midrash assumed that the patriarchs knew the entire Torah and "learned" it just as they did. One of the matters that they are anachronistically assumed to have studied, in all its halakhic detail, is the law of the *eglah arufah*, which concerns "a slain person . . . lying in the field [when] it is not known who has smitten him/her" (Deut. 21:1–9). In such a case, the Torah commands, the elders of the city closest to the place of the crime shall take a heifer and break its neck in a "rough valley." "And all the elders of that city nearest to the scene of the crime shall wash their hands over the beheaded heifer . . . and shall say, 'Our hands have not shed this blood, nor have our eyes seen it. Forgive, O Lord, Thy people Israel whom Thou hast redeemed and suffer not innocent blood to remain in the midst of Thy people Israel'" (Deut. 21:6–8).

Sifre, a collection of midrashim on Deuteronomy cited by Rashi, asks (with respect to verse 7): "Would it enter anyone's mind that the elders . . . are suspected of blood-shedding? [Surely not!] But the meaning of the declaration is: We never saw him and knowingly let him depart without food or escort [if we had seen him, we would not have let him depart without these]." When Joseph tells his brothers to mention to Jacob that they were "learning" the laws of the *eglah arufah* at the time of Joseph's disappearance, we may surmise that he is rebuking his father and justifying his silence. Didn't you send me to the brothers knowing the dangers involved? Weren't you aware of the hatred between us? Didn't it strike you and forewarn you that I answered your request to visit my brothers at Shechem with the single word of trepidation, uttered by Father Abraham before the binding of your own father: *Hinneni*, "Here I am" (Gen. 37:13)? And when I disappeared in that rough field, did you do anything? Did you investigate? Did you ask for forgiveness for letting me go without escort?

Joseph did not say those things, of course. Had he done so, it would only have made his father defensive and angry. He just gave him a sign that he was really Joseph by reminding him what he was "learning," obviously under Jacob's tutelage, when they were separated so many years before.

Between a Son and His Late Father:
A Midrash on Reconciliation

An even more dramatic reconciliation is suggested by a midrash that addresses the verse "And Israel offered sacrifices unto the God of his father, Isaac" (Gen. 46:1). Jacob is about to embark upon his last journey, to Egypt, to be with his beloved Joseph. And before leaving the Land of Israel, the man who was renamed Israel by an angel offers sacrifices and evokes the name of his father together with that of (Isaac's) God. The midrashic teacher Rabbi Yehoshua ben Levi wonders why Isaac is mentioned and not Abraham and he describes his search for an answer. The midrash then mentions various approaches to the matter:

> R. Yehoshua ben Levi said: I went round to all the masters of Agaddah in the south asking them to tell me the meaning of this verse, but they could not elucidate it for me, until I stood with Judah b. Pedaya
> . . . who explained to me that when one encounters a teacher and his disciple walking on the way [one should] greet the disciple first and then the teacher. R. Huna said: when R. Yehoshua b. Levi came to Tiberias he asked R. Yohanan and Resh Lakish about it. R. Yohanan said, the reason is that a person owes more honor to a parent than to a grandparent. Resh Lakish said, he offered sacrifices concerning the covenant promising the [development of the family into] tribes [originally promised to Isaac but fulfilled through Jacob who had twelve sons].
>
> Bar Kappara and R. Jose b. Patras [also discussed this]: One of them said, [it should be understood this way. Jacob declared]: As my father was eager for delicacies, so am I. The other [understood it differently and] said: Just as my father made a distinction between his children, so do I. [Isaac favored Esau and I, Joseph.] Then I [R. Yehoshua b. Levi] reconsidered and declared [that what Jacob said

was]: My father had the care of only one soul whereas I have the care of seventy souls.

R. Judan made two comments and R. Berakiah also commented. R. Judan said [that Jacob declared]: My father blessed me with five blessings and the Holy One, blessed be He, correspondingly appeared five times to me and blessed me. [R. Judan's other comment]: I thought He would permit me the actual enjoyment of these blessings. What were these blessings? "Let nations serve thee and nations bow down to thee . . . " [but now I see that] their application is postponed to Joseph [who indeed enjoyed power]. R. Berakiah [had another idea and] observed: The Holy One, blessed be He, never unites His name with a living person save with those who experience suffering [hence, the dead Isaac and not the living Jacob is mentioned in connection with God] and Isaac [would have deserved to be mentioned even if still alive because he] did indeed experience suffering. The rabbis said, We look upon him as though his ashes were heaped in a pile upon the altar. (*Genesis Rabbah* 84:5)

The fact that Jacob mentioned only his father Isaac while offering sacrifices to God and did not refer to Him as the God of Abraham seems strange to R. Yehoshua ben Levi. He entertains a number of answers offered to him by other sages.

The first three are informed by a rather impersonal kind of reasoning. R. Yehudah b. Pedaya sees here a general rule of etiquette. If you are in a hurry, greet a disciple (in this case, Isaac) before the master (i.e., Abraham), since everyone knows that the master is more revered and that greeting the disciple also reflects on the master's status, whereas just greeting the master may be perceived by the disciple as an insult. R. Yohanan also explains Jacob's behavior as a simple case of good manners. "Greet a parent before a grandparent." Resh Lakish is also still some distance away from touching on the tense relationship between this particular child and this particular parent. His explanation is that Jacob wanted to be sure that God's original covenantal promise made to Isaac, that there would be twelve tribes, would still be fulfilled through him even if he left Eretz Yisrael, which his father was explicitly told not to do.

In the comments of Bar Kappara and R. Jose b. Patros we are brought face to face with the ambivalence, if not actual animosity, between this son and this father. Jacob, by way of explaining to God his descent into Egypt, "reminds" God that Isaac loved the delicacies that Esau provided. So why should Jacob be different and not go "down" to Joseph, his son, who would provide him with delicacies in these years of famine? And didn't Father Isaac discriminate between sons? Here one hears the anguish and the specious pleading: All right! I love one son more than the others. But so did my father who discriminated against me!

The excuse that Jacob gives for leaving the land, according to R. Jose, is hardly less bitter. It has Jacob saying: So my father didn't leave Eretz Yisrael. But how many souls did he have to worry about feeding, and how many have I! There is pique here, and self-pity. Perhaps we hear active dislike: He only worried about himself. (After all, what about Rebecca, and what about his other son?)

R. Judan and R. Berakiah bring Jacob back from the abyss. Jacob is imagined recalling that his father did bless him. Moreover, it was certainly not by chance that God appeared to him the same number of times as his father blessed him. Thus, despite everything, his relationship to God does owe a great deal to his father. Moreover, some of the blessings bestowed upon him are actually meant for Isaac's grandsons. One cannot cut the cord of generations; God, through His blessings, maintains their continuity.

Finally, Jacob remembers that his father, in whom he finds so much to criticize and who evokes some bitter emotions, was, after all, the man who "gave him his God," who, throughout Jacob's life, will be alluded to as his father's God. Also, Isaac was a man who suffered much, a matter that Jacob could hardly have comprehended as a child and as a young man. But Isaac is no longer alive. The flawed relationships are behind him. So there are ample reasons why the son, like God Himself, may now link the divine Name with him. Jacob, intimate the sages, can now gain some understanding of Isaac's suffering, especially through the perspective of his father's great ordeal, the *Akedah*, which left him, in some senses, dead. It is now possible for Jacob to leave hurt and injury behind, to remember only Isaac's blessings, his share in the future, and Jacob's own share in the past, evoked by his father's memory.

Standing now in Beersheva before his last journey, Jacob understands that his God is the God of his father, Isaac. We may imagine him reconciled.

Teachers as (Former) Children

I have already said that children do not always have an easy time with those who pass the tradition on to them. There are hurtful things associated with these fathers and mothers and teachers as well as pleasant and inspiring ones; there may be elements of "night": frightening and overpowering, or unsupportive and distant. And when the children become parents and mentors and are themselves passing on a tradition, there are complications; there is static. We do not exactly do as our parents did, though we secretly hope they would have done much as we do in our circumstances, despite all our criticism of what *they* did. We mobilize daring and courage to be our own selves, yet, because we want continuity between generations that will give us a place to stand and someone with whom to associate an enduring spirituality, we also want blessing and approval. And then, there are perceived weaknesses of our own to be overcome or endured, that parents could not and did not understand. Also, although we hope that the blessings of the past we convey to our children and pupils will make God's presence accessible to them, we do not know exactly when that blessing will appear or what form it will take. We are not even always sure what the blessings we articulate actually mean, how they will be understood by our children and pupils, now and throughout the course of their lives.

Yet we try, as parents and teachers, not to be discouraged or defeated by that. We are, in fact, always in the process of acquiring a perspective, and we are preparing our children and pupils for the fashioning of their own. When teaching Torah, we try to resist the temptation of making it all a fairy tale, where everybody lives happily ever after. Torah is about life; it is complicated, just as we are, and its truth is to be found, as Hirsch would say, "wherever we find ourselves." Among the things it teaches us is that it is (almost) never too late to grow up, to reach the stage of faith at which self-pity is vanquished and where outrage at the complexities of life is left behind. And when one does grow up, learning to cope without hardness of heart or cynicism, one stands, not before blurred images and romantic conceptions of a distant past, but before the God of one's immediate parents, as they were, as we may now understand them.

Looking back at those in our immediate past with whom we shared experiences and sometimes shared hurt, each of us sees a slice of his or her own imperfect life. And that is the life each of us must bring to his or her teaching, parenting, journeying, accepting, and giving. It is the only life for covenant and Torah that we possess. It is all we have been given.

16

CAN ILLNESS HAVE MEANING? COMMUNITY, SOLITUDE, AND PROVIDENCE

IN HER CLASSIC STUDY entitled *Illness as Metaphor*, the anthropologist Susan Sontag, notes that it was not only in "the speculations of the ancient world" that diseases were "most often an instrument of divine wrath." Our modern secular age, she finds, is given to the same tendency to make illness into a metaphor and attribute blame to the ill. We are all aware of the advice casually given to the ill, that they "learn to take it easy," and not to "eat themselves up" as though heart and cancer patients (respectively) are, somehow to blame for their illnesses. And, in most recent years, there is the stigma attached to AIDS patients. Sontag cites various opinions that ascribe to the ailing person responsibility and even guilt for his or her illness. For example, she cites the renowned American psychologist Karl Menninger, who wrote that illness "is in part what the world has done to a victim, but in a larger part it is what the victim has done with his world and with himself."[1] To this Sontag responds that "such preposterous and dangerous views manage to put the onus of the disease on the patient and not only weaken the patient's ability to understand the range of plausible medical treatment but also, implicitly, direct the patient away from such treatment."

Sontag may be overstating her case: There is much learned inquiry suggesting that illness is at least aggravated by psychological states of mind. Of course, too, the risks of contacting many diseases can be drastically reduced by eliminating various health hazards. Nevertheless, Sontag's is a case that must be stated. It is one that may also be drawn into dialogue with what is certainly one of the most perplexing sections of the Torah, Leviticus 12:1–14:57, read in the synagogue as two portions of the week, *Tazria* and *Metsora*. Both of these portions deal mainly with the various manifestations of a strange disease called *tzara'at*, translated as "leprosy," and with what seems to be a strange culture of heartlessness toward both the malady and its victims. The difficulty posed by these portions is particularly acute for the adult who looks upon the experiences of life, especially, the most isolating, lonely, and often terrifying, as a path to self-education and self-understanding, and who seeks normative insight and direction in the Torah.

On the face of it, what we have here is what Sontag sharply denounces: priests declaring the ailing "clean" or "unclean"; detailed descriptions of unsavory symptoms; the banishment of the sick to a no-man's land "outside the camp" of Israelite habitation; the ill being required to wear torn clothing and to uncover their heads, marks of mourning and shame, respectively. Even worse, the lepers are obliged to warn others away, by yelling and/or marking their garments *tamai*, "unclean." Hence, these unfortunates are not only untouchable but also, except for the inspecting priest and other lepers, unapproachable.

The purification rite for a healed leper, with its one slaughtered bird and one released one, its cedar wood, crimson cloth, and hyssop branch, seems merely to round out the surrealistic scenario. Moreover, if the laws pertaining to the leprosy of persons can be explained away as ancient—even exotic—attempts at medical diagnosis and hygiene by guarding society against contagion, what should one say about the "leprosy" of clothing and even of buildings?

Several biblical commentators explain leprosy as a natural disease, and there seems to be some evidence for this view in the Bible. After all, there are two intriguing biblical narratives about persons who seem simply to have been unfortunate sufferers from the illness: Na'aman, the Aramite general (2 Kings 5), and four hapless men of Samaria who are inadvertent agents of salvation for Israel (2 Kings 7).

The Nature of Illness:
Religious and Moral Interpretations

Nonetheless, the vast majority of sages and exegetes assume that the illness the Torah calls *tzara'at* was not a natural illness at all, but a miraculous punishment for social wrongdoing, especially, *lashon hara*, "speaking ill of others." For this view, they could adduce a number of points. To begin with, the Torah specifically relates Miriam's leprosy to slanderous remarks she and Aaron (ostensibly to a lesser extent and more passively) made against their brother Moses (Num. 12) and warns us to "remember what God did unto Miriam" (Deut. 24:8–9). Second, Moses himself suffered a temporary spell of leprosy for slandering the Israelites by telling God that they "will not believe me . . . for they will say, The Lord has not appeared unto you" (Exod. 4:1). Third, exegetes had to agree that the leprosy of clothes and buildings discussed by the Torah were so unnatural that only a miraculous explanation made sense. Finally, they could point out that some of the biblical and talmudic halakhot were incongruent with appropriate medical procedure or even with simple quarantine measures. If the ancient priest was simply a kind of doctor, why did he make declarations upon and about the leper rather than simply treating him or her? After all, the Torah itself, on the basis of Exodus 21:19 ("you shall cause him to be fully healed") was understood to mandate medical treatment for the stricken. Why then, with regard to this illness, was he or she only "pronounced" ill and then isolated and humiliated? Moreover, if the reason for the quarantine was to prevent the spread of contagious diseases, why did the halakhah stipulate that a bridegroom should not be examined during the week of his wedding festivities, or any person during the days of festivals, including the intermediate days of festivals *(hol hamoed)*? One can hardly imagine contexts more dangerous for the spreading of contagious diseases than wedding weeks and pilgrim festivals! Furthermore, the Torah commands that the priest shall have a house suspected of plague infection cleared of all its contents *before* he comes to examine it "so that nothing in the house become unclean [at the moment of the priestly pronouncement]" (Lev. 14:36).

Hence, Maimonides, doyen of rationalistic thinkers and halakhic codifiers, who himself ruled that "one who is ill has not only the right but the duty to seek medical aid," determines with regard to leprosy:

> It is said in the Talmud that the leprosy described in the Torah comes as punishment for slander. . . . It is evidently not something natural, certainly not a common disease, for garments and homes are of brute matter and could not possibly be affected by organic leprosy, but we are dealing here with supernatural and miraculous effects, just as with the accusing water of bane and bitterness *(sotah)*. (Maimonides, *Commentary to the Mishnah, Nega'im* 12:5)

And once having established that the disease in question was indeed "wondrous," our sages, thinkers, and commentators looked at every feature of the illness through this prism. Thus, Na'aman contracted it for his sins and the four lepers who saved Samaria were identified as Ghizai, servant of Elisha, whose master afflicted him for his deceit and greed, and likewise his three sons (2 Kings 5). These sons were said to be culpable because they ostensibly heard Ghizai demanding presents from Na'aman as a reward for his having been healed, yet remained silent.

And once it is clear that the sins that cause leprosy are the various social ones that sow dissension among people (*Tanhuma, Metsora* 4), especially slander, everything falls into place. Just as the serpent sowed dissension between husband and wife with his tongue in Eden and was henceforth denied contact with human society, so is the leper isolated from the community. Because the slanderer "chatters and chirps," persons being restored to the community after their recovery must bring two birds to the Temple, for they too chatter and chirp. They bring cedar wood because the cedar tree is a symbol of haughtiness and pride. As crimson cloth gets its color from a worm and the hyssop is the lowliest of plants, so must the recovered patient step down from pride. Thus, in brief, is the way Rashi explains it in his commentary on the purification ceremony of the (healed) leper.

The commentaries on our *parashot*, "portions," contain a wealth of insight, not only about the evils of slander, but also about the complex relationship between society and those of its delinquent members, who corrode it with antisocial behavior. For example, the Torah commands that the priest go out to inspect the leper, but it also orders the leper to go—or be brought to the priest. The early sixteenth-century commentator Rabbi Obadiah Sforno explains the discrepancy between these prescriptions by suggesting that they meet in the middle: The priest goes out of the camp for the inspection but the leper must come to the closest place possible to "the camp" so as not to cause undue hardship for the priest. But why, one may ask, should the priest be troubled at all? Why not have the leper examined in the priest's domain? One Hasidic teacher, Sifte Cohen,[2] suggests that the priest must go out to lepers to show them respect, a measure of compensation for the humiliation inflicted upon them. Society has put the slanderer in his or her place, but it must not be forgotten that this person has feelings. Society is still responsible for this person and cannot be indifferent to the dignity even of a wrongdoer. However, since plague afflicts people because of their arrogance, it will not be spiritually helpful for the sick person to see the priest coming all the way to where she or he is. The patient too must make a humbling effort and walk in the direction of the priest.

The understanding of illness as divine and punitive in origin seems here to generate many profound insights and to solve various exegetical problems in our Torah reading. But isn't such an understanding a moral and educational problem in itself? How dare one impose the onus of moral delinquency on those who suffer from disease, whether they are lepers, cancer or heart disease sufferers, or victims of AIDS? Educators, for example, are constantly faced with the problem of how to maximally integrate children who are physically or mentally handicapped into (school) society. These children, like such adults, frequently experience the natural tendency of the healthy to shut them out, to blame them for being the way they are, to resent the discomfort and embarrassment experienced in their presence. Doesn't the conception of plague as a supernaturally imposed affliction justify the callousness of the healthy? By what right is the physical and mental suffering of the afflicted augmented by placing them "outside the camp"?

The Relationship of Illness to Covenant

A good place to begin thinking about these questions seems to be the legislation pertaining to "afflicted" houses. Many commentators have noted that the laws of leprous houses is introduced in Leviticus with an almost festive proclamation: "When you come into the land of Canaan that I am giving you as a possession, I shall put [literally, 'give'] the affliction of leprosy in a house in the land of your possession" (Lev. 14:34).

Why is the affliction announced as though it were a gift (*v'natati*, "I shall give")? Why is it only in the land of Canaan that this affliction will be "given"? And why only upon Israelites? Sforno, in his commentary on that verse, states that "the idea is that the plague was inflicted to draw the victim's attention to sins he had committed." Such plagues, as the midrashic writer of *Sifra* observes, "bore a message for them." And the nineteenth-century exegete Rabbi Meir Leibush Malbim finds this reminiscent of God's special relationship to the house of David: "I shall be a father to him and he shall be a son to Me; if he commits iniquity, I shall chasten him with the rod of men and with the plague" (2 Sam. 7:14).

The plague can thus be viewed as if it were a gift, an expression of God's love, enabling us to take stock of our lives. In this connection, we must note Nachmanides' (Ramban's) statement in his commentary on Leviticus 13:47.

> This [leprous discoloration of garments] is not at all natural and occurs nowhere in the world [except for the Land of Israel] and this is also true with regard to the plague of houses. But when Israel is wholehearted with the Lord, His spirit will always be upon them to guard the wholesome appearance of their bodies, their garments, and their homes. If, however, anyone should commit a crime or sin, his body or garment or home will be stained by this taint, showing that the divine Spirit has departed from him.

Leprosy is here presented as the dark side of the gift of Providence!

This idea of providential punishment is radically developed by Sforno in his commentary on Leviticus 13:47. After repeating the idea that this disease applies only to Israel because of its special moral charge as a chosen people, Sforno explains the view expressed in the Talmud that there never was and never will be a leprous house (*Sanhedrin* 71a). "When choosing the people of Israel as His peculiar treasure, He warned them that any departure from the mode of life He commands would incur punishment. On the assumption that the majority of the people will abide by His will, He, in His mercy, will remind the straying individuals of their dereliction."

This reminding will happen in stages, says Sforno. First the garments will be contaminated, then the houses, and finally the bodies of the sinful. In seeing divine retribution moving from property to the person, Sforno follows *Midrash Tanhuma*, although there houses are said to be afflicted before garments.[3] But Sforno then proceeds to turn the matter upside down: "However, as no generation ever satisfied the assumption that the majority of Israel will

abide by His will, this special state of mercy never became operative, and there have never been leprous homes, as some in the Talmud say (*Sanhedrin* 71a) that the *parashah* of leprous homes *never*
applied."

And now we may return to Rambam, whose *Commentary to the
Mishnah* was just cited. In his later, comprehensive code, *Mishneh
Torah*, Maimonides relates the entire issue of leprosy to the specific
case of Miriam:

> "Take heed of the plague of leprosy. . . . Remember what the Lord
> your God did to Miriam by the way as you came forth out of Egypt"
> (Deut. 24:9), which means: bethink carefully what befell Miriam . . .
> the prophetess, who spoke ill of her younger brother, whose senior
> she was by many years, and whom she had reared so selflessly, endan-
> gering even her own life to save him from the Nile: she did not slan-
> der in malice, she only mistook his station as a prophet to be on the
> same level as most prophets, whereas Moses himself did not take it
> amiss, as the Torah asserts: (Num. 12:3), "Now the man Moses was
> very meek." And yet Miriam was at once afflicted with leprosy. From
> this you may infer a fortiori to what punishment those people are li-
> able who slander with malice aforethought, talking big and loose.
> Therefore it behooves everyone who pursues a direction in his life to
> shun such company and keep his distance from that kind of talk, lest
> he be caught in the snare of the wicked and their stupidity. (*Mishneh
> Torah, Sefer Ahavah, Hilkhot Tumat Tzara'at* 10:10)

The Torah, states Rambam, teaches and warns us ("Remember
. . . ") about slander through the far-fetched case of Miriam, whose
righteousness was unquestioned and whose sin was minute.
Miriam, the selfless older sister, herself a prophetess, inadvertently
speaking ill of a person who took no offense! If even she was struck,
what about us, less than prophets and hardly selfless, speaking
against those vulnerable to insult and hurt by evil talk *(lashon hara)!*
Of course, Maimonides can no longer warn the sinner of leprosy,
an ancient "miraculous" sickness. Rather, the malignancy about
which we are warned seems to be synonymous with slander itself:

The sickness is to be "caught in the snare of the wicked and their stupidity." Hence we are led to imagine that the punishment is causally related to the "sickness": If we slander, we shall find ourselves isolated; people will keep away from us. Maimonides seems to be giving us a different focus, on a direction in life that maintains (spiritual) health.

If we see illness as miraculously addressing itself to those whom God loves, who *deserve* to be taught a lesson by God, then we might consider viewing the diseases of leprosy as in certain respects analogous to all disease and misfortune and paradigmatic of them. All diseases may indeed be seen as natural, requiring examination, and, at times, quarantine. But they, like everything in the life of a religious person, are never *simply* natural. A religious person, upon becoming ill, is bidden to "search out his/her deeds." He or she hopes to be worthy of learning something from them and, likewise, seeks ways to express his or her gratitude for rehabilitation. I vividly recall a lesson, many years ago, with the late and revered teacher Nehama Leibowitz, on 2 Samuel 12, which tells of David's sin with Batsheva and the death of their child, as foretold by the prophet Nathan. Nehama, in her provocative and exciting teaching fashion, asked us, her students: Why did the child die? Is the child to be held responsible for the sins of the parents? No, she answered her own question emphatically: *He probably died of a viral infection.* The prophet, declared Leibowitz, explained to David that he was to understand the death of the child as related to his sin. *He was to interpret it as God's demand for his repentance.* This understanding commanded by God was not an illusion or a psychological orientation. It was a command of God, communicated through His prophet.

The Individual Within a Supportive Community

The idea we have traced briefly, from Maimonides and Nachmanides, through Sforno and Leibowitz, is that we should, in pondering the events of our own lives, wonder what God "is saying to us" through them. We should do that even though we know that those events have natural causes; even though we understand that it is presumptuous for us to think of ourselves, of our communities, and of our societies as worthy of God's "miraculous" attention.

But whether illness can be miraculous or not, there is a necessary distinction to be drawn between the existentially paradoxical way in which we are to understand and respond to our problems and misfortunes and what scientists may declare to be the facts of given circumstances. The Torah is not a medical textbook, but it instructs us how to live with one another and before God. The ideal society is one in which God teaches every individual, within and through the righteous society in which she or he lives, how to view sin and how to "return" from it. A society that is itself sick is hardly in a position to judge and condemn the suffering, and there may never be a society that deserves to do that. It is, then, only the individual who has the right and perhaps the duty to be introspective upon falling ill; it is the individual who is invited to use the means put at his disposal by the Torah, which becomes accessible to him or her through the community, for such introspection.

Not only can the individual strive for a desired relationship to God through Torah and the community that teaches him or her Torah, but the community can and must be supportive of its members through Torah. Our *parashot*, as understood by our sages and commentators, teach the person who experiences life in community but has recently experienced angst and solitude and suffering: This is a way you may look upon your affliction. Possibly, the community intimates, you have learned something through it; perhaps you have gained a different perspective through it. But we shall never judge you. All but the most utopian and righteous society, which apparently never existed (hence, "the leprous house never was and never will be") must relate to the misfortunes of others only through commanded medical treatment, compassion, and concern. "The priest must go out" to those who are suffering, those who feel isolated and lonely in their pain but who yet may learn from it, even in the sometimes horrible solitude it imposes.

R. Yitzhak Suggests a Third View

The narrative that precedes the portions *Tazria* and *Metsora* tells of Nadav and Avihu, two sons of Aaron, who died when they "offered strange fire before the Lord" (Lev. 10:2). After this tragedy, the Torah relates that Moses comforted the stricken father and conveyed God's consolation to him: "I shall be sanctified by those who are close to me." This statement has been interpreted to mean that the intentions of these young men were good; hence, they died "before the Lord," as righteous people. Others understand their death as punishment. Nadav and Avihu, it is suggested, were impudent. They wished to usurp the authority and power of their elders.

But one midrash suggests a third view: On the verse "All things come alike to all; there is one event to the righteous and to the wicked; to the good and to the clean and to the unclean; to him who sacrifices and to him who does not sacrifice; as is the [lot of the] good so is [that of] the sinner: and he who swears [has no different a lot than] the one mindful about oaths" (Eccles. 9:2), R. Yitzhak declares: ". . . to the righteous": these are the sons of Aaron, as it is written (Mal. 6): "For in peace and straightness he went with me and turned many from sin" (*Leviticus Rabbah* 20:1).

We do not know why Nadav and Avihu died, says the midrashic teacher. All things come alike to all. His view is not simply stoic. In the context of our *parashot*, it intimates that, at the very center of our ignorance and perplexity, there is a norm. Those young priests were righteous, even if they died as sinners might have. Whatever, if anything, is being "said" to the sufferer, whether the suffering is "given" or inflicted, is only for him or her to discover, and for prophets possibly to discern. Perhaps she or he is drawing comfort from quiet heroism or seeking the strength to learn from misfortune. We, as friends, teachers, parents, or children, may lean, like the midrashist, on Ecclesiastes. We do not know why there is suffering and sickness. We only know that it is part of what human existence is like.

But what we do know and see, in addition to inexplicable suffering and pain, is the need of most sufferers to be together with others, to be as active, healthy, and normal as possible. We know, too, that every healthy child must be given to understand, however gently, that it "could be him or her" and that this possibility is also part of what life, however inexplicably, is all about. Through the commandments and the norms of community, we can teach children how they may, now or potentially, be helped to cope with affliction. An ideally holy community might even be "graced" with miraculous diseases that offer it protection and legislate distance from those who work at corrupting it. In such a society there may be clear signs and procedures, acknowledged by all but delinquent individuals, implemented by a trustworthy and righteous leadership.

But it seems plausible, so Sforno tells us, that such a society never existed. Perhaps from the very beginning, all we have had is the Torah, which can serve as our guide on the endless road to holy life and holy community. Such a searching community will not impose "signs" upon individuals or judge them for their illnesses, but will reach out to them through commandments. It will heal the sick, "go out" to them and bring them as close as possible, regardless of what the patient him/herself is shown and given to understand.[4]

Therefore, when a person who has recuperated from illness or has been through some dangerous situation gets up before the public to pronounce the blessing of thanksgiving *(Birkat Hagomel)*, he or she will bless God "who has granted good things *to the undeserving* and has granted me every good."[5] The individual admits that his or her shortcomings place him or her in God's debt. But the community, in responding to this blessing, *which is always said in public*, refers not at all to that situation of debt. Pointedly oblivious to theological issues of merit or guilt, it just declares: "May He who has granted you every good, grant you only good."

This dialogue of blessing says it well. You, the sufferer, may or, perhaps, are commanded to look inward. We, your community, are here to live a life of Torah with you: to support you and to bless you.

17

LIVING UNTIL ONE
HUNDRED AND
TWENTY: ON DYING

How a human being has fathomed something of the meaning of life may be reflected in the ways that person faces the proximity of death, and how she or he lives toward it. Riemer recalls a conversation with a friend about a dying person that reflects significantly upon that person's life:

A dear friend of mine observes the anniversary of his father's death each year on the seventh day of Passover. We sat together one year reminiscing about his father, and he recalled to me his memories of the last day of his father's life. His father was conscious until near the end, and so, knowing that it was a festival, he said his prayers including the *Hallel*, the psalms of thanksgiving and rejoicing. When he finished reciting the *Hallel* he felt weary and so he said the *Vidui*, the confessional. Soon afterward he died. . . . I wonder which words of the *Hallel* [psalms] spoke most directly to his heart on that last day of his life. Was it a phrase like "Grievous in the sight of the Lord is the death of His faithful ones"? Or was it perhaps a line like "What shall I give back to the Lord for his goodness to me?" Or was it a phrase like "Answer me, O Lord, for I am Your servant, the child of your handmaid,

Undo my chains"? Or was it perhaps the line, "From the narrow place I cried out, 'Lord!'? He answered me with great enlargement."[1]

Leaving aside the good fortune of that man, who was blessed with being conscious and in command of his mental faculties on the day of his death, we may wonder what in his education and self-education made it possible for him to act as he did, to perhaps even choose the verse that bestowed significance on that moment, and to have a way, perhaps uniquely his own, to interpret it and to be addressed by it.

Life and Death

In recent years, there has been much significant writing about attitudes toward death in our culture, and even about the place of death and dying in teaching. Existential philosophers, anthropologists, psychologists, and educators have emphasized that cultural and religious discourse about death reflects and articulates the ways in which people *live*; how they approach meaning in their lives.

In the chapter, we shall explore these questions through the medium of midrashic reflections on the death of Moses, the "man of God," who lived until "one hundred and twenty" and at one point clearly wished to go on living. Moses becomes the subject of high drama about the issue of human mortality. The Midrash suggests that Moses refused at first to accept the edict that he, too, would die. His overwhelmingly rich life seemed at first to make death unbelievable and outrageous. What our teachers of the Midrash do with the subject of dying, with a focus on Moses' last days, is a good point of departure for thinking about the subject that we often perceive, at least for ourselves, as unthinkable.

Shorn of Authority: Moses Prepares for Death

The end of Deuteronomy is about the warnings and blessings Moses gives to the people of Israel who are about to cross the Jordan into the Promised Land. But the midrashic tradition turns it partially into the saga of the great teacher's last day. As we shall see, this midrashic drama is rich in profound reflections upon life and death. It exposes to view a "world" in which a specific kind of social heroism is at home. It speaks of what makes life meaningful and of what makes death an aspect of life, not to be denied.

The Torah's epic of Moses' last day is introduced with the following:

> And Moses went and spoke all these things to Israel, and he said to them: I am now one hundred and twenty years old; I can no longer come and go, and the Lord has said to me, you shall not cross this Jordan. The Lord your God Himself will cross over before you, and He Himself will destroy these nations from before you and you shall dispossess them, and Joshua shall go before you, as the Lord has spoken. (Deut. 31:1–3)

Moses goes from tribe to tribe, preparing each in turn for life without him, reassuring them that God "will not fail you or forsake you" (v. 6). Moses seems calm, speaking with the voice of paternal wisdom and reason, even with a certain detachment. Do not overly fear or regret my death, he says. I can no longer carry out the tasks of leadership. Moreover, since God has proscribed my crossing the Jordan, my death must necessarily precede your entrance into the Land. The time for both my demise and your conquest has arrived. As for the leadership you need, do not fear: God Himself will protect you, and Joshua too will be there to go before you.

But there is a prior episode that intimates a different state of affairs and mind. There, Moses pleads to be allowed into the Land until God sternly tells him: "Enough! Do not speak to me further about this matter." Then, in a kind of partial acquiescence, God agrees to Moses' entreaty "to see the good land that is beyond the Jordan." Moses is told that he may look at it. "Go up to the summit of Pisgah and lift up your eyes to the west and to the north and to the south and to the east and see [the Land] with your own eyes, for you shall not go over the Jordan" (Deut. 3:24–29; compare Num. 27:12–13).

There seems to be a note of sarcasm in God's willingness to relent, as if He were saying, "You want to see the Land? All right,
then look at it." We shall return later to this passage and to Moses'
ascent to Pisgah.

For teachers of the Midrash, the passages of the Torah dealing
with Moses' impending death suggest the turmoil, the arguments,
even the cosmic ferment accompanying it, and they find in them
Moses' ultimate reconciliation to the human condition that he
shares with all mortals. To several sages, even the fact that Moses
went from tribe to tribe before his death to reassure and bless them
is suggestive. Why did Moses not simply convene the people, as he
had done shortly before, when he re-ratified the covenant with
them? As the thirteenth-century French commentator Hizkuni
(Rabbi Hizkiah ben Manoah), asks it in his commentary on
Deuteronomy 31:1: Why did Moses have to trouble himself by going from tribe to tribe? Why didn't he simply assemble them by
blowing the trumpets that he had made specifically for calls to assembly (Num. 10:1–10)? Hizkuni finds the answer in the following
midrash:

> Said R. Joshua in the name of R. Levi of Sikhnin: As for the trumpets
> that Moses made in the desert: Because Moses was about to die, the
> Holy One concealed them so that Moses would not blow upon them
> and get [the people] to come to him, as it is written (Eccles. 8:8):
> "And there is no rule over [or, rather, on?] the day of death." (*Tan-
> huma, Beha'alotekha* 10)[2]

R. Joshua and R. Levi understand the verse that muses on the
lack of human control with regard to the date of death as teaching
that the dying person loses all rulership on that day. Moses cannot
assemble the people, for he has been suddenly shorn of authority.
God has hidden the instruments of power. And Moses has no
choice but to walk from tribe to tribe. It may well have been an occasion of some embarrassment, perhaps even bitterness. The bearer
of blessing and comfort could hardly help wondering whether some
of the people, especially the younger ones, were not thinking be-

hind their reverential smiles of welcome: The old man again. What does he want now?

Moses Pleads for Life

As we see Moses going from tribe to tribe on his last day, he has become reconciled to his death. But what happened before that? The sages of the Midrash tell us: "When Moses realized that God's decree concerning his death had been sealed, he drew a circle in the ground, stood inside it and declared, 'Lord of the universe I will not move out of this circle until you repeal the decree.'"

Moses prays and cries out "until the heaven and the earth and all creation shook," and God has to order the gates of prayer closed. Moses then moves from prayer to pleading and bargaining. "All I want is to see a little of their happiness after all the years of pain in the wilderness." God is not impressed. Then Moses tries a different tack: "If You do not let me cross the Jordan," he says, "You discredit your own Torah. Your own law commands the employer to pay his hired servant on the day he finishes his work. Is this my payment from You for forty years of toil trying to make Israel into a holy and faithful nation?" "This is still My decree," God responds.[3]

Moses lowers the stakes but continues to bargain. "Let my bones be brought into the Land, like the remains of Joseph." God answers: "Moses, when Joseph went down into Egypt, he did not hide the fact that he was a Hebrew, but he told everyone his identity. However, when you arrived in Midian, you appeared like an Egyptian" (Exod. 2:19). Moses does not relent: "Let me be like one of the beasts of the field which eats the grass, drinks the stream waters, and gazes out on the world. . . . Let me fly like a bird that goes in all directions searching for its food and that comes back to its nest at day's end."[4] This is the pleading we read about in Deuteronomy 3, as filled in by the midrashic teacher. This, our midrash imagines, is the context of God's losing patience with Moses and giving him the curt reply of that chapter: "Enough! Do not speak to me further about this matter."

Moses is then portrayed as crying bitterly for mercy. God, who has always been won over by Moses' pleas for mercy, moves to a therapeutic approach: The Physician brings the patient whom He knows so well to an awareness that restores him to his former heroism:

> Moses, you remember that I made two oaths. The first was to destroy Israel after they worshiped the Golden Calf, and the second was that you would die here, and not enter the Promised Land. The first oath relating to Israel I annulled when you prayed, "Forgive, I pray you." And now again you ask me to annul a decree because of your prayer. You are holding the rope at both ends. If you want me to accept your present prayer, then you must forgo your first one. But if you stick with your first prayer, then withdraw the present one. When Moses heard this he said, "Lord of the Universe! Let Moses and a thousand like him die before a single fingernail of one of Israel be hurt."[5]

Then Moses tries another approach. "Is it right that the feet that ascended on high and the face that looked at the divine Presence and the hands that received Torah from Your Hands should sleep in the dirt?" "Such is My plan," God responds, "and this is the law of life. Each generation will have its own teachers and its own leaders. Until now it was your lot to minister before Me. Now it is the lot of Joshua."[6]

At this point Moses set up his final bargaining position. If indeed it is destined that Joshua will lead the next generation, he, Moses, will become his disciple. God, who knows the soul of His servant, agrees to that. Moses goes to Joshua's tent and listens to Joshua teaching the Torah. He embarrasses Joshua by his commanding presence, and until God tells the disciples that they must now learn Torah from Joshua, they refuse to leave Moses' side. So Joshua sits at the head, Moses at his right, and the sons of Aaron at his left as he expounds Torah. It is an awkward situation for Joshua, for Moses, and for the disciples, but Moses seems to accept it and the others have no choice.

And then, finally, comes the moment at which Moses becomes reconciled to his death.

> Afterwards as they walked away from the tent, Moses was at Joshua's left and they entered the Tabernacle. The cloud of God's Presence descended between them in the Tabernacle. When it departed, Moses asked Joshua, "What was the divine Word that God spoke to you?" Joshua turned to Moses and said, "I am not permitted to divulge it even as I did not hear the divine Word when God spoke to you." Hearing this, Moses cried bitterly: "Better a thousand deaths rather than a single jealousy. O Lord of the universe, until now I sought life, but now I am ready to return my soul to You."[7]

This midrash portrays a man who is in the midst of life. He cannot accept the advent of death and at first denies it, even becoming "isolated"—standing alone in a circle of prayer that pits him against the foundations of the created order. He then expresses anger: Is this his reward for forty years of work in the wilderness? He then tries to bargain for continued life, under any and all circumstances. After that, he becomes depressed and, finally, he is reconciled. The "stages of dying" as they have been spelled out by Elisabeth Kuebler-Ross in her renowned *On Death and Dying*, are all represented and articulated here.[8] (Nevertheless, in one version of the midrash, Moses suffers a setback or, perhaps, a penultimate victory. For when God sends Samael, the angel of death, to take his soul, Samael finds Moses "writing the ineffable divine Name in a scroll," and the radiance of his face strikes terror into Samael's heart.)

A very different approach is suggested in the midrashic elaboration on the Mishnaic tractate *Avot*:

> The Holy One, blessed be He, said to the angel of death: Go and bring the soul of Moses to Me. [The angel of death] went to the dwelling place of Moses, searched for him, but could not find him. He went to the sea and asked, "Has Moses come here?" The sea answered, "Since Israel passed through me, I have seen nothing of him."

He went to the mountains and hills and asked them, "Has Moses come here?" They answered: "Since Israel received the Torah at Mount Sinai we have seen no more of him." He went to Sheol and Destruction and asked them, "Has Moses come here?" They answered, "His name we have heard but himself we have not seen." He went to the ministering angels and asked them, "Has Moses come here?" They answered, "God understands his way and He knows his place" (Job 28:23). God has put him in safekeeping for life in the world to come, and no creature knows his whereabouts.

Joshua was sitting and worrying about Moses, until the Holy One said to him: "Joshua why are you worried about Moses? Moses my servant is dead" (Josh. 1:2). (*Abot de-Rabbi Natan*, 12)

To this divine response to Joshua, another midrash adds, "He is dead, but indeed it is I who have lost him and not you."⁹

This midrash, in its several versions, seems to offer a different approach than the previous one, in which Moses bargains for his life but is finally reconciled to his death. Here, the angel of death is foiled: He looks for Moses in all the wrong places. God seems, in fact, to have sent him on a wild-goose chase. God Himself brings about Moses' death with His "Word," and He announces Moses' death to Joshua, who is worried about his teacher's disappearance, while the hapless angel of death is still looking for him. A related midrash has Yocheved, Moses' mother, also running from sea to hill to desert, asking each in turn, "Where is my son, where is Moses?"

Educating Toward Death—Or Denying It

How may we approach these two clusters of midrashim? What can they tell us about death and its relationship to life? How shall we educate about death, as part of the consciousness of every thoughtful living person and as the inevitable occurrence at the end of every life?

In general, we in Western society tend to ignore, deny, or disguise death. As the renowned philosopher-anthropologist Ernest Becker has written, we have no overarching concept of heroism, of the life well lived, that has not been dissipated by the loss of our faith and the abandonment of their internal visions.

> Modern man is drinking and drugging himself out of awareness, or he spends his time shopping, which is the same thing. As awareness calls for types of heroic dedication that his culture no longer provides for him, society contrives to help him forget. Or, alternatively, he buries himself in psychology in the belief that awareness all by itself will be some kind of magical cure for his problems. But psychology was born with the breakdown of shared social heroisms: it can only be gone beyond with the creation of new heroisms that are basically matters of belief and will, dedication to a vision.[10]

With the loss of these faiths and visions has come denial, for without a vision of the good and heroic life, death can have no meaning and becomes merely a focus of chaos and terror. And the occasion of death itself, in our life experience always happening to others, becomes something unpleasant, almost a misdeed on the part of the deceased, an acutely irritating accident that is best politely ignored. Yet, no amount of repression makes death go away, for we cannot but realize that we too will die. Becker notes Gregory Zilboorg's statement: "Underneath all appearances, the fear of death is universally present. . . . We may take for granted that [it] is always present in our mental functioning." Yet it is repressed because the monster of meaninglessness arises before us through the apparition of death. And this very meaninglessness makes death more frightening. "Insomuch as dying today is considered to be less meaningful, more final and thus more frightening, it is to be avoided by all available means" including "life-support systems" which make the experience of dying more mechanical and impersonal.[11]

The rabbinic sages, from within their faith and vision, saw things differently. Characteristically, their vision was largely couched in halakhic normative terms: When there is no burial society in a town, even scholars are bidden to stop their Torah study to attend to the dead. One who sees a funeral procession and does not accompany it for a short distance is "mocking the dead." "Comforting the mourners" was a staple of community life, necessary both for the mourners and for the community, and for the spiritual well-being of the individual soul, its inner order and focus.

Obviously, the habits of denial and disguise make the rabbinic tradition of encountering death appear out of place. A society wherein visitors are urged not to visit the bereaved in order not to bother them would be hard put to understand one in which participation in the life event of death, by accompanying the dead at the funeral and visiting the family during the week of mourning (shiva), is not only appropriate but also self-understood. Since death is something unpleasant for modern people, a kind of blunder, it makes sense not to see burial and consolation as part of the cycle of life. Indeed, in such a society as ours, the conception of the cycle of life retreats altogether, becoming relegated to distant or primitive cultures, of interest only to anthropologists.

The demise of these value actions is not simply to be nostalgically bemoaned as leading people to drugs and obsessive shopping. To restore communal virtues, such as mourning together, one must recoup communal sensibility. Especially for contemporary people, the road to communal sensibility and to a comprehensive philosophy of life passes through the prism of the individual and of his or her conceptions of a worthy and authentic life.

Conversely, such a philosophy of life and hence, of education, if sought and partially attained, cannot bypass the subject of death. For death in human consciousness is all about the vulnerability and uncertainty of the project of a well-lived life and the frightening specter of the possible absurdity of the entire matter. It is about one's notions of what it is, what it *means* to have lived a fulfilled life. In the language of Jewish tradition, it means having an idea of what one is wishing upon a person when expressing the hope that she or he may live until "one hundred and twenty."

We may now return to our midrashic texts. Clearly, there are several assumptions that underlie both clusters.

First, everyone dies. Death is not something that happens only to other people. That is a difficult lesson to learn, though, subliminally, we know it always. Even Moses, in reporting God's edict that the generation of the desert would die (Num. 14:28–39), does not wish to "realize" that that edict is likely to include him.

Second, the death of a person is part of his or her life. It cannot be thought about or understood outside of that context. Moses knows his powers to change reality and thus cannot avoid thinking that he can put off or conquer death. As he looks for the meaning of the edict of his death and burial outside the Land of Israel, Moses is forced by God to ask himself why he refrained from identifying himself as an Israelite in Midian. He cannot fathom that someone who has conversed with God is still ruled by the seemingly absurd and brute facts of the human situation. How can the body that stood before God on the highest rungs of prophecy be given over to decay and decomposition?

Third, death is starkly personal and solitary. In the metaphor of our midrashim: Moses "disappears," and he is nowhere to be found, even by his mother, Yocheved. He is alone with God. Joshua is sad but probably relieved; the Israelites mourn Moses for thirty days, and then, the Torah tells us pointedly, "the days of weeping in the mourning for Moses were ended" (Deut. 34:8). But at the same time, coping with dying and death has a pervasive social context, and the dying person faces an inescapable social reality that must be confronted. Can Moses really "learn" from Joshua? (Should an old person pay the steep price attached to living with the children?) How should Joshua cope with his old teacher, who is now to become his disciple? (What does role change vis-à-vis the old mean for the younger generation?)

What is the old Moses' responsibility to his former role of leader of the Israelites? Can he sacrifice the people for his own survival without relinquishing his integrity? Does he still have the power to assemble them, or have "the instruments of power" with which he may beckon them been taken from him?

Commandments That "Keep the World Going": Education for Social Heroism

The mishnah that opens tractate *Peah* and is a staple of Torah learning in the liturgy of the morning service well describes the reality and the vision of the Jewish human life in which death plays a role and, symbolically, a central one:

> These are the things the benefits of which a person enjoys in this world, while the stock [or principal] remains for [payment in] the world to come: honoring [one's] father and mother, deeds of loving-kindness, timely attendance at the House of Study morning and evening, hospitality to wayfarers, visiting the sick, dowering the bride, accompanying the dead to the grave, devotion in prayer, and making peace between people.

Of all of these, the mishnah teaches that "a person eats the fruits of them in this world while the 'principal' remains for the world to come. And the study of Torah is equal in worth to all of them" (*Peah* 1).

The commandments enumerated here have three things in common: They address a human situation of need and vulnerability; they turn to each person with the demand to hold the precarious fabric of social life together, and they promise that in a world held together by these commandments, each individual will enjoy their fruits in this world, for we all live in vulnerability and precariousness. At the same time, these commandments make of their devotees responsible and caring persons: They refine their souls, and make them worthy of the world to come. All of these mitzvot constitute the network of a shared social heroism that is also a personally held vision of character and meaning.

Let us be specific about cases. The Mishnaic teachers certainly had in mind that the Torah promises "length of days" for the honor paid to parents, and they believed that the existence of the family and society depended on it. There can be no "length of days" for a society that pulls back from responsibility for these fragile social groupings. Yet it is natural and sometimes simple, especially in ages of economic self-sufficiency and self-reliance, to rebel. ("Who do they think they are? Anyone can be a parent. I too may become one, but do I deserve respect?") Deeds of loving-kindness are an exquisite recognition of the need of the other without turning it to advantage;

punctual attendance at the House of Study makes communal prayer possible, for without the presence of the often elusive tenth person, that prayer cannot come into being. Each one of us may be the wayfarer in need of a warm meal and a bed. Most of us will be ill at some time, seeking companionship and verification of our worth, sometimes in undignified circumstances. Each person longs for the day of happiness that weddings represent, yet poverty may make a mockery of it, intimating that the joy of celebrating and starting families is only "make believe." All of us will die. Each of us, as well as society at large, requires the devoted prayers of each member of the community for the always precarious public welfare; all people's lives are sometimes soured by quarreling and misunderstanding, and all wonder whether the hope that the world of affection and understanding can be put back together again is merely an illusion.

There are some people who fervently fulfill all of these mitzvot, without exception, under almost all circumstances and in all stages of life. Nonetheless, the nonfulfillment of these mitzvot can be explained and even justified in a prosaic and antiheroic world. "Honor my parents? Even though they thwarted my personal development?" "There are others who have time for charity, but I have to make a living." "I can't get up that early and communal prayer doesn't do anything for me." "I need some privacy at the end of the day." "I hate hospitals." "Let the bride take a bank loan like everyone else." "I didn't go to the funeral because I hardly knew her." "I can get along without so many communal aspirations." And "I don't butt into other people's relationships."

Yet the actions described here, each one with its coterie of social heroes, virtually keeps the world going. Conversely, at each of the stages of life noted here, the lack of a common vision and vision action can lead to collapse, nonexistence, and chaos. Then, when the world has been destroyed, it makes sense to ask, What world? Then, as Becker would say, comes the appropriate time to refer the matter to psychologists who may raise awareness of nothingness and give us the courage to break out of alleged illusions.

The social heroism pinpointed by our mishnah is potently symbolized by death, even if it almost gets lost amid the abundance of world-maintaining mitzvot there. In the presence of death collapse and the anguish of meaninglessness are nowhere else so close at hand. Nowhere do the questions that arise out of human fragility and vulnerability arise so urgently, lead so quickly to despair, tempt so urgently to repression. And with repression comes negation of the vision and an evasion, not only of the dead and of those who mourn them, but also of brides, wayfarers, and the ill. Especially the ill.

But why should the contemporary individual appropriate this particular kind of social heroism? Why not simply face the facts, with or without the help of psychology? Why, in the face of pervasive death, be a hero?

We shall shortly return to that question, but first: This mishnah states that learning Torah makes this social heroism and its fruits, as well as the project of self-making (the principal laid up for the world to come) accessible. We must, then, first return to our study of Torah, specifically, the midrashim about Moses.

As we know, the death of Moses is part of his life. God forces him to reflect on the nature of his leadership. He rethinks, and perhaps regrets, some features of his past. ("Why *didn't* I identify myself as a Hebrew in Midian?") His impending death returns him to events in his past and raises the issue of his relationship with future generations and future leaders. He gains a different perspective. Yet it is precisely the nature of this perspective that distinguishes between the two groups of midrashim.

In the first case, Moses is in the midst of life and expects, however unreasonably, to stay there. Death comes as an intruder, in the shape of an unanticipated and unfair catastrophe. When the angel of death approaches, Moses is radiant, writing God's ineffable Name or otherwise engaged in "doing" Torah. He has no time for death, and it is only when direct contact with the divine Presence is denied him that life loses its meaning for him and becomes expendable.

In this first group of midrashim, which seem to take their cue from Deuteronomy 3:24–29, coming to terms with death requires the dying person to go through "stages" of dying. In that scheme of things, the role of others is substantial and significant. Joshua must manage with having Moses on his right, and the disciples must learn to ignore Moses' greater knowledge while Joshua teaches them. Situations arise that are awkward and embarrassing. The dying person must be confronted, appeased, bargained with, taught awareness. Moses, in these midrashim, certainly keeps God busy; indeed, even the Almighty is driven at one point to say: "Enough! Do not speak to me further about this matter."

In the case of the midrashim in *Abot de-Rabbi Natan*, the ambiance is vastly different. The angel of death does not find Moses in any of the places where he (and we) would expect him to be. The angel of death goes first to the sea, hoping to locate his victim there. The sea, for Moses, is the place of lifting his rod and splitting the waters; it is a high point in his life with God and Israel. As for most people, then, the sea represents the element of daring and adventure in Moses' life. It symbolizes the ability to go forward even in desperate situations.

The angel of death then goes to the mountains. They represent, perhaps, the pinnacle of achievement, of having reached the heights. Again, that is more true of Moses than of others: The mountain is the place where God revealed the Torah to him. But Moses is no longer there. And when the angel of death looks for Moses in the depths of despair, the situation is the same. In fact, though the depths have heard of Moses, for he has been in the vicinity, he was never really there. He never completely despaired. In any case, he is not there now.

Nor is Moses among the ministering angels. The ministering angels, I suggest, represent the world of rarefied ideas. What the sea is to adventure and mountains are to achievement, the ministering angels are to spiritual seeking and, perhaps, detachment. Moses also knew about that; he had been there. He had argued with angels, spoken to God, reached unparalleled heights of spiritual understanding, at times having to stand at a distance from his people. But although the ministering angels state this with appropriately angelic theological finesse, their response to the angel of death is simple: Moses is not here now. He is not with us anymore.

Being at any of these places—the sea, the mountains, the depths— or being with the ministering angels is being in the midst of life, still expecting high adventure, great achievement, being ready for despair but also hoping for philosophical and spiritual breakthroughs and enlightenment. Someone who has stepped back from these places has permitted him/herself to be partially an observer, to see things from a distance. At the same time, we may expect such a person to actively practice the mitzvot of world maintenance. She or he has experienced the importance of those mitzvot and has, one hopes, both eaten the fruits of them and been shaped by them. But such a person, for example, in the home of his or her adult children, will not demand to sit at the head of the table, though thankful when son or daughter insist she or he be the first at *netilat yadayim*, the "washing of hands," before meals, as a sign of world-maintaining respect.[12] Such a person, no matter what chronological age he or she has reached, is perhaps only moments away from "one hundred and twenty," the age at which Moses could calmly explain to the tribes that he could no longer lead but that the world would go on, nevertheless, without him.

If the midrashic tradition of stages—denial, anger, bargaining, and depression—reflect the situation of Deuteronomy 3, then, at the end of the Torah, we meet a Moses who, having been truly reconciled, is "one hundred and twenty years old."

Ascending Mount Pisgah

The change in Moses can explain the transfiguration of his ascent on Mount Pisgah to see the Land. The idea arose, we recall, as God's advice to Moses at the beginning of Deuteronomy, that he go up there to see the Land. When Moses finally does it, moments before his death, the sarcasm that might be read into God's original suggestion ("You want to see the Land? Very well, then, go and look at it. From afar!") is no longer there.

And Moses went up from the steppes of Moab to Mount Nebo, to the summit of Pisgah opposite Jericho, and the Lord showed him the whole land: Gilead as far as Dan; all Naftali; the land of Ephraim and Menasseh; the whole land of Judah as far as the Western Sea; the Negev; and the Plain—the Valley of Jericho, the city of palm trees—as far as Zoar. And the Lord said to him: This is the land of which I swore to Abraham, Isaac and Jacob, "I will assign it to your off-spring." I have let you see it with your own eyes, but you shall not cross over to it. And Moses the servant of God died there, in the land of Moab, at the word of the Lord. (Deut. 34:1–5)

This is not what we were led to expect in Deuteronomy 3! When Moses finally ascends, God is at his side, showing him the Land in all its variety and beauty, assuring him that the promise made to the patriarchs will be fulfilled. It seems to me that now the view "from afar" is also a comfort and a perspective. Moses, God seems to be saying, you have done all that was asked of you, and without you the events of your lifetime could not have happened. But the conquest is not your problem. You may rest now. Just enjoy the view. Trust me, you who are the trusted of my house. You need no longer maintain the world. You, like the patriarchs before you, have been a hero in my world, and like them, you shall be rewarded.

"It Is I Who Have Lost Him"

An education about death is thus like the teaching of hospitality, devoted prayer, and making peace between people. It is a teaching about life, a vision of social and individual heroism. Also, it is a hope, but no certainty, of living in an attitude of world building and world maintaining—until "one hundred and twenty."

But is the vision that sustains the heroic mode a true one? That question, for contemporary people, has no objectively detached answer. It can only be answered through the lives of those who accept the commandments of world maintenance, who study Torah to discover how to do so, and who together constitute a holy community, dedicated to the truth of their vision. That there is a God who is, at the least, coauthor of all truly worthy visions and worlds of meaning, as well as the educator of heroes, is best known in our time by seeing who God's friends are and learning from them.

Perhaps the teachers of the Midrash understood this proximity to God's friends as a perennial condition of religious faith. Recall what our midrash finds God to say to Joshua when He informs him that Moses has died: "He is dead, but indeed it is I who have lost him and not you."

18

What Is Worth
Knowing?
Learning Torah
"for Its Own Sake"

⟨⟩ The preparation of the young for a life of
learning and religious action and their initiation into what
is inherently valuable engages the tradition of Torah with great
force. The sages of the Talmud coined the term *Torah lishmah*,[1]
"Torah for its own sake," to depict learning and the observance of
the commandments performed with a religious intention, without
expectation of external reward. The concept of *lishmah* clearly
points to the realization of a (religious) human potential. It is with
an exploration into this concept that I conclude this discussion of
self-education.

In Search of Reasons for the Commandments

In his exhaustive study of Talmudic theology, Ephraim E. Urbach
explains that the rabbinic sages did not only explicate the Torah's
commandments but constantly explored and reexplored their inner
meaning. The sages, he finds, were much engaged in discovering

cogent philosophical, social, or moral reasons *(te'amim)* for the mitzvot. In some ways, this search for the significance of the commandments was similar to the theological project of such culturally Hellenized Jews as Philo of Alexandria, who defended the "philosophy" of Judaism and its legal code enthusiastically. Yet Urbach finds a substantial difference between the two. The universe of discourse of the Alexandrian Jews was the Greek philosophical one, with its axioms of logic, reason, and autonomy. There, commandments, in general and in particular, had to have plausible "reasons" to maintain their authority and their relevance. For the sages, in contrast, the binding character of the commandments themselves always preceded the "reasons" and the commandments held their normative ground even where there were no plausible grounds for them. Moreover, the sages insisted, sometimes enthusiastically, that some mitzvot were indeed incomprehensible and mysterious.[2]

The classic example of a mitzvah that eluded reason finding and reasonableness in rabbinic literature is the mysterious red heifer *(parah adumah)* (Num. 19). The commandment that mandates using the ashes of the red heifer to purify those who have become ritually impure is called "*the* statute *(hok)* of the Torah." As we have seen in Chapter 8, a statute is said to have no "reason" other than that God, for His reasons, commanded it. How can the ashes of the red heifer purify the ritually unclean and, conversely, pollute the ritually clean? And why specifically a red heifer? One may raise interesting conjectures, connected perhaps to the Golden Calf and the need for catharsis after transgression, but one finds no rational answers.

A midrash relates that Rabbi Yohanan ben Zakkai, the sage who established the academy at Yavne at the time of the destruction of the Second Temple, had the following conversation with a skeptical Gentile on the touchy subject of the *parah adumah*:

> A certain Gentile questioned Rabbi Yohanan ben Zakkai: "These things that you do seem like magical practices. A heifer is brought and slaughtered and burned and pounded and its ashes are collected and when one of you is defiled by the dead, two or three drops are

sprinkled upon him [with the ashes] and you say to him: 'You are clean.'" He [the rabbi] replied: "... Have you not seen anyone into whom the spirit of *pezzazit* [the demon of madness and epilepsy] has entered?" He [the Gentile] said, "Yes." R. Yohanan ben Zakkai asked him, "And what do you do [in such cases]?" He replied, "We bring roots and fumigates, place them under him and spray water upon [the demon spirit] and it flees." Said the rabbi, "Do not your ears hear what your mouth is speaking? Such too, [like that demon] is 'the spirit of uncleanliness.'" ... When the Gentile had left, R. Yohanan ben Zakkai's disciples said to him, " Master, him you have thrust aside with a reed [i.e., dismissed with a paltry argument]. But what explanation will you offer us?" Said he to them: "By your lives! Neither does the dead person defile nor does the water purify. Rather, this is the decree of the Holy One, blessed be He. [He has said] ... 'I have ordained a statute, I have issued an edict, and you may not question My edict.'" *(Pesikta de-Rabbi Kahana, Piska 4, Parah)*

For the uncomprehending outsider, who wants to know what the red heifer is good for, Rabbi Yohanan ben Zakkai draws a (false) comparison and concocts a "reason" within the context of witchcraft. Obviously, the sage does not himself believe in this connection; even his disciples recognize the argument as "a reed." So, speaking to these initiates, he simply states that there are mitzvot that have no reasons except to bear witness, by their commanded character, to the relationship between God and Israel. Rabbi Yohanan ben Zakkai might similarly have answered a Gentile who asked why Adam and Eve were forbidden the fruits of the Tree of Knowledge. He might have asked him: "Have you never come into contact with dangerous plants and poisonous fruits? And kept away from them? So too were Adam and Eve to do." And his students might have responded: "And now, Master, what is the real reason?" To which the sage might have said: "The tree is not dangerous and the fruit is harmless. But God has ordered a statute that poses a question to them: Will you act for the sake of Heaven? Is God's will a good enough reason for you to act in one way rather than another?"

The inability to formulate a plausible reason for a particular commandment, to tell what it's good for, has historically had a favorable consequence that itself looks like a reason, namely, that it generates an insider's sense of noblesse oblige. We are the ones who do strange things because they are God's decree. For members of the community, the statement that "they are God's decree" is a "reason," because it confers identity. By virtue of such strange commandments, Jews become more than mere senior citizens in Western culture or contributors to its civilization: They are the ones who have been tuned in to Rabbi Yohanan ben Zakkai and the red heifer. They are the ones for whom the "arbitrary" commandment not to eat of the Tree of Knowledge is a paradigm of all Torah.

But does it still work that way for most Jews? What does the reason of "no other reason than that it is God's decree" signify? Is that more or is it less than a commonsense (ethical, social, psychological) one? Why be different for no *good* reason? Modern Jews are increasingly inclined to raise such questions. And with regard to our particular midrash: If the Gentile is being brushed off because he could not understand (the truth) anyway, maybe there is not that much to understand. What is the status of a truth that only insiders can understand? In an age of multiple identities and many blurred ones, an age in which we claim to understand and sometimes even to sanction adolescent rebellion and self-choosing, young people especially will ask: If there are no reasons that make universal sense for the study of Torah and the performance of the commandments, why do these things? What are they good for?

If the study and the action demonstrate devotion to God, what actually is such devotion? What does it mean to say that a certain action is God's edict? Or is the notion of God's edict simply a flight from human freedom and autonomy? Isn't an act done for the sake of Heaven culturally incongruent? How does "for the sake of Heaven" point in the direction of something inherently worthy in human action and character?

These questions, though uniquely contemporary, are at the heart of a crucial debate in the world of the Talmudic sages as well. As we shall see, they are also related to a perennial and interesting educational issue, namely: On what basis may we claim that some things are worth teaching and learning even if they serve no extrinsic purpose or have no function, but simply belong to a realm of (alleged) inherent value?

We must, however, be careful to avoid anachronisms and apologetics. We must keep in mind that, unlike many moderns, the sages believed that obeying God's edicts, simply because they were commanded, was inherently worthwhile, in fact, the most significant human activity imaginable. Hence their discussion of the problem of reasons moved in the opposite direction from that of contemporary skeptics. Their problem was not whether one should observe commandments and study Torah if there were no good reasons for doing so. Rather, they wondered whether good reasons that were ulterior and extrinsic to Torah study and practice—such as hope of social approval, honor, reward, or conversely, fear of being shamed and punished—were acceptable motives for study and action or whether they were pernicious, corrupting, and ultimately destructive of the religious purpose of these activities. Of course, they knew that the Torah itself sometimes attached to its commandments rewards for doing them and sanctions for disobeying them. Nevertheless, the name they gave to studying Torah and "doing mitzvot" for no reason but the interior value or the commanded character of these activities was *lishmah*, "for its own sake." Studying and acting because it was worth one's while in some extrinsic fashion, they called *lo lishmah*, "not for its (or their) own sake."

Perhaps the clearest statement of this position was articulated by a midrash on the words "to love the Lord your God" (Deut. 11:13): "You might say, I am going to study Torah in order to become rich, or in order to be called 'Rabbi' or in order to receive a reward in the world to come. Therefore Scripture says, 'to love the Lord your God,' whatever you do should only be done out of love" (*Sifre, Piska* 41).

Learning for Intrinsic Value

One may wonder where the Talmudic sages and later teacher-commentators found grounds for the sometimes heatedly argued posi-

tion that only the performance of the commandments and the study
of Torah for their own sake were genuinely valuable. For how could
anyone reading the text of the Torah doubt that a major theme,
even there, is *lo lishmah*? Does not the Torah repeatedly urge Israel:
Do this and you shall live; do that, and you shall surely die? This
refrain is first heard in the Garden of Eden and resounds until almost the end of Deuteronomy, where Moses warns Israel about
backsliding and the terrible price in destruction and suffering to be
paid for it. Are not the terrifying warnings in Leviticus 26 and
Deuteronomy 28, in the portions of *Behukotai* and *Ki Tavo* respectively, crystal clear? If you turn your back on the covenant and the
commandments, we are told, instead of being blessed in the city
and in the field, you will be cursed here and there, becoming an object of mockery, a driven leaf, scattered among the nations. The
Torah obviously seems to be saying that it pays to be good. Like
children urged to good behavior by irate parents, Israel is apparently scolded into obedience.

Yet the rabbis' careful study of the Torah and reflection on their
own spiritual lives led them to discover an internal tension within
the text itself: between *lishmah*, the inherently valuable, and *lo
lishmah*, the instrumental. For example, they found that the commandment to love the Lord your God with all your heart, soul, and
might made no sense in the world of ulterior motivation. Could
one truly love (God or anyone) because it served some extrinsic
purpose or carried some reward, especially if the love was to be
with all one's heart, soul and being? When that love could lead to
death? We find the classic expression of that unconditional love—
and that question—in the story of Rabbi Akiva's martyrdom:

> When Rabbi Akiva was taken out to be killed by the Romans, it was
> the time for the reading of the *Shema*, and they kept flaying his flesh
> with iron combs, yet he accepted upon himself the yoke of the king-
> dom of Heaven [i.e., he recited the first passage of the *Shema*]. His
> disciples said to him: "Even now, master?" He said to them: "All my
> days I was troubled by this exposition [of the verse]: 'With all your
> soul'—[as meaning] 'even if He takes your soul from you.' I said, if

only it were within my power to fulfill this. And now that it is in my power, shall I not fulfill it?" (*Berakhot* 61b)

Indeed, the first paragraph of the *Shema* (Deut. 6:4–9), which commands total love of God and the routine ritual acts of spiritual dedication that articulate it, makes no mention of reward or punishment. This paragraph does not cajole with extrinsic benefits of any kind. The Torah does not say that love of God is good for social stability, conducive to spiritual health, or a sure way to Paradise. Even in the gruesome case of Rabbi Akiva, the heavenly voice that spoke as he expired merely exclaimed that he should be accounted "happy" because his spirit had left him while proclaiming the unity of God.

Yet the text that constitutes the second paragraph of the *Shema* is as pointedly *lo lishmah* as the first is *lishmah*.

And it shall come to pass . . . if you shall hearken diligently unto My commandments . . . to love the Lord your God and serve Him with all your heart and soul, that I will give the rain of your land in its season . . . and I will give grass in your fields for your cattle, and you will eat and be satisfied. Take heed lest your hearts be deceived and you turn aside and serve and worship other gods, and the anger of the Lord be kindled against you and He shut up the heaven so that there will be no rain, and the ground will not yield its fruit and you perish quickly off the good land that the Lord gives you. (Deut. 11:13–21)

How can these orientations, even within the *Shema* that the halakhah bids us recite twice daily, be reconciled? The seeming contradiction between these two orientations, as between these two passages, requires negotiation in order to understand the goals of religious life and to maintain the integrity of such a life. So, the following questions arose for discussion even in Talmudic times: Is the life of Torah a way of individual and social perfection? If so, and in spite of that, does human nature require that the Torah first, and always, be a way of setting social standards and establishing sanctions for delinquency, even if the notion of reward and punishment undermines and corrupts the spiritual ideal? Or is there a way to accommodate the inherent ideal of Judaism with the somber facts of human nature and social imperfection? Is the only proper way to study Torah and observe the commandments to do them "for their own sake," without expecting rewards or fearing punishment? However, since the Torah itself gives reasons for so many commandments, must it not also be laudable, though less so, to do these things for good reasons, even if they are extrinsic?

And what is to be understood by "for its own sake"? Is the spiritual perfection of the human being as an aim of the mitzvot a *lishmah* feature, or is it also a form of self-aggrandizement? Are the moral goals the sages found in the mitzvot part of what these mitzvot intrinsically mean? Which ways of bringing people closer to the Torah and its inner meaning, which rewards and instrumental uses of the Torah and its commandments, are legitimate?

Is There a Place for Instrumental Learning?

We begin with the statement of Antigonos in the *Ethics of the Fathers*: "Do not be like servants who minister to their master upon condition of receiving a reward, rather be like servants who minister to their master without the condition of receiving a reward" (*Avot* 1:3). To Antigonos, it is as simple as that. The mitzvot are to be observed for their own sake, not for any particular benefit but because they are located within the context of a master-servant relationship. Ben Azzai later expresses a related thought, but his idea has further ramifications: "The reward of a mitzvah is a mitzvah, and the reward of a transgression is a transgression" (*Avot* 4:2). The things we are to do have inherent value; if good, they enhance the doer, leading him or her to further acts of value; if bad, they corrode the soul. Similarly, the Talmudic sage Rabbi Eliezer understood the verse "Happy is the person who fears God, who takes great delight in His commandments" (Ps. 112:1) to refer to the person who takes delight "in His commandments but not in the reward of His commandments" (*Avodah Zarah* 19a). Rabbi Benayah states this idea more radically and draws operative conclusions with specific reference to the study of Torah: "Whoever engages in the study of Torah *lishmah*, his Torah becomes for him an elixir of life ... and whoever engages in Torah *lo lishmah*, not for its own sake, his [study] becomes a deadly poison for him" (*Ta'anit* 7a).

Rava of Babylonia is similarly uncompromising about studying Torah "not for its own sake." "Whoever engages in [the study of] Torah *shelo lishmah* [not for its own sake], it would have been better had he not been born." Are these sages engaged in hyperbole or do they have specific delinquencies in mind that go beyond the *lo lishmah* reason of wanting to enter the world to come? We may assume for the moment that their idea of *lishmah* and *lo lishmah* differed significantly from that of the Talmudic sage Rav. For Rav Yehudah said in the name of Rav: "A person should always engage in [the study of] Torah and [the observance of] mitzvot even if not for their own sake, for [the study and acting] 'not for their own sakes,' *(lo lishmah)* will lead to [doing them for their own sakes *(lishmah)*]" (*Pesahim* 50b). What, then, is the argument between them?

Stages of Learning:
From Childhood to Maturity

Maimonides, in his comprehensive code, *Mishneh Torah*, incorporates both opinions. He begins by citing the same *Sifre* as above (*Piska* 41) and then draws his conclusions:

> The sages of old said, Perhaps you may think to say, "I will study Torah in order to become rich, in order to be called rabbi, in order to receive reward in the world hereafter?" Hence it is said, "to love the Lord your God" (Deut 11:13). Whatever you do, you must do only out of love. . . .
>
> Whoever engages in Torah in order to receive reward or in order to escape punishment: this is engaging [in Torah] *lo lishmah*. And whoever engages in it not because of fear, and not in order to receive reward, but only because of love for the Lord of all the earth who commanded thus is engaging in Torah *lishmah*. And the sages said,

one should always engage [in Torah] even if it be *lo lishmah*, for by means of *shelo lishmah* he will get to *lishmah*. (*Mishneh Torah, Hilkhot Teshuvah* 10:4–5)

Our question is not yet answered. How does this harmonizing permissiveness with regard to *lo lishmah* deal with the harsh judgment of R. Benayah, who calls it poison, and Rav, who believes it would have been better for one who acts *lo lishmah* not to have been born?

In an earlier work, his *Introduction to the Mishnah (Perek Helek)*, Maimonides does supply a remarkable pedagogic answer to the question. He himself implicitly asks, Why does the Torah constantly give reasons that are not "for the sake of" study and action (*lishmam*) but are founded upon fear, if the ideal the Torah posits is to study and carry out the commandments only for the sake of Heaven (love)? Maimonides builds his argument upon a commentary on the statement in the mishnah that opens chapter 10 in tractate *Sanhedrin*. That mishnah declares that "all Israel have a share in the world to come," except for those whose doctrines or deeds deprive them of it.

Maimonides proceeds to categorize the various beliefs found among Jews as to what this "world to come" might be, ranging from notions of lush gardens in Paradise to a messianic age accompanied by a resurrection of the dead. Maimonides rejects all of these "strange" beliefs, which are largely based on "impossible things" that defy the laws of nature and philosophical sense. In order to explain why the Torah and the sages seem to permit people to entertain notions about the world to come that are tainted by "deplorable" ideas, Maimonides presents a parable:

Imagine a small child who has been brought to his teacher so that he may be taught the Torah, which is for his ultimate good because it will bring him to perfection. However, because he is only a child and because his understanding is deficient, he does not grasp the true value of that good, nor does he understand the perfection which he can achieve by means of Torah. Of necessity, therefore, his teacher, who has acquired greater perfection than the child, must bribe him by means which the child loves in a childish way. Thus the teacher may say, "Read [i.e., study] and I will give you some nuts or figs; I will give you a bit of honey." . . . Eating these delicacies is far more important to him studying, and a greater good.[3]

In the course of time, the child's conception of what is desirable changes. At that point of his development, he is best won over with promises of beautiful clothes or money. Still later, "his teacher may say to him . . . 'study so that you may become president of a court, a judge, so that people will honor you and rise before you as they honor So-and-So.' [The child] will then try hard to study in order to achieve his new goal . . . to achieve the honor, the exaltation and the praise that others might confer upon him." Only afterwards will the bright and sensitive student understand that "the end [purpose] of wisdom is neither to acquire honor from other men nor to earn more money. . . . The truth has no purpose other than knowing that it is truth." But knowing that it is truth is, as we have seen, not enough:

> Since the Torah is truth, *the purpose of knowing it is to do it.* A good person must not wonder, If I perform these commandments, which are virtues, and if I refrain from these transgressions, which are vices which God commanded us not to do, what will I get out of it? This is precisely what the child does when he asks, "If I read [i.e., study] what will you give me?" The child is answered in some such way because, when we know his limited understanding and his desire for something other than a real goal, we answer on the level of folly, as it is said in Proverbs 26:5, "Answer the fool according to his folly."[4]

Maimonides recognizes that not everyone can achieve a pristine knowledge of the truth, which must be "done" as well as comprehended. Therefore, the Torah gives sanction to study and observance for such extrinsic reasons as reward and punishment and gives at least lip service to Rav's hope that those who act *lo lishmah* will thereby be led to acting *lishmah*: "In order that the common folk might be established in their convictions, the Sages permitted them to perform meritorious actions with the hope of reward, and to avoid doing evil out of fear of punishment . . . until eventually the intelligent among them come to comprehend and know what truth is and what is the most perfect mode of conduct."5

Maimonides has addressed himself here to many of the relevant issues. He offers an explanation for the Torah's manifold promises and threats: They are a pedagogic device to bring immature human beings to noble actions. These actions, accompanied by study and reflection, will be slowly recognized as possessing an internal excellence. The contemplation and practice of this excellence is the greatest reward and the pinnacle of human potential. The ultimate goal of Jewish life, then, is to serve God for the sake of serving Him alone, but the road traveled to get there is instrumental *(lo lishmah)*.

Maimonides reminds us that the study of Torah is "for its own sake" *only if* it is translated into practice. The dry and uncommitted study of the truth is a betrayal of truth, for it must be translated into noble living. Here Maimonides intimates one possible understanding of the radical statement of the Babylonian sage Rava, "Whoever engages in [the study of] Torah *shelo lishmah* [for instrumental purposes], it would have been better had he not been born," namely, that studying "not for its own sake" signifies studying without intending to do (the mitzvot) but rather to provoke. This student of Torah learns in order to ridicule and undermine the practice of Judaism. This person has been corrupted by his or her inability to understand that knowledge alone, without practice, is worthless and dangerous.

We should note once again that this invaluable and indispensable practice is not aimed at achieving anything extrinsic to it. It is for its own sake. The Torah is "known" for the sake of knowledge of Torah and its being acted upon is part of what "knowing" it means.

What may we learn from this controversy with regard to the self-education of people who are on their own, after the education of childhood, that is, "training" and initiation has done its best with them?

1. As Urbach teaches us, the sages were always looking for reasons *(te'amim)* for the commandments. These commandments, in

general and in their particulars, would refine us. They believed the mitzvot would make us more compassionate, instill gratitude in us, teach us to deal justly and respectfully with one another, and protect us from the "evil impulse." The universe of *lishmah*, that is, observing the commandments "for their own sake" too, has its internal reasons. And underlying them is the promise of understanding truth and living it.

2. So that this ideal will penetrate consciousness, there are some commandments about which the search for reasons proves futile. Then inherent motivation *(lishmah)* moves to a different level of significance: of pure devotion, "love," and accepting "the yoke of the kingdom of Heaven."

3. The study and practice of Torah for its intrinsic value *(lishmah)* is always preferable to instrumental learning and practice *(lo lishmah)*, but children cannot be expected to act for intrinsic reasons they do not yet know or understand. And some people, alas, will never be mature enough to act "for the sake of Heaven." The fact that the recitation of the first two paragraphs of the *Shema* is required suggests that all Jews are included in the life of covenant. Nevertheless, the desirable direction is from the *yoke of the commandments* (as the second—instrumental—paragraph of the *Shema* is termed) to the *yoke of Heaven*, which is represented by the first paragraph of unconditional love.

4. "For its own sake" *(lishmah)*, suggests the inherent reason of devotion, but it may also indicate how to guard against the corruption of study or practice. For example, studying Torah not for the sake of practicing it is sterile, and a student who has no intention of carrying out the Torah's teachings deserves condemnation. It is with regard to such a person that Maimonides interprets Raba's statement, "It would have been better had he not been born."

(5) The instrumental, *lo lishmah*, which is basically denigrated, though sometimes (grudgingly) permitted, is that in which the student or the practitioner of Torah asks: What's in it for me? How will this serve my purpose of being rewarded? Yet the approval of such externally motivated, *lo lishmah*, behavior is grounded in the hope that it is only a stage of development and maturation.

A Theory of Knowing and
Doing "for the Sake of Heaven"

The *lishmah–lo lishmah* controversy illuminates a crucial debate in the world of education that points to the self-education that, one hopes, will follow upon it, namely, How may given curricula be justified? Is their purpose simply to prepare young people for the tasks and problems they will face in adult life by making them skilled, competent, and effective? Or are there fields to be studied and learned only so that they may be reflected, perhaps much later, in the character of the educated person? Are there subjects that have some "inner worth," shaping society in light of some social ideal or helping individuals to fashion themselves as somehow "fully" and uniquely human?

In his theory of human personality as composed of diverse "sentiments," which point toward diverse aspirations in life, the mid-twentieth-century American psychologist-philosopher Gordon Allport[6] pointed to the distinction between the "intentions" that characterize the religious sentiment in human beings and the "goals" that characterize other sentiments.

The goals of most other "sentiments," that is, fields of desire and motivation, are usually relatively clear-cut. One can learn how to achieve these goals, and one may recognize the moment of their achievement. If I want to be a great scholar, a desire arising in the "knowledge sentiment," I locate the scholars with whom I should study, the universities that offer the best chances of progress, and the professions that offer adequate scope for action, accomplishment, and recognition.[7] If I wish to be a great football player, my being wooed by an outstanding football team tells me that I have "arrived." If sentiments like love of adventure or curiosity drive me to plan a trip to France, I make financial and other calculations, clear my calendar, buy a ticket, arrange for accommodations, and organize an itinerary. Once I have decided on my plan, I either carry it out successfully or fail. But I will easily recognize success or failure. Either I get to my destination, enjoy myself, satisfy my curiosity about France and the French, and indulge my sense (and "sentiment") of adventure, or I do not. It may turn out that the whole venture was a bad idea. I should never have planned the trip. But in any case, after it is over, I relegate it to being a happy or sad memory and move on to other things.

As the religious sentiment matures, says Allport, it can no longer be satisfied by the achievement of such goals, of "having," getting, and achieving. It mobilizes the relevant forces of the entire human personality to move in the direction of a mode of *being*. The "being" that I strive for is one that is meant only for me, although I have never been there. I have a wellspring of desire and love for my intention, but little knowledge of it, for it lies in an uncertain and undefinable future. I may well ask, Is the intention really worthy? How can I know? To what extent is it achievable? How shall I move toward its achievement?

What I need here is not a travel guidebook or the most important research papers in my chosen field but a sacred textbook and people who are themselves a "text." I need a tradition and some human embodiments of it that I can trust. Yet this enterprise, of moving toward an "intention," is never simple. Too much trust may mar my enterprise of being a certain type of human being while also being myself. The goal is not limited; it requires all of me. I shall probably never know to what extent I was successful, and it will be a miracle if a "voice from Heaven" tells me at the moment of my death what success means and that I have somehow achieved it. What I am looking for is not pride of accomplishment or an interesting experience, but the Tree of Knowledge, which is ultimately intertwined with the Tree of Life.

Learning to Distinguish Between Knowledge for Use and Knowledge for Understanding

As we have seen, one of the great educational issues centers on usefulness and intrinsic worth in the curriculum. Should some subjects be studied simply because they are valuable in themselves, or must all fields of study justify themselves before the bar of use and function?

The twentieth century, in which we crossed innumerable and incredible frontiers of accomplishment, was not kind to "intrinsically valuable" studies. Such subjects, and especially the humanities, have been stigmatized: They are good only for impractical creatures or for those who are not very bright. Conversely, they are said to be favored by snobs and reactionaries.

Yet those are the "subject matter" of the religious intention. One studies them "for their own sake," without thought of rewards (of achievement), but only in order to deal better with questions about the meaning of life and the meaning of one's life within one's community of intention.

This "subject matter" is given a bad name by elitists who wish to study it without feeling themselves responsible to the question, how one *lives* by it. There is no more insidious form of *lo lishmah* than that. Nor is humanistic education well served by those who refuse to recite the second—*lo lishmah*—paragraph of the *Shema*, who refuse to recognize the value of discrete goals that are not for the sake of Heaven. Seeing everything in light of existential, "high cultural," and pietistic intentions, they move into ivory towers, meant only for themselves, or into fortresses of fanaticism. Then there are those who spurn all reasons, even moral ones, who have no conception of human potential beyond their circle of savants. Perhaps even worse are those who defend such learning by *lo lishmah* arguments, that pledge allegiance to Latin because it helps people learn Italian or to Talmud because it ostensibly trains the mind.

The distinction between knowledge that is useful and knowledge that is valued as intrinsically good—what we are calling *lo lishmah* and *lishmah*—is well expressed and defended by the Australian philosopher of education M. A. B. Degenhardt:

> It is hard to see why we should regard knowledge as "significant" or "serious" for any reason other than the fact that it can fuse with other knowledge to become part of the overall view a man takes of the world he inhabits and of himself in that world. In his daily living a man may be unlikely to *use* knowledge about his early ancestors, the

size of the universe, or the meaning of great art. Yet such knowledge can still be important to his life: important not as inert knowledge unrelated to how he lives and merely contemplated for its own sake; rather it is knowledge that helps to shape a man's view of things in general so as to become part of the very texture of how he understands and lives his life. Such areas of knowledge are significant and valuable to a man because they can become part of his "worldview" or "philosophy of life."[8]

The value of such knowledge, says Degenhardt, is not that it is "an end in itself." Rather, it is "serious or significant insofar as it makes a difference to how one lives," even though it is not "useful" in the ordinary sense of the word. For it is not knowledge that is to be used to some further end. "Rather, it is the kind of knowledge that helps us to determine our ends. By this I mean that it gives us that picture or understanding of things in terms of which we can decide what to do with our lives, what aims to set ourselves, what ends to live for."[9]

The Allport and Degenhardt conceptions seem to make good sense of the *lishmah–lo lishmah* issue and to provide a universal context for it. Their theses can help us understand how study, ostensibly "for its own sake," can really be *lo lishmah*, why children and others with immature religious sentiments cannot (yet) understand the meaning of *lishmah*. This discussion even places, for wide communicability, the notion that we hold our intrinsic values more in "love of God" than knowledge or understanding of Him. We do not understand "statutes" (those things we are to do for no "reason" other than that God commanded them), but they are an avenue of articulating devotion for us, and they help us to express who we are.

For Jews, as for others who cultivate comprehensive "intentions" and seek to learn what ends to live for, describing the proximity of their internal language to other ones and translating, as the great philosopher and educator Emmanuel Levinas would have said, "from Hebrew to Greek"[10] is only the beginning of wisdom. To understand intellectually that all human beings ask about the relationship between the Tree of Knowledge and the Tree of Life, which is also the relationship between discipline and freedom and harmony, is not yet to answer the question or even to ask, Which knowledge deserves obedience and submission? What life of creativity and autonomy is attainable? Whom do I trust to teach me when I am searching for the meaning of my life? on the way to confronting its frighteningly unclear "ends" and its dialectic of "knowledge" and "life"? Christian scholastics? Secular humanists? The rabbinic sages? The text of the Torah and those commentators that gather around the page, intent on being seen and heard in the great conversation of ends and guiding us toward the paths that lead to these ends?

Jewish education and Jewish life will continue meaningfully if the conversation around the text of the Torah continues, if Torah is "learned" and then practiced *lishmah*, for its own sake. That means, for the sake of a significant moral, intellectual, spiritual, and, yes, religious existence that can make itself understood in the world forum of search and value but that lives toward its own meanings and ends, in the hope of increasingly understanding them. This conversation of study and practice listens to Rabbi Yohanan ben Zakkai as he discusses the red heifer and to Rabbi Akiva as he interprets the *Shema* and—in the seemingly absurd act of acceptance that marks Akiva's last moments—as he carries his learning into active intention.

Listening, of course, is not always agreeing. Fortunately, on the perpetually yellowing, yet mysteriously fresh, page on which sages of all generations discuss ultimate intention with the text of the Torah, there is always some controversy, always something new to learn. And there is, miraculously, always room for more.

Postscript:
The Tree of
Knowledge and the
Tree of Life

THE GREAT HISTORIAN of Jewish mysticism, Gershom Scholem, has pointed to the centrality of the two trees in Eden in the kabbalistic tradition for understanding the tensions inherent in human self-realization. Scholem writes:

> What do the two trees in Paradise represent? Even in biblical metaphor, wisdom, identified by Jewish tradition with Torah, is designated as Tree of Life (Prov. 3:18); thus opens the whole realm of topology. The trees in Paradise are not merely physical trees; beyond that they point to a state of things which they represent symbolically. In the opinion of the Jewish mystics both trees are in essence one. They grow out in two directions from a common trunk. . . . The two trees are different aspects of the Torah, which have their common origin in revelation. . . . The law which is concealed in the life of this Tree [of Life] is that of a creative force manifesting itself in infinite harmonies, a force that knows no limitations or boundaries. The sin of Adam was that he isolated the Tree of Life from the Tree of Knowledge to which he directed his desire. Once the unity of the two trees in men's lives was destroyed, there began the dominion of the

Tree of Knowledge. . . . [This] corresponds to a condition of this
world in which distinctions must be made before the unity of life can
be regained: the distinctions between good and evil, commandment
and prohibition, holy and profane, pure and impure.[1]

One need not follow the mystic model to its conclusion, with its
possibly antinomian intimations that in messianic times, the focus
of revelation will be within the Tree of Life, with its expansive harmonies. However, we may learn from the imagery of the kabbalists
that there is a tension between the revelation of restriction (of commandment and prohibition), which is symbolized by the Tree of
Knowledge, and the revelation of creativity, harmony, and the absence of boundaries—symbolized by the Tree of Life. We may also
learn from the notion that both trees, despite the apparent contra-
dictions between them, "grow out of a common trunk," and that
they should not, and perhaps ultimately cannot, be separated. They
stand at the very center of the garden and, hence, at the center of
human concern. Despite the seeming antitheses and the tangible
tension between caution, restriction, and the setting of boundaries,
on the one hand, and freedom, daring, openness, and harmony, on
the other, they are both aspects of Torah and of human existence.

Education, we have seen, is about both trees, and educated persons may be said to have an inkling of the challenge conveyed by
the image that the two trees are one. Their education invites them
to look to the heroic models of the patriarchs and matriarchs, who
are bound by a specific and cherished family covenant, yet seek the
truth on their own, untroubled by the fact that they are pioneers on
the road as yet untraveled. In the family circle, educated persons
have learned a language that initiates and restrains, yet it liberates
by making communication possible and rendering the world,
through the mediation of the family, trustworthy.

In our search for models of educational thinking and practice, we
have seen Moses, the teacher, teaching initiative and responsibility
even when no one has any experience with doing what must be
done, by articulating the apparently soothing but actually demanding lesson that "God is always with you," but only if you are there

for Him. In the story of young Esau and Jacob, we see the danger of restricting the education of one child to what may be normative for the other. We have followed the community as it initiates the child into its patterns. We have asked how much Tree of Knowledge "honor" is needed, for children and adults, lest we die as social beings. Conversely, we have dwelt on the need to cultivate the dignity of children, to open many vistas for them, to place them in the shade of the Tree of Life. Yet we have also expressed concern that attention to dignity alone, bereft of honor, will propel them to flee from freedom and draw them into totalitarian "Edens" ruled by serpents who walk erect and look all too human.

The educational problem of identity, what is "inside" and what "outside," a dominant theme of several chapters, and the kindred issues of particularism and universalism can be related to the notion of the two trees as interlinking. This interlinking suggests that one should avoid seeing the Tree of Knowledge—with its clear, fixed, and "particularistic" categories of holy and profane, with its intimation of the world as divided into "inside" and "outside"—as the sum total of Torah. Such an exclusive concern with the Tree of Knowledge may, all too often, lead to the conclusion that what is good, holy, pure, and noble is to be found exclusively in the realm that defines and commands *us*, and that all else is trivial. In a world in which the Tree of Knowledge, with its restraints and distinctions, is routinely uprooted in the name of a messianic Tree of Life, which allegedly teaches that "anything goes," one can understand where the educational orientation of exclusive concern with the Tree of Knowledge comes from. But acceding to it is dangerous and may be deadening.

The final section of my study dealt with the individuation of the human being who has been socialized and who is now responsible for what she or he becomes. We have seen that "education for mitzvot," in itself vintage Tree of Knowledge and the staple of religious experience, serves not only to foster and articulate loyalty and piety but is also a portal to the well-being of the soul, to its diverse "perfections," wherein each individual attempts to discover what is really *lishmo*, "for its own sake," for the sake of what he or she hopes to become. *Lishmo*, I suggest, is where the two trees meet. There the commandments, the norms of community, the restrictions, and the obligations point toward directions in which we can "go" with them. The interlocking roots of the two trees point to the paradox of being free and responsible. When that is achieved—because of what parents and teachers have done, because of what the individual makes of what they did, in sickness and in health, in the midst of life and toward its end—then education has succeeded, and those who are educated have "a share in the world to come," which Jewish tradition also, poignantly, calls Eden.

Finally, the study of Torah. In the Introduction, I referred to the two blessings recited by the one who "ascends" to the reading of the Torah. Before the reading, we bless God, "who has chosen us from among the nations and given us His Torah." Again, vintage Tree of Knowledge. Upon the conclusion of the reading, the person called to the reading blesses God, "who has given us a Torah of truth and has planted eternal life in our midst," a phrase that overtly ties Torah to the Tree of Life.

I have attempted to show how membership in the family and in the people mandates study of Torah. But the Bible of the Synagogue, which perceives the "language" of Judaism shining through its diverse "literatures," throughout its worlds of midrash, analysis, reasoning, and moral deliberation, strives to assure that the Torah of chosenness—the Torah that is an intimate road to knowledge and that is the cherished treasure of a people that "rejoices in its commandments"—will also remain a Torah of expansive truth, of reasons for the mitzvot in all their heuristic meanings, pointing in their particularity toward ultimate harmonies.

I have argued that in education, the Tree of Knowledge comes first, and the distinctions it makes and the specific commitments it demands illuminate the path to the Tree of Life. For this reason I have assumed that texts about leprosy should, in the questions they pose and the symbols they evoke, be as seriously instructive as academic bible scholarship that insists on the expansive freedom of inquiry; that the red heifer should not be shunted aside for instructive midrash on inherent value, but should, rather, nourish it. Likewise, the universal predicaments associated with mortality should not be isolated from such halakhot as inviting aged parents at the dinner table to be the first for the ritual washing of hands. For, if the Torah of our education is *only* universal truth—requiring mere human decency, moral spontaneity, and, ultimately, reason, to be understood and appropriated—why stick with Judaism? Conversely, if this Torah is only about having been divinely chosen and about halakhic competence, how will loyalty and pride not blunt commitment to truth? Can there be education without both community and truth? Can universal truth that really matters be kept apart from the agendas and memories of communities and from the ways they teach? And can communities flourish when they themselves cease to be communities of learning?

I have explored some ways in which such questions are raised and resolved in the "language" of Jewish tradition and tried to show why fresh reflection upon them is called for in this generation, as in previous ones. I suggested that the modes of Torah study—its questions, controversies and resolutions—may also initiate fruitful discussions about contemporary Jewish education.

Now, in the manner of Torah study, I close this book with these questions, knowing that there will be no closure on them. The conversations with Torah continue.

APPENDIX:
THE CHAPTER,
THE VERSE,
AND THE "PORTION"

Tree of Knowledge, Tree of Life may remind some readers of the sermonette, or "word of Torah" *(dvar Torah)*, they want to deliver on some Sabbath morning or at some community occasion where "something needs to be said," whether to express joy or give voice to sorrow. To focus matters somewhat, I here mention the major texts of the Torah that explicitly lay the foundations for the thematic development of each chapter. And, in addition to citing chapter and verse, I note which "portion of the week" the passage comes from, so that its possible usefulness for studying and speaking will be more readily obvious. Those texts of the Torah that arise in the discussion only implicitly, say as proof texts for midrash, are not mentioned here unless they clearly lead us back to Bible study, but the sources are, of course, noted in the body of the book. I hope this "key" to further reflection and discussion will prove useful.

TABLE A.1   Key to the Sources and the "Portions of the Week"

Chap.			
	Introduction	Genesis 2:15–17	Portion of Bereshit
	Chapter 1 The story of Abraham and Sarah	Genesis 11:26–32; 12–23	Portions of Noah (end) Lech Lecha, Vayerah, Haye Sarah
	Also, on the in- fertility of Rachel and Jacob's re- buke	Genesis 30	Portion of Vayetze
	Chapter 2 On three of the four children of the Haggadah	Exodus 12: 25–27; 13:8; 13:14	Portion of Bo
	The fourth child	Deuteronomy 6:20–6:21	Portion of Va-Ethannan
	Chapter 3 The story of the Akedah	Genesis Chapter 22	Portion of Va-yera
	The Torah's text for the midrash of the 'Captain'	Numbers 15:37–41	Portion of Shelah
	Chapter 4 The problem of Esau	Genesis 25	Portion of Toledot
	On Amalek 'who did not fear God'	Exodus 17:8–16 Deuteronomy 25:17–19	Portion of Beshallah Portion of Ki Tetse
	Chapter 5 At the Red Sea	Exodus 13:17–22; 14, 15	Portion of Beshallah
	Chapter 6 On Creation On the festivals	Genesis 1–3 Leviticus 23	Portion of Bereshit Portion of E'mor

Chapter 7

On Aaron, his clothing and his (Yom Kippur) service	Exodus 27:20 – 30:10 Leviticus 16	Portion of Tetsavveh Portion of Aharei Mot, or, Yom Kippur reading

Chapter 8

The role of law in human life	Exodus 15:22–26 Exodus 21–24	Portion of Beshallah Portion of Mishpatim

Chapter 9

The ideal person	Deuteronomy 10:12–13	Portion of Ekev

Chapter 10

Jacob and Esau	Genesis 27; 28; 32:1 Genesis 35	Portions of Toledot and Vayetse Portion of Vayishlah

Chapter 11

On the Land of Israel	Deuteronomy 30:3–5	Portion of Nitsavim
On Joseph and his family in Egypt	Genesis 47–50	Portion of Vayehi

Chapter 12

The universal and the particular	Genesis 6–9	Portions of Bereshit (end) and Noah

Chapter 13

Bible scholarship and faith	Exodus 32:11–34:35	Portion of Ki Tissa
On the 'tent' outside the camp	Numbers 11:24–26; 12:4; Deuteronomy 31:14–15	Portions of Be-ha'alotekha and Vayelekh
	Exodus 38:21	Portion of Pekudei

Chapter 14

The story of Joseph	Genesis 37–50	Portions of Vayeshev, Mikkets, Vayiggash, Vayehi

Chapter 15

On the beheaded heifer   Deuteronomy 21:1–9   Portion of Shofetim

The midrashic take-off   Genesis 46:1   Portion of Vayiggash
is on:

Chapter 16

On leprosy in the   Numbers 12, Deuter-   Portions of Be-
Torah's narrative   onomy 24:8–9, Exo-   ha'alotekha, Ki Tetse,
                         dus 4:1–7   Shemot

On laws of leprosy   Leviticus 13:1–14:57 Portions of Tazria and
                                               Metsora

On Nadav and Avihu   Leviticus 10:1–7   Portion of Shemini

Chapter 17

On dying   Deuteronomy   Portions of Vayelekh,
                         31:1–3; Deuteron-   Va-Ethannan, Pinhas
                         omy 3:24–29; Num-
                         bers 27:12–14

                         Deuteronomy 34   Portion of Vezot
                                               Haberakhah
Chapter 18
'For Its Own sake'

For the first two para- Deuteronomy 6:4–9;   Portions of Va-
graphs of "the Shema"   Deuteronomy   Ethannan and Ekev
                         11:13–21   Portion of Hukkat

On the red heifer   Numbers 19

READING OVER MY
SHOULDER

READERS MAY HAVE NOTED that certain writers were my own teachers, whether by way of face to face instruction or through the written word, and they will perhaps wish to go to the masters directly rather than relying on the disciple. As I mentioned in the Preface, one of my great teachers was Nehama Leibowitz ("Nehama" to all her pupils). Fortunately for those who wish to study with her, six books of biblical-midrashic study, arranged according to the "portion of the week," have been published in English, covering the entire Torah. They are entitled *Studies in Bereshit* [Genesis] (1974); *Studies in Shemot* [Exodus], two volumes (1976); *Studies in Vayikra* [Leviticus] (1980); *Studies in Bamidbar* [Numbers] (1980); and *Studies in Devarim* [Deuteronomy] (1980). All are published by the Torah Department of the World Zionist Organization, Jerusalem. Readers who have no access to her voluminous Hebrew studies can easily spend years of Sabbaths with the English ones.

We have seen Rashi to be the "staple" of Torah study. There are translations of Rashi's Torah commentary in English. Look at *Chumash and Rashi*, translated and annotated by A. M. Silberman in collaboration with M. Rosenbaum (New York: Feldheim, 5745 [1985]). Also available in English translation is Nachmanides (Ramban) on the Torah, translated and annotated by Charles B. Chavel (New York: Shilo Publishing House, 1974). For the commentary of Samson Raphael Hirsch in English, see *The Pentateuch*, explained by Rabbi Samson Raphael Hirsch, translated by Isaac Levy (London: Isaac Levy, 1958–1962). I should not fail to mention the Jewish Publication Society's five volumes on the Bible, each volume (and book of the Torah) being explained and interpreted by a different academic scholar: Genesis *(Bereshit)* is accompanied by the commentary of Nahum Sarna (1989) as is Exodus *(Shemot)* (1991); Leviticus *(Vayikra)* has the commentary of Baruch A. Levine (1989); Numbers *(Bamidbar)*, that of Jacob Milgrom, and Deuteronomy *(Devarim)*, that of Jeffrey H. Tigay (1996). This obviously makes for very different reading than, say, Rabbi Hirsch's commentary. For more traditional commentary, there is still the venerable Hertz Chumash: *The Pentateuch and Haftorahs*, English Translation and Commentary by J. H. Hertz (London: Soncino Press, 1976), as well as *the Soncino Chumash* (London: Soncino Press, 1966), which abridges classic commentators. Both are useful to the English reader perusing the "portion of the week."

A large proportion of my midrashic sources are taken from the compilation entitled *Midrash Rabbah* (on the books of the Pentateuch and on the "scrolls" of the Bible). *Midrash Rabbah* is translated into English by Rabbi D. H. Friedman (London: Soncino Press, 1961); a multivolume work, it bears the simple title, *The Midrash*. Although I have relied on the Hebrew original in most of my citations, I list them by chapter and passage, and these remain constant in all editions, whether Hebrew or translated. Many other midrashic collections may now be found in translation: the *Mekhilta de-Rabbi Yishmael* (on Exodus); *Midrash Tanhuma* (on the Torah); *Sifra* (a rabbinic commentary on Leviticus); *Sifre* (a rabbinic commentary on Numbers and Deuteronomy), among others.

Two midrashic-aggadic works that I have frequently consulted in translation are *Tanna debe Eliyyahu*, translated by William G. (Gershon Zev) Braude and Israel J. Kapstein (Philadelphia: Jewish Publication Society, 5741 [1981]), and *The Fathers According to Rabbi Nathan (Abot de-Rabbi Natan)*, translated and annotated by Judah Goldin (New Haven: Yale University Press, 1955). Goldin's work deals with what scholars call Version A of this midrashic collection.

The first great work of Midrash and Aggadah I was privileged to read is Louis Ginzberg's monumental seven-volume *Legends of the*

Jews (Philadelphia: Jewish Publication Society, 1942). Ginzberg sketches a "running plot" of the Bible cum midrash that is fascinating. He also invites the reader to locate his sources (in Volumes 5 and 6) and supplies an index in Volume 7. Differently textured is the great anthology of H. N. Bialik and Y. H. Ravnitzky, *Sefer ha-Aggadah*, happily now available in English as *The Book of Legends*, translated by William G. Braude (New York: Schocken Books, 1992). And how can I leave out the oft-cited work of Thomas Mann, *Joseph and His Brothers*, also a monumental Midrash of sorts?

On the subject of Midrash and rabbinic literature in general, two other volumes available in English should be noted. One is Ephraim E. Urbach's two-volume *The Sages: Their Concepts and Beliefs* (Jerusalem: Magnes Press, 1975), a truly encyclopedic work. The other, more monographic, work is Judah Goldin, *Studies in Midrash and Related Literature*, edited by Barry L. Eichler and Jeffrey H. Tigay (Philadelphia: Jewish Publication Society, 5748 [1988]). For more extensive reading lists on Midrash and other areas of Jewish study, the reader is referred to Barry Holtz's, *Back to the Sources: Reading the Classic Jewish Texts* (New York: Summit Books, 1984). For this volume Holtz brought together some of the best voices in Jewish scholarship, on almost every "classic" dimension of Jewish study. Each chapter offers the reader extensive bibliographic information and advice. Holtz himself provides both the chapter and the bibliography for Midrash. That bibliography takes us only to the mid-1980s, but it is extremely valuable.

Those who have developed the culture of "studying the portion of the week" in contemporary Jewish life are too numerous to mention. Besides Nehama, I should like to mention a teacher who gets insufficient credit for his contribution to the field, namely, Rabbi S. B. Jacobson, a Bible teacher in Tel Aviv in the mid-twentieth century. His essays on the portion and on the prophetic readings that are attached to them are always lucid and suggestive. In English his volume on "the portion of the week" is *Meditations on the Torah* (Tel Aviv: Sinai Publishing, 1969).

Among the great Jewish scholars who have changed the way we look at Jewish history, one cannot fail to mention Gershom Scholem, historian of Jewish mysticism, and Jacob Katz, historian of Jewish modernity. Of Gershom Scholem, in English, I advise looking (at the very least) at *The Messianic Idea in Judaism* (New York: Schocken Books, 1971). For Jacob Katz, I recommend as a start *Exclusiveness and Tolerance: Studies in Jewish-Gentile Relations in Modern Times* (London: Oxford University Press, 1961). There are many others: I mention these only because their ideas helped shape some of the theses in this book.

The thinkers that most speak to me are those whose approach is dialogical, such as Martin Buber and Franz Rosenzweig. I suggest looking, to begin with, at Buber's *Israel and the World: Essays in a Time of Crisis*, 2d ed. (New York: Schocken Books, 1963), and *On Zion: The History of an Idea* (New York: Schocken, 1975). For Franz Rosenzweig, his slim book of essays and letters, *On Jewish Learning*, edited by N. N. Glatzer, 2d ed. (New York: Schocken Books, 1963), may be a good introduction, specifically on theological-educational issues.

I feel a strong affinity to Jewish and non-Jewish writers who are concerned with the relationship between traditional faith and modernity, and who are not ready to sacrifice either of them. Hence my interest in Emil L. Fackenheim, especially in his seminal work, *To Mend the World: Foundations of Post-Holocaust Jewish Thought* (New York: Schocken Books, 1982, 1989); Joseph B. Soloveitchik, *The Lonely Man of Faith* (New York: Doubleday, 1995), and the (especially halakhic) writings of Eliezer Berkovits. See particularly *Not in Heaven: The Nature and Function of Halakha* (New York: Ktav Publishing House, 1983). Then there are the non-Jewish writers who speak much of the same "language," however different the "literature": Peter L. Berger, in, for example, *A Rumour of Angels: Modern Society and the Rediscovery of the Supernatural* (Garden City, N.Y.: Anchor Books, 1970), Ernest Becker, and Charles Taylor. I highly recommend reading Becker's groundbreaking book, *The Denial of Death* (New York: Free Press–Macmillan, 1973), and Charles Taylor, *The Ethics of Authenticity* (Cambridge, Mass.: Harvard University Press, 1991). Among educational thinkers, I suggest reading Israel Scheffler, Thomas F. Green, and R. S. Peters. Scheffler's *In*

Praise of the Cognitive Emotions and Other Essays in the Philosophy of Education (New York: Routledge, 1991) seems like a good place to begin reading the works of this thinker. For Peters, the classic is *Ethics and Education* (London: Gallen and Unwin, 1966). As for Green, a fairly new and stimulating work is *Voices: The Educational Formation of Conscience* (Notre Dame, Ind.: University of Notre Dame Press, 1999).

I am grateful to these and many others who made it possible for me to think afresh about Jewish tradition and the question of its transmission and renewal. I thought I should mention at least some of the people who, for me, are teachers as well as scholars.

GLOSSARY

aggadah   the nonlegal portions of Talmudic and midrashic literature

Akedat Yitzhak   philosophical commentary on the Bible of R. Yitzhak (Isaac) Arama (late fifteenth century)

asara harugai malkhut   the ten martyrs put to death by the Romans after the unsuccessful Bar Kohhba uprising to regain Jewish independence (132–135 C.E.)

Abot de-Rabbi Natan   a midrashic work organized as a commentary on *Avot*, or *Pirke Avot (The Ethics of the Fathers)*

Baba Batra   Talmudic tractate that constitutes the "last [third] gate" (*baba*, "gate"; *batra*, "last") in the Talmud section "Damages," dealing mainly with torts and damages; *Baba Batra* follows *Baba Kamma* and *Baba Metzia*

Baba Kamma   the Talmudic tractate that constitutes the "first gate" (*kamma*, "first") in the Talmudic section "Damages," dealing mainly with torts and damages

Baba Metzia   the tractate that is the "middle gate" (*metzia*, "middle") of the Talmudic section "Damages," dealing mainly with torts and damages

Berakhot   the tractate of the Talmud dealing with blessings and prayer

bet midrash   "House of Study," the institution of Talmudic Judaism for the study of Torah

Braita   laws and discussions of the Oral Tradition that are not incorporated into the Mishnah, yet figure prominently in the Gemara, the bulk of the Talmud, which consists of discourse on the Mishnah in the generations after its compilation

brit milah   circumcision

Debe Eliyahu Rabbah   an *aggadic* work of the late tenth century, rich in ethical teachings and insights; an appended shorter work is entitled *Seder Eliyahu Zuta*

drash   the homiletic mode of biblical exegesis

Elohim   the name of God that is often used to refer to Divinity in its manifestation in nature (rather than in history)

Eretz Yisrael   the Land of Israel, the "promised land"

Four Species   the *etrog*, "citron"; *lulav*, "palm branch"; *hadassim*, "myrtle branches"; and *aravot*, "willow branches"; they figure prominently in the liturgical celebration of Sukkot, the Feast of Tabernacles

349

galut   exile from the Land of Israel

Gittin   Talmudic tractate dealing mainly with laws of divorce

Ha'amek Davar   biblical commentary of the nineteenth-century **Rabbi Naftali Zvi Berlin**, also known by the acronym **"Netziv"**

Haggadah (of Passover)   the narrative prayer book used at the Seder celebration on the eve of Passover

Hagigah   Talmudic tractate dealing with the laws of festivals and pilgrimage to Jerusalem

halakhah   Jewish law as a whole or a specific legal ruling or usage; adjective, halakhic

HaShem   "the Name," a pious appellation for God

Hilkhot Teshuvah   a section of Maimonides' *Mishneh Torah* dealing with the laws of repentance

Hizkuni   Rabbi Hizkiah ben Manoah, the last of the great medieval French biblical commentators (thirteenth century)

hok   that aspect of Jewish law identified with inexplicable laws, divinely decreed; plural, *hukim*

kabbalistic   adjective referring to mystical writings and doctrines of Judaism

Kedushin   a tractate of the Talmud dealing essentially with the laws of marriage

Kohen Gadol   the High Priest who officiated in the Temple in Jerusalem

korbanot   sacrifices, offered in the Temple

lashon hara   literally, "evil tongue," referring to gossip and malicious talk

lishmah   action and/or study carried out "for its own sake"; its opposite is action and/or study not done for its own intrinsic purpose, *lo lishmah*; plural of *lishmah*, *lishmam* or *lishman*

mahloket   controversy among sages and other students of Torah, which is said to be a rewarding activity only if conducted "for the sake of Heaven"

Maimonides   Rabbi Moses ben Maimon, leading halakhic scholar, codifier, and philosopher of medieval Jewry (twelfth century); also known by the acronym "Rambam"

Mekhilta   early midrashic compilation on Exodus; its complete name is *Mekhilta de-Rabbi Yishmael*

Midrash   rabbinic literature of Talmudic and post-Talmudic times based on a mode of scriptural interpretation that homiletically expounds words and verses; "a midrash," a single homiletic teaching

Midrash Rabbah   midrashic compilation consisting of midrashic statements and conversation, mainly compiled in the post-Talmudic era; *Midrash Rabbah* includes collections on each of the five books of the Torah and each of the five scrolls read in the synagogue on appropriate festivals, and in the case of Lamentations, on the Fast of the Ninth of Av (Esther, Song of Songs, Ruth, Lamentations, and Ecclesiastes)

Minhah   the afternoon service

mishkan   the "dwelling for the divine Presence," the sanctuary erected for divine service during the forty years of wandering in the wilderness

Mishnah   the traditions and teachings of "Oral Torah" compiled and edited by Rabbi Judah the Prince (212 C.E.); a single passage of the Mishnah is "a mishnah"

Mishneh Torah   the comprehensive code of Talmudic law compiled by Moses Maimonides

mishpat   that aspect of Jewish law associated with rational judgment

mitzvot   commandments; singular, mitzvah

Mussaf   the "additional" morning service recited on Sabbaths and festivals

Nachmanides   Rabbi Moses ben Nahman, leading thirteenth-century medieval scholar and commentator, also known by the acronym "Ramban"

Nedarim   the tractate of the Talmud dealing mainly with vows and the laws governing the making of vows

Noahide commandments   moral laws incumbent on all humans

ohel mo'ed   the "tent of meeting," the tabernacle of divine service throughout the yeatrs of wandering in the winderness

parah adumah   the "red heifer," a biblical law of purification that, for the Talmudic rabbis, exemplified the concept of *hok*, that is, laws that are to be obeyed as divine decrees (Num. 19)

Parashat Hashavua, or **"the *Parashah"***   "portion of the week"; that section of the Torah read in the synagogue in any specific week

Pe'ah   the tractate of the Talmud dealing with agricultural laws, specifically, with the law that requires leaving a corner *(pe'ah)* of each field for the poor

Pesahim   the tractate of the Talmud dealing with Passover

Pesikta de-Rabbi Kahana   midrashic compilation dealing with biblical selections read on holidays and special Sabbaths (e.g., the three prophetic texts read on the Sabbaths before the ninth of Av)

Pirke Avot, **or** *Avot*   a short Mishnaic tractate recording the views of early sages on questions of proper ethical conduct; hence, often called *The Ethics of the Fathers*

Rambam   see Maimonides

Ramban   see Nachmanides

Rashi   acronym for Rabbi Shlomo ben Yizhaki, the leading and most widely studied exegete of Scripture and Talmud in medieval Jewry (eleventh century)

Rosh Hashanah   the festival of the New Year; also known as Yom Hazikaron, the Day of Remembrance

Sanhedrin   the tractate of the Talmud dealing with procedures and purposes in courts of law

Seder Eliyahu Zuta   see *Debe Eliyahu Rabbah*

Sefer ha-Aggadah   a comprehensive anthology of *aggadic* texts found in the Talmud (both the Jerusalem Talmud and the Babylonian Talmud) and in the classic

midrashic works of antiquity and the early middle ages; edited by Haim Nahman Bialik, first poet laureate of modern Israel, and J. H. Ravnizki

Sforno, Obadiah   great Italian commentator in Renaissance times, whose philosophical humanism is evident in his biblical exegesis

Shabbat   the Sabbath; also the Talmudic tractate dealing with the laws of the
Sabbath

Shema Yisrael   the opening words of the first of three biblical passages that are
recited morning and evening by observant Jews, proclaiming the unity of God;
often referred to as *the Shema*

Shekhinah   a term for the "divine Presence," the indwelling spirit of God

Shmini Atzeret   the concluding festival of Sukkot, coming on the eighth day after the beginning of that festival—hence known as the Eighth Day of Solemn
Assembly

Shulhan Arukh   the halakhic code of law written by Rabbi Joseph Karo in the
sixteenth century and still considered authoritative among Orthodox Jews

Sifra   a midrashic compilation relating to the text of Leviticus

Sifre   midrashic texts on Numbers and Deuteronomy

sod   the mystic mode of interpreting the Torah

Sotah   a tractate of the Talmud dealing largely with the biblical law in relation to
an adulterous woman: her identification, her rights, and her punishment

talmid hakham   literally, "a disciple of the wise"; in actual usage, "a learned and
wise person"; plural, *talmide hakhamim*

Talmud   the normative "Oral Torah" consisting of the Mishnah and the Gemara;
the Palestinian Talmud was redacted in the Land of Israel during the latter part
of the fourth century, the Babylonian Talmud, which is longer, at the end of the
fifth century and at the beginning of the sixth century

Tanhuma   a midrashic compilation on the five Books of Moses (Pentateuch)

Tannaic   relating to the views recorded in the Mishnah (and related literature) of
the Tanna'im, sages of the early Talmudic period; their views are discussed by
later sages, the Amora'im, in the Gemara

teshuvah   repentance, returning to the ways of God

tikkun hagoof and *tikkun hanefesh*   represent the Torah's "intention," according
to Maimonides, namely, that we work to achieve the "well-being of the body"
and the "well-being of the soul," the latter consisting of intellectual self-realization and the former, social order and morality

Torah Temimah   biblical commentary of Rabbi Baruch Halevi Epstein, a nineteenth-century exegete and halakhic scholar

tzaddik   a righteous person (in contrast to the *rasha*, a wicked one)

tzara'at   the disease that is usually called leprosy, as described in Leviticus

Yalkut Shimoni   a midrashic compendium on the entire Bible, compiled in the
late thirteenth or early fourteenth century

yetzer ra, or *yetzer hara*   the "evil impulse" depicted in rabbinic literature, as countered by the *yetzer tov* (or *yetzer hatov*), the good/righteous impulse in the human personality

yir'at shamayim   literally, the "fear of Heaven"; a trait characterizing the righteous person

Yom HaAtzma'ut   Israel's Independence Day

yom tov   literally, "a good day," a common term for the festivals of Judaism

Yoma   the Talmudic tractate dealing with the laws pertaining to Yom Kippur

NOTES

Introduction

1. Robert M. Hutchins, *The Conflict in Education in a Democratic Society* (Westport, Conn.: Greenwood Press, 1972), pp. 81–82.

2. Philosophers of education, since they are engaged by these questions, are not directly concerned with the question How shall we transmit what is deemed worthy, useful, and true? On that question, the floor is given to psychological, sociological, and pedagogic theorists and to the parents, teachers, and other educators who intuitively or consciously translate theory into practice. The hope is, of course, that philosophers will occasionally talk to these varied professionals, observe them at work, and become familiar with the "field," especially with teachers' psychological sensitivity, pedagogic wisdom, and scholarly knowledge of "the material," all of which trigger conversation and make education happen.

3. Martin M. Buber, *I and Thou* (New York: Charles Scribner's Sons, 1970), p. 62.

4. For this concept, see Michael Oakeshott, "The Study of 'Politics' in a University," in *Rationalism in Politics and Other Essays* (London: Methuen and Co., 1962), pp. 301–333. I have expanded his concept of language to include the realm that Oakeshott calls civilization. The theological applications are my own, though I am indebted for my train of thought to Franz Rosenzweig, especially his letter "The Commandments: Divine or Human?" in *On Jewish Learning*, ed. N. N. Glatzer (New York: Schocken Books, 1955), pp. 119–124. For my previous discussion of language and literature in the context of education, see Michael Rosenak, *Roads to the Palace: Jewish Texts and Teaching* (Providence, R.I.: Berghahn Books, 1995), chap. 2.

5. An interesting example of how language gives a world picture that must confront experienced difficulties is the liturgical poem recited on the High Holidays (Rosh Hashanah and Yom Kippur), during the *Mussaf* (additional) morning service: "And all believe . . . ," which consists of numerous statements that "all believe" about God, such as that God answers all who call upon him in truth, that God is the only judge, is merciful, and so on. Immediately thereafter, the worshiper is directed to the petitionary prayer "Let Your fear fall upon all Your crea-

355

tures. . . . ," with an implied list of things that must be mended in the world, so that what "all believe" can indeed become self-evident.

6. Whenever the word *language* or the word *literature* is used, whether italicized or not, the reference is to the term as explained above, unless another use is specifically noted.

7. In general, I follow the *Encyclopedia Judaica* style for transliterations of Hebrew names and words, but I also try to take into consideration what is most comprehensible for the reader.

8. This inductive access to language is often found in ideational rationales for halakhic decisions or in ideational descriptions of aspects of Jewish life. See, for example, Joseph B. Soloveitchik, *Halakhic Man*, trans. Lawrence Kaplan (Philadelphia: Jewish Publication Society, 1984).

9. Alasdair MacIntyre, "The Idea of an Educated Public," in *Education and Values*, The Richard Peters Lectures, Institute of Education, University of London, 1985, pp. 15–36.

10. There are numerous disparaging comments by rabbinic sages in the Talmud about the *am ha-aretz*, the "ignorant person" who is unreliable in religious practice and disrespectful to sages, and also evidence that the *am ha-aretz* thought poorly of the sages in return. See, for example, *Pesahim* 49b.

11. Modern scholars and teachers as well have examined what, throughout its culture of lavish controversy, can yet be said to characterize this "language's" way of doing literature, but whether their findings may be seen as a continuation of the literature of Torah or are necessarily a break with it is a subject of controversy. See, for example, Moshe Greenberg, "Can Modern Critical Bible Scholarship Have a Jewish Character?" *Studies in the Bible and Jewish Thought* (Philadelphia: Jewish Publication Society, 5755 [1995]) pp. 3–8.

12. Talmud as such generally refers to the Babylonian Talmud, though Talmudic citations sometimes appear with the prefix "BT" (Babylonian Talmud), especially after mention has already been made of the Palestinian, or "Jerusalem," Talmud.

13. Jakob J. Petuchowski, "The Bible of the Synagogue," *Commentary* 27 (1959): 142–150.

14. For a previous discussion from which I have learned much, despite my fundamental disagreement with the author's theological conclusions, see Erich Fromm, *You Shall Be as Gods* (New York: Holt, Rinehart and Winston, 1966).

Chapter 1

1. Thomas Mann, *Joseph and His Brothers*, Vol. 1: *The Tales of Jacob*, trans. H. T. Lowe-Porter (London: Sphere Books Ltd., 1968), p. 21.

2. "Letter to Obadiah the Proselyte" and "Letter to Hasdai Halevi," in *A Maimonides Reader*, ed. Isadore Twersky (New York: Behrman House, 1972), pp. 475, 477–478.

3. Yehudah Halevi, *The Kuzari: An Argument for the Faith of Israel* (New York: Schocken Books, 1964), Book 4, para. 16.

4. Ibid.

5. Ibid., para. 17.

6. The student of the psalm under discussion will note how the sages understood what appears to be a blatantly secular song about a foreign bride and her royal husband to be an allegory of the relationship between God and Israel.

7. Nel Noddings, *Caring: A Feminine Approach to Ethics and Moral Education* (Berkeley: University of California Press, 1984), pp. 1–6.

8. In his commentary on Genesis 17:10, Nahum Sarna states that the phrase "every male among you shall be circumcised" "intentionally excludes ... female circumcision, found in many parts of the world." Nahum M. Sarna, ed., *The JPS Torah Commentary, Genesis* (Philadelphia: Jewish Publication Society, 5749 [1989]), p. 125.

9. André Neher, "Rabbinic Adumbrations of Non-violence: Israel and Canaan," *Studies in Rationalism*, ed. Raphael Loewe (London: Routledge and Kegan Paul, 1966), p. 177.

10. Commentary of Moshe Aryeh Mirkin, *Genesis Rabbah*, Vol. 2 (Tel Aviv: Yavneh Publishing House, 1971), chap. 1, on 60:16.

11. Nehama Leibowitz, *Studies in the Book of Genesis in the Context of Ancient and Modern Jewish Bible Commentary* (Jerusalem: World Zionist Organization, Department for Torah Education and Culture in the Diaspora, 5723 [1962]), pp. 334–335.

Chapter 2

1. Franz Rosenzweig, *The Star of Redemption*, trans. William W. Hallo from the 2d ed. (Boston: Beacon Press, 1964), pp. 317–318.

2. My source for comparing the various rabbinic texts here is E. D. Goldschmidt, *Haggadah shel Pesah v'Toldotehah* [The Passover Haggadah: Its Sources and History] (Jerusalem: Bialik Institute, 1969), pp. 22–29.

3. This is the opinion of Rav; one should not move from one circle *(havurah)* to another. Shmuel considers *afikoman* to be the nuts and dainties generally eaten after festive meals. BT *Pesahim* 119b.

4. Goldschmidt, *Haggadah shel Pesah*, cites the scholar-rabbis D. Z. Hoffman (1886) and L. Finkelstein (1943) as suggesting this merger of distinct sources.

5. Emil L. Fackenheim, *God's Presence in History: Jewish Affirmations and Philosophical Reflections* (New York: New York University Press, 1970), p. 21.

6. Yehudah Halevi, *The Kuzari: An Argument for the Faith of Israel* (New York: Schocken Books, 1964), 6:15.

7. Martin M. Buber, *I and Thou* (New York: Charles Scribner's Sons, 1970).

Chapter 3

1. In *Pragmatism and the Meaning of Truth*, William James presented the tender-minded and the tough-minded as sharply differentiated psychological types. Only some of the characteristics he listed are relevant for the discussion here. For example, although our tender-minded person is a "free willist" rather than a "fatalist," as in James's characterization, his portrayal of the tough-minded "skeptical" temperament is not herein, as James would have it, countered by the tender-minded person's "dogmatism." William James, *Pragmatism and the Meaning of Truth* (Cambridge, Mass.: Harvard University Press, 1909; reprint, 1975), pp. 12–15

2. The midrash (*Genesis Rabbah* 58:5, cited by Rashi on Genesis 23:2) arrives at this conclusion after noting that the story of Sarah's death follows immediately upon the *Akedah* narrative, with only a short family genealogy, intimating the marital match that God is planning for Isaac, separating the two stories.

3. Samuel Hugo Bergman, *The Quality of Faith: Essays on Judaism and Morality*, trans. Yehudah Hanegbi (Jerusalem: World Zionist Organization, 1970), "The Sacrifice of Isaac and Contemporary Man," p. 29.

4. The rabbinic interpretation makes the requirement of wearing fringes incumbent only upon adult males, unlike the other commandments in this passage that are assumed to apply equally to men and women. In liberal versions of modern Judaism, the wearing of the *talit* by some women suggests a rethinking of whether women too should consider themselves obligated by it.

5. Rabbi J. B. Soloveitchik, "Kol Dodi Dofek" [My beloved knocks], in *Ish ha'E-munah* [*The Man of Faith*] (Jerusalem: Mossad Harav Kook, 5731 [1970/1971]), pp. 65–71.

6. Emil L. Fackenheim, *God's Presence in History: Jewish Affirmations and Philosophical Reflections* (New York: New York University Press, 1970), pp. 3–34.

7. Peter L. Berger, *A Rumour of Angels: Modern Society and the Rediscovery of the Supernatural* (Hammondsworth, Middlesex, England: Penguin Books, 1971), pp. 72–73.

Chapter 4

1. Elhanan Bunim Wasserman, *Kovetz Ma'amarim* [Collected essays] (Tel Aviv: Sifriati Ltd., n.d.), pp. 40–41.

2. Ibid.

3. Ibid.

4. Eliyahu E. Dessler, *Mikhtav MeEliyahu* [*A Letter of Elijah*], Vol. 3, ed. A. Carmel and A. Halperin (Bnai Brak, Israel: Committee for the Publication of the Writings of Rabbi E. E. Dessler, 1964), pp. 360–361.

5. Ibid., p. 361.

6. Ibid.

7. For an interesting exposition of this approach, see Aaron Kotler, *How to Teach Torah* (Lakewood, N.J.: Rabbi Aaron Kotler Institute for Advanced Learning, 1972).

8. *The Pentateuch*, explained by Rabbi Samson Raphael Hirsch, trans. Isaac Levy (London: Isaac Levy, 1958–1962), Vol. 1, p. 425, on Genesis 25:27.

Chapter 5

1. John Dewey, *How We Think: A Restatement of the Relation of Reflective Thinking to the Educative Process* (Boston: Heath, 1933), p. 13.

2. Not all commentators see the *zir'ah* as a hornet. Some, for example, understand it as a plague (e.g., Ibn Ezra and R. Saadyah Gaon).

3. Although it is difficult to give up such a "secret weapon" and some sages indeed believe that the reassuring hornet stood "on the far side of the Jordan" and aimed its poison at the enemy from there, the realities suggest otherwise. As R. Baruch Halevi Epstein, in his commentary, *Torah Temimah*, points out: "[had it fought for Israel, even from across the Jordan] then all the wars that Joshua fought for seven years would have been superfluous, since the hornet would have killed [the enemies] in an instant!" (on Exodus 23:28).

4. Hence we find the rabbis of the school of R. Ishmael, after the destruction of the Temple, bluntly "rereading" the biblical verse "Who is like You among the gods *(ba'elim)* O Lord" (Exod. 15:11), as "Who is like You among the silent *(ba'ilmim)*." Yet Jewish theology has generally balanced this realism with an insistence on God's presence, even in the hour of his silence. See, for example, André Neher, *The Exile of the Word: From the Silence of the Bible to the Silence of Auschwitz* (Philadelphia: Jewish Publication Society, 5741 [1981]).

5. The late Yehudah Elitzur, of Bar Ilan University, Ramat Gan, Israel, shared this explanation of the defeat with me.

Chapter 6

1. Norbert Samuelson, Review of Emil L. Fackenheim's *Quest for Past and Future*, *CCAR Journal*, no. 65 (April 1969): 46–47.

2. Martin Buber, "The Way of Man According to the Teaching of Hasidism," in *Religion from Tolstoy to Camus*, ed. Walter Kaufmann (New York: Harper Torchbooks, 1961), p. 426.

3. Abraham Joshua Heschel, *God in Search of Man: A Philosophy of Judaism* (New York: Farrar, Straus & Cudahy, 1955), p. 328.

4. Philip H. Phenix, *Intelligible Religion* (New York: Harpers, 1954), chap. 3.

5. Yehudah Halevi, *The Kuzari: An Argument for the Faith of Israel* (New York: Schocken Books, 1964), 1:11–13.

Chapter 7

1. This passage is quoted (in Hebrew) from *Shevet Yehudah*, a late medieval chronicle, mainly of persecutions throughout Jewish history, in the *Rinat Yisrael* prayer book for Yom Kippur (Allon Shvut and Tel Aviv: Yad Shapira and Moreshet, 1982), pp. 274–275.

2. Peter L. Berger, Brigitte Berger, and Hansfried Kellner, *The Homeless Mind* (Hammondsworth, Middlesex, Eng.: Penguin Books, 1973), "Excursus: On the Obsolescence of the Concept of Honor," p. 84.

3. Ibid., pp. 82–84.

4. Ibid., p. 85.

5. Quoted here as found in Nehama Leibowitz, *Studies in Shemot* [Exodus], Vol. 2 (Jerusalem: World Zionist Organization, 1976), p. 526.

6. The quotation is from a liturgical poem recited after the Avodah service.

7. Note how they required priests to be prepared for the Yom Kippur service, as spelled out in the Mishnah (*Yoma* 1:3–7): "At the conclusion of this somewhat rigorous preparation, they said to him: 'My lord High Priest, we are delegates of the Court, and you are our delegate and the delegate of the Court. We adjure you by Him that made His name to dwell in this house [i.e., the Temple] that you change nothing [in the order of the service] of what we have said to you.' He turned aside and wept [that they suspected him of sectarian tendencies] and they turned aside and wept [for having suspected him]" (1:5).

8. This prayer is based on Psalms 51:13.

Chapter 8

1. Ze'ev W. Falk, *Law and Religion: The Jewish Experience* (Jerusalem: Mesharim Publishers, 1981), p. 192.

2. Leo Strauss, "What is Political Philosophy?" *What Is Political Philosophy and Other Studies* (Chicago and London: University of Chicago Press, 1959), p. 10.

3. John Kekes, *Facing Evil* (Princeton, N.J.: Princeton University Press, 1990), pp. 230–231.

4. See, for example, the Hirsch's commentary on Genesis 18:19: "*Mishpat* is what each person has the right to claim [on ethical grounds, from another person." Note that Abraham can tell even God that He "dare not" go against *mishpat* (Gen. 18:25). *The Pentateuch*, explained by Rabbi Samson Raphael Hirsch, trans. Isaac Levy (London: Isaac Levy, 1958–1962), Vol. 1, p. 320.

5. The modern commentator A. S. Hartum, on Exodus 15:25, suggests that the rescue from thirst in this passage lays the foundations for the fundamental principle that "the salvation of the people depends on obeying God." That is certainly in line with the approach that insights arise in human consciousness in situations wherein one "calls from the depths."

6. A. J. Heschel, *Torah min Hashamayim b'Aspaklarya shel Hadorot* (often referred to as *Theology of Ancient Judaism*), Vol. 2 (London: Soncino Press, 1965), unnumbered introductory page.

Chapter 9

1. Martin Buber, *Tales of the Hasidim: Early Masters* (New York: Schocken Books, 1961), p. 251.

2. This story appears in *Midrash Tanhuma, Pekudai.*

3. *Niddah* 17b.

4. Deborah Weisman, "Bais Ya'akov As an Innovation in Jewish Women's Education: A Contribution to the Study of Education and Social Change," in *Studies in Jewish Education* 7, ed. Walter Ackerman (Jerusalem: Magnes Press, 1995), pp. 278–299. In introducing the subject why such noble women as Sarah Schneier (the founder of the Beth Yaakov school system) are denied Talmudic study, the director explains, "Such is the demand of Judaism. A modern European woman couldn't possible understand this, but we would be doing a grievous injustice if we obscured this fact from our girls who are being instructed in pure, complete Judaism. . . . We will say openly that the Jewish male has more responsibilities and commandments incumbent upon him and is, therefore, worthy of high status, according to the principle, 'One who is called upon to perform a certain act and does so is greater (more meritorious) than another who performs the same act without having been so commanded.'" Citations are from pp. 292.

5. Whether that includes women and to what extent is the subject of much Jewish controversy and polemics in the current generation.

6. Yonah Frankel, *Iyyunim b'Olamo haRuchani shel Sippur ha-Aggadah* [*Explorations in the Spiritual World of the* aggadic *Story*] (Tel Aviv: Hakibbutz Hameuchad, 1981), pp. 66–69.

7. A *braita* is a passage of early (Tannaic) literature that was not included in the Mishnah as edited by Rabbi Judah the Prince at the beginning of the third century C.E.

8. Ben-Zion Luria, "*Mihu Menahem?*" [Who is Menahem?], *Sinai* 55, no. 6, Elul 5724 [1963]: 299–305.

9. One of the issues that agitated the rabbinic sages (who were Pharisees) about the Hasmonean line was that its members were of the priestly line and were disqualified thereby, in the sages' opinion, from holding both the priestly and the royal reins.

Chapter 10

1. See *Crisis and Leadership: Epistles of Maimonides*, trans. and notes by Abraham Halkin, discussion by David Hartman (Philadelphia: Jewish Publication Society, 5745 [1985]), p. 97.

2. Thomas Mann, *Joseph and His Brothers*, Vol. 1: *The Tales of Jacob*, trans. H. T. Lowe-Porter (London: Sphere Books Ltd., 1968), citations from pp. 130–131.

3. *Pesikta de-Rabbi Kahana, Piska* 4, *Parah*. See discussion of the red heifer, Chapters 8 and 18.

4. See Rashi's commentary on Genesis 18:1.

5. Rabbi Avraham Isaac Kook, *"Ne'um b'Petihat Hamikhlalah b'Yerushalayim"* [Address upon the opening of the Hebrew University in Jerusalem], *Ma'amare Haraya* [*Essays of Rabbi Avraham Isaac Hacohen Kook*], Vol. 2 (Jerusalem: Golda Katz Foundation, 5744 [1983/1984]), pp. 306–308.

6. Rav A. Y. Kook. *Selected Letters*, trans. Tzvi Feldman (Ma'aleh Adumin, Israel: Ma'aliot Publ., 1986), citations from pp. 191–192.

Chapter 11

1. The Omer is a grain offering brought to the Temple on the morning of the second day of Passover, thereby making permissible the eating of the new harvest (Lev. 23:10). The first fruits were offered by the farmer in the early summer (Deut. 26:2), and the two loaves were brought to the Temple on the festival of Shavuot to allow the consumption of the new harvest there.

2. Maimonides, *Mishneh Torah, Hilkhot Milakhim* 11:1, as found in *A Maimonides Reader*, ed. Isadore Twersky (New York: Behrman House, 1972), p. 222.

3. Ibid.

4. Nahum M. Sarna, *Understanding Genesis: The Heritage of Biblical Israel* (New York: Jewish Theological Seminary of America and McGraw-Hill, 1966), p. 222.

5. Marshal Sklare, "Intermarriage and the Jewish Future," *Commentary* 37, no. 4 (April 1964), 50.

6. Ephraim E. Urbach, *Muda'ut shel Mercaz V'tefuzot b'Toldot Yisrael Umashma'-utah Beyamainu* [Center and Periphery in Historic Jewish Consciousness: Contemporary Implications] (Jerusalem: Institute of Contemporary Jewry, Hebrew University, 1975).

7. Quoted in Salo W. Baron and Joseph L. Blau, *Judaism: Post-Biblical and Talmudic Period* (New York: Liberal Arts Press, 1954), pp. 51–52.

8. Apparently, because they had been in hiding, they had not been able to celebrate Sukkot that year in the month of Tishre. It was thus celebrated on the days of the dedication (Hanukkah) that year (2 Macc. 10:5–6). Other explanations have also been suggested. A. S. Hartum, in his commentary on the Apocryphal Books, suggests that Hanukkah was originally called Sukkot, for it, like Sukkot, was an eight-day holiday marked by the recitation of psalms.

Chapter 12

1. Nahum M. Sarna, ed., *The JPS Torah Commentary, Genesis* (Philadelphia: Jewish Publication Society, 5749 [1989]), pp. 48–49.

2. On this interpretation, see commentaries of Hizkuni (R. Hizkiah ben Manoah) and Nachmanides (Ramban) on Genesis 9:13.

3. Whether it is only "the righteous" of the nations (who accept the Noahide laws as revealed) or also "the wise" who have a share in the world to come has been the subject of much polemic, especially since Maimonides appears to rule that only the righteous have such a "share." See Eugene Korn, "Gentiles, the World to Come and Judaism: The Odyssey of a Rabbinic Text," *Modern Judaism* 14 (1994): 265–287.

4. E. E. Urbach, "Bakashat Ha'emet K'hovah Datit" [Searching for Truth as a Religious Obligation], in *Hamikrah v'anahnu* [*The Bible and Us*], ed. Uriel Simon (Tel Aviv: Dvir Publishers, 1987), pp. 24–25.

5. The "sons of God" (Gen. 6:2) are variously understood as the mighty who did whatever they pleased or as those who did God's will. Rashi cites both midrashic traditions. Ramban unequivocally sees them as "openly acting with corruption."

6. "Katzia" may be the name of the king or of his country, perhaps Carthage. See commentary of Moshe Aryeh Mirkin, *Genesis Rabbah*, Vol. 2 (Tel Aviv: Yavneh Publishing House, 1971), on 33:1.

7. This idea will, of course, be denied by those who deny that there is an inherent relationship between religion and morality, a position that I am maintaining here.

Chapter 13

1. Moshe Greenberg, "Reflections on Interpretation," in *Studies in the Bible and Jewish Thought* (Philadelphia: Jewish Publication Society, 5755 [1995]), pp. 232–233.

2. Peter Ochs, "An Introduction to Postcritical Scriptural Integration," in *The Return to Scripture in Judaism and Christianity* (New York: Paulist Press, 1993), pp. 3–4.

3. Greenberg, "Can Modern Critical Bible Scholarship Have a Jewish Character?" in *Studies in the Bible and Jewish Thought*, p. 6.

4. Jacob Milgrom, ed., *The JPS Torah Commentary, Numbers* (Philadelphia: Jewish Publication Society, 5750 [1990]), p. 386.

5. The letter is from 1927. Although it is often cited in English, I have not seen an English translation of it. "*Ahdut haMikra*" [The Unity of Scripture], in *Naharayim: Mivhar Mikhtavim* [Selected Letters], trans. with notes by Yehoshua Amir (Jerusalem: Mossad Bialik, 5721 [1960]), pp. 26–27.

6. Franz Rosenzweig, "The Builders: Concerning the Law," in *On Jewish Learning*, ed. N. N. Glatzer (New York: Schocken Books, 1955), p. 81.

7. R. Shlomo Goren, *Torat haMikra: Derashot al Parashot Hashavua* [The teaching of Scripture: Discourses on the weekly portions] (Jerusalem: Ha'idra Rabbah Umesora L'am, 5756 [1995/1996]), pp. 149–154, 312–314.

8. Ibid.

9. Milgrom, *JPS Torah Commentary, Numbers*, p. 386; and Goren, *Torat haMikra*, pp. 149–154.

10. Goren, *Torat haMikra*, p. 313

11. Menachem Haran, "The Nature of the 'Ohel Moed' in Pentateuchal Sources," *Journal of Semitic Studies* 5 (1960): esp. 54–58.

12. Michael Rosenak, *Commandments and Concerns: Jewish Religious Education in Secular Society* (Philadelphia:: Jewish Publication Society, 5747 [1987]).

13. Gershom Scholem, "Three Types of Jewish Piety," *Ariel: Review of Arts and Letters in Israel*, no. 32 (1973): 76–97.

Chapter 14

1. Isaiah Leibowitz, "Education for Mitzvot," in *Readings in Jewish Thought* (in Hebrew), ed. David Weinstein and Michael Yizhar, Vol. 1 (Chicago: College of Jewish Studies, 1964), pp. 56–60.

2. Moses Maimonides, *Guide to the Perplexed (Moreh Nevuhim)*, sect. 3, chap. 27.

3. Ibid., sect. 3, chap. 54.

4. Ibid.

5. Ibid.

6. Ibid.

7. Ibid.

8. David Hartman, *Maimonides: Torah and the Philosophic Quest* (Philadelphia: Jewish Publication Society, 5737 [1976]), p. 205.

9. I. Leibowitz, "Education for Mitzvot," p. 59.

10. Van Cleve Morris, *Existentialism and Education: What It Means* (New York: Harper and Row, 1966), p. 114.

11. Ibid.

12. Thomas Mann, *Joseph and His Brothers*, Vol. 4: *Joseph the Provider*, trans. H. T. Lowe-Porter (London: Sphere Books Ltd., 1968), p. 607.

13. Erik H. Erikson, *Identity: Youth and Crisis* (New York: W. W. Norton & Co., 1968), chap. 3, esp. pp. 139–141.

14. Bruno Bettleheim, *The Uses of Enchantment: The Meaning and Importance of Fairy Tales* (New York: Vintage Books, 1977), esp. pp. 102–111.

15. Maurice Samuel, *Certain People of the Book* (New York: Union of American Hebrew Congregations, 1977), chap. 8, "The Brilliant Failure."

16. According to commentators working by the rule of elimination, those who sold Joseph must have been Simon and Levi. Reuven was, as we know, against it, as was Judah. That left, of the older sons of Leah, only Simon and Levi. It must be assumed that the only "remaining" son of Rachel, Benjamin, was too young to be part of the discussion. See Nechama Leibowitz, *Studies in Bereshit* [Genesis] (Jerusalem: World Zionist Organization, Dept. of Torah Education and Culture, 1974), p. 564.

17. Although Joseph's mother, Rachel, was no longer alive, Rashi places Bilhah, who had raised Joseph, in the role of the moon.

18. N. Leibowitz, *Studies in Bereshit* [Genesis], quotations here are from p. 459.

19. Ibid., pp. 459–460.

20. Ibid., p. 564. Liebowitz cites a passage in *Pesikta Rabbati.*

Chapter 15

1. R. Samson Raphael Hirsch in his collected writings devotes much attention to "symbolism in the commandments." Of special interest with regard to the "psychology of day" versus "psychology of night" is his discussion of circumcision. See *Timeless Torah: An Anthology of the Writings of Rabbi Samuel Raphael Hirsch* (New York: Samson Raphael Hirsch Publications Society by Feldheim Books, 1957), pp. 388–400.

2. For my understanding of the concept *yirat shamayim*, "fear of Heaven," see Michael Rosenak, *Roads to the Palace: Jewish Texts and Teaching* (Providence, R.I.: Berghahn Books, 1995), chaps. 6–8.

3. The midrashist is punning. *Lehodot* means both "to thank" or "to give praise" *and* "to confess."

Chapter 16

1. Susan Sontag, *Illness as Metaphor* (New York: Vintage Books, 1979), pp. 45–46.

2. This and a number of other commentaries on this line are discussed in Yehudah Nahshoni, *Hagut b'Parashat Hashavu'a (Vayikra, Bamidbar, Devarim)* (Bnai Brak, author, 1981), pp. 457–458.

3. The "model" used here is reminiscent of another set of plagues, those that struck Pharaoh and Egypt before the Exodus. There, too, the afflictions began at some distance from human beings and only after Pharaoh had persisted in his stubbornness, struck the humans.

4. That healing does not apply, as we have seen, in cases of miraculous illness. In those cases, society, as represented by the priest, will, before inspection, minimize its effect, for example, by removing everything from the leprous house in advance so that there be no financial loss and postponing inspection until after the pilgrim festivals and after the week of wedding feasts.

5. *Hayavim* is here translated as "the undeserving," as in many prayer books, rather than its usual translation as "the guilty."

Chapter 17

1. Jack Riemer, ed., *Jewish Reflections on Death* (New York: Schocken Books, 1975), pp. 5–7.

2. Extensive midrashim on Moses' death are found in *Yalkut Shimoni, Tanhuma,* and *Deuteronomy Rabbah* as well as in other collections. I here draw on the composite narratives of Haim Nahman Bialik and Yehoshua H. Ravnitzky in their *Sefer ha-Aggadah.* The English edition is *The Book of Legends,* trans. William G. Braude (New York: Schocken Books, 1992), p. 104.

3. Bialik and Ravnitzky, *Sefer ha-Aggadah,* p. 104.

4. Ibid.

5. Ibid.

6. Ibid.

7. Ibid.

8. For these stages, see Elisabeth Kuebler-Ross, *On Death and Dying* (London: Macmillan Press, 1969).

9. Louis Ginzberg, *Legends of the Jews,* Vol. 3 (Philadelphia: Jewish Publication Society, 5715 [1954]), p. 475, quotes this statement from several midrashic sources.

10. Ernest Becker, *The Denial of Death* (New York: Free Press, 1973), p. 284.

11. Cary D. Kozberg, "Comforting the Bereaved: An Analysis," *Journal of Reform Judaism* 34, no. 139 (Fall 1987): 39–52.

12. "When the father is aged and the son takes him to his house, the son remains seated at his normal place as previously, but the father nonetheless is to perform the ritual washing of the hands *(netilat yadayim)* first and to receive the first portion of food, as well as other designations of honor at the table." *Arukh Hashulhan* [Code of Law], of Rabbi Yehiel Michel Epstein, *Yoreh Deah* 240:11). For a discussion on this issue, see "'Do Not Cast Us Away In Our Old Age': Adult Children and their Aging Parents," *Melton Journal* (Jewish Theological Seminary of America) (Autumn 1994): 12, 20.

Chapter 18

1. The word *lishmah* will vary in spelling according to grammatical requirement. *Lishmah* refers to study of Torah or observance of a specific commandment, both of which are grammatically feminine. *Lishmo* may refer to a grammatically masculine act, and *lishmam* or *lishman* are plural.

2. Ephraim E. Urbach, *The Sages: Their Concepts and Beliefs,* trans. Israel Abrahams, Vol. 1 (Jerusalem: Magnus Press, 1975) p. 388.

3. Maimonides, "Introduction to *Perek 'Helek,'*" in *A Maimonides Reader,* ed. Isadore Twersky (New York: Behrman House, 1972), p. 404.

4. Ibid., p. 405.

5. Ibid., p. 406.

6. For an explication of these ideas, see Gordon W. Allport, *The Individual and His Religion: A Psychological Interpretation* (New York: Macmillan Paperback, 1960), and *Becoming: Basic Considerations for a Psychology of Personality* (New Haven: Yale University Press, 1955).

7. Of course, where the "knowledge sentiment," or the moral sentiment, is the one that "organizes" and takes charge with regard to the entire personality, the final intention will also be "open" and heuristic, as would be the case with the mature religious sentiment.

8. M. A. B. Degenhardt, *Education and the Value of Knowledge* (London: George Allen and Unwin, 1982), p. 85.

9. Ibid.

10. Emmanuel Levinas, *In the Time of the Nations* (Bloomington, Ind.: Indiana University Press, 1994), pp. 52, 173.

Postscript

1. Gershom Scholem, *The Messianic Idea in Judaism* (New York: Schocken Books, 1971), pp. 69–70.

Index